Religion and Education in Europe

Religious Diversity and Education in Europe

edited by

Cok Bakker, Hans-Günter Heimbrock,
Robert Jackson, Geir Skeie, Wolfram Weisse

Volume 3

Globalisation and plurality are influencing all areas of education, including religious education. The inter-cultural and multi-religious situation in Europe demands a re-evaluation of the existing educational systems in particular countries as well as new thinking at the broader European level. This new book series is committed to the investigation and reflection on the changing role of religion and education in Europe. Contributions will evaluate the situation, reflect on fundamental issues and develop perspectives for better policy making and pedagogy, especially in relation to practice in the classroom.

The publishing policy of the series is to focus on the importance of strengthening pluralist democracies through stimulating the development of active citizenship and fostering greater mutual understanding through intercultural education. It pays special attention to the educational challenges of religious diversity and conflicting value systems in schools and in society in general.

Religious Diversity and Education in Europe is produced by two European research groups, in which scholars are engaged in empirical and theoretical research on aspects of religion and education in relation to intercultural issues:
* **ENRECA: The European Network for Religious Education in Europe through Contextual Approaches**
* **REDCo: Religion in Education. A contribution to Dialogue or a factor of Conflict in transforming societies of European Countries**

The series is aimed at teachers, researchers and policy makers. The series is committed to involving practitioners in the research process and includes books by teachers and teacher educators who are engaged in research as well as academics from various relevant fields, professional researchers and PhD students. It is open to authors committed to these issues, and it includes English and German speaking monographs as well as edited collections of papers.

Book proposals should be directed to one of the editors or to the publisher.

Robert Jackson, Siebren Miedema,
Wolfram Weisse, Jean-Paul Willaime (Eds.)

Religion and Education
in Europe

Developments, Contexts and Debates

Waxmann Münster / New York
München / Berlin

Bibliographic information published by Die Deutsche Bibliothek
Die Deutsche Bibliothek lists this publication in the
Deutsche Nationalbibliografie; detailed bibliographic data
are available in the Internet at http://dnb.ddb.de.

Religious Diversity and Education in Europe, volume 3

ISSN 1862-9547
ISBN 978-3-8309-1765-6

© Waxmann Verlag GmbH, 2007
Postfach 8603, D-48046 Münster

www.waxmann.com
info@waxmann.com

Book cover: Pleßmann Kommunikationsdesign, Ascheberg
Print: Zeitdruck GmbH, Münster

Printed on age-resistant paper,
acid-free according to ISO 9706

Acknowledgements

The editors and contributors would like to thank colleagues and PhD students for their substantial assistance in producing this book. Dr. Jack Priestley, University of Exeter, has undertaken much valued work in improving the language of contributors whose first language is not English. Dörthe Vieregge has given us a great deal of technical assistance, with the support of Dr. Christine Müller. Volker Bach has contributed some excellent translation work. We are very grateful to all of them. We also express our thanks to the European Commission for its substantial financial support for our REDCo project, including assistance in publishing this book. Last, but not least, we thank the Waxmann Publishing House, especially the Director, Dr. Ursula Heckel, and Beate Plugge. We are grateful for their encouragement to initiate a new book series on Religious Diversity and Education in Europe, of which this book is a part.

Contents

Wolfram Weisse
The European Research Project on Religion and Education "REDCo".
An introduction..9

PART I: EUROPEAN HORIZON

Robert Jackson
European Institutions and the Contribution of Studies of Religious Diversity
to Education for Democratic Citizenship 27

Jean-Paul Willaime
Different Models for Religion and Education in Europe 57

Dan-Paul Jozsa
Islam and Education in Europe. With Special Reference to Austria, England,
France, Germany and the Netherlands 67

PART II: CONTRIBUTION TO DIALOGUE OR CONFLICT?
HISTORICAL AND CONTEXTUAL ANALYSIS

Jean-Paul Willaime
Teaching Religious Issues in French Public Schools.
From Abstentionist *Laïcité* to a Return of Religion to Public Education 87

Gunther Dietz
Invisibilizing or Ethnicizing Religious Diversity? The Transition of
Religious Education Towards Pluralism in Contemporary Spain....................103

Fedor Kozyrev and Vladimir Fedorov
Religion and Education in Russia. Historical Roots, Cultural Context
and Recent Developments 133

Pille Valk
Religious Education in Estonia 159

Robert Jackson and Kevin O'Grady
Religions and Education in England: Social Plurality, Civil Religion and
Religious Education Pedagogy...181

Ina ter Avest, Cok Bakker, Gerdien Bertram-Troost and Siebren Miedema
Religion and Education in the Dutch Pillarized and Post-Pillarized
Educational System: Historical Background and Current Debates 203

Geir Skeie
Religion and Education in Norway 221

Thorsten Knauth
Religious Education in Germany: a Contribution to Dialogue or Source of Conflict?
Historical and Contextual Analysis of the Development since the 1960s.......................243

PART III: COMPARATIVE ANALYSIS

Siebren Miedema
Contexts, Debates and Perspectives of Religion
in Education in Europe. A Comparative Analysis..267

List of authors...285

Wolfram Weisse

The European Research Project on Religion and Education 'REDCo'. An Introduction

Introduction

In most European countries we have long assumed that an increasing secularisation would lead to a gradual retreat of religion from public space. This tendency has reversed itself in the course of the past decade as religion returned to public discourse. Regardless of the wide variety of conditions prevailing in different European countries it appears more and more important to study the increasingly influential factor of 'religion and religiosity' and its ambivalent potential for both dialogue and social conflict and tension.

There is a rising public awareness of the necessity to seek dialogue with all that can aid us in preventing conflict and supporting peaceful coexistence in a multireligious society. And more and more scholars, who formerly did not touch the field of religion, are taking up this field. Colleagues from the political sciences, from sociology, from law and from philosophy show an increasing interest. An outstanding example for me is Jürgen Habermas. For decades he refused to take religion into account within his theory of communicative action. For a couple of years now he has been writing more and more on religion and its function for mutual understanding (see Habermas, 2005).

Since September 11th 2001, the dangers arising from religious isolation and confrontation and the instrumentalisation of religion for political purposes have become clear to a wider public. However, religious values can equally serve as the foundation of the peaceful coexistence of various religions and to justify respect for the human dignity of others, regardless of their religious and political convictions. They can thus act as a pillar for civility.

This also requires efforts in intercultural and interreligious education. The political scientist Hasenclever from the University of Tübingen even extends the claim. He argues that a positive correlation between religious education and democratic conduct can be shown. The lesser the degree of religious education, the greater is the potential for religious differences to be instrumentalised as a tool for political mobilisation (Hasenclever, 2003, p. 204).

A study by the European Monitoring Centre on Racism and Xenophobia shows empirical support for this (European Monitoring Centre on Racism and Xenophobia, 2005). This makes religious education a vital field within which this question can be addressed: The degree to which religion serves (or could potentially be made to serve) as a criterion of exclusion in schools and universities must be investigated as well as to what degree religious dialogue in education can promote potentials for the peaceful coexistence of people in Europe. This is especially important regarding people of different cultural and religious backgrounds for whom we need to map out educational strategies to recognize each other and to learn from each other, rather than perpetuate divisions (Ricoeur, 2006).

These questions are the main focus of an international research-project called REDCo: 'Religion in Education. A contribution to Dialogue or a factor of Conflict in transforming societies of European countries'. It is connected with the thematic frame of the EU-program, 'Citizens and Governance in a knowledge-based society' for the years 2004–2006, where one section deals with 'Values and Religions in Europe'. Our application from April 2005 has been rated positively: We got that official information from the European Commission in Brussels in September 2005 and started our project in March 2006. The REDCo-project is funded by the research department of the European Commission over a period of three years with a total of 1.188.000.000 Euro. Ten projects from eight different European countries are participating. The author of this article is the coordinator of REDCo.

This book is the first outcome of the REDCo-project. It is directed to an analysis of the preconditions of our research. It outlines the discussion-process in all of Europe and the developments, contexts and debates in the respective countries. In the introduction I will give an insight into the aims, the theoretical background and the structure of REDCo. In the end of the introduction I will explain the idea behind this book and report on the first steps of our research and give an outlook on the structure of our way ahead.

REDCo: Insight into a European Research Project[1]

Aims and Frame of the EU-Program

The REDCo-project's main aim is to establish and compare the potentials and limitations of religion in the educational fields of selected European countries and regions. Approaches and constellations that can contribute to making religion in education a factor promoting dialogue in the context of European development will be addressed.

Our project aims at analysing conceptual and practical approaches to mutual understanding in the field of religious education. The correlation between low levels of religious education and a willingness to use religion as a criterion of exclusion and confrontation was pointed out before. We plan to look into how theoretical and practical approaches in schools and universities that encourage openness towards others and mutual respect across religious and cultural differences can be strengthened. Looking into the future, we cannot hope to solve this task at the national level alone. A European perspective needs to be established by means of comparative studies. This is the stated aim and corresponds to the outcome structure of our project.

Theoretical, conceptual and empirical analysis will help to lay the foundation for our understanding of the contribution religion in education can make towards the current transformation processes in various European countries. By comparing different approaches we hope to gain the necessary historical perception and analytical clarity to address the core questions of dialogue and conflict in Europe and to find ways to stimulate a process of growing European identity/ies.

---

1   In this section I am going to reproduce parts of the texts contained in our application to Brussels, but partly in another order, shortened and revised.

Which are our main research questions?

Mainly in the initial phase we will direct our attention to the following basic questions:

- What is the historical background of religion in education in the participating countries? Does this history show more potential for conflict or opportunities for dialogue?
- Which legal and institutional frameworks for religion in education currently exist in the different countries and regions?
- What approaches used in participating countries have potential for a perspective in the development of European identities?

In the main phase we will focus on theoretical and empirical research guided by the following questions:

- Which conceptual approaches to religion in education can be further developed as a basis for a form of religious education in schools and universities that aims at dialogue and understanding without excluding difference?
- Which empirical findings at national and European level point towards those elements of religious education that enhance dialogue and understanding without ignoring existing tensions between people of different religion, culture and political opinion?
- How can these theoretical and empirical findings be combined in order to provide strong and sustained impulses throughout Europe?

Mainly in the last phase of our project we will work out the results and draw on the following perspectives:

- How can the findings be formulated in a manner that they can be adopted and utilised by institutions at the national and European level?
- What can the findings add to the development of our goals for a peaceful coexistence of people from different cultural, religious and political backgrounds in Europe?
- What growth potential for elements of a European identity do the findings hold?

Our project represents a necessary approach to address the core question, how religions and values can contribute to dialogue or tension in Europe. It contributes to concerns addressed by the following programmes of the European Commission.

In the FP6 Specific Programme 'Integrating and Strengthening the European Research Area', Priority 7: Citizens and Governance in a knowledge based society (European Commission, 2004, p.2) the following primary objectives are framed:

> 'The activities carried out in this thematic priority are intended to mobilise in a coherent effort, in all their wealth and diversity, European research capacities in economic, political, social sciences and humanities that are necessary to develop an understanding of, and to address issues related to, the emergence of the knowledge-based society and new forms of relationships between its citizens, on one hand, and between its citizens and institutions, on the other.'

We see our project located at the centre of one of these objectives. In our project highly qualified researchers in the humanities and social sciences will cooperate in a pre-defined thematic and methodological approach in order to gain better insight into how European citizens of different religious, cultural and political backgrounds can live together and enter into dialogue of mutual respect and understanding, developing their respective evolving positions. These possibilities are to be examined in the context of educational institutions.

The REDCo-project is located in special area 7.2.1 'Values and religions in Europe' of the above mentioned Priority 7 programme of the EU. Here it is stated (European Commission, 2004, p. 16 f.):

> 'European societies have a long history of dialogue and coexistence as well as of tensions between different cultures, values and religions. The objective is to better understand the significance and impact of values and religions in societies across Europe and their roles in relation to changes in society and to the emergence of European identities.' (Emphasis in the original).

This is the core issue our project addresses. Looking at religion in the context of education, we will look at the position and importance of religions and religious values in various European countries with their very different traditions. Our main aim is to look at the challenges facing religious education in the context of the current change in European societies and its importance for dialogue and mutual understanding without disregarding potential problems. We believe it is vital in this context not only to further develop theoretical approaches, but to also look for possibilities for successful dialogue in the actual encounter situations that occur daily at schools throughout the European Union. Taking account of confrontational as well as dialogue potential, this will allow us to develop impulses for the future peaceful coexistence of people of different religions. The area 'values and religions in Europe' specifies in addition:

> 'STREPs and/or CAs should explore the role of different values, religions and cultures in European societies from historical perspective; their different perceptions within and across communities (e.g. ethnic, religious, national minorities, immigrant communities) – including gender aspects – either as an enrichment or a threat to their own identities.'

This is precisely our intention. In the context of historical development, we will concentrate on questions of religions and religious values. Differences will not be studied in the abstract or through history (there are numerous studies of this kind from both theological and religious studies perspectives), but in their impact on modern Europe and the lives of its citizens. We plan to research empirically how differences within European societies can be taken into account without creating conflict or exclusion. Empirical studies targeting students between 14 and 16 years old will look into their own perceptions of dialogue or conflict within the different national contexts. These will include a dual focus of the subjects' own perspectives on the one hand and of analyses of observed teaching in both dialogue and conflict situations on the other hand. Our student selection will also allow for gender-specific results. It is particularly from those studies we expect to gain insight into whether and how religious- and value-based identity development can coexist or clash with openness for other positions.

Finally the EU-text on values and religions in Europe states:

> 'The processes leading to tolerance or intolerance and xenophobia – and their relation to changes in society – could be examined in this regard. The role of symbols and cultural heritage in the transmission and diffusion of different values (secular and religious) could be examined as well. Research could also explore how religion is sometimes being used as a political instrument and a factor in social mobilisation, solidarity or discrimination. The challenges posed by religious, ethnic and cultural diversity to legal, educational and political systems in European countries and possible ways to ensure peaceful coexistence of different value sys-

tems should be examined. The differing ways in which European countries address these issues and implement various policies and practices in this context could be examined in a
comparative perspective as well as their degrees of success in achieving them.'

As stated before, our project aims to analyse conceptual and practical approaches to mutual understanding in the field of religious education.

Countries Involved and the Consortium

The plurality of religion and education in European regions is mirrored in the countries
we have chosen to study. The wide religious and societal spectrum covered by these
countries and the challenges of social transition they face can be briefly summarised as
follows:

- Germany, with two established churches (Catholics and Protestants) and Norway
  with one (Lutheran) are moving towards religious pluralism.
- The Netherlands and England/Wales both have established churches (Reformed, respectively Anglican), but can also look back on a long (though not unchallenged) tradition of religious pluralism.
- Traditionally majority-Catholic France has a laical system facing a rising number of
  challenges through the increasing relevance of religion in public discourse. Spain as a
  predominantly Catholic country faces an increasing religious and interreligious openness which is mirrored in an increasing public discourse on new forms of Catholic
  RE and new approaches to an Islamic RE.
- Russia and Estonia both have strong religious traditions (Lutheran in Estonia, Orthodox in Russia) which have long been marginalised by Communism. In recent years,
  both societies have become increasingly open towards religious influences.

This book provides an insight in the developments and contexts of RE in the countries
mentioned above. All project leaders (the 'consortium') have a deep experience in the
field related to the project and have previously co-operated fruitfully. Their respective
disciplines are: Theology, Islamic studies, education, religious education, sociology, political science, ethnology and anthropology. They are determined to cooperate in theoretical and empirical studies, knowing that only interdisciplinary and international cooperation can bring about new results nowadays. Shared responsibility is combined with
special functions:

- The project coordinator – the author of this introduction – has been active in international research projects for a long time. He and Thorsten Knauth, the co-leader for the
  project in Hamburg, will contribute their special background on the concept and practice of intercultural dialogical religious education and their experiences with the
  analysis of videotaped RE-lessons to the REDCo-project.
- Robert Jackson from Warwick University is the leading expert in religious education
  in England with close ties to Norway and most of the other European countries. He is
  currently involved in a Council of Europe project on bringing the dimension of religious diversity to intercultural education across Europe. His 'interpretive approach'
  will be used as theoretical background for the project.

- Jean-Paul Willaime from the Sorbonne is the dominant figure both in academic and public discussions on religious education in France. He will shed light on different approaches in European countries, whether and how a new form of a concept of laicity could provide impulses for the development of European identity.
- Siebren Miedema from the Free University Amsterdam, his colleagues Ina ter Avest and Cok Bakker (University of Utrecht) are highly recognised in both theoretic questions (e.g. the non-foundational approach) and in empirical research with regard to qualitative studies on pupils and teachers. They are also experts on the correlation of empirical analysis at school and a theory of multicultural and multireligious education.
- Geir Skeie from the University of Stavanger is an outstanding systematic educationalist, who contributes to the relevant field of citizenship education and the contribution to the formation of religious identity within intercultural identity-management.
- Pille Valk from the University of Tartu is an expert for the study of the possibilities and limits of religious education in a post-Communist state. This relates to theoretical work and to her expertise on a comparative study with the instrument of quantitative methods.
- Muhammad Kalisch from the University of Münster is one of the few researchers in Europe with a high expertise on approaches of an authentic, but contextual European Islam. He and Dan-Paul Jozsa have first hand experience of the challenges of appropriate approaches to teacher training for Muslims, which is adapted to the multicultural reality of European societies. He is an expert for a dialogical approach in Muslim RE.
- Udo Steinbach from the German Institute for Middle East Studies is an outstanding expert for basic questions of intercultural understanding, both seen from a European and from an outside perspective. He has the capacity to identify elements of a European identity in the field of religion and education and especially look to possibilities for further development with the potential to foster dialogue instead of separation. He adds an outside-view to the group, namely from the perspective of Arab states.
- Vladimir Fedorov and his colleague Fedor Kosyrev from the Russian Christian Academy for Humanities in St. Petersburg are experts for the change from communism to the post-socialistic society in Russia. They are experts in both fields: in the religious developments in their country and the challenges of the 'laboratory' for RE in Eastern Europe. They will offer their analysis of religious education in Russia as a new form of experimenting with new approaches to/forms of, and didactic material for RE.
- Gunther Dietz from the University of Granada is an internationally recognized expert of ethnographic methods. He also has a high academic reputation in systematic approaches of comparative studies in the field of religion, culture and gender-issues.

Framework of International Research and State-of-the-Art

In terms of research, work has been done in several countries to date. Efforts to stimulate cooperative research work in different countries have been started in recent years by several more or less formal international networks. However, comparative European analysis on religion and education and its relevance for different societies or in the wider European context are still in their beginnings.

The following international networks provide space for an exchange of research in the field of religious education and values:

The 'International Seminar on Religious Education and Values' (ISREV) has existed since 1978. Its focus was originally directed to research in Western Europe and the English speaking countries of North America and Australasia. Researchers with common methodological approaches initially worked on themes like young people's attitudes towards Christianity and stage development. Only in recent years has more attention been given to interreligious and intercultural questions. Most members of our consortium are members of ISREV.

The international research network 'Inter-Religious and Intercultural Education' (IRE) has been working since 1994. Colleagues from Western European and Southern African countries form this group. Here questions of dialogical RE, of the correlation between interreligious an intercultural education, of religion and citizenship education have been dealt with.[2] A special emphasis is put on different perspectives arising from the varying conditions in European and Southern African countries. Most members of our consortium are members in IRE, Jackson and Weisse are the founders of it.

The 'European Network for Religious Education through Contextual Approaches' (ENRECA) works precisely in the field of our project. Its aims are published under the title: 'Towards Religious Competence. Diversity as a Challenge for Education in Europe' (Heimbrock et al., 2001). About half of the project leaders of our consortium are members of ENRECA.

In the context of these networks, various comparative studies have been conducted.[3] However, these do not usually take a European perspective but rather focus on a comparison of individual countries – e.g. Germany and Poland or Germany and the United States (Faern et al., 2004; Osmer & Schweitzer, 2003). One of the rare European studies has been a comparison of the position of Judaism, Christianity and Islam in European curricula, funded by the Herbert-Quandt-Stiftung (Kaul-Seidman et al., 2003). This study offers a good background analysis for our project, but its thematic focus is very different from ours (it focuses on school curricula and takes a more prescriptive and normative approach as opposed to our descriptive, empirical study).

Increasing efforts to exchange research results and impulses between different countries are made, but no coordinated European effort existed up to date.

---

2   Dialogical RE: Weiße, W. (1996); Correlation: Andree et al. (1997), Chidester et al. (1999), IRE (2005); Religion and citizenship: Jackson (2003).
3   For elements of comparative approaches see Jackson (2004d), Weisse (1997, 187 ff.), Council of Europe (2004).

There is a considerable deficit in Europe-wide comparative approaches to religion and education. This has been concluded by an important conference in Lund in March 2004. The findings of this conference have fittingly been titled 'Towards a European perspective on Religious Education' (Larsson & Gustavsson, 2004). In the common statement 'Religious Educational Research for the Future' of that conference the following perspectives or European research on religious education are outlined.

Inter alia the statement stresses the need

> '1) to be well informed about the pluralistic, multicultural and multireligious or secularised society; 2) to be good listeners to the voices of people, first of all young people; 3) to develop adequate educational approaches' (Religious Educational Research for the Future, 2004, p. 354).

Special attention is given to three priorities: To develop both empirical and theoretical research in religious education, to overcome the restriction to 'small milieus' of RE research, and to strive for better co-operation among the existing institutions (Religious Educational Research for the Future, 2004, p. 356).

Those challenges formulated in Lund in 2004 encourage a project like ours: We focus on interreligious learning as well as on the views of young people, propose to do analytical work on educational approaches, we combine empirical and theoretical research, we foster and establish cooperation among our team (consortium), we work in cooperation with different institutions and disseminate our findings to them.

Comparative studies are important for our approach as they show both the potential for dialogue-centred teaching within the range of historically developed institutions of religious education and its institutional and ideological limitations.

The Understanding of 'Religion' in Education and the Theoretical Background

We use the term religious education in a broad sense. It covers academic teacher training as well as both philosophical and practical aspects of religious and value education at schools. Our main focus with regard to schools will be the subject 'Religious Education (RE)', but we will also keep hold of the option to look at religion and religiosity in other subjects. We indicated this broader definition of religious education by using 'religion in education' as part of the title of our project. We focus on the contribution of RE both to personal development as well as to social responsibility and social cohesion. In the context of different understandings of what 'religious education' means (e.g. a more confessional orientated approach vs. a more religious studies approach) in different regions of Europe, all members of the consortium share an appreciation of religious and cultural difference as a positive factor, as well as a collective concern for the question about common values.

When studying religion, we will not focus on abstract belief systems or 'world-religions' but rather concentrate on the forms of religions and world-views as presented by the adherents themselves. With reference to Emmanuel Levinas, we are directing our attention to 'neighbour-religions' (Weiße, 2003) – the views of neighbours in classrooms, in the region, in the state, and the whole of Europe. The world religions are present in the 'neighbour-religions', and thus our approach permits us to study them in their current forms with their potentials for dialogue and conflict. Thus we find appropriate ways of dealing with plurality, diversity, and difference. With a non-foundationalist view we stress the value of personal expressions and dialogue related to religious identity formation (Miedema, 2004). Identity formation must be looked upon in view of a positive orientation, but also with regard to inherent dangers (e.g. the exclusion of others).

Religions and world views will be studied in their function for individual and collective identity management both in certain regions and with a perspective to open up towards a European perspective (Skeie, 2001). In the context of these questions we also take up gender issues.

Our main theoretical background will be the interpretive approach to the study of religious diversity (Jackson, 1997, 2004, 2006).

The key concepts in this approach are:

- *Representation:* Religions should be presented not as homogeneous.
- *Interpretation:* Students should not be expected to set aside their own presuppositions, but should compare their own concepts with those of others.
- *Reflexivity:* Students should re-assess their own ways of life; they should be constructively critical of the material they study (see Jackson & O'Grady in this book).

The interpretive approach allows for a combination of ethnographic and educational approaches to RE, and is especially useful for achieving a rich and empirically grounded analysis of the local practice and individual interpretations.

With a focus on religious diversity, conceptualising this through 'representation', 'interpretation' and 'reflexivity', it covers the individual as well as the group level. It also allows for theoretical reflection including a discussion of how certain aims, contents and methods in religious education may or may not contribute to peaceful coexistence in a multicultural Europe both through curriculum design and in classroom practice.

The subject of our study can be understood in the context of citizenship education, although we underline, that religious education is not the same as citizenship education. Members of the applicant group have already demonstrated the importance of religious education centred on intercultural dialogue and current social issues for this. Two points were particularly stressed in this context: Religious education complements civic education. It has the potential to incorporate European and global ideas of citizenship and helping children debate issues relevant to a plural society (Jackson, 2003).

Religious education in the form of interreligious education has shown to be able to contribute to intercultural understanding, tolerance and harmony (Weiße, 2003).

Religious education plays an important role in European societies with a long history of church-state-interaction, but could also be seen as a ferment for change and a resource for values in European societies both with a strict separation of church and state like France and others with an anti-religious political tradition, like Estonia (Willaime, 2004a, b, c; Valk, 2002a, b).

The Structure of our Research: Common Backgrounds, Special Projects with Cooperation and Networks

In formulating our specific projects we ensured that – in spite of the differences of states and regions – we have important factors in common, so that a comparative study will be possible. We share the theoretical background, the analysis of historical and societal background, the methods and methodological setting, the analysis on the views of the pupils, the classroom analysis and the perspective of a restructuring at university-level.

Theoretical background: As outlined above, our main theoretical stimulus will be the interpretive approach to the study of religious diversity, but we also refer to the theoretical backgrounds of 'neighbour-religions', of 'non-foundationalism' and of 'identity-formation'. These approaches complement each other.

Historical and societal background: We will all begin with an analysis of the special historical and societal backgrounds in our states and/or regions of Europe, focusing on the contribution of religion in education to dialogue and/or to conflict. Thus we will see where we have common ground and where we have different backgrounds regarding the basic questions of our project. We combine this analysis with a study of the ideas and the development of European identity (focusing on the documents of the European Council).

Methods and methodological setting: We all use the same repertoire of methods and analyse our findings in a triangulation (Flick, 2004). For text analysis, we refer to mainly hermeneutical methods. For empirical methods, we all use the following: Participant observation, semi-structured interviews, questionnaires (qualitative and quantitative), videotaping of RE-lessons for interaction analysis. Within this repertoire, special methods, like e.g. action-research, will be used as well. The shared methods will also be used in different proportions by the different project groups, but nevertheless there is sufficient similarity for valid comparisons to be drawn. All our projects look at religious education for school students in the 14 to 16 years age group in various countries. Arrangements have been made to apply a shared core methodology (participant observation, semi-structured interviews, and classroom interaction) to similar questions while allowing specialised tasks to be addressed with a mix of quantitative and qualitative methods appropriate to the purpose. We all use hermeneutical as well as empirical methods. We combine analyses of concepts of RE with the concrete views of pupils: We observe them, we interview them, we ask for written answers in questionnaires, and we analyse their interaction. With this combination, we can capture both the perspective 'from above' and the perspective 'from below', and will combine both perspectives in a triangulation.

Analysis on the views of pupils: A qualitative and quantitative analysis on the views of pupils in participating countries will be carried out. The age of the pupils will be 14 to 16 years. The gender perspective will be one of the elements for the structure of research questions and for the analysis. In addition and in connection with the empirical analyses in the special projects we plan an empirical study for our overall project. It consists of both a qualitative and a quantitative approach:

Qualitative study: In the first half year of the project, three or four questions will be worked out in order to record pupils' views on the societal function of religion, on their experience with religion in education, and their wishes to include or exclude religion from education. All questions will focus on the possibilities of dialogue and/or conflict. In the first half year of the project those questions will be answered in a written form (about one to two pages per pupil) by about 70 pupils in each country (in Germany 140 pupils).

Quantitative analysis: On the basis of the results of the qualitative analysis, questions will be worked out for a quantitative questionnaire. This will be answered by 200 pupils in each country (in Germany 200 in Hamburg and 200 in the region of Münster).

Dissemination: We will use the material of the empirical studies for various forms of dissemination. This includes publications, but also exhibitions. How do we do that? The project partners take the analysis of the country-related qualitative study back to their research fields and ask the pupils for comments on the preliminary analysis, in order to include their views and maybe add new aspects to the analysis. At the same time four or five pupils per school whose answers were particularly interesting will be asked if they agree to be photographed. This will be the source for photos to be combined with the main positions of pupils. Photos of pupils combined with significant answers and photos of the classroom, school and surroundings will be structured for both exhibitions related to the different countries and an exhibition which includes regions or all countries.

Classroom analysis: On the basis of participant observation and the videotaping of RE-lessons, an analysis of interaction patterns in the classroom (14–16 years age group) will be possible. Our research structure and the analyses include gender perspectives. We will focus on incidents exemplifying both successful dialogue and conflict in lessons. From the recorded incidents, an interpretation will be structured bottom-up. On the basis of this material and of additional professional filming a 30-minute-film will be produced.

Restructuring at University level: One of the perspectives which will be based on our results is related to questions of how universities are able to cope with religious plurality and in which direction structural changes would be required in order to prepare future teachers to deal in a better way with religious and cultural difference.

Perspectives for the Work of REDCo and Dissemination

Previous single efforts and the analyses offered in this book now allow us an increasingly clear and structured view of the different situations of religious education in various countries throughout Europe. Hereon our project aims to carry out joint research in several countries simultaneously for the first time. We will aim at

- answering the increasingly urgent question of how dialogue between cultures and religions can be fostered and gaps bridged in the context of religion in education,
- gaining an impression of the possibilities and limits of interreligious dialogue at the conceptual and empirical level,
- in particular, gaining such an impression for the age group of 14 to 16-year olds which will be decisive for future developments in public opinion,
- combining national studies of very different profiles (see above 'choice of countries') with a comparable theoretical, methodical and thematic approach,
- not limiting ourselves to university researchers, but from the beginning aim at the inclusion of cooperation partners in schools and information and dialogue with stake-

holders in the education system, various religious groups, the general public, the media and politics.

The members of the consortium are deeply involved in both national and international research on our subject. Our network has been designed with this aim in mind. We are also in contact with colleagues within and outside of our countries who are doing research work in the field of intercultural religious education. They will be kept informed on our project and its progress. We will discuss the research work of colleagues and younger researchers who are contributing to the broader field of our project.

The findings of this programme will contribute to a better understanding of how religions and questions of religion and religiosity for children, young people and students can be anchored in the educational process so as to promote an appreciation of the value of difference and an understanding of the values held in common and develop mutual respect.

The focus of the project will be on ways to develop an understanding in the field of religion and value systems that can serve both as an orientation for personal development and as a means to develop an appreciation of the processes of democratic citizenship and social cohesion. This dual focus remains open for the development of a collective 'European identity' (which must be understood as plural and dialogic rather than monolithic).

The members of the consortium will use the following contact points at the national and European level to disseminate interim results and provide innovative impulses.

- We use discussions and presentations within the structure of international networks for Religious and Values Education (see above in the 'state of the art' information on ISREV, IRE, and ENRECA) for the dissemination of our activities and will propagate the relevance of our findings,

- discussions with representatives of schools, education authorities and curriculum commissions in order to improve awareness of the issues of interreligious education and conflicts involving religion. This may address fundamental basics of school organisation, but will also include concrete impulses for immediate improvement.

- Developing outlines of necessary changes at national and European level resulting from our conceptual and empirical studies. This analysis will particularly investigate strategies to further classroom dialogue, as well as approaches to a more dialogue-centred teaching required for teacher training institutions.

- Presentation and discussion at congresses, symposia and university seminars in order to improve awareness of the relevance of our study and promote a pan-European perspective on religion in education.

- Entering the public arena in order to highlight the need for and possibility of approaches to dialogue and encounter in religion and education. This will also help to counter divisive and confrontational developments.

Beyond the results with regard to single countries, our project will open perspectives for pan-European research. Our findings may shed light to the profiles and the differences between countries and their main emphases, thus improving our understanding of the path towards developing a European identity. The need for this is evident not least of all by the calls of various European institutions.

Developing education for democracy has been a vital issue in the more than 50 years' history of the Council of Europe. Within this context, education for democratic citizenship and, more recently, intercultural and interreligious education are playing increasingly important roles. This development can be outlined as follows:

In the Declaration by the European Ministers of Education on Intercultural Education in the New European Context (Athens, Greece, 10–12 November 2003) the importance of intercultural education for the development of the unity and diversity of European societies is emphasised. The issue was particularly addressed by the launch of the project 'The New Intercultural Challenge to Education: Religious Diversity and Dialogue in Europe'. In the course of this, a conference on 'The Religious Dimension of Intercultural Education' was held in Oslo on 6–8 June 2004 during which the Director-General of Education, Culture, Youth, Sport and Environment in the Council of Europe, Gabriella Battaini-Dragoni, pointed out the particular importance of religious education. The different institutional and legislative structures within which religious education takes place in various European countries are not easy to unify, given their different historical developments, but, as she states,

'... we will I hope find greater commonalities in good practice in the classroom' (Battaini-Dragoni, 2004, p. 11). Religions matter 'because the matter of religion – whatever orientation we each adopt – goes to the heart of our emotions and identities ...' (Battaini-Dragoni, 2004, p. 13).

This can often lead to great conflict, but in this respect,

'... even policymakers, can learn from children' (ibid).

This clearly shows the need for the kind of research our project proposes. The same need is also addressed by other activities of the Council of Europe. The latest study published by the European Monitoring Centre on Racism and Xenophobia emphasises the increasing degree of rejection cultural and religious minorities meet in Europe (European Monitoring Centre on Racism and Xenophobia, 2005). In order to counteract increasing tension and combat the entrenchment of prejudice, opportunities for dialogue and encounter must be supported in schools. This is particularly important for school students still in the process of forming their opinions, for whom encounters with people of different religions and interreligious learning can be an important step towards

- respecting other positions (even in disagreement) rather than absolutising one's own opinion,
- not regarding religion and culture as monolithic but rather as determined by a multiplicity of human beings in daily practice and as changeable,
- establishing bars against the ideological abuse of religion and its instrumentalisation for political conflict.

It is particularly these topics which we will be able to offer impulses and solutions for in the context of interreligious education by conducting research which has rightly been called for within the EU.

The project will address ways of studying religion for all students in publicly funded schools as well as developing methods for dealing positively with religious plurality in schools that have a religious foundation.

In its comparative, empirical results, this project will decisively contribute to the formulation of standards as well as quality criteria for the ongoing national and EU processes of formulating guidelines for the institutionalization of inter-religious education and diversity management in religious education. In all participating countries, the domains of secular/religious education are currently being redefined vis-à-vis religious diversification/pluralisation and the 'Europeanization of Islam'. In this context, 'best practices' are still scarce. Thus, pilot projects such as the ones studied here will inform educational policy-making by identifying a set of standard quality criteria for determining the inter-religious character of educational measures, curricula, intra-school settings and extra-school arrangements.

First Steps of REDCo and the Aim of this Book

So much for the basic ideas of our REDCo-project. We have started our project in March 2006 and will run it till February 2009. Through the funds of the EU we are able to hire more than a dozen younger researchers, who will largely contribute with their abilities and power to the success of REDCo. For EU funded projects a tight time schedule must be followed. According to our application, reports of our work ('deliverables') must be communicated every half year to the headquarters of the EU in Brussels. Main results, the 'milestones', must be reached within a time span, which is fixed from the very beginning. A work-structure like this may be regarded as too strict; nevertheless it provides a clear basis for the research in a group, working in quite different regions of Europe. In such a network with twelve project leaders and additionally even more researchers funded by the EU such a transparent and clear design seems to be adequate and helpful.

The contributions of this book are based on reports after the first half year and form the first milestone. We are aware of the fact, that comparative research on religion in education in Europe must be founded on analyses of the different settings in our European countries. This has been widely neglected until now. That is why we present the historical and societal backgrounds of religion and education in this volume, focussing on the contribution of religion in education to dialogue and conflict. Our analyses are the prerequisite and a bridge towards the planned empirical and theoretical work.

We include a whole section on European discussions in the first part of our book. This is the horizon, in which our work takes place. Bob Jackson highlights the discussions within the Council of Europe and other European Institutions in a sort of participant observation: He analyses documents of discussion-processes, he has mostly been directly involved in himself. So he presents a view from within as well as an analysis from the outside. Jean-Paul Willaime refers to different groups and models for religion and education in Europe, in order to structure existing tendencies in the European field. The contribution of Dan-Paul Jozsa is directed to a theme, which gains more and more relevance for religion and education in the whole of Europe: The way of dealing with Islam in schools, in Universities and in societies.

The second and main part of our book contains historical and contextual analyses of religion and education in our different countries. The contributions pay attention to the following items:

- The historical tradition and socio-political background of religion in education, including church/religion-state-relations, goals of education in state, family and church, and the geographical position.

- The present context of religion in education, including the nature and degree of multiculturalism, the impact of globalisation and pedagogical trends.

- The aims and debates of religions in education, including changing aims of RE and open questions, especially referring to the legal framework, policies and pedagogies that address issues of dialogue and conflict.

- Perspectives with the potential of religion in education as a contribution to dialogue in school and society.

At the end of the book one of the editors refers to the contributions of this book, compares them and formulates a preliminary summery.

This book forms the first expression of the REDCo-project and paves the way for our research ahead. We would like to express our gratitude to the EU for the strong support. We are aware of the responsibility linked with a funding, which is higher than for any project in our field until now. Although we have a lot to do, in order to fulfil our workplan with deliverables and milestones, we are open to contacts and cooperation with other colleagues. We are in contact with other research-projects and have already started additional projects, affiliated to REDCo. This relates e.g. to questions of Muslim schools and their potential to contribute to isolation or to an openness and dialogue in two European countries (The Netherlands and England) and South Africa.

The REDCo-project with its team focuses on a comparative research directed to questions of dialogue and conflict in the field of religion and education in Europe. But we are open to the cooperation with other colleagues, including regions outside Europe. And we know that our research will be strengthened by the advisory group, the critical friends and other colleagues, interested in our theme. We are starting a project with a strong focus on comparative research, where a lot more needs to be done in the future. So we see REDCo as a first comprehensive step in an ongoing research-process.

References

Andree, T., Bakker, C., & Schreiner, P. (Eds.) (1997) *Crossing Boundaries: Contributions to Interreligious and Intercultural Education* (Münster, Comenius Institut).

Battaini-Dragoni, G. (2004) Opening, in: Council of Europe (Ed.) *The Religious Dimension of Intercultural Education* (provisional edition) (Strasbourg, Council of Europe Publishing) 11–14.

Chidester, D., Stonier, J. & Tobler, J. (Eds.) (1999) *Diversity as Ethos: Challenges for Interreligious and Intercultural Education* (Cape Town, ICRSA, University of Cape Town).

Council of Europe (Ed.) (2004) *The Religious Dimension of Intercultural Education* (Strasbourg, Council of Europe Publishing).

European Commission (Ed.) (2004) FP6 Specific Programme *Integrating and Strengthening the European Research Area*, Priority 7: Citizens and Governance in a knowledge based society, Work Programme 2004–2006 (Brussels).

European Monitoring Centre on Racism and Xenophobia (Ed.) (2005) *Majorities' Attitudes To-wards Minorities:* Key Findings form the Eurobarometer and the European Social Survey (Vienna, EUMC).

Faern, M., Ziebertz, H.-G. & Pasierbek, W. (2004) Perceptions of Religious Education among Polish and German Young People: An Empirical Perspective, in: R. Larsson & C. Gus-tavsson (Eds.) *Towards a European Perspective on Religious Education:* The RE research conference March 11–14, 2000 University of Lund (Stockholm, Artos & Norma) 175–190.

Flick, U. (2004) *Triangulation: Eine Einführung* (Wiesbaden, VS Verlag für Sozialwissen-schaften).

Habermas, J. (2005) *Zwischen Naturalismus und Religion: Philosophische Aufsätze* (Frankfurt am Main, Suhrkamp).

Hasenclever, A. (2003) Geteilte Werte – Gemeinsamer Frieden? Überlegungen zu zivilisierenden Kraft von Religionen und Glaubensgemeinschaften, in: H. Küng & D. Senghaas (Eds.) *Friedenspolitik: Ethische Grundlagen internationaler Beziehungen* (München, Piper) 288–318.

Heimbrock, H.-G., Scheilke C.T., & Schreiner, P. (2001) *Towards Religious Competence: Di-versity as a Challenge for Education in Europe* (Hamburg, Lit-Verlag).

IRE (2005) Contributions of the International Network for International and Intercultural Educa-tion (IRE), Stellenbosch-Conference March 2004, *Scriptura. International Journal of Bi-ble, Religion and Theology in Southern Africa*, 89 (2/2005) (section 1), 233–374.

Jackson, R. (1997) *Religious Education: An Interpretive Approach* (London, Hodder and Stough-ton).

Jackson, R. (2004) *Rethinking Religious Education and Plurality: Issues in Diversity and Peda-gogy* (London, RoutledgeFalmer).

Jackson, R. (2006) Understanding religious diversity in a plural world: The interpretive approach, in: M. de Souza, K. Engebretson, G. Durka, R. Jackson & A. McGrady (Eds.) *Interna-tional Handbook of the Religious, Moral and Spiritual Dimensions of Education*, (The Netherlands, Springer Academic Publishers), 399–414.

Jackson, R. (Ed.) (2003) *International Perspectives on Citizenship, Education and Religious Di-versity* (London, RoutledgeFalmer).

Kaul-Seidman, L., Nielsen, J.S. & Vinzent, M. (2003) *European identity and cultural pluralism: Judaism, Christianity and Islam in European curricula*, Supplement: Country reports (Bad Homburg v.d. Höhe, Herbert-Quandt-Foundation).

Kelle, U. & Erzberger, C. (2003) Making inferences in mixed methods: The rules of integration, in: A. Tashakkori & C. Teddlie (Eds.) *Handbook of mixed methods in social & Behav-ioural research* (Thousand Oaks) 457–488.

Larsson, R. & Gustavsson, C. (2004) *Towards a European Perspective on Religious Education.* The RE research conference March 11–14, 2004, University of Lund (Stockholm, Artos & Norma).

Miedema, S. (2004) Beyond Foundationalism: A Plea for a New Normativity in the Philosophy of Religious Education, in: R. Larsson & C. Gustavsson (Eds.) *Towards a European Per-spective on Religious Education*, (Stockholm, Artos & Norma) 36–45.

Osmer, R.R. & Schweitzer, F. (2003) *Religious Education between Modernization and Global-ization: New Perspectives on the United States and Germany* (Grand Rapids).

Religious Educational Research for the Future (2004), in: R. Larsson & C. Gustavsson (Eds.) *Towards a European Perspective on Religious Education.* The RE research conference March 11–14, 2004, University of Lund (Stockholm, Artos & Norma) 353–356.

Ricoeur, P. (2006) *Wege der Anerkennung: Erkennen, Wiedererkennen, Anerkanntsein* (Frankfurt am Main, Suhrkamp).

Schiffauer, W., Baumann, G. Kastoryano, R. & Vertovec, S. (Eds.) (2002) *Staat – Schule – Ethnizität. Politische Sozialisation von Immigrantenkindern in vier europäischen Ländern* (Münster/New York/München/Berlin, Waxmann).

Skeie, G. (2001) Citizenship, Identity politics and Religious Education, in: H.-G. Heimbrock, C. Th. Scheilke & P. Schreiner (Eds.) *Towards Religious Competence: Diversity as a Challenge for Education in Europe* (Münster, Lit Verlag) 237–252.

Valk, P. (2002a) *Eesti kooli religiooniõpetuse kontseptsioon* [Concept of Religious Education for Estonian Schools], Dissertationes Theologiae Universitatis Tartuensis (Tartu, Ülikooli kirjastus).

Valk, P. (2002b) Geo-Political Approach to Christian Education in Contemporary Eastern Europe (together with T. Lehtsaar), in: W. Gräb & B. Weyel (Eds.) *Praktische Theologie und protestantische Kultur in Berlin* (Gütersloh) 511–522.

Weisse, W. (1997) Religious Education in multiperspective view of the participants, in: T. Andree, C. Bakker & P. Schreiner (Eds.) (1997) *Crossing Boundaries, Contributions to Interreligious and Intercultural Education* (Münster, Comenius Institut) 187–190.

Weisse, W. (2003) Difference without discrimination: Religious Education as a field of learning for social understanding? in: R. Jackson (Ed.) *International Perspectives on Citizenship, Education and Religious Diversity* (London, Routledge/Falmer) 191–208.

Weisse, W. (Ed.) (1996) *Interreligious and Intercultural Education: Methodologies, Conceptions and Pilot Projects in South Africa, Namibia, Great Britain, the Netherlands, and Germany* (Münster, Comenius Institut).

Willaime, J.-P. (2004a) *Europe et religions : les enjeux du XXIe siècle* (Paris, Fayard).

Willaime, J.-P. (2004b) Participation à la table ronde animée par D. Borne Le religieux et l'école en France, *Revue Internationale d'Education*, Sèvres, 36, juillet 2004 (Dossier "Ecole et religion"), 49–69.

Willaime, J.-P. (2004c) Peut-on parler de 'laïcité européenne?', in: *La laïcité à l'épreuve. Religions et libertés dans le monde* (dirigé par J. Baubérot) (Paris, Universalis) (2004), 53–63.

Robert Jackson

European Institutions and the Contribution of Studies of Religious Diversity to Education for Democratic Citizenship[1]

The International Context

Issues about the study of religion in public education are being discussed internationally as never before. The discussions include specialists in religion, but also many outside the professional field of religious education – politicians, civil servants, NGOs and other groups within civil society as well as educators concerned with fields such as citizenship and intercultural education. This is partly due to the global attention given to religion as a result of the events of September 11, 2001 in the USA, their causes, on-going consequences and associated incidents that have affected people in many parts of the world. In Europe, it also relates to the challenge of transcultural diversities (Robins, 2006) and the growing climate of racism in some states (MacEwen, 1995), much of it directed against Muslims, exacerbated by 9/11 and its consequences (Modood, Triandafyllidou & Zapata-Barrero, 2006).

Of course, positive events involving religion also have an impact on public consciousness in relation to issues within civil society, whether through the constructive activities of inter-faith networks, or the example of outstanding personalities such as the Dalai Lama in relation to peace and environmental issues[2] or Archbishop Desmond Tutu as Chairman of the Truth and Reconciliation Commission of South Africa (Tutu, 2000). It is also interesting that several research projects are being conducted at the moment on the theme of religion as social capital (Putnam, 1995), aiming, for example, to explore the extent to which faith organisations and members contribute to, or appear as obstacles to, 'the bridging and linking of social capital required to achieve well-connected communities'.[3]

In the present discussion, there is no intention to imply that the study of religion in schools should be solely justified through attention to social and political events and issues. I agree with the Delors Report in considering that education should include learning to know, learning to do, learning to live together and learning to be (UNESCO, 1996). It is arguable that religious education should be concerned with all of these, especially the fourth. The present discussion focuses on the third, but does not ignore the others. The discussion responds to recent and widespread international interest in the study of religions in schools, with particular attention to European institutions, prompted by various political events and social issues. This is why close attention is given to citizenship education.

---

1   An earlier version of this chapter was presented as a plenary paper at the International Seminar on Religious Education and Values Conference on 'Religious Education in a World of Religious Diversity', Driebergen, Netherlands, 3rd August 2006.
2   http://www.dalailama.com/ accessed 15 May 2006.
3   For example, 'Faith as Social Capital: Connecting or Dividing?' Joseph Rowntree Foundation, 2005. http://www.jrf.org.uk/bookshop/eBooks/9781861348388.pdf accessed 14 June 2006.

Religious Education and Citizenship Education:
Diversity in Europe

Having placed the debate in a global context, I will now concentrate on issues concerning religion and public education in Europe. These will be considered in parallel with developments in citizenship education, a field which also responds to social issues.

First, I will illustrate some different approaches to religious education and citizenship education in individual states. The differences between them reflect particular factors in each state, including historical tradition (especially the history of Church/State relations in the case of religious education), the nature and degree of 'multiculturalism' in society and other cultural factors, socio-political structure, economic system, and international/global influences, all of which interplay with factors such as educational values, aims and funding arrangements. I will then go on to consider broader European approaches, developed through European networks of researchers and educators, and especially through projects associated with European institutions. There will be some reference to EU/EC funded research, but most space will be devoted to developments within the Council of Europe. Both institutions are concerned with European integration, understood in terms of fostering a society in which citizens feel that they belong to Europe while they also feel rooted in regional and national traditions and cultures. European integration thus includes identifying and establishing a minimum of common values, as legislated in the European Convention of Human Rights, but respects the preservation and development of regional and national cultural elements, including the integration of various kinds of cultural diversity within and across individual states. European collaborative work in education can thus provide models for policy makers and curriculum developers that present a broad European vision, but which may not be fully applicable in all countries.

Religious Education in Europe

Of course, the role of religion in education has been seen rather differently in the various European states. Friedrich Schweitzer has pointed out the need for careful comparative study of religious education (or its equivalents) as a research tool for informing developments in policy and practice (Schweitzer, 2006). He has also, rightly, pointed out the pitfalls of such studies if done superficially, especially in relation to linguistic issues such as the different meanings given to 'religious education' and diverse usages of particular terms such as 'confessional' (and its equivalent in other European languages) across different systems.

Despite the field of comparative study being in its infancy, there have been a number of publications aiming to give a picture of educational provision in relation to religion across European states (eg Kodelja & Bassler, 2004; Schreiner, 2002; Willaime & Mathieu, 2005). On the basis of these sources one might make some points about the diversity of policy and practice in Europe from different angles. One might, for example, distinguish between the different ways in which states accommodate religion within their educational systems and develop policy accordingly. There are 'confessional' systems in which religious bodies are given responsibility for religious education. For example, in Germany, the churches have a supervisory responsibility for religious education, but within a constitutional framework of equal rights and non-discrimination. The 'confessional' system is different in the Netherlands, where schools have the right to teach the religion of the sponsor, and different again from, say, Slovakia, where schools teach what is recognised as the religion of the state – in this case Roman Catholicism. In some instances, as in Poland, religious education is an optional subject, taught by insiders, according to the tenets of particular denominations (mainly Roman Catholicism). Teachers' qualifications are defined by the church in question, in agreement with the Ministry of National Education and Sport (Eurydice, 2006). Then, there are non-confessional systems where religious bodies have no role in public education. For example, in public education in France, there is no subject devoted specifically to the study of religion, and any teaching covering religion in subjects such as history or philosophy must be purely informational (Estivalezes, 2005, 2006). Sweden presents another example of non-confessional religious education. As with France, there is no direct involvement in education from religious bodies, but in contrast to the French situation, religious education is seen very much in relation to the personal development of children and young people (Larsson, 2000). There are also 'mixed' systems, as in England and Wales, where fully publicly funded schools have a form of religious education which aims at impartiality in its treatment of religion, while mainly state-funded voluntary aided schools may teach and promote the religion of the sponsoring body (Jackson, 2000).

A familiar way of making distinctions is from the point of view of the aims of the subject. The distinction is sometimes made between educating into, about and from religion (cf Hull, 2002). Educating into religion deals with a single religious tradition, is taught by 'insiders' and often has the objective of enabling pupils to come to believe in the religion or to strengthen their commitment to it. Educating about religion confines itself to using descriptive and historical methods, and aims neither to foster nor to erode religious belief. Educating from religion involves pupils in considering different responses to religious and moral issues, so that they may develop their own views in a reflective way. Here the main objective might be seen as enabling pupils to develop their own point of view on matters relating to religion and values. On this taxonomy, the Italian system would be an example of educating into religion (Gandolfo-Censi, 2000), the Estonian system would exemplify educating about religion (Valk, 2000), while the English community school system would combine educating about and educating from religion (QCA, 2004).

Another way of distinguishing between varieties of religious education is in relation to broad geographical regions – such as the northern countries influenced mainly, in terms of religious history, by Protestantism, the southern mainly Catholic-influenced countries, and the former communist states recovering and reshaping earlier traditions (Orthodox and Catholic for example) following the demise of communism. There is a real danger of over-simplification here, of course. It is in the north, however, that most research and development has been done so far in the field of religious education (Larsson & Gustavsson, 2004). Times are changing rapidly, as we know from the wide variety of new work represented in the International Seminar on Religious Education and Values (ISREV), the European Network for Research on Religious Education through Contextual Approaches (ENRECA) and other networks. Some Russian scholars aim to produce a non-confessional cultural approach to recovering Orthodox tradition (Kosyrev & ter Avest, forthcoming), while French social scientists re-examine the concept of laïcité in relation to the accommodation of religion within public education (Debray, 2002; Estivalezes, 2005, 2006). Turkey which, like the Russian Federation, spans the continents of Europe and Asia, has a lively debate over the development of models of religious education appropriate for public education (Kaymakcan, 2006).

Clearly, these simple taxonomies do not provide a completely reliable basis for comparative study. The more detail that is uncovered in each system or approach, the more one realises the dangers of easy comparison. It is also evident that there would be difficulties in finding a common European approach to religious education.

Citizenship Education in Europe

Citizenship education is high on the agenda of European governments although, as with religious education, understandings of its nature and purposes are diverse across the continent. Whether influenced primarily by fears of the young's disengagement with political processes, by concerns about social cohesion in culturally diverse societies, or by political change in former communist countries, citizenship education has emerged, either as a discrete curriculum subject or as a dimension of the wider school curriculum (Paludan & Prinds, 1999). On a major Council of Europe project in Education for Democratic Citizenship (EDC) (which we will return to below), citizenship education is inclusive of human rights education, civic education, peace education, global education and intercultural education as well as activities in which participation in society can be learned, exercised and encouraged.[4] There is an increasing number of sources of information about citizenship education in different European states. For example, the International Association for the Evaluation of Educational Achievement (IEA) has conducted an international *Civic Education Study*.[5] More than 140,000 pupils, teachers and school principals from 28 countries took part in the study, and two major reports were issued by the IEA in 2001 and 2002.[6] Of the 28 countries researched, 23 were European.

The study found some general trends. For example, students in most countries showed some understanding of democratic values and institutions but often with little depth of understanding. Students with the most civic knowledge were most likely to be open to participate in civic activities as adults, while schools modelling democratic practice were the most effective in promoting civic knowledge and engagement. Patterns of trust in government-related institutions varied widely across countries (Torney-Purta, Lehmann,

---

4   http://www.coe.int/T/E/Cultural_Co-operation/education/E.D.C/ accessed 15 May 2006.

5   Formed 31 years ago, IEA is a non-profit, private association which carries out international comparative studies on schools. Policy makers and educators use data from IEA studies to assess the impact of alternative curricular offerings; monitor the quality of schooling worldwide; identify effective schools and learn how to improve their own educational systems, and better understand the instructional learning process.

6   For further information see: http://www2.hu-berlin.de/empir_bf/iea_e.html and http://www.wam.umd.edu/~iea/ both accessed 15 May 2006.

Oswald & Schulz, 2001). The study showed a gap between policy and practice in many cases, especially in relation to participation and active learning. Only about 25 per cent of pupils across all countries reported that they were often encouraged to state their own views during lessons, with an equal proportion stating that such discussion occurs rarely or never (Kerr, 2003, p. 21).

A second important source is a Eurydice project on citizenship, sponsored by the European Commission. The EC Directorate-General for Education and Culture, in 2003, established a working group focusing on an 'Open Learning Environment, Active Citizenship and Social Inclusion' (European Commission 2003). In 2004, this group requested information on citizenship education via the Information Network on Education in Europe (Eurydice).[7] A wealth of relevant data were provided from 30 European countries, in the form of a final report analysing how citizenship education is taught in schools (Eurydice, 2005), plus numerous accounts of the treatment of citizenship education in individual countries.[8]

The final report, *Citizenship Education at School in Europe*, recommends that the term citizenship education should be detached as far as possible from its legal connotation, 'embracing all members of a given society, regardless of their nationality, sex, or racial, social or educational background'. The report also notes that in different states citizenship education may be offered as a separate subject, integrated into conventional subjects (including religious and moral education) or be seen as a cross-curricular theme. There is also a growing view that the idea of citizenship should be pursued through whole school policies and increasing support for the 'democratic school' in which teachers, parents and pupils are involved in school management and decision-making. There is also widespread support for citizenship education's role in developing political literacy through dealing with issues such as democracy and human rights and for increasing active participation by pupils (Eurydice, 2005, p. 59-62). A trawl through individual reports shows that approaches linking citizenship education and religious education reflect the range of conceptions of both fields found across Europe.[9]

The Council of Europe project on Education for Democratic Citizenship has also conducted a survey of current policy and practice in citizenship education among member states. The findings draw attention to the 'implementation gap' between national policies and syllabuses and what is actually experienced by students (Council of Europe, 2004b).

The findings of the studies mentioned above bear out Terence McLaughlin's distinction between 'maximal' and 'minimal' interpretations of citizenship education

---

7   Eurydice is a network of institutions collecting, monitoring, processing and circulating comparable information on education systems and policies across Europe. Eurydice was established in 1980 by the European Commission and member states as a strategic mechanism to foster co-operation, through improving understanding of educational systems and policies.

8   Downloadable from http://www.eurydice.org accessed 10 June, 2006.

9   For example, religion is mentioned in relation to social exclusion or discrimination (Belgium [Flemish]); diversity (Italy); understanding religious values (Denmark); strengthening values (Slovakia); understanding religions (Slovenia) and respecting each other's religions (Bulgaria). Links between religious and citizenship education are seen through visits to neighbourhood or community groups including religious bodies. Some countries make no reference to religious education in their official documentation on citizenship education (eg Poland, Estonia, the Netherlands and Malta).

(McLaughlin, 1992). In this, a 'minimal' approach presents the subject as knowledge-based, with a particular civics-related content to be transmitted in a formal and didactic manner. A 'maximal' approach, in contrast, emphasises active learning and inclusion, is interactive, values-based and process led, allowing students to develop and articulate their own opinions and to engage in debate. The IEA, Eurydice and Council of Europe studies show a spectrum of practice between the two extremes. McLaughlin observes that the 'minimal' interpretation is open to various objections; the most notable being '...that it may involve merely an unreflective socialisation into the political and social *status quo*, and is therefore inadequate on educational, as well as other, grounds' (McLaughlin, 1992, p. 238).[10]

Research on Effective Citizenship Education

There is considerable support in the European Union and the Council of Europe for a more 'maximal' interpretation of citizenship education. When we consider pedagogy, there is strong research evidence, from Europe and the USA in particular, endorsing the effectiveness of 'maximal' approaches. A key source is two close analyses of published research in citizenship education by Ruth Deakin Crick and her collaborators (Deakin Crick et al., 2004, 2005; Deakin Crick, 2005).[11]

In the 2004 study, Deakin Crick and her colleagues provide a review of evidence giving information of how citizenship education is implemented in schools.[12] This review included different types of empirical studies published by early 2003. The overall question addressed was 'What is the impact of citizenship on the provision of schooling?' This was taken to mean learning and teaching; school context and ethos; leadership and management; curriculum construction and development and external relations and community. Fourteen studies were selected for detailed analysis.

With regard to learning and teaching specifically, seven studies were considered especially relevant. These indicated that dialogue and discourse relating to shared values, human rights and issues of justice and equality were effective methods, and that the quality of discourse is a key factor in learning. In such dialogue the teacher acts as a facilitator, rather than a purveyor of information; the students are encouraged to express their

---

10   See also Kerr, 1999, 12f on distinguishing between education about, through and for citizenship.

11   The research was conducted under the auspices of the Evidence for Policy and Practice Information and Co-ordinating Centre (EPPI-Centre), set up in 1993 to address the need for a systematic approach to the organisation and review of evidence-based work on social interventions. Both reports are published on EPPI-Centre's website as part of The Research Evidence in Education Library (REEL) (http://eppi.ioe.ac.uk/EPPIWeb/home.aspx?page=/reel/intro.htm).

12   Following Gearon (2003) she points out that there was little or no UK research on citizenship education before the 1990s, but some research and writing in fields such as values education, character education and PSHE, and in fields operative since the 1970s, called collectively by Gearon 'implicit citizenship education' – peace education, global/world studies, human rights education and political education. In particular, there was very little research on practice at the school level and little attempt to integrate citizenship education into broader educational philosophies and practices.

views, often drawing on their own life experiences. The studies reveal that such participative, conversational activity sustains achievement and that students become engaged when the experience is challenging, attainable and relevant to their own lives. A necessary condition is that there need to be ground rules for dialogue and discussion, ensuring inclusion and respect for others. The studies suggest the need for opportunities for students to engage with values issues across all curriculum subjects and experiences. Deakin Crick notes that this approach may challenge existing conventions and power structures within the school, and that teachers and leaders are likely to need additional training and support in order to acquire the necessary professional skills, preferably through a whole-school strategy, including an agreed framework of values (Deakin Crick, 2005, p. 72).

The 2005 study reviewed the impact of citizenship education specifically on student learning and achievement. The review focused on a detailed analysis of 13 research studies, two UK based, with a broader context provided by 35 research studies. Most of these were from the USA (22), five from the UK, two from Australia and one each from New Zealand, Portugal, Canada, Thailand, Ireland and Romania. Findings are consistent with those of the earlier review. The evidence indicates that approaches using dialogue and discussion are especially effective in enhancing learning and in increasing students' motivation and engagement. A co-operative learning environment that empowers students is shown to lead to increased self-confidence, greater self-reliance and more positive behaviour. Moreover, students' participation increases when lesson content relates to their own personal experiences. In gaining awareness of the situations of others, students are enabled to analyse and reflect on their own personal stories and experiences. On the question of teaching, as with the 2004 report, the review acknowledges a need for support for teachers in developing their expertise in facilitation and dialogue.

What is remarkable in this research is the consistent finding that there is a close connection between pedagogies that affirm the autonomy of young people and give them voice and responsibility (cf Hallett & Prout, 2003; Prout, 2001) and an increase in student motivation and engagement. This is also a finding of an ESRC research project on teaching and learning (Flutter and Rudduck, 2004).

Religion, Citizenship and Public Education in European Institutions

Having given a sketch of the diversity of both religious education and citizenship education in Europe, I will now concentrate on these fields as dealt with at the European level, focusing on work undertaken under the auspices of the Council of Europe.

With regard to the European Union, the preamble to the EU's first ever Constitution, (agreed at a summit on 18 June 2004, but rejected by referenda in France and the Netherlands), says the EU draws its 'inspiration from the cultural, religious and humanist inheritance of Europe, from which have developed the universal values of the inviolable and inalienable rights of the human person, democracy, equality, freedom and the rule of law'.[13] The Vatican and several Roman Catholic countries led by Poland pressed, without

---

13   http://europa.eu/constitution/en/ptoc1_en.htm#a1.

success, for the Constitution's preamble to refer to Europe's Christian heritage. Since the statement about religious heritage was not a factor in the French and Dutch rejection of the Constitution, it seems unlikely that the text will change in relation to religion in any future draft. In article 10 of the Constitution, there is a guarantee of freedom of thought, religion and conscience: 'Everyone has the right to freedom of thought, conscience and religion. This right includes freedom to change religion or belief and freedom, either alone or in community with others and in public or private, to manifest religion or belief, in worship, teaching, practice and observance.' One would expect EU policies with regard to religion and education to reflect these principles (Willaime 2005).

In developing a more integrated approach to the place of religion in public education, the importance of informal and semi-formal European networks of scholars and professional associations should be mentioned. With regard to religious education, for example, the International Seminar on Religious Education and Values (ISREV),[14] the European Association for Religious Education through Contextual Approaches (ENRECA)[15] and the International Network for Inter-religious and Intercultural Education[16] have been important. These networks have furnished opportunities for the discussion of new research ideas and research in progress at the European level and have provided the basis for bids for European funding for research. These include a successful bid to the EU Framework 6 programme for a collaborative European research project on 'Religion in Education: A Contribution to Dialogue or a Factor of Conflict in Transforming Societies of European Countries' (REDCo), which will be completed in 2009.[17] In relation to professional organisations, The Co-ordinating Group for Religious Education in Europe (CoGREE)

---

14   The International Seminar on Religious Education and Values (ISREV) was founded in 1978 and has met biennially since that time. Originally it included western Europeans and north Americans. The membership is now much more international. See http://www.isrev. org/ (accessed 8 August 2006).

15   The driving figure behind the establishment of ENRECA was Professor Hans-Günther Heimbrock. Heimbrock, Scheilke and Schreiner (2001) is ENRECA's first book; Miedema, Schreiner, Skeie and Jackson (2004) explains the ENRECA's goals; see also http://enreca.isert-network.com/docs/index.htm (accessed 1 June 2006). ENRECA now has its own European Book Series on 'Religious Diversity and Education in Europe', published from Germany by Waxmann. The first titles published were Zonne (2006) and Afdal (2006).

16   The International Network for Inter-religious and Inter-cultural Education was set up in 1994, soon after the election of a democratic government in South Africa, and had its first meeting at the University of Hamburg. The aim was to promote links between Southern African and Northern European research groups working in fields connecting religion and education in culturally diverse democratic societies. The seminar brought together Northern European and Southern African members of research and development groups working in the fields of religion, education and cultural diversity. Publications include Andree, Bakker and Schreiner (1997); Chidester, Stonier and Tobler (1999); Jackson (2003a); Weisse (1996) and contributions to a special issue of Scriptura: International Journal of Bible, Religion and Theology in South Africa, 89 (2), 2005.

17   Bringing together research groups from 10 European universities in seven countries, the REDCo project aims to identify policies and pedagogies that can contribute to making religion in education a factor promoting dialogue in the context of European development. This is the first major international project on religious education to gain funding from the European Commission, reflecting the changing attitude towards bringing studies of religion into public education (Jackson 2006a; see also Chapter 1 of this volume and http://213.131.236.148/web/3480/3481/index.html).

brings together a range of European professional associations in the field.[18] With regard to citizenship education and its constituent fields, bodies such as the International Association for Intercultural Education (IAIE) have had a similar synthetic function.[19]

The Council of Europe

Another major influence on educational developments in Europe is the Council of Europe. Since the Council is currently taking a strong interest in both the study of religious diversity in schools and education for democratic citizenship, it is worth explaining how it operates since, unlike the EU/EC, it integrates project development with political decision making and support. The Council is an inter-governmental organisation founded in 1949 and based in Strasbourg, France. It comprises 46 member states currently and its aims include protecting human rights, pluralist democracy and the rule of law and seeking solutions to problems such as discrimination against minorities, xenophobia and intolerance (Council of Europe, 2004c). The Council's work leads to European conventions and agreements in the light of which member states may amend their own legislation. The key political bodies of the Council are the Parliamentary Assembly, the Committee of Ministers and various specialist conferences of Ministers.

The Parliamentary Assembly is made up of Members of Parliament (not Members of the European Parliament) from the member states, appointed or elected within their own countries, with cross party representation and with the number of MPs per country determined by its relative population size. The Assembly meets for a week four times a year. Its many functions include the consideration of proposals from specialist groups and projects, and making recommendations to the Committee of Ministers. Unlike the European Parliament, its powers extend only to investigation, recommendation and advice.

The Committee of Ministers, comprising the Foreign Affairs Ministers of member states or their permanent diplomatic representatives (based in Strasbourg), is the Council's decision making body. Its functions include determining action to be taken following recommendations by the Parliamentary Assembly and conferences of specialist ministers (such as the Standing Conference of Ministers of Education, which meets every three years). The Committee of Ministers meets twice a year, but their permanent diplomatic representatives meet weekly. The Committee's decisions are relayed as recommendations to member governments or are incorporated into European conventions and agreements which are legally binding on governments ratifying them.

At the administrative level, the Council is organised under four directorates, including the Directorate of Education, Culture and Heritage, Youth and Sport (DGIV).[20] Ideas for projects or results of projects are channelled by the Directorates and their various committees, as appropriate, for consideration by the Parliamentary Assembly, the Committee of Ministers or one of the conferences of specialist ministers, such as the Standing Con-

---

18   http://www.cogree.com/ accessed 6 June 2006.
19   See http://www.iaie.org/ accessed 6 June 2006.
20   The others are: the Directorate of Legal Affairs (DGI), the Directorate of Human Rights (DGII) and the Directorate of Social Cohesion (DGIII).

ference of Ministers of Education (the Ministers of Education from the parliaments of the member states). There is also a Commissioner for Human Rights, who operates (in organisational terms) independently from the Directorates.

From the point of view of official projects, the Council of Europe offers a structure which fully integrates development and political processes. Project proposals are approved by the Council's political institutions and project findings and recommendations are considered and approved by them or sent back for further development. There is an expectation that, in turn, member states will implement policies set out in declarations or be influenced by them in policy development. The Council is thus a powerful instrument for European integration within its fields of operation.

The Council's projects on Intercultural Education and the Challenge of Religious Diversity and Dialogue in Europe and on Education for Democratic Citizenship will now be considered, as will a discussion on the possible establishment of a European Centre for Religious Education.[21]

Intercultural Education and the Challenge of Religious Diversity and Dialogue in Europe

Within the Council, a view of intercultural education has gradually emerged, concerned with developing competences and attitudes enabling individuals to respect the rights of others, developing skills of critical empathy and fostering dialogue with others from different backgrounds (Council of Europe, 2002). This approach was developed in projects in history, education for democratic citizenship, modern foreign languages and the Roma, but did not include attention to religion. Religion was avoided because of the different relationships between religion and state across Europe, because of the diversity of current arrangements in member states on the place of religion in schools – reflecting histories involving religious conflict – and especially because, as a public body, the Council has to maintain neutrality with regard to the expression of views on the truth or falsity of religious claims.

However, at the political level, the atrocities of September 11, 2001 triggered a shift in policy. Through the Committee of Ministers, the Council of Europe formulated its response to include safeguarding fundamental values and investing in democracy. In relation to the latter, the then Secretary General, Walter Schwimmer, affirmed that intercultural and interfaith dialogue would become a key theme for the Council, proposing:

> ...action to promote a better understanding between cultural and/or religious communities through school education, on the basis of shared principles of ethics and democratic citizenship (Council of Europe, 2002).

9/11 thus can be regarded as a symbol for the entry of the study of religion as a new priority for European public policy on education. However, the paper proposing the Council's first project involving religion as part of intercultural education saw reflection on the events of 9/11 as offering a very limited amount in educational terms: 'The study of re-

---

21   A general discussion of education policies within the Council of Europe is provided in Bîrzéa (2005).

ligions here could show that all the main world religions categorically reject terrorism as a legitimate political tactic, but could do little more.' Rather the Council's Working Party took the view that:

> It is better to see the connection between extremist religion and political conflict and social disruption as a wake-up-call to tackle the quite different and less acute, but still widespread and serious, problem of poor community relations within Europe: where mutual mistrust, intolerance, racist incidents, and discrimination mainly take an ethnic form, but sometimes a religious one (Council of Europe, 2002).

The new priority was therefore an extension of previous efforts to combat racism and promote democratic citizenship within the Council agreed at the Vienna Summit in 1993.[22] However, the Council had '… no overall intercultural concept, strategy or recent normative text capable of easy extension specifically to cover religious diversity as well', recognising that 'existing activities do not deal with issues of religion in education', and concluding that 'a new activity is required; and the importance and complexity of the subject indicate making it a full-scale project' (Council of Europe, 2002).

In early 2002, the Council set up a working party to examine the issues, prior to the establishment of a project suggesting methods and approaches for integrating the study of religion into intercultural education in the public domain. The Working Party's action plan reflects the view that all countries face common challenges expressed in different environments, that they have much to learn from each other and that they should be prepared to review their policies in dialogue with the relevant stakeholders.

The key condition for including religion as a pan-European topic in education was that, despite different views on religion at the personal and societal levels, all could agree that religion is a 'cultural fact' and that knowledge and understanding of religion at this level is highly relevant to good community and personal relations and is therefore a legitimate concern of public policy. This was not a form of intellectual reductionism, but a pragmatic recognition that the fact of the presence of religions in society was the lowest common denominator with which all European states could work in an educational context. Had this strategy not been adopted, the project would not have gone forward.

The Working Party's proposals were discussed at a forum on 'Intercultural education and the challenge of religious diversity and dialogue' in Strasbourg in September 2002 and subsequently, in modified form, adopted by the Committee of Ministers. Experts in religious and intercultural education from different parts of Europe met in Paris in June 2003 in order to identify the key issues in relation to religious diversity and the religious dimension of intercultural education, to tease out the implications of these issues for pedagogy and to make policy recommendations for the Education Ministers' conference on intercultural education to be held in Athens in November 2003. One conspicuous feature of this workshop was the initial suspicion by some of the intercultural educators of the aims and motives of specialists in religious education. It soon became clear that, as a result of their academic specialisation and national focus, many in each field were ignorant of the work of the others; there was especially an ignorance of work done on open and impartial approaches to the study of religions in schools. Once intercultural educators

---

22   http://www.coe.int/T/e/human_rights/ecri/5-Archives/2-Other_texts/2-Vienna_Summit/ Declaration/Declaration_Vienna_Summit.asp accessed 15 May 2006.

became aware of the range of pedagogical and theoretical work that had been done in seeking to present religious material impartially, a genuine dialogue was established, and the complementary skills of the different constituencies were appreciated mutually.

In terms of policy, the working group that included members from Italy, the Netherlands, Germany, Greece, the UK, Latvia and Denmark recommended that, whatever the system of religious education in any particular state, children should have education in religious and secular diversity as part of their intercultural education, regardless of where specifically this was included in the curriculum. This element of the curriculum should include, for example, encouraging tolerance for different religious and secular points of view, education in human rights, citizenship and conflict management, and strategies to counter racism and discrimination in a religiously diverse world.[23] The 2003 Athens Conference of the European Ministers of Education endorsed the project and also recognised its significance in promoting dialogue beyond Europe.

Issues related to the project were discussed at a high profile conference on 'The religious dimension of intercultural education', held in Oslo in June 2004. Participants included educational decision-makers from most member states and from observer states, education professionals and representatives of civil society involved in intercultural education. Speakers included the Prime Minister of Norway and the Council of Europe's Director General for Education, Culture and Heritage, Youth and Sport. The conference proceedings were published by the Council (Council of Europe, 2004a).

Following the conference, the Council appointed a group of specialists in religious and intercultural education to work together to produce a guide for teachers, teacher trainers, administrators and policy makers to deal with the issue of religious diversity in Europe's schools (Council of Europe, 2006). The first section deals with theoretical perspectives that teachers and others need to be aware of in considering the dimension of religious diversity in intercultural education. The second begins to relate the conceptual elements of intercultural education to various approaches to teaching and learning. The third section considers wider questions of religious diversity in schools, including school governance and management, dealing with how to apply intercultural education principles (participation, inclusion and respect for human rights) in different educational settings. The final section includes some examples of current practice in some member states of the Council of Europe.

---

23   This group also recommended that states should:
- encourage schools to develop policies with respect to diversity (including religious diversity) promoting equity based on the national and local situation and within the legal framework of the country
- collect and disseminate examples of good practice of school policies.
- encourage schools to develop curricula that reflect cultural diversity, including religious and linguistic diversity.
- provide initial and continuing teacher education that reflects the reality and needs of teachers preparing children for participation in an open society and of teachers working in multicultural schools.
- encourage schools to develop a critical attitude towards textbooks and electronic means of information and to develop criteria for the selection and use of resources.

At the end of the project, the Steering Committee for Education will submit a draft recommendation to the Committee of Ministers on the management of religious diversity in schools, based on the project's approach. The final Ministerial recommendation will provide a set of principles that can be used by all member states. As with other work within the Council of Europe, the process of interdisciplinary and international collaboration was as important as the product. There are now established procedures for including studies of religious diversity as a dimension of intercultural education at the European level.

The Council of Europe and Education for Democratic Citizenship

The Council of Europe has considered education for democratic citizenship (EDC) to be a priority in relation to its mission to strengthen pluralistic democracy, human rights and the rule of law in Europe. The EDC project was officially launched by the Heads of State and Government of the Council of Europe's member countries in Strasbourg in October 1997. At the time of writing, (2006), the project is now in its third phase. The first phase, covering 1997-2000, set out to identify values and skills needed to become responsible citizens and to examine how they could be acquired and transmitted to others. By September 2000 publications had been produced clarifying concepts, practices and methods, identifying and promoting citizenship sites (including schools), presenting various studies and teaching materials, and establishing a network including decision makers, experts, practitioners and NGOs. The first phase resulted in the production of a range of publications including Audigier (2000), discussing basic concepts and competences for citizenship education, Carey and Forrester (2000), considering 'sites of citizenship' and Dürr, Spajic-Vrkaš and Martins (2000), exploring different contexts for learning for democratic citizenship, and considering methods and practices, including core concepts, values and skills. Here, Education for Democratic Citizenship is seen as inclusive of many aspects of Human Rights Education, Civic Education, Peace Education, Global Education and Intercultural Education as well as activities in which participation in society can be learned, exercised and encouraged. The results of phase one were endorsed by the Standing Conference of European Ministers of Education in Cracow in October 2000.

The second phase covered the period 2000-2004, concentrating on the development of EDC policies, establishing networks, producing and disseminating materials and preparing for the European Year of Citizenship in 2005. In 2002, the Council of Europe Committee of Ministers adopted the proposal that member states should make EDC a priority of educational policy and reform (Council of Europe, 2004b, p. 13). The EDC group produced a systematic review of policy on EDC in six regions of Europe,[24] a 'toolkit' for policy makers and practitioners (including Huddleston & Garabagiu, 2005) and a key text on learning about and practising democratic participation in the school (Dürr, 2005).

The European Year of Citizenship through Education (2005) marked the culmination of the first two phases of the EDC project and set out to encourage the implementation of

---

24   The policy review was piloted in South Eastern European countries and then applied in the Northern, Western, Southern, Central and Eastern regions. The results of these studies are published in Council of Europe (2004b), as is a synthesis of them.

agreements by politicians who undertook to adapt the 2002 Committee of Ministers' Recommendation on EDC to their own states' education systems. The year included a range of activities, some in collaboration with international organisations such as the EU and UNESCO.

The third phase of the project (2006–2009) aims to promote sustainable policies, support good practice and encourage co-operation between and within the member States. The programme includes the further development of guidelines, tools and policy recommendations and is especially concentrating on developing ideas for democratic governance in educational institutions (Bäckman & Trafford, 2006).

The EDC project has not dealt directly with religion as an aspect of citizenship education. This is partly because the project is primarily concerned with generic issues, and may also be because of the view that religion was the centre-piece of the project on Intercultural Education and the Challenge of Religious Diversity and Dialogue in Europe – intercultural education being considered to be a sub-set of EDC. However, the absence of religion from direct consideration in the EDC project is a pity, since there are various reasons for addressing issues of religion within citizenship education – issues concerning values, human rights, peace and the global environment, as well as existential questions – that are not specific to the intercultural dimension (Blaylock, 2003; Gearon, 2006; Ipgrave, 2003; Jackson, 2003a; Jackson & Fujiwara 2007).

Proposal for a European Centre for Religious Education

Mention should also be made of discussions prompted by the then Commissioner for human rights, Mr. Alvaro Gil-Robles, who set up a series of annual meetings to discuss the role of religious bodies in promoting human rights and addressing social issues in member states. The meetings brought together representatives of the main religions traditionally present in Europe, representatives of the authorities of the Council of Europe's member states, academics and politicians (including some members of the Committee of Ministers). These annual seminars began in 2000, turning their attention to religious education at the meetings in Malta (2004) and Kazan in the Russian Federation (2006).

The Maltese consultation discussed the possibility of establishing a foundational programme for religious education in all member states of the Council, and considered the establishment of a European Centre for Religious Education focusing on human rights (McGrady, 2006). The recommendations of the Maltese seminar were considered by the Parliamentary Assembly in 2005 (http://assembly.coe.int/Main.asp?link=/Documents/AdoptedText/ta05/EREC1720.htm), which made specific recommendations to the Committee of Ministers, including that it should:

- examine the possible approaches to teaching about religions at primary and secondary levels, for example through basic modules which would subsequently be adapted to different educational systems (13.1.)
- promote initial and in-service teacher training in religious studies …(13.2.)
- envisage setting up a European teacher training institute for the comparative study of religions (13.3.)

- encourage the governments of member states to ensure that religious studies are taught at the primary and secondary levels of state education (14.)

Such an education should include ensuring that pupils are informed impartially about religious diversity in Europe and aware of the human right of freedom of religion or belief (including the right to have no religion) (14.1, 2). The objective of this form of teaching should be to promote understanding, not to instil faith, even in countries having a state religion (14.4). Teachers providing this kind of education, from whatever discipline, would need specific training (14.5). Teacher training (for an impartial education in European religious diversity) should be provided within each state, and generic syllabuses (produced under the auspices of the Council of Europe) should be adapted to each country's particular needs and to the different ages of children (14.6).[25]

The 2006 seminar, on 'dialogue, tolerance and education: the concerted action of the Council of Europe and the religious communities', at Kazan in the Russian Federation (22–23 February), took the discussion further.[26]

The 2005 recommendations of the Parliamentary Assembly were discussed by the Committee of Ministers on May 24th 2006. The Ministers welcomed the recommendations in principle, but set them in the context of various policy statements on developing intercultural dialogue (within and beyond Europe), including the religious dimension, relating them to the Council's wider activities in fields such as pedagogy and teacher education in intercultural education and history, which incorporate the dimension of religious diversity. Attention was drawn to the Council's project on the intercultural education and religious diversity (see above), especially to its output on *Religious Diversity and Intercultural Education: A Reference Book for Schools* (Council of Europe 2007), which encourages impartiality, open mindedness and a critical approach.

Although not stated explicitly, it is clear that the Committee of Ministers considered that the recommendations from the Parliamentary Assembly, relating only to teaching about religions, were too narrow in relation to the establishment of a European Centre. The Chair of the Education Steering Committee, whose observations were appended to the Committee of Ministers' response, reiterated the Steering Committee's interest in set-

---

25   Parliamentary Assembly, 4 October 2005 Recommendation 1720 (2005) http://assembly. coe.int/Main.asp?link=/Documents/AdoptedText/ta05/EREC1720.htm accessed 9 June 2006.

26   The conclusion to the seminar report states that:
       In the majority of Council of Europe member states the new generations do not even receive an education in their own religious heritage, much less that of others. For this reason, it had previously been suggested to establish an Institute capable of contributing to the development of teaching programmes, methods and materials in the member states. At the same time this Institute would serve as a research centre on these matters. It should also be a training centre for instructors, a meeting place and a forum for dialogue and exchange. Course content should be defined in close collaboration with representatives of the different religions traditionally present in Europe (Anon 2006).
       Participants discussed the nature of such a centre (it should be independent, but organised within the structures of the Council of Europe), the kind of curriculum that might be taught there, the place that religious communities might have in a consultative role (the group envisaged an advisory body from the religious communities who could work with the Council of Europe), and the Centre's organisation, management and staffing. For example, the group envisaged an advisory body from the religious communities who could work with the Council of Europe.

ting up a network, centre or 'pôle' of excellence for the training of education staff in the Council of Europe's fields of competence, such as education for democratic citizenship and human rights, history teaching and intercultural education. The Chair noted that training for teachers on education about religion could be featured more prominently in the centre's programme.[27]

Summary

I have outlined issues of policy and practice regarding the place of religion in public education internationally and in Europe, noting the view expressed within the Council of Europe that 9/11 was a 'wake-up-call' with regard to the study of religions in relation to social and cultural issues, precipitating a move towards the inclusion of studies of religions in public education across Europe. This shift in policy especially prompts the question of the relationship between studies of religion in education and citizenship education and related areas such as intercultural education.

At the level of European policy and pedagogy, I have, in particular, traced developments in the fields of education about religious diversity and citizenship education within the Council of Europe. On the positive side, the benefits of interdisciplinary work were noted, involving specialists in religious and intercultural education who have worked together fruitfully on a project bringing the dimension of religious diversity to intercultural education. The joint work did much to dispel stereotypes of research and development in religious education, facilitated the dissemination of pedagogical ideas derived from the RE field to wider constituencies and raised awareness among religious education specialists of the academic isolation of their field.

Also of particular benefit is the Council of Europe's role in European integration. This does not aim for homogeneity across European education systems. Rather it requires the application of human rights principles to educational issues in order to develop models for policy and practice that are adaptable for use in particular national settings. The Council's arrangements for integrating recommendations from projects into the European political process are a key element in this, especially in terms of influencing policy development in member states. Examples illustrating the roles of the Parliamentary Assembly, the Committee of Ministers and the Standing Conference of Ministers of Education in consolidating and applying ideas from projects have been given.

Negatively, it was noted that, while much good work is being done in the Council of Europe on Education for Democratic Citizenship, so far there has been no specific collaborative work focusing on EDC involving both religious education and EDC specialists. This is partly because the EDC project has concentrated on generic issues, and partly because the EDC project regards intercultural education to be a sub-set of EDC – and, of course, the Council already has a project on intercultural education and religious diversity. It would be beneficial to have a forum within the Council of Europe where specialists in the two fields (and other related areas) could share research findings and peda-

---

27   http://assembly.coe.int/Main.asp?link=/Documents/WorkingDocs/Doc06/EDOC10944.htm
       accessed 13 June 2006.

gogical studies, debate issues and develop ideas for policy and practice. Religious education has much to offer such discussions, since there has been a significant amount of theoretical and empirical research on the relationship between the two fields initiated by specialists in religion (eg Gearon, 2003; Jackson, 2003a; Jackson & Fujiwara, 2007; McGrady, 2006; Ouellet, 2006).

I outlined the proposals for a European Centre for Religious Education, developed by a group convened by the Council's Commissioner for Human Rights and approved by the Parliamentary Assembly. General approval to the principles underlying this proposal was given by the Committee of Ministers, but it was also clear that the Ministers saw the proposal as too narrow and isolated from other related concerns of the Council. Mention was made of the possibility for the development of a European interdisciplinary Centre bringing together expertise in a range of fields, including citizenship education, intercultural education, human rights education and the study of religions. As indicated above, the establishment of such a Centre would provide rich opportunities for more international and interdisciplinary work, including the study of religions. The Council of Europe commissioned a feasibility study which recommended the establishment of such an interdisciplinary Centre. Subsequently, a major international conference on 'Dialogue of Cultures and Inter-Faith Co-operation' (the Volga Forum) included in its final declaration the statement that 'the participants expressed their support for the project aiming at setting up, in the framework of the Council of Europe, a pôle of excellence on human rights and democratic citizenship education, taking into account the religious dimension'.[28]

Discussion

If such a Centre were established, I would put four related issues immediately on the agenda for consideration. The first concerns the representation of religion as a 'cultural fact', the second is concerned with teaching about religions in a social climate of growing racism, the third relates to the use of pedagogies giving agency to children and young people and the fourth deals specifically with the issue of whether children and young people should share their own beliefs and commitments in exploring issues related to identity. Each of these issues is relevant to the debate about religion in the public sphere, and especially to the discussion of the study of religions in public education in Europe and the relationship between an open, critical religious education and a broad citizenship education which incorporates intercultural and human rights education and related fields.

---

28   The conference was held in Nizhniy Novgorod in the Russian Federation, September 7-9, 2006, under the auspices of the Ministry of Regional Development of the Russian Federation, the Inter-Faith Council of Russia and the Council of Europe. The quotation is from the 'Volga Forum Declaration', Final Document of the International Conference 'Dialogue of Cultures and Inter-Faith Cooperation', paragraph 4.
     http://www.strasbourg-reor.org/modules.php?name=News&new_topic=42&file=article &sid=352   http://www.coe.int/T/DC/Press/news/20060908_declaration_volga_en.asp   (both accessed 12 October 2006).

Religion as a Cultural Fact

The generic Council of Europe perspective for the intercultural project, as reflected in the ground rules developed by politicians and civil servants, takes a cultural view of religion. That is, religion is represented as a 'cultural fact'. The maintenance of strict impartiality in the face of contested religious and secular beliefs is a position that one would expect to find adopted by a formal political institution manifesting the values of constitutional democracy in the institutional public sphere (Habermas, 2006).

For the Council of Europe, religion is seen as a topic to be dealt with at the level of culture – within intercultural education, itself perceived as a subset of Education for Democratic Citizenship. The documentary evidence from the Council of Europe confirms that the 'religion as a cultural fact' position is neither an epistemological stance nor a secular assumption, but a *procedural* strategy for dealing publicly with an intractable problem that had previously kept religion out of the general European discussion and out of policy development and curricula in much European public education (Council of Europe, 2002).[29]

There are developments in the Council of Europe's relationship with religions, in that there is an increasing openness to consultation with religious organisations. The Volga Forum Declaration notes that the participants:

> welcomed the newly established policy of the President of the Parliamentary Assembly of the Council of Europe of inviting religious leaders and consulting with religious organisations on relevant topics. They felt that the time had indeed come for the Council of Europe to develop appropriate mechanisms for an open, transparent and regular dialogue with religious organisations (Volga Forum Declaration, Final Document, paragraph 6, September 2006).[30]

This is a positive move in the sense that dialogue between those of different religious and secular outlooks, using both religious and secular language, is fully appropriate at the level of public debate (Habermas, 2006).

The important point is that the Council of Europe should maintain its impartiality and independence and should not be over-influenced either by secularists or by those promoting religious stances and worldviews. On the one hand, there is a need for scrutiny of policies and materials produced in the Council's name in order to monitor any tendency towards reductionism – that is to check that there is no assumption that religion can *only* be interpreted in cultural terms.[31] On the other hand, there is equally a need to ensure that religious bodies do not propagate their own beliefs via the Council of Europe or in any other way compromise its impartiality and commitment to fair deliberation on the part of *all* citizens.

---

29   The issue of faith-based religious education is a separate issue. One view expressed within the Council of Europe, based on human rights arguments, recognises the complementary nature of faith-based education (mainly in the private sphere) and a generic public education 'about' religion (McGrady 2006).

30   http://www.strasbourg-reor.org/modules.php?name=News&new_topic=42&file=article&sid= 352 http://www.coe.int/T/DC/Press/news/20060908_declaration_volga_en.asp accessed 12th October 2006.

31   Moreover, the appreciation of religion as a 'cultural fact' should not inhibit the observation in classroom practice that many religious people believe their convictions to be true.

Religion and Racism

There has already been some work done on religious education in relation to racism, including what Tariq Modood (1997) has called 'cultural racism' (e.g. Council of Europe 2007; Jackson 1997, 2004; Milot, 2001; see also Runnymede Trust, 1997 and Richardson, 2004 on 'Islamophobia'). However, post 9/11, European countries have seen a revival of far right political parties, some of them getting quite close to the political mainstream – in Austria, the Netherlands, Denmark, Belgium and France, for example (MacEwen, 1995; Mason 2002). Muslims and Islam are the main target for such groups (Modood, Triandafyllidou & Zapata-Barrero, 2006). Moreover, the perpetration of atrocities by radical Muslims in European locations, and the threat of further attacks, has led to a hardening of policy towards 'multiculturalism' by some European governments, which has played into the hands of the extreme right. Reports in popular newspapers, interpreting the remarks of politicians, can reinforce stereotypes of Islam and foster an atmosphere of deep intolerance,[32] What sets out to be a reasonable debate, according to the politicians concerned, can precipitate a change in climate permitting segments of the media to cultivate a fear of 'difference', and allowing the perpetuation of stereotypes and generalizations that are characteristic of 'cultural racism' and 'Islamophobia'

Such forms of racism can only be addressed fundamentally through the leadership and policies of governments. However, schools and other educational institutions offer one area of public space where racist assumptions can be studied and challenged in a rational manner. There is still much work to be done here. There are, of course, key issues relating to whole school policies and values which need further consideration, but religious education (at least in some education systems), citizenship education, human rights education (Gearon, 2006), peace education (Jackson & Fujiwara, 2007) and associated fields, are curriculum areas which have the potential to address forms of racism that focus on religion and culture. For example, the Spanish scholar Francisco Diez de Velasco has suggested that religious education has the potential to become 'a laboratory for peace education' (Diez de Velasco, 2007). Fulfilling that potential would require interdisciplinary study and close attention to pedagogy, especially in developing approaches which include self-reflection as well as learning to listen to the voices of others and to be critical of stereotypical and insensitive representations of religions. Thus we turn now to issues related to pedagogy that require further consideration.

Agency of Pupils and Pedagogical Styles

Issues of pedagogy need to be considered in relation to views of the child or young person. There is a general issue of whether participative methods which give independence and agency to students are universally acceptable, and a specific issue as to whether methods drawing on personal views of children and young people on *religious matters in particular* are appropriate in all countries.

---

32   Eg Ban it! Daily Express, 21 October, 2006.

What is striking about the Council of Europe's work on Education for Democratic Citizenship is its emphasis on a 'maximal' approach that gives agency to students, and which has implications for the organisation and procedures of the whole school and for governance, as well as for classroom methods and styles of teaching and learning. We have seen that strong support for a student-centred pedagogy also comes from independent reviews of European research on approaches to citizenship education. Deakin Crick's analysis of research relating to teaching and learning, in the context of citizenship education, links the exploration of personal issues with broader social issues and provides evidence that the participation and motivation of students increases when lesson content relates to their own personal experiences and that students are enabled to analyse and reflect on their own personal stories and experiences through gaining awareness of the situations of others.[33]

The general approach of the Council of Europe EDC project and the findings from the research projects reported by Deakin Crick reverberate with much research and development in religious education which takes a hermeneutical turn. Theoretical work influenced by hermeneutics,[34] ethnographic research on young people's identity in the context of religious diversity,[35] and pedagogical research on the practice of religious education[36] are all highly relevant to an analysis of the relationship between a critical religious education and the kind of 'maximal' citizenship education advocated in the research reported by Deakin Crick and in the Council of Europe EDC project.[37] The body of theoretical work affirms the exploration of individual identity issues as a key feature of religious education, and links issues important to young people with broader questions of value. Evidence from ethnographic studies of children and young people confirms the importance of attention to individual identity issues in representing accurately individual young people's stances on religion and ethnicity. Data from such focused qualitative studies are a powerful counter to stereotypical portrayals of religions and provide an important source for religious, intercultural and citizenship education. The research studies on pedagogy in religious education referred to above also show the efficacy of approaches that include the exploration of identity issues, even with younger children. Ipgrave's work in England, on dialogue in the primary school, draws heavily on children's own perspectives and experiences (2003, 2005). As with Leganger-Krogstad's research in Norway (2000, 2001, 2003) and Weisse's work in Germany (2003), Ipgrave makes connections between children's explorations of identity at the individual level and broader social issues. Referring to Iris Young's writing (Young, 1990), I also argue that, in inte-

---

33   Research on the values of European youth also shows that most young people rate the value of personal autonomy highly (Kay and Ziebertz 2006).

34   Eg Jackson 1997, 2004; Meijer 1995, 2006; Ouellet 2006; Skeie 1995, 2006; Wright 2006.

35   Eg Jackson and Nesbitt 1993; Nesbitt 2004, 2006; Østberg 2003, 2006.

36   Eg Ipgrave 2003, 2005; Jackson 1997, 2004; 2006b; Leganger-Krogstad 2000, 2001, 2003; O'Grady 2003, 2005; Weisse 2003.

37   See the view that exploration of fundamental questions also contributes to citizenship education (eg Ipgrave 2003) and the view that religious education has much to offer considerations of global citizenship (Jackson 2003b). Note also that some research conducted in the broad religious education field is highly relevant to the exploration of the relationship between religious and citizenship education at the conceptual level. Geir Afdal's monumental study of 'tolerance' comes to mind (Afdal 2006).

grating religious and citizenship education, pedagogies that give voice to children, thus promoting 'differentiated citizenship', should be favoured (Jackson, 2003, 2004). Moreover, O'Grady's action research studies with adolescents, conducted in schools in the north of England, demonstrate that a pedagogy relating students' ethical concerns and personal pre-occupations to material from the study of religions and to wider social issues can be highly motivating to students (O'Grady, 2003, 2005).

Despite this impressive body of theory and research related to hermeneutical and pupil-centred approaches to religious and citizenship education, it is currently not possible to apply or develop it in all parts of Europe. The diversity of national systems reflects various pedagogical traditions related to each country's historical experience, and student-centred approaches are at odds with traditional practice in some European states. Some colleagues from France and Spain tell me that, currently, the kind of student-centred approaches advocated by the Council of Europe EDC project, reflected in the research reported by Deakin Crick, would be difficult to apply in public school classrooms in their countries, although this would depend to some extent on particular circumstances, such as the age of children and the subject under study (in France, it would be easier to do in philosophy than in some other subjects, for example). Comparative education specialists would need to analyse whether this tendency is a matter of 'cultural assumption' or whether there are other reasons for it. For example, in explaining why the IEA study on citizenship education showed that only around 25 per cent of pupils surveyed were encouraged or allowed to share their personal views, it would be instructive to investigate how far the various national traditions on pedagogy reflect different perspectives (including theological perspectives of various kinds) on the nature of authority and the nature of childhood. It would be valuable to know how much support there is for the idea of the child as an autonomous agent, a view which has gained support through theoretical and empirical studies in the sociology of childhood (eg Christensen, 2004; Hallett & Prout, 2003; Prout 2001).

There are some important points to pursue and develop here about the nature of learning: a hermeneutical view *requires* movement between the learner's views and those to be found in material that is studied, such as material from the religions, or movement between personal issues and wider social issues or broad issues of tradition. It does not separate activities of understanding and reflection (representation, interpretation and reflexivity [Jackson, 1997, 2004, 2006b]) but presents these as complementary and integrated processes.

Children's Personal Views on Religion

When we turn to the specific issue of the study of religions in education, we find additional objections to approaches which give children agency and voice, even within a 'democratic' classroom where the teacher acts as an impartial facilitator. These are that the exploration of issues related to identity issues of children and young people encroach on the field of private space and potentially undermine parental wishes. For example, the French discussion sees the study of religion in schools as 'teaching about religion', as imparting a body of knowledge that is regarded procedurally as independent of the students in the classroom (Estivalezes, 2006). The principle of laïcité, which is linked to the separation of public and private domains, demands the impartiality and neutrality of teachers (Debray, 2002). Students have more freedom to express their own religious convictions than teachers, although it is arguable that the 2004 law against the wearing of religious symbols has restricted it. Moreover, the way in which laïcité is represented often makes it difficult in practice for young people to discuss their own personal views in class. As one French colleague put it, 'There is a fear of assigning religious identities to pupils: we don't want to force them to reveal whether they are Jewish, Muslim or Christian and, sometimes, most of them are just indifferent; I think this might be one of the reasons why we don't want too much of a pupil-centred approach'. Nevertheless, discussion of the interpretation of the concept of laïcité is currently part of the French debate, including the issue of whether religious expression should be confined to private space (such as the family or religious community) or should be integral to public life within civil society; thus there is potentially some room for movement (Debray, 2002; Estivalezes, 2006). For reasons close to those stated above, it would also be difficult currently to take a fully hermeneutical approach in countries such as Spain, Turkey and Estonia, just as it would in some non-European states, such as the Republic of Korea or the USA.

We have already noted that the ideal of European integration, as expressed within the EU and the Council of Europe, does not demand or expect total uniformity in educational matters. What is important is that a dialogue is maintained, especially through collaborative work on European research projects (such as the EC REDCo Project) and through the Council of Europe. In discussing pedagogical issues in the European context, it would be worth considering dialogue in the context of wider international debates related to the study of religions and citizenship education. We might, for example, gain some insight from another country struggling to find pedagogies for the study of religion in public education, namely the USA.[38] Over the last 30 years or so, there has been some movement in the United States towards inclusion of religion in the curriculum of publicly funded schools. Arising from the religious liberty principles of the First Amendment to the United States Constitution, the view has been developed 'that age-appropriate study about religion should be a part of all public and private elementary, secondary and university education' (American Assembly, 2000, p. 14). Teaching models so far developed are of the 'teaching about' variety, aiming to increase pupils' understanding of different religions in history and society as well as to increase tolerance and sensitivity toward people of different faiths and philosophies. Advocates of this approach would be wary of methods which relate material studied to students' own beliefs and assumptions and with the development of their religious or spiritual identities. This would be regarded as a deviation from the requirement that public schools should be entirely neutral in areas of religion. Bruce Grelle, a leading authority in the debate about religion in public education, in considering the American situation in relation to my own interpretive approach (Jackson, 1997, 2004, 2006b), suggests an alternative way of making the connection between knowledge and understanding and pupils' personal lives. He does this precisely through

---

38   There are also interesting developments in the Canadian province of Quebec that are very
      relevant to the European debate (see Milot 2001; Ouellet 2000, 2001, 2006).

linking religious education to citizenship education, with an emphasis on the rights and responsibilities of citizenship in a pluralistic democracy, rather than on the sharing of personal views. 'Teaching about diverse religious and secular worldviews and ways of life', argues Grelle, 'becomes a venue for helping students understand their rights to religious liberty or freedom of conscience as well as their responsibility to protect those same rights for their fellow citizens' (Grelle, 2006).

Grelle's ideas provide an example of an adaptation to a strictly 'teaching about' approach, tailored to the American context, resulting from an international dialogue about pedagogy. It is hoped that the Council of Europe will continue its important work by promoting dialogical thinking of this type across the European states and between the Council of Europe and other countries, in the Arab world, for example, in an interdisciplinary context. This could be achieved under the Council's current organisational arrangements, but ideally should be facilitated through the establishment of a Centre bringing together educators and researchers dealing with religion in public education and scholars from other fields, such as education for democratic citizenship.

References

Afdal, G. (2006) *Tolerance and Curriculum*, Religious Diversity and Education in Europe series (Münster, Waxmann).

American Assembly (2000) *Matters of Faith: Religion in American Public Life* (New York, American Assembly).

Andree, T., Bakker, C. & Schreiner, P. (Eds.) (1997) *Crossing Boundaries: Contributions to Interreligious and Intercultural Education* (Münster, Comenius Institut).

Anon (2006) Unpublished 'Conclusions' following the seminar on 'dialogue, tolerance and education: the concerted action of the Council of Europe and the religious communities' Seminar organised by the Commissioner for Human Rights, Mr Alvaro Gil-Robles, Kazan, Russian Federation, 22–23 February.

Audigier, F. (2000) *Basic Concepts and Core Competencies for Education for Democratic Citizenship* (Strasbourg, Council of Europe).

Bäckman, E. & Trafford, B. (2006) *Democratic Governance and Educational Institutions* (Strasbourg, Council of Europe).

Daumann, G. (1999) *The Multicultural Riddle: Rethinking National, Ethnic and Religious Identities* (London, Routledge).

Beauchamp, M. (2002) Guidelines on religion in public schools: an historic moment, *Spotlight on Teaching*, 17 (2), 2, 4, 10.

Bîrzéa, C. (2005) *Learning Democracy: Education Policies within the Council of Europe* (Strasbourg, Council of Europe).

Blaylock, L. (2003) Why citizenship needs to take its spiritual and religious frontiers more seriously, *Teaching Citizenship*, Summer, 24–29.

Carey, L. & Forrester, K. (2000) *Sites of Citizenship: empowerment, participation and partnerships*, Strasbourg, Council of Europe.

Chidester, D, Stonier, J. & Tobler, J (Eds.) (1999) *Diversity as Ethos: Challenges for Interreligious and Intercultural Education* (Cape Town, Institute for Comparative Religion in Southern Africa).

Christensen, P. (2004) Children's participation in ethnographic research: issues of power and representation, *Children and Society* 18, 165–176.

Council of Europe (2002) *Education for intercultural and interfaith dialogue: Proposal for a new project*, unpublished working document prepared by the Secretariat, Educational Policies and European Dimension Division, Directorate of School, Out-of-School and Higher Education, Directorate General IV.

Council of Europe (Ed.) (2003) *Adopted Texts on Education for Democratic Citizenship and Human Rights* (revised version) (Strasbourg, Council of Europe Publishing).

Council of Europe (Ed.) (2004a) *The Religious Dimension of Intercultural Education* (Strasbourg, Council of Europe Publishing).

Council of Europe (Ed.) (2004b) *All European Study on Education for Democratic Citizenship Policies* (Strasbourg, Council of Europe Publishing).

Council of Europe (2004c) *The Council of Europe: 800 Million Europeans* (Strasbourg, Council of Europe).

Council of Europe (Ed.) (2007) *Religious Diversity and Intercultural Education: A Reference Book for Schools* (Strasbourg, Council of Europe Publishing).

de Souza, M., Engebretson, K., Durka, G., Jackson, R. & McGrady, A., (Eds.) (2006). *International Handbook of the Religious, Moral and Spiritual Dimensions of Education* (The Netherlands, Springer Academic Publishers).

Deakin Crick, R. (2005) Citizenship education and the provision of schooling: a systematic review of evidence, *International Journal of Citizenship and Teacher Education*, 1 (2), December, 56–75.

Deakin Crick, R., Coates, M., Taylor, M. & Ritchie, S. (2004) *A Systematic Review of the Impact of Citizenship Education on The Provision of Schooling*, Research Evidence in Education Library (REEL) (London, EPPI-Centre, Social Science Research Unit, Institute of Education).http://eppi.ioe.ac.uk/EPPIWeb/home.aspx?page=/reel/review_groups/   citizenship/review_one.htm (accessed April 2006).

Deakin Crick, R., Tew, M., Taylor, M., Durant, K. & Samuel, E. (2005) *A Systematic Review of the Impact of Citizenship Education on Learning and Achievement*, In: Research Evidence in Education Library (London, EPPI-Centre, Social Science Research Unit, Institute of Education).http://eppi.ioe.ac.uk/EPPIWeb/home.aspx?page=/reel/review_groups/ citizenship/review_two.htm (accessed April 2006).

Debray, Régis (2002) *L'Enseignment du Fait Religieux dans L'École Laïque: Rapport au Ministre de l'Éducation Nationale* (Paris, Odile Jacob).

Diez de Velasco, F. (2007) Religion, identity and education for peace: Beyond the dichotomies: Confessional/non confessional and global/local, in R. Jackson & S. Fujiwara (Eds.) (2007) *Peace Education and Religious Plurality: International Perspectives* (London, Routledge).

Dürr, K. (2005) *The School: A Democratic Learning Community* (Strasbourg, Council of Europe).

Dürr, K., Spajic-Vrkaš, V. & Martins, I. F. (2000) *Strategies for Learning Democratic Citizenship* (Strasbourg, Council of Europe).

Estivalezes, M. (2005) L'enseignement religieux en France: Un état des lieux de la situation contemporaine, in: J-P. Willaime, & S. Mathieu (Eds.) *Des Maîtres et des Dieux: Ecoles et Religions en Europe*, (Paris, Belin), 223-235.

Estivalezes, M. (2006) Teaching about religion in the French education system, in: M. de Souza, K. Engebretson, G. Durka, R. Jackson & A. McGrady (Eds.) *International Handbook of the Religious, Moral and Spiritual Dimensions of Education* (The Netherlands, Springer Academic Publishers), 475-486.

European Commission (2003) *Open Learning Environment, Active Citizenship and Social Inclusion*. Implementation of Education and Training 2010, Work Programme: Progress Report (Brussels, European Commission).

Eurydice (2005) *Citizenship Education at School in Europe*, The Information Network on Education in Europe (Eurydice) (Brussels, European Commission) (available online at: http://www.eurydice.org accessed May 2006)

Eurydice (2006) *Spanish enquiry on the teaching of religious education in the 10 new Member States of the European Union* (Cyprus, Slovakia, Slovenia, Estonia, Hungary, Latvia, Lithuania, Malta, Poland, Czech Republic), Eurydice at NFER website http://www.nfer.ac.uk/eurydice/ (accessed April 2006).

Flutter, J. & Rudduck, J. (2004) *Consulting Pupils: What's in it for Schools?* (London, RoutledgeFalmer).

Gandolfo-Censi, G. (2000) Italy, in: P. Schreiner (Ed.) *Religious education in Europe* (Münster, ICSS and the Comenius Institut), 107–9.

Gearon L. (2003) *Citizenship Education: A Professional User Review of Research* (Nottinghamshire, British Educational Research Association).

Gearon, L. (2006) 'Human rights and religious education: Some postcolonial perspectives' in: M. de Souza, K. Engebretson, G. Durka, R. Jackson & A. McGrady (Eds.), *International Handbook of the Religious, Moral and Spiritual Dimensions of Education* (The Netherlands, Springer Academic Publishers), 375–385.

Grelle, B. (2006) Defining and promoting the study of religion in British and American schools, in: M. de Souza, K. Engebretson, G. Durka, R. Jackson & A. McGrady (Eds.) *International Handbook of the Religious, Moral and Spiritual Dimensions of Education* (The Netherlands, Springer Academic Publishers), 461–474.

Habermas, J. (2006) Religion in the public sphere, *European Journal of Philosophy*, 14 (1), 1–25.

Hallett, C. & Prout, A. (Eds.) (2003) *Hearing the Voices of Children: Social Policy for a New Century* (London, RoutledgeFalmer).

Heimbrock, H. G., Scheilke, C. & Schreiner, P. (Eds.) (2001) *Towards Religious Competence: Diversity As A Challenge For Education In Europe* (Münster, Lit Verlag).

Huddleston, E. & Garabagiu, A. (Eds.) (2005) *Education for Democratic Citizenship 2001-2004: Tool on Teacher Training for Education for Democratic Citizenship and Human Rights Education* (Strasbourg, Council of Europe).

Hull, J. (2002) The contribution of religious education to religious freedom: a global perspective, in: H. Spinder, J. Taylor & W. Westerman (Eds.) *Committed to Europe's Future: Contributions from Education and religious Education*: A Reader (Münster, Coordinating Group for Religious Education in Europe (CoGREE) and the Comenius Institut) 107–10.

Ipgrave, J. (2003) Dialogue, citizenship, and religious education, in: Robert Jackson (Ed.) *International Perspectives on Citizenship, Education and Religious Diversity* (London, RoutledgeFalmer), 147–68.

Ipgrave, J. (2005) Pupil-to-pupil dialogue as a tool for religious education in the primary classroom, in: R. Jackson & U. McKenna (Eds.) *Intercultural Education and Religious Plurality*, Oslo Coalition Occasional Papers (1) (Oslo, The Oslo Coalition on Freedom of Religion or Belief), 39–42.

Jackson, R. (1997) *Religious Education: An Interpretive Approach* (London, Hodder and Stoughton).

Jackson, R. (2000) Law, politics and religious education in England and Wales: some history, some stories and some observations, in: M. Leicester, C. Modgil & S. Modgil (Eds.) *Spiritual and Religious Education* (London, Falmer) [Education, Culture and Values (Vol 5)], 86–99.

Jackson, R (2002) Religious education and education for citizenship, Editorial, *British Journal of Religious Education*, 24 (3), 162–9.

Jackson, R. (Ed.) (2003a) *International Perspectives on Citizenship, Education and Religious Diversity* (London, RoutledgeFalmer).

Jackson, R. (2003b) Citizenship, religious and cultural diversity and education, in: R. Jackson (Ed.) *International Perspectives on Citizenship, Education and Religious Diversity* (London, RoutledgeFalmer), 1–28.

Jackson, R. (2004) *Rethinking Religious Education and Plurality: Issues in Diversity and Pedagogy* (London, RoutledgeFalmer).

Jackson, R. (2006a) New EU research on religious education, Editorial, *British Journal of Religious Education*, 28 (2), 111–113.

Jackson, R. (2006b) Understanding religious diversity in a plural world: the interpretive approach, in: M. de Souza, K. Engebretson, G. Durka, R. Jackson & A. McGrady (Eds.), *International Handbook of the Religious, Moral and Spiritual Dimensions of Education* (The Netherlands, Springer Academic Publishers), 399-414.

Jackson, R. (forthcoming) *Education and Religious Diversity: The Interpretive Approach in an International Context* (Münster , Waxmann).

Jackson, R. & Fujiwara, S. (Eds.) (2007) Peace Education and Religious Plurality: International Perspectives (London, Routledge).

Jackson, R. & Nesbitt, E. M. (1993) *Hindu Children in Britain* (Stoke on Trent, Trentham).

Kay, W. K. & Ziebertz, H.-G. (2006) A nine-country survey of youth in Europe: selected findings and issues, *British Journal of Religious Education*, 28 (2), 119–129.

Kaymakcan, R (2006) Religious education culture in modern Turkey, in: M. de Souza, K. Engebretson, G. Durka, R. Jackson & A. McGrady (Eds.), *International Handbook of the Religious, Moral and Spiritual Dimensions of Education* (The Netherlands, Springer Academic Publishers), 449-460.

Kerr, David D. (1999) Citizenship education: an international comparison, *International Review of Curriculum and Assessment Frameworks Archive*, www.inca.org.uk/thematic.asp (Accessed online, 2/2/04).

Kerr, D. (2003) Citizenship: local, national and international, in: L. Gearon (Ed.) *Learning to teach citizenship in the secondary school* (London, RoutledgeFalmer), 5-27.

Kodelja, Z. & Bassler, T. (2004) *Religion and Schooling in Open Society: a Framework for Informed Dialogue* (Ljubljana, Open Society Institute).

Kosyrev, F. & ter Avest, I. (forthcoming) 'Religious Culture' as a school subject, *British Journal of Religious Education*.

Larsson, R. (2000) Sweden, in: P. Schreiner (Ed.) *Religious Education in Europe* (Münster, ICCS and Comenius Institut), 159-64.

Larsson, R. & Gustavsson, C. (Eds.) (2004) *Towards a European Perspective on Religious Education* (Stockholm, Artos & Norma).

Leganger-Krogstad, H. (2000) Developing a contextual theory and practice of religious education, *Panorama: International Journal of Comparative Religious Education and Values*, 12 (1), 94–104.

Leganger-Krogstad, H. (2001) Religious education in a global perspective: a contextual approach, in: H.-G. Heimbrock, P. Schreiner & C. Sheilke (Eds.) *Towards Religious Competence: Diversity as a Challenge for Education in Europe* (Hamburg, Lit Verlag), 53–73.

Leganger-Krogstad, Heid (2003) Dialogue among young citizens in a pluralistic religious education classroom, in: Robert Jackson (Ed.) *International Perspectives on Citizenship, Education and Religious Diversity* (London, RoutledgeFalmer), 169–90.

Leicester, M. (1992) Antiracism versus the new multiculturalism: Moving beyond the interminable debate, in: J. Lynch, C. Modgil & S. Modgil (Eds.) *Cultural Diversity and the Schools: Equity or Excellence? Education and Cultural Reproduction* (London, Falmer).

MacEwen, M. (Ed.) (1995) *Tackling Racism in Europe: An Examination of Anti-Discrimination Law in Practice* (Oxford, Berg).

McGrady, A. (2006) Religious education, citizenship and human rights, in: M. de Souza, K. Engebretson, G. Durka, R. Jackson & A. McGrady (Eds.), *International Handbook of the Religious, Moral and Spiritual Dimensions of Education* (The Netherlands, Springer Academic Publishers).

McLaughlin, T. H. (1992) Citizenship, diversity and education: a philosophical perspective, *Journal of Moral Education*, 21 (3), 235–50.

Mason, B. (2002) *The rise of the European right*, BBC News, http://news.bbc.co.uk/1/hi/world/europe/1944157.stm accessed October 20, 2006.

May, S. (Ed.) (1999) *Critical Multiculturalism: Rethinking Multicultural and Antiracist Education* (London, Falmer Press).

Meijer, W. A. J. (1995) The plural self: a hermeneutical view on identity and plurality, *British Journal of Religious Education*, 17 (2), 92–99.

Meijer, W. A. J. (2006) Plural selves and living traditions: a hermeneutical view on identity and diversity, tradition and historicity, in: M. de Souza, K. Engebretson, G. Durka, R. Jackson & A. McGrady (Eds.), *International Handbook of the Religious, Moral and Spiritual Dimensions of Education* (The Netherlands, Springer Academic Publishers), 321-332.

Miedema, S., Schreiner, P., Skeie, G. & Jackson, R. (2004) The European Network for Religious Education through Contextual Approaches (ENRECA): Its Policy and Aims, in: U. Nembach, H. Rusterholz & P. Zulehner (Eds.) *Informationes Theologiae Europae: Internationales Ökumenisches Jahrbuch für Thelogie, Volume 13* (Frankfurt am Main, Peter Lang), 227–32 and *Panorama: International Journal of Comparative Religious Education and Values*, 16 (Summer/Winter 2004), 10–14.

Milot, M., (2001) Etude des religions et éducation citoyenne: enjeux politiques et juridiques, in M. Pagé, F. Ouellet et L. Cortesão, *L'éducation à la citoyenneté* (Editions du CRP, Faculté d'éducation, Université de Sherbrooke), 203-212.

Modood, T. (1997) '"Difference", cultural racism and antiracism', in P. Werbner and T. Modood (Eds.), *Debating Cultural Hybridity* (London, Zed Books), 154-72.

Modood, T., Triandafyllidou, A. & Zapata-Barrero, R. (Eds.) (2006) *Multiculturalism, Muslims and Citizenship: A European Approach* (London, Routledge).

Modood, T. & Werbner, P. (Eds.) (1997) *The Politics of Multiculturalism in the New Europe: Racism, Identity and Community* (London, Zed Books).

Nesbitt, E. (2004). *Intercultural Education: Ethnographic and Religious Approaches* (Brighton, Sussex Academic Press).

Nesbitt, E. (2006) Ethnography, religion and intercultural education, in: M. de Souza, K. Engebretson, G. Durka, R. Jackson & A. McGrady (Eds.), *International Handbook of the Religious, Moral and Spiritual Dimensions of Education* (The Netherlands, Springer Academic Publishers), 387-398.

O'Grady, K. (2003) Motivation in religious education: a collaborative investigation with year eight students, *British Journal of Religious Education* 25 (3), 212–23.

O'Grady, K. (2005) Pedagogy, dialogue and truth: intercultural education in the religious education classroom, in: R. Jackson & U. McKenna (Eds.) *Intercultural Education and Religious Plurality*, Oslo Coalition Occasional Papers (1) (Oslo, The Oslo Coalition on Freedom of Religion or Belief), 25–33.

Østberg, S. (2003) *Pakistani Children in Norway: Islamic Nurture in a Secular Context*, Monograph Series (Leeds, University of Leeds, Community Religions Project).

Østberg, S. (2006) Islamic nurture and identity management: the lifeworld of Muslim children and young people in Norway, in: M. de Souza, K. Engebretson, G. Durka, R. Jackson & A. McGrady (Eds.), *International Handbook of the Religious, Moral and Spiritual Dimensions of Education* (The Netherlands, Springer Academic Publishers), 501-512.

Ouellet F., (2000) *L'enseignement culturel des religions. Le débat* (Editions du CRP, Faculté d'éducation, Université de Sherbrooke).

Ouellet F., (2001) Les questions touchant le sens dans l'éducation à la citoyenneté, in M. Pagé, F. Ouellet et L. Cortesão, *L'éducation à la citoyenneté* (Editions du CRP, Faculté d'éducation, Université de Sherbrooke), 243–258.

Ouellet, F (2006) Religious education and citizenship in postmodern societies, in: M. de Souza, K. Engebretson, G. Durka, R. Jackson & A. McGrady (Eds.), *International Handbook of the Religious, Moral and Spiritual Dimensions of Education* (The Netherlands, Springer Academic Publishers), 363–374.

QCA (2004) *Religious Education: the Non-Statutory National Framework* (London, Qualifications and Curriculum Authority).

Paludan, P. & Prinds, E. (1999) *Evaluation of Education in Citizenship and Moral Judgement* (Copenhagen, Danish Ministry of Education).

Parekh, B. (2000) *Rethinking Multiculturalism: Cultural Diversity and Political Theory* (Basingstoke, Macmillan).

Prout, A. (2001) Researching children as social actors: An introduction to the children 5-16 research programme, *Children and Society*, 16 (2), 67–76.

Putnam, R. D. (1995) Bowling alone: America's declining social capital, *The Journal of Democracy*, 6 (1), 65–78.

Rattansi, A. (1999) Racism, postmodernism and reflexive multiculturalism, in: S. May (Ed.) *Critical Multiculturalism: Rethinking Multicultural and Antiracist Education* (London, Falmer Press).

Richardson, R. (Ed.) (2004) *Islamophobia: Issues, Challenges and Action, Commission on British Muslims and Islamophobia*, (Stoke on Trent, Trentham Books),

Robins, K. (2006) *The Challenge of Transcultural Diversities* (Strasbourg, Council of Europe Publishing).

Runnymede Trust (1997) *Islamophobia: A Challenge for Us All* (London, Runnymede Trust).

Runnymede Trust (2000) *The Future of Multi-Ethnic Britain: The Parekh Report* (London, Profile Books).

Schreiner, P. (Ed.) (2000) *Religious Education in Europe* (Münster, ICCS and Comenius Institut).

Schreiner, P. (2002) Different approaches – common aims? current developments in religious education in Europe, in: P. Schreiner, H. Spinder, J. Taylor & W. Westerman (Eds.) *Committed to Europe's Future: Contribiutions from Education and Religious Education: A Reader* (Münster, Coordinating Group for Religious Education in Europe (CoGREE) and the Comenius Institut), 95–100.

Schweitzer, F. (2006) Let the captives speak for themselves! More dialogue between religious education in England and Germany, *British Journal of Religious Education*, 28 (2), 141–151.

Skeie, G. (1995) Plurality and pluralism: a challenge for religious education, *British Journal of Religious Education*, 25 (1), 47–59.

Skeie, G. (2003) Nationalism, religiosity and citizenship in Norwegian majority and minority discourses, in: R. Jackson (Ed.) *International Perspectives on Citizenship, Education and Religious Diversity* (London, RoutledgeFalmer), 51–66.

Skeie, G. (2006) Plurality and pluralism in religious education, in: M. de Souza, K. Engebretson, G. Durka, R. Jackson & A. McGrady (Eds.) *International Handbook of the Religious, Moral and Spiritual Dimensions of Education* (The Netherlands, Springer Academic Publishers), 307–319.

Torney-Purta, J., Lehmann, R., Oswald, H. & Schulz, W. (2001) *Citizenship and Education in Twenty-eight Countries: Civic Knowledge and Engagement at Age Fourteen: Executive Summary* (Amsterdam, International Association for the Evaluation of Educational Achievement (IEA)). http://www.wam.umd.edu/~jtpurta/exec_summ/Exe%20Sum%20embargoed.pdf.

Torney-Purta, J., Schwille, J. & Amadeo, J. (1999) *Civic Education across Countries: Twenty-Four National Case Studies from the IEA Civic Education Project* (Amsterdam, IEA).

Tutu, D. (2000) *No Future Without Forgiveness: A Personal Overview of South Africa's Truth and Reconciliation Commission* (New York, Doubleday).

UNESCO (1996) *Learning: the Treasure Within* (the Delors Report), The report to UNESCO of the International Commission on Education for the Twenty-first Century (Paris, UNESCO).

Valk, P. (2000) From the Soviet atheism to the national identity: a specific background for the religious education in Estonia, *Panorama: International Journal of Comparative Religious Education and Values*, 12 (1), 78–93.

Weisse, W. (Ed.) (1996) *Interreligious and Intercultural Education: Methodologies, Conceptions and Pilot Projects in South Africa, Namibia, Great Britain, the Netherlands and Germany* (Münster, Comenius Institut).

Weisse, W. (2003) Difference without discrimination: Religious education as a field of learning for social understanding, in: R. Jackson (Ed.) *International Perspectives on Citizenship, Education and Religious Diversity* (London, RoutledgeFalmer), 191–208.

Willaime J-P., (2005) *Europe et Religions. Les Enjeux du XXIe Siècle* (Paris, Fayard).

Willaime, J-P. & Mathieu, S. (Eds.) (2005) *Des Maîtres et des Dieux: Ecoles et Religions en Europe*, (Paris, Belin).

Wright, A. (2006) Critical realism as a tool for the interpretation of cultural diversity in liberal religious education, in: M. de Souza, K. Engebretson, G. Durka, R. Jackson & A. McGrady (Eds.), *International Handbook of the Religious, Moral and Spiritual Dimensions of Education* (The Netherlands, Springer Academic Publishers), 333–347.

Young, I. M. (1990) *Justice and the Politics of Difference* (Princeton (NJ), Princeton University Press).

Ziebertz, H.-G. & Kay, W. K. (Eds.) (2005) *Youth in Europe 1: An International Empirical Study about Life Perspectives* (Münster, Lit Verlag).

Zonne, E. (2006) *Interreligiöses und Interkulturelles Lernen an Grundschulen in Rotterdam-Rijnmond, Religious Diversity and Education in Europe series*, (Münster, Waxmann).

Jean-Paul Willaime

Different Models for Religion and Education in Europe[1]

The relationship between school and religion, like that between state and church, is a matter of national sovereignty in each European country and the EU does not have any uniform approach towards teaching religion in public schools. Yet, as we will see, though the breadth of the different national solutions is great, there is a degree of European integration in this field, as in many others. Be it for social or legal reasons, we discern an effective convergence in the way European countries attempt to meet the challenges facing public education in secularised, pluralistic societies.

In the first part, we will develop certain general questions on teaching about religion in Europe. In the second part we will then present the three principal approaches we can see in order to, in the third, explore the directions that different national policies are currently taking. This will allow us, in conclusion, to state whether, and to what degree, we can identify European convergences beyond the historical diversity of individual nations.

General Observations

1) School instruction about religious faith is a strong indicator of the way church-state and school-religion relations are constructed inside a given national framework. Thus, in countries where national identity is strongly tied to a particular confession (such as Lutheranism in Denmark, Orthodoxy in Greece, or Catholicism in Italy) there are notable effects on the way school education is understood. We note especially that, in some countries, the very definition of the goals of school education encompasses the religious dimension. For example:

The Greek constitution, which was framed 'in the name of the Holy Trinity, consubstantial and indivisible' and which, in article 3.1., indicates that 'the dominant religion in Greece is that of the Eastern Orthodox Church of Christ', closely associates the development of the religious consciousness of students with that of their national consciousness:

---

1   We allow ourselves to revisit the work issued by an international colloquium which we organised in the context of the Institut Européen en Sciences des Religions in October 2004: *Des maîtres et des dieux. Ecoles et religions en Europe* (sous la direction de Jean-Paul Willaime avec la collaboration de Séverine Mathieu), Paris, Belin, 2005. See also: Gerhard Robbers (Ed.), *State and Church in the European Union*, Second Edition, Baden-Baden, Nomos Verlag, 2005. (the presentation of each of the 25 EU countries contains information regarding religious instruction in schools), Peter Schreiner, *Religious Education in Europe: A Collection of Basic Information about RE in European Countries*, Münster, Comenius Institut/Intereuropean Commission on Church and School, 2000 and Jean-Paul Willaime: *Europe et religions. Les enjeux du XXIe siècle*, Paris, Fayard, 2004, 'Cultures, religions, laïcités. Divergences et convergences des modèles nationaux', in *'Faire' des Européens ? L'Europe dans l'enseignement de l'histoire, de la géographie et de l'éducation civique* (Alain Bergounioux, Pascal Cauchy, Jean-François Sirinelli, Laurent Wirth dir.), Paris, Delagrave, 2006, p.69-82.

'Instruction constitutes a fundamental mission of the state. Its purpose is the moral, cultural, professional and physical education of the Hellenes as well as the development of their national and religious consciousness and their formation into free and responsible citizens' (Article 16.2.).

In *Great Britain*, the Education Act of 1988 sets out that the overall curriculum of public school education is to promote 'the spiritual, moral, cultural, mental and physical development of students in school and society'. The fact of adding 'spiritual development' to the list of general educational goals cannot fail to stress the proximity of school and religious faith.

In Germany, the goals of public education in several Länder are defined in connection with religion. Thus, in the Land of Hessen, the educational mission of the public school is defined as embedded in 'the Christian and Humanist tradition' while, in Baden-Wurttemberg, it is stated that instruction is to take place 'in responsibility before God and Christian love'.

Regarding Italy, the Concordat of 1984 states in article 9.2.:

'The Italian Republic, recognising the value of religious culture and taking into account the fact that the principles of Catholicism are part of the historical patrimony of the Italian people, continues to ensure within the school system the instruction in the Catholic religion in non-university public schools of all levels and types'.

Though the role and prerogatives of the state in matters of school education are strongly emphasised everywhere, in some countries, such as Ireland, the constitution particularly stresses the importance of parents' rights in this field:

'The state recognises that the primary and natural educator of the child is the family and promises to respect the inalienable right and duty of parents to ensure, within their means, the religious and moral, intellectual, physical and social education of their children.

2. The parents are free to ensure that education, be it privately, be it through private schools or through schools recognised or established by the state'.

Though the central government invariably exercises some responsibility in educational matters, in many countries regional or local authorities play an important role. Thus in *Germany*, though education is placed 'under the supervision of the federal government' (article 7.1. of the Grundgesetz, the constitutional law), it is the responsibility of the Länder. This is also evidently the case in Switzerland, where every canton constitutes a separate state within the Helvetic Confederation. Religious instruction in those countries needs to be studied at the regional level.

Finally it needs to be stated that the distinction between public and private schools does not necessarily mirror that between lay and religious schools. Europe has public confessional and interconfessional schools as well as private secular ones. In some countries, such as Belgium with its extensive network of Catholic schools, the contribution of religious schools to public education is vitally important. Article 2 of the first additional protocol of the European Declaration of Human Rights forbids, among other things, all state monopolies on education, stating:

'Nobody may be refused the right to education. The state, in the exercise of the functions it assumes in the domain of education and instruction, shall respect the rights of parents to ensure an education and instruction conforming to their religious and philosophical convictions'.

However, it places no financial obligations towards private education on the state. The scope of this study is limited to religious instruction at non-confessional public schools.

2) However great the diversity of state-church and school-religion relations in the various European countries may be, and however many national approaches to the treatment of religion in education they may have, they are all confronted with similar challenges. Secularisation, and the increase in the number of people declaring themselves 'of no religion' (see the European Studies of Moral Values), the lack of religious acculturation among school students and their loss of contact with religious life, the existence of strong Muslim minorities in some countries, an overall religious pluralisation manifest in European societies through the presence of all sorts of religious groups and networks, worries about sectarian splinter groups of various kinds, the current interrelationship of religion and politics in various international conflicts, Antisemitism and Islamophobia, and the question of limits to religious expression in the educational context are issues facing European societies. They are seeking to address them by rethinking how schools approach, treat and teach religion. Faced with these challenges, not only was the necessity to understand and live with and beyond our respective differences stressed, but also and above all, with increasing strength, the need to give much more importance to the study of religions in the school curriculum. Though there has not always been a Europeanization of responses, there is a Europeanization of the challenges facing each national approach to religion in school education.

3) There is also a European consensus about the need to strengthen the role of religious knowledge in public school education. In Recommendation 1720, adopted on 4 October 2005, the Parliamentary Assembly of the Council of Europe declared:

'6. Education is essential to combat ignorance, stereotyping, and incomprehension of religions. Governments must also do more to guarantee freedom of conscience and religious expression, to encourage religious instruction, to promote dialogue with and between religions, and to further the cultural and social expression of religions'.

'7. The school is an important element in the education and the formation of the critical faculties of future citizens, and also in intercultural dialogue. It shall lay the foundation of tolerant conduct based on respect for the dignity of every human being. It shall teach its students the history and philosophy of all major religions in a measured and objective fashion, respecting the values of the European Convention of Human Rights, and it shall fight fanaticism, effectively. It is essential to understand the history of political conflicts on the name of religion'.

'8. The understanding of religion is an integral part of understanding the history of humanity and its civilisations. It is entirely different from belief in one particular religion or its practice. Even the countries in which one confession largely predominates must teach the origins of all religions rather than privilege one or promote proselytising'.

Thus in spite of a high degree of difference which shows no sign of disappearing, there is a broad consensus in Europe on the need for instruction on religions in public schools.

4) Regarding the question of school instruction on religion, the situation in France differs markedly from that in other European countries. In practically all those countries, including those which joined the EU in 2004, there exist courses dedicated to the study of a religion or religious matters in general, managed by teachers having received special training for the purpose. These courses, be they confessional or non-confessional, form an especially designated school subject (religious education, Religionsunterricht ...). By

opting to introduce the study of religious matters across existing school subjects without introducing either a specific new subject or a specifically trained teaching body, France represents an original solution in Europe. Though, through its laical and interdisciplinary approach to religious education, France distinguishes itself strongly from those countries that developed a confessional system of religious instruction (Alsace-Lorraine excepted), it is meanwhile no longer alone in this. By now, numerous courses of religious education have evolved, as we shall see, towards non-confessional approaches integrating the plurality of religions, even giving equal treatment to atheist Humanism. In the matter of non-confessional religious education, France is thus not isolated in Europe, yet that non-confessional, interdisciplinary instruction has been conceived differently there.

Three Situations Existing in Europe

When it comes to religious education in schools, European countries can be grouped into the following three categories: 1) *no religious instruction in schools*; 2) *confessional religious instruction*; 3) *non-confessional religious education*. In each of these categories, though, there are differences between the various national systems. The first category is unique to France. Although the situation in some other countries, such as Hungary, comes close, they cannot be included in the same group (in Hungary, confessional religious instruction can effectively be given in school hours, even if the instructors are not part of the school faculty). For the situation in France, we refer to the presentation given by Mireille Estivalèzes. It is, then, through a variety of confessional and non-confessional courses that religious education is given in schools throughout the rest of Europe.

In the essay collection 'Des maîtres et des dieux. Ecoles et religions en Europe', the Italian jurist Silvio Ferrari summarises the characteristics of confessional religious education in Europe thus:[2]

> 'Religious instruction is organised and controlled by religious communities which are charged with the training and selection of educators, the drafting of curricula, and the approval of materials (Austria, Belgium, Cyprus, Spain, Greece, Malta, Poland, Portugal, Czech Republic). In some countries (e.g. Hungary, Italy, Latvia, Lithuania, Germany, Finland), state and religious communities cooperate in the abovementioned tasks. In these systems, religious instructors require a certification by the religious communities (this is the case in Austria, Belgium, Germany, Spain, Greece, Hungary, Italy, Latvia, Lithuania, Luxembourg, Malta, Poland, Portugal, the Czech Republic and Slovakia). Most frequently, religious instruction is an optional or elective school subject. Where it is obligatory, students have the right to receive dispensation (Germany, Austria, Cyprus, Finland, Greece, Malta, Slovakia). Confessional religious instruction is subject in organisational and economic respects to the state (which remunerates instructors and provides localities and school time). The problem is that this state organisation is selective and that only certain religions may be taught. Thus, the question of the selection criteria poses itself' (2005, p. 36).

---

2   We follow the incisive analysis undertaken by Silvio Ferrari in Des maîtres et des dieux. Ecoles et religions en Europe (sous la direction de Jean-Paul Willaime avec la collaboration de Séverine Mathieu), Paris, Belin, 2005, p. 31–39): 'L'enseignement des religions en Europe: un aperçu juridique'. Subsequent references to this essay will be by page number only for simplicity.

Under these systems, each country must determine which religions may be taught in schools. Most use both historical and statistical criteria to enable them to make this decision (Spain now recognises the Catholic, Protestant, Jewish and Muslim faiths owing to their historical importance). It is thus not surprising at all to see that the main problems arising from this structure to stem from the handling of minority religions and that recently established faiths need to be taken into account. Silvio Ferrari points out that where such systems are established, we have also found the willingness to listen to other religions (such as in Italy, in Spain or Portugal), yet this quickly comes up against the practical limits of the system (set by the small number of students, their diffusion, the effective training and choice of teachers etc.). In bi-confessional countries (such as Switzerland or Germany) we can see the tendency towards a Protestant-Catholic ecumenicalisation of religious courses. Finally, confessional religious instruction itself increasingly includes, among its core elements, the study of religion in general and knowledge of other religions, even though these are still filtered through a teacher trained in a particular religious tradition. However, although of necessity some degree of confessionality continues to exist, in practice, it plays very little part in the actual coursework. We must not forget that teachers of religion are, in effect, obliged to take account of the wishes of their students who might desert them if the course does not come up to their expectations. Thus, participant pressure equally works towards a secularisation, with many sessions transforming into general discussions of the existential questions that interest young people today.

The third category is represented by non-confessional religious education. We meet this particularly in Northern European Protestant countries. There, religious education used to be confessional, though under the direction of the state, not the church (in a system of close alignment of Lutheran national churches to the state according to the 'Volkskiche' model). Yet, as Silvio Ferrari explains, 'secularisation has slowly transformed this confessional instruction into a non-confessional one. Thus in Sweden, religious education, originally having been instruction in the Protestant faith, was changed into 'instruction in Christianity' (1919), the 'study of Christianity' (1962), the 'study of religion' (1969) and finally into 'education on the questions of life and existence' (1980). Sweden thus offers a very characteristic example of an originally confessional curriculum secularising from within'. We can observe a similar development in the Swiss cantons such as Zurich and Lucerne and in the German Land of Hamburg, where a 'religious education for everyone' (Religionsunterricht für alle) is developing. In England and Wales, a confessional 'religious instruction' has morphed into non-confessional 'multifaith religious education' with programmes including elements of the principal religious traditions present in the country: many syllabuses include Christianity in its various forms together with Judaism, Islam, Hinduism, Buddhism and Sikhism, and may also include other traditions. Since the implementation of the 1988 Education Reform Act, it has been a requirement that religious education in state-funded community schools should be both pluralistic and non-confessional. Various pedagogical approaches have been developed as a consequence. For example, a pedagogical approach developed by Robert Jackson,[3]

---

3   Aside from his contribution to Des maîtres et des dieux 'L'évolution vers un enseignement religieux multiconfessionnel en Grande-Bretagne' (2005, p. 101–111), we refer to his works: Re-

uses the findings of cultural anthropology and develops a deontology respectful of the conscience of all students, while preparing them for citizenship in a pluralist society.

According to Silvio Ferrari (2005, p. 35), the characteristics on non-confessional religious education in Europe are the following:

> 'Religious education is organised and controlled by the state which is charged with the training selection and remuneration of instructors, the definition of curricula and the approval of materials (possibly, as is the case in the United Kingdom, in consultation with the religious communities). In these countries, educators do not require a certification by the religious communities. Religious instruction is obligatory, but dispensation is possible. No alternative courses are provided... The non-confessional character of the courses does not preclude particular emphasis being placed on Christianity (as is the case in Denmark or the United Kingdom)' (Ferrari, 2005, p. 35).

Across the Channel the Education Act of 1988 specifies that *religious education* 'must reflect the fact that the religious traditions of Great Britain are principally Christian while including in its curriculum the practice of the other great religions represented in the country'. In Denmark, a similar adherence to Christian dominance can be observed, though the subject, especially in higher secondary education, is largely open to religious pluralism.

The Direction of Current Developments

The diversity present in Europe is no obstacle to notable developments. Thus we have already noted a process of deconfessionalisation and secularisation in religious education in some countries characterised by traditions of confessionalism. Throughout, three main lines of development are noticeable:

1.) **A growing integration of religious education, be it confessional or not, with the overall educational goals of the school and its specific mission**. In most countries, religious instruction is required to contribute to the education of students towards responsible citizenship in pluralist societies. In *Belgium* we see the confessional religious instruction curriculum espouse the same ideals of emancipation and autonomy as the secular ethics curriculum, both coming together, at least in their stated intentions, to promote a shared ideal of citizenship. Thus we read the following text in a brochure published by the Francophone Community in Belgium titled *Les cours de morale et de religion. Des lieux d'éducation*:[4]

> 'Whether it is in religious experience, the memory of a people, or secular culture, human existence is always confronted by the same fundamental questions. Birth, life, and death invariably pose the same great metaphysical problems. Social inequalities, the refusal of democratic rights, and crimes against humanity impose new demands on justice. The progress of technology, medicine, surgery, and genetics poses new ethical questions.

---

ligious education: an interpretative approach (London, Hodder and Stoughton, 1997) and Rethinking Religious Education and Plurality: Issues in Diversity and Pedagogy (London, Routledge Falmer, 2004).

4   At the end of this brochure, six contact addresses are given for: Non-Confessional Morality, Catholic Religion, Israelite Religion, Protestant Religion, Islamic Religion and Orthodox Religion.

There are values that every one of us, in all our difference, may call upon, ideals that we continue to uphold to unite us in common action:

- The dynamic of liberation, understood as the liberation of thought, where unfreedom produces a reduction, impoverishment, oppression and negation of the human.

- The indefatigable quest for peace, fraternity, justice, friendship and love

- The development of democratic engagement to develop dialogue and tolerance in the spirit of mutual respect and understanding of differences

- An education towards citizenship, understanding of and for human rights and fundamental liberties.

The school needs to center on the human being. Ethical and religious instruction is a subject of education which, while respecting all their different convictions, favour integration into a pluralist society. Within a coherent educational action plan, they allow us to fight indifference, fanaticism, dogmatism, intolerance, violence, negativism, and other dehumanising evils of our time'.

The Council of Europe, through its Commission of Human Rights, is particularly sensitive to that aspect. Concluding a seminar dedicated to 'Human rights, culture, and religion: Convergence or Divergence? Dogma, norms and education' organised by the Commission (Louvain-le-Neuve 9-10 December 2002), the participants declared:

'The religions, playing an important role in the education of young people, must in their instructions in equal measure teach the value of human rights, promoting knowledge and respect. In order to ensure the highest possible quality in an educational subject as important as it is sensitive, the participants believe that it is time to set up a dedicated place of learning where a methodology for the integration of human rights in religious education and the integration of religious matters into education in general can be developed'.

2.) **The second great tendency is an increased openness, in different degrees, to the religious and philosophical plurality of European societies**. This is particularly evident in the initiatives in many European countries to either organise a Muslim religious education, where religion is part of the school curriculum, or to better take account of the Muslim faith in the overall school curriculum. As we have outlined earlier, the most important example here is the British development of multifaith religious education and the internal secularisation of religious instruction courses in general which it represents. The fact that it is becoming ever more difficult not to approach religious faith in all its diversity in the school environment requires a socio-historical objectivity towards religion that, in some ways, mirrors the pluridisciplinary and laical approach taken in France.

In Europe, there are two approaches towards a non-confessional religious education which can be categorised respectively as secular and laical. The first, which is increasingly unfolding in Great Britain (especially in England and Wales and in Scotland, which has its own education system), develops an approach towards religion along non-confessional lines, adopting a position derived from the Humanities and viewing religion as a regular dimension of the human experience to be understood through empathy, but also, in England and Wales, encouraging the idea that students might learn form religions whilst studying them in an impartial way. From this perspective, non-religious options (atheist conceptions of the world and Secular Humanist philosophy) are on an equal footing with religious ones; they do not constitute an encompassing system for everyone, but rather philosophical systems that take their place at the same level as, not above, religions. The second approach, developed in France, privileges an approach towards religion through its works, its cultural traces, and its inclusion in the different school subjects while refusing to take specific account of religion in its own dimension through a dedicated subject (though the approach through various disciplines does not in itself preclude this). In this case, the school opens itself to the religious dimension of history and culture without constituting religions and secular philosophies as subjects in their own right. In all other countries, meanwhile, for all the differences in modality and internal development, we are looking at the model of a dedicated school subject. Behind the difference between the secular and laical approach lie layers of singular historical experiences with the interrelationship of politics and religion which, in turn, have contributed to shaping the different relations between political and scholastic culture on the one hand and religion on the other. Secular approaches can progress as well as laical ones, just as laical approaches are capable of gradually converging with secular ones.

Where confessional religious instruction exists, we have seen the insertion of such courses into scholastic culture forcing them to subscribe to the goals of school education in democratic and pluralist societies. Religion in school – and it does not matter here which religion this is – comprises those religious expressions compatible with human rights and a democratic ordering of society. Thus in Turkey, the laical state now believes that the establishment of Islamic instruction in its schools will form the best defence against radical Islamism. An ambitious and far-reaching plan – its successful realisation is hardly as clear-cut as this – it must especially not lose sight of the fact that human rights are also women's rights. However, insofar as the integration of religious instruction into the general school curriculum renders it, so to speak, 'reasonable', how far is this so? While all issues are not yet resolved, its exclusion from general education leaves the subject to its own internal logic, and the maintenance of confessional courses in schools which are difficult to justify. Passing through the filter of a historical approach and free critical examination, do not secular and laical approaches both contribute much more to understand religious and philosophical stances and to education in human rights and democratic citizenship?

3.) **Finally, the third great characteristic of current developments is the fact that they raise tensions and engender conflicts.** National systems grown from historical roots have found themselves buffeted by sociological developments, and the necessary adjustments are not always made without conflict peacefully. They activate or reactivate fissures on issues like the place of religion in society, especially the question of the place of Islam. Two countries are especially significant in this respect: Spain and Russia. In Spain, the privileged status of Catholic religious instruction in public schools (e.g. the grade received being taken into account for promotion into higher grades) is under attack from the left who, aside from criticising the difficulties it causes in offering equivalent courses for religious minorities, intend to replace it with a course of non-confessional religious studies. As in other countries, the establishment of Muslim religious instruction in public schools is beset with difficulties. In Russia, the partisans of a curriculum dedicated to 'the foundations of Orthodox culture' are supported by the Russian Orthodox Church in their opposition to the introduction of a course of comparative religious history. The state authorities are carefully equivocating between these two positions which have re-opened a debate on the nature of national identity. In Germany, the reintroduction of confessional religious instruction in the Eastern Länder following reunification has also produced conflicts (e.g. the controversy in Brandenburg around the course on 'life education, ethics, science and religion' proposed as an alternative to confessional religious instruction). The question poses itself how alternative courses for students not following this or that confession can be organised. Be they called Ethics, Non-confessional Morals, Values – even the naming of such courses is not without its own problems (not least in that subject names implicitly express a conception of the relationship between a course of morals and one of religion, either as alternatives or as closely associated subjects).

Conclusion: European Convergence or Divergence?

According to Silvio Ferrari, 'there does not appear to be today in Europe a significant demand for the abolition of religious instruction in schools in those countries where it is given, either on a confessional or non-confessional basis ...' (2005, p. 38). This view is confirmed by recent developments in former Communist Bloc countries where, in the course of their various paths towards democracy, the role and place of religion is being redefined by establishing (mostly confessional) religion curricula in state schools. However, that does not stop Silvio Ferrari from arguing that confessional religious instruction in school, deeply anchored in the legal tradition of European countries, requires reform. As Ferrari remarks:

> '...the school as an institution at the service of different demands made upon it by civil society', is in dire need of reform if it is to withstand the exigencies of pluralist societies and conform to European rules seeking to enforce non-discrimination of all individuals regardless of their religious belief or non-belief. 'It is especially necessary to render it entirely non-obligatory, to take account of more religions, and to see to it that state support is given on a more equal basis; According to the situation in different countries, it may be placed within or outside of school hours, be paid for by the state or not. Only if these conditions are respected can confessional religious instruction survive to play a positive role in a situation increasingly characterised by religious pluralism', the Italian jurist concludes (2005, p. 39).

The first convergence we can observe in Europe is an internal development within the confessional courses of religious instruction themselves. They continue to exist, but develop under a double constraint: a *sociological* one, in that the religious and philosophical pluralisation of European societies obliges them to include ever more alternative religions and non-religious positions into their curricula, and a *legal* one, through the importance of the principle of non-discrimination on religious or philosophical grounds (as well as others such as gender or race) in international law, especially in the European Convention of Human Rights. Although the confessional religious instruction courses do evolve, they remain dominant on the European scene. Many former East Bloc countries introduced them to their school systems in the 1990s (Poland, Latvia, Lithuania etc.) whereas few, like Estonia, privilege a non-confessional religious education or, like Slovenia, forbid all confessional instruction in their schools. However, such confessional instruction can also evolve into a non-confessional model, as seen in Sweden, Switzerland, and especially England and Wales. This gradual development or more sudden reverse towards a non-confessional curriculum may just as well be coming about through the convergence of the contents of confessional and non-confessional religious education. Yet one essential question remains: that of the relationship between academic and religious authorities. Do the former teach religious education independently, or do the latter in some fashion or other exert control over it? This question is an important indicator of the degree of secularisation in religious education.

The other great European convergence is the development of non-confessional religious education through the establishment of secular and multi-disciplinary approaches to religious faith. This development is encouraged by European authorities and mirrors, in some ways, the French experience, although it takes place within the context of an established subject. There is, in our view, nowhere that European integration is felt more strongly than in this development where non-confessional approaches meet the legal and sociological changes we see in Europe. As the educational challenges of European societies are increasingly formulated in terms of 'How can we live together with our differences' (be they cultural, religious etc.), having the ability to discuss all religions with all students increasingly appears to be a pedagogical and civic necessity in pluralist and secular societies.

References

Estivalèzes, M. (2005) L'enseignement religieux en France. Un état des lieux de la situation contemporaine, in: J.-P. Willaime, (Ed.) & S. Mathieu *Des maîtres et des dieux. Ecoles et religions en Europe* (Paris, Belin) 223–235.

Ferrari, S. (2005) L'enseignement des religions en Europe: un aperçu juridique, in: J.-P. Willaime, (Ed.) & S. Mathieu *Des maîtres et des dieux. Ecoles et religions en Europe* (Paris, Belin) 31–39.

Jackson, R. (1997) *Religious education: an interpretive approach* (London, Hodder and Stoughton).

Jackson, R. (2004) *Rethinking Religious Education and Plurality: Issues in Diversity and Pedagogy* (London, Routledge Falmer).

Jackson, R. (2005) L'évolution vers un enseignement religieux multiconfessionnel en Grande-Bretagne in: J.-P. Willaime, (Ed.) & S. Mathieu *Des maîtres et des dieux. Ecoles et religions en Europe* (Paris, Belin) 101–111.

Robbers, G. (Ed.) (2005) *State and Church in the European Union* (second edition) (Baden-Baden, Nomos Verlag).

Schreiner, P. (2000) *Religious Education in Europe: A Collection of Basic Information about Religious Education in European Countries* (Münster, Comenius Institut/Intereuropean Commission on Church and School).

Willaime J.-P. (2004) *Europe et religions. Les enjeux du XXIe siècle* (Paris, Fayard).

Willaime, J.-P. (Ed.) & Mathieu S. (2005) *Des maîtres et des dieux. Ecoles et religions en Europe* (Paris, Belin).

Willaime J.-P. (2006) Cultures, religions, laïcités. Divergences et convergences des modèles nationaux, in: A. Bergounioux, P. Cauchy, J.-F. Sirinelli, L. Wirth (Eds.) *'Faire' des Européens? L'Europe dans l'enseignement de l'histoire, de la géographie et de l'éducation civique* (Paris, Delagrave) 69–82.

Dan-Paul Jozsa

Islam and Education in Europe

With Special Reference to Austria, England, France, Germany and the Netherlands

Introduction

The situation and the history of Islam in the different European countries are heterogeneous. In almost all European countries Muslims are a minority, exceptions being Albania, with 70% of the population being Muslims and Turkey, with 99.8% Muslims.

In some Eastern European countries Muslims form big minorities, with over 10% of the population: Bosnia and Herzegovina, with 40% Muslims, Bulgaria, with 12.2%, Kazakhstan, with 47% , Macedonia, with 33.3%, Montenegro, with 10-17.5%, Russia, with 10-15%.

In a number of especially Western European countries Muslims form substantial minorities with a percentage of over 1%: Austria, with 4.2% Muslims, Belgium, with 4%, Croatia, with 1.3%, Denmark, with 2%, France, with 5-10%, Georgia, with 9.9%, Germany, with 3.7%, Greece, with 1.3%, Italy, with 1.7%, Luxemburg, with 2%, Netherlands, with 5.5%, Norway, with 1.8%, Slovenia, with 2.4%, Spain, with 2.5%, Sweden with 2.2-4.4%, Switzerland, with 4.3%, United Kingdom, with 2.7%. In all other European countries Muslims account for under 1% of the total population. The percentage of Muslims living in the EU is approximately 5%.[1]

Islam is today Europe's second largest religion after Christianity and the history of Muslims in Europe dates back to the 8th century (Hunter, 2002). Although the presence of larger numbers of Muslims in Western Europe is in modern times a new phenomenon due to economical and political migration after the Second World War, Muslims have been living continuously in Europe for centuries and we only have to go back in time to the Middle Ages to see large numbers of Muslims living also in Western Europe in the countries of modern Italy, Spain, and Portugal. But still Europe is generally perceived as being Christian, at least culturally. Some also talk nowadays about the Jewish-Christian cultural heritage of Europe (e.g. Marranci, 2004). Unfortunately this is sometimes stated

---

1 Sources: mainly CIA (2006), but also USDS (2005) and Ende and Steinbach (2005). Actual data is not available for Serbia and Montenegro. These two countries have separated on June 3, 2006. The percentage of Muslims in the former State Union 'Serbia and Montenegro' was 19%. Note that the numbers given refer to Muslims living in the respective country and not to Muslim citizens and that the data is heterogeneous with respect to the date of collection and to the definition of the term 'Muslim'. Some of the numbers, especially those regarding West European countries, define as 'Muslims' all people with a migration background from a country with Islam being the predominant religion. For example the 3.7% Muslims in Germany include all the people with migration background from Turkey, Iran, Iraq, Pakistan etc. living in Germany no matter if they regard themselves as Muslims or not.

to exclude Islam from the cultural heritage, the intellectual history of Europe and from European Identity (see Ballard, 1996).

The use of the argument of differences in culture and fundamental values between Turkey, as a predominantly Muslim country, and the actual member states of the European Union, which are at least historically Christian, in the bitter debate about the question whether Turkey should or should not become a member of the European Union highlights this issue in a significant manner (see Cremer, 2006). Nevertheless the Recommendation 1162 (1991) of the Parliamentary Assembly of the Council of Europe (PACE) on the contribution of the Islamic civilisation to European culture acknowledges the role of Islam in Europe:

> 'in addition to Christianity and Judaism, Islam in its different forms has over the centuries had an influence on European civilisation and everyday life, and not only in countries with a Muslim population such as Turkey ... Islam has, however, suffered and is still suffering from misrepresentation, for example through hostile or oriental stereotypes, and there is very little awareness in Europe either of the importance of Islam's past contribution or of Islam's potentially positive role in European society today. Historical errors, educational eclecticism and the over-simplified approach of the media are responsible for this situation... ' (PACE, 1991).

Islam is not only widely perceived as foreign to Europe, which is understandable for Western European countries, due to the relatively new presence of larger numbers of Muslims, but also as hostile, aggressive and frightening. Out of the Non-Muslims in Germany, France, Russia, Spain and the UK 78%, 50%, 72%, 83% and 48% respectively associate Muslims with being fanatical. And 52%, 41%, 59%, 60% and 32% respectively associate Muslims with being violent (PGAP, 2006a). Historically the reasons for this perception are varied and it is argued that they are also deeply rooted in history, the image of Islam in the European consciousness and in Christian theology.[2] But Muslims'own understanding of Islam in some of the Islamic law and theological schools as well as in some of the modern Islamic political movements is another reason for this image of Islam in Europe and western countries in general.

A hostile perception of Islam in Europe became more obvious and the tensions between the Muslims and Non-Muslims in society, which manifested themselves in some countries also in political and judicial actions like laws prohibiting the wearing of conspicuous religious symbols in schools, intensified after the September 11, 2001 attacks. Further acts of terrorism, some of them taking place in Europe, like the March 11, 2004 Madrid train bombings and the July 7, 2005 London bombings, which were understood as being also religiously motivated, aggravated the situation of Muslims in Europe in different ways and drew the public's and the politicians' attention in different European countries more and more also to questions regarding Islam and education, Islam in education or, as the case may be, Islamic religious education in public or private schools and in mosques or educational institutions of Islamic communities.

One of the main questions in this context may be, if including Islam in the religious education or in the educational curriculum of the public and private schools has a positive impact in integrating Muslim minorities in Europe and reducing the conflict potential

---

2   See Watt et al. (1980) for a general discussion of the subject and Tworuschka (1986) and Vöcking (1988) for an analysis of the presentation of Islam in religious schoolbooks in Germany.

therein. This is argued for example by Hobson and Edwards (1999), who say that the lack of religious education in France would be responsible for some of the problems faced by France with regard to its Muslim population. Interestingly enough the report of Régis Debray to the French Minister of Education in 2002 recommended exactly to introduce the teaching of religious subjects in French public schools, knowledge of this subjects being understood as belonging to a good general education, necessary to understand our world and society and to be able to cope with the contemporary challenges. Regarding Islam he writes: 'Laicity is a chance for Islam in France, and French Islam is a chance for laicity.'[3]

The Recommendation 1720 (2005) 'Education and Religion' of the Council of Europe also fosters the implementation of an integrative religious education approach which includes Islam and also other religions beside Christianity and Judaism out of an acknowledgement of shared and common values, of the positive role religions can play in shaping the future of Europe and of the social problems, which are mainly responsible for intolerance, fanaticism and extremism. The text states:

> '... democracy and religions should not be incompatible. In fact they should be valid partners in efforts for the common good. By tackling societal problems, the public authorities can eliminate many of the situations which lead to religious extremism. Education is essential for combating ignorance, stereotypes and misunderstanding of religions ... By teaching children the history and philosophy of the main religions with restraint and objectivity and with respect for the values of the European Convention on Human Rights, it will effectively combat fanaticism...Knowledge of religions is an integral part of knowledge of the history of mankind and civilisations... Even countries with one predominant religion should teach about the origins of all religions rather than favour a single one ... Education systems generally – and especially the state schools in so called secular countries – are not devoting enough resources to teaching about religions ... The Assembly observes moreover that the three monotheistic religions of the Book have common origins (Abraham) and share many values with other religions, and that the values upheld by the Council of Europe stem from these values.' (PACE, 2005).

The landscape of the religious education organised in mosques and in educational institutions of Islamic communities is too vast and heterogeneous for it to be dealt with here; furthermore this topic has only been subject to a small amount of systematic scientific research up to this day. This type of education, widely represented also in Europe, is controversial, because of the general opinion that extremist and fundamentalist views are taught and propagated exactly through some of these institutions. Some authors argue that the 'interaction between the East and the West' which takes place in these educational institutions is beneficial to Islamic education and Islam in general (Makdisi, 1981) and that mainly these institutions play a central role in propagating peaceful coexistence in the respective societies in which they act (Wardak, 2002). This is not only plausible but is in fact in accordance with day to day experience, but still too little is known in general about the teaching curricula and the pedagogic methods used, etc., to give a broad overview or a comprehensive estimation on this subject.

---

3   'La laïcité est une chance pour l'islam en France, et l'islam de France est une chance pour la laïcité.' (Debray, 2002).

The treatment of Islam in public and private schools in Europe differs from country to country and is embedded in the general approach to religious education in the respective country, which is not only determined by pedagogical considerations but also by the religious landscape or the religious structure of the society, the shape of the education system, the role and value of religion in the state, the relationship between state and religious communities, the underlying philosophical assumptions regarding the meaning of religion, the legal statutes regarding religious education, etc.(see Schreiner, 2004, 2005).

If one wants to classify the different approaches to Islam in religious education, one can do this in the common classification schemes used for religious education in general. One can differentiate from a philosophical-pedagogical perspective between education into Islam, about Islam, from Islam and through Islam. If one looks to who is responsible for religious education one can differentiate between religious education in the solely responsibility of religious communities, in the solely responsibility of the state and with shared responsibility between state and religious communities. One can distinguish between confessional and non-confessional approaches, i.e. between approaches where Islam is the only religion deepened in the classes or not, but also between approaches where only one Islamic school of law and/or theology is taught and those where different Islamic schools are subject in the classes. Finally one can differentiate also according to who pays for the education, according to the different types of schools (private, public), according to the language in which the subject is taught (official language(s) of the country in which the religious education is given, the language of the country of origin of the pupils or their parents, another language (Arabic) …) etc. (e.g. Schreiner 2000, 2004, 2005, 2006).

Subsequently an overview will be given about the situation in selected countries. Special attention will be paid to the state of affairs in Austria, England, France, Germany and the Netherlands. The main reason for this choice is that the approaches in these countries cover the main models to integrate Islam in Education in Europe.[4]

In Austria confessional, state funded Islamic religious education in the responsibility of an Islamic organisation is analogue to Jewish, Buddhist and Christian religious education of different denominations. In England religious education in public schools is non-confessional with a multi-religious approach and emphasises on Christianity. State funded private Islamic schools are only few. As well as public schools with a majority of Muslim pupils the private schools can emphasise on Islam in the agreed syllabuses. In France there is no such subject as religious education in the state schools. The few private Islamic schools as well as the Christian and Jewish ones have confessional religious education. In Germany different approaches are in place, ranging from confessional to multi-religious religious educations. In the Netherlands confessional Islamic religious education is given in the numerous state funded, private Islamic schools but sometimes also in public schools.[5]

---

4   For the situation in Spain see the article of Gunther Dietz in this book, for the situation in Russia the article of Fedor Kozyrev and Vladimir Fedorov.

5   Confessional religious education sometimes also in public schools can be found in a majority of countries like: Austria, Belgium, Bosnia and Herzegovina, Bulgaria, Czech Republic, Cyprus, Finland, Germany (partially), Greece, Hungry, Ireland, Italy, Latvia, Netherlands, Poland, Por-

Islamic Religious Education in Austria

In the K. u. K. Monarchy Islam of the Hanafi school – it was the main school of jurisprudence in the Ottoman Empire and it is still the main school in nowadays Turkey – was recognised by law as 'religious community' (*Religionsgemeinschaft*) in 1912 after the annexation of Bosnia and Herzegovina in 1908.[6] After the First World War the K. u. K. Monarchy was divided. The emerging Austria didn't abolish the law regarding the legal status of Islam, although no significant numbers of Muslims lived on its territory. Beginning with 1968, when already considerable numbers of Muslims lived in Austria, mainly immigrants from Turkey, Bosnia and Herzegovina and Kosovo, negotiations were started to implement the law of 1912. In 1979 the 'Islamic Religious Community in Austria (IRCA)' (*Islamische Glaubensgemeinschaft in Österreich*) was legally recognised as 'religious community' and is since then the only organisation to represent Muslims in their relation to the state.

The legal status of 'religious community' confers on the respective community a number of privileges and rights, among them being the right to establish confessional private schools and to give religious education in public schools. Since the school year 1982/83 the IRCA provides Islamic religious education in public schools according to §1 'Religious Education Law' (Religionsunterrichtsgesetz[7]). Today there are also some Islamic private schools in Austria among them being also a college (Gymnasium).[8] The salaries of the teachers in private schools are paid integrally by the state.

Every Muslim in Austria is regarded by law as a member of the IRCA and has the right to use all services provided by the IRCA, regardless if she or he is a registered and/or dues-paying member of the IRCA or not (IGGÖ, 2005b). This implies that all Muslim pupils have the right to attend Islamic religious education which is solely provided by the IRCA, which is responsible for all contents, teaching curricula and syllabuses. There is an obligation that all syllabuses are published by the Ministry of Education and Cultural Affairs. The teachers and the institutions that provide the religious education and the teacher training etc. are financed by the state, according to the law. Note that every recognised religious community in Austria is subject to the same legal statutes; there is no exception or discrimination; all that is stated here regarding the legal status of Islamic religious education applies to all 13 recognised faith communities (see Schreiner, 2000).

---

tugal, Romania, Serbia, Slovakia, Spain, Switzerland (partially), Turkey. If there is Islamic religious education at all it is sometimes only taught in private schools, like it is the case for example in Greece and Romania. Non-confessional religious education (at least) in public schools is in place in: Armenia, Denmark, England, Estonia, Iceland, Norway, Scotland, Sweden, Switzerland (partially), Wales. No religious education is given in public schools in: Albania, France (with the exception of Alsace-Moselle), Montenegro, Slovenia (see Schreiner, 2000, 2004, 2006; Lienemann and Reuter, 2005).

6   The English translation of the law of 1912 is available at: http://www.derislam.at/islam.php?name=Themen&pa=showpage&pid=6 (accesed 27 August 2006).

7   For a presentation and discussion of the law see Schakfeh (2001).

8   See the information of the IRCA at: http://www.derislam.at/islam.php?name=Themen&pa=showpage&pid=125 (accesed 27 August 2006).

At present there are ca. 40,000 Muslim pupils attending Islamic religious education. There are ca. 350 teachers who teach Islamic religious education in ca. 2700 schools ('Standorten') (IGGÖ, 2005a). Religious education is regarded as a compulsory subject in all public schools. Non-Muslim pupils are also free to attend Islamic religious education and Muslim pupils are free to attend religious education classes of other recognised faith communities or to opt out from religious education (this is possible only in the first 10 days of a school year). There is no alternative subject to religious education, but there are plans to introduce Ethics as a general alternative subject (Schreiner, 2000).

The aims or Islamic religious education in public school are seen by the IRCA as being mainly:[9]

- To provide a good and genuine understanding of Islam according to high pedagogical standards, to promote own critical thinking of the pupils, who should achieve an attitude of moderation and of consciousness of their own responsibility in the society, which leads to ethical behaviour based on mutual respect and understanding.
- To encourage the formation of a personal identity based on the shared values of the heterogeneous society faced by the pupils and make them realise that being a good Muslim is not opposed to being a good Austrian and European.
- To promote an inner-Islamic dialogue through teaching different Islamic traditions and confronting the pupils with the different historical responses to religious questions; to make clear that diversity is a chance, which can be fruitfully used to develop a specifically Muslim character in Austria; to establish equal opportunities for everybody, men and women;
- Out of a positive attitude to diversity in Islam, to contribute to the affirmation of the religious, ethnical and cultural diversity in Austria and Europe; to encourage participation of the young generation in society to establish a peaceful coexistence in mutual respect.

One of the main problems for the IRCA was, and in some ways it still is, to provide qualified teachers. At the beginning, in the 1980s, the teachers were mainly Austrian Muslims without a specialised training in teaching Islamic religious education. After bad experiences with this approach, the attempt was made to employ specialised teachers from Turkey, but this solution also proved inadequate. According to Schakfeh (2002) the main problem with the teachers from Turkey was due to their lack or very poor command of the German language. After this experience the IRCA came to the conclusion that an own religious-pedagogical Academy might be the best solution to cope with the problem.

After short negotiations with the Austrian government started in 1997 the establishment of the 'Islamic Religious-Pedagogical Academy' (IRPA) (Islamische Religionspädagogische Akademie) was approved by the Austrian Ministry of Teaching and Cultural Issues (Bundesministerium für Unterricht und kulturelle Angelegenheiten). The IRPA is a confessional private teaching institution under public law, located in Vienna and funded by the state (Shakfeh, 2002).

The teachings of the IRPA are limited to religious and theological subjects. For pedagogical subjects and other subjects in general human sciences the students of the IRPA

---

9   See IGGÖ (2005a).

attend the general courses of the Pedagogical Academy in Vienna (Kiefer, 2005). The length of the studies to become a teacher in Islamic Religion is 8 semesters, i.e. 4 years. The study includes special subjects as: Arabic, Quranic sciences, Quranic exegesis (tafsir), prophetic traditions (hadith), Islamic law (fiqh), methodology of law (usul al-fiqh), history of Islam, history of culture, didactics of Islamic religious education etc., but also general subjects such as: religious pedagogy (Religionspädagogik), general pedagogy (Erziehungswissenschaften), teaching methods (Unterrichtswissenschaft), pedagogical psychology, pedagogical sociology, general comparative religion (vergleichende Religionskunde), political education (politische Bildung), law regarding schools (Schulrecht), German language and informatics etc. (Shakfeh, 2002).[10]

The IRCA wishes to represent all Muslims in Austria, and wants the provided religious education to be a general inter- or over- confessional one. But virtually the religious education is confessional insofar as only the general Sunnitic understanding appears in the curricula, and the same seems to apply also for the religious teaching of the IRPA, which is conducted in cooperation with the Egyptian University of al-Azhar, which sticks to a traditional Sunnitic understanding of Islam.[11] This might be one of the reasons why some Muslim pupils – in some districts like Salzburg – up to 30% opt out of Islamic religious education (Kiefer, 2005). This seems to be also one of the reasons why only a small percentage of ca. 1% of the Muslims living in Austria are registered members of the IRCA.

Kiefer (2005) regards the dependence in teaching of the IRPA from the al-Azhar University to be only appropriate as a transitory solution. To develop a genuine Islamic approach and a theological understanding responding to the specific situation in Austria and Europe it will be necessary for the IRPA in the future to free itself from the tutelage of the al-Azhar. Still the evaluation of the experiences with Islamic religious educations seems to be mainly positive due to the fact that Islam is perceived as 'normal' in the every day school life and that it is apparent that it fosters identity formation of the Muslim pupils in an integrative way as part of the Austrian society (Schaible, 2004).

Islam in Religious Education in England

According to the Education Reform Act of 1988 religious education is part of the core curriculum. In all non independent schools in England except voluntary aided schools with a religious foundation, religious education has to be nondenominational, the schools and the teaching must refrain from attempting to convert pupils. The shape and content of religious education is decided on a local basis. Locally agreed syllabi have to reflect the predominant place of Christianity but also to take into account the other principal religions in the UK including Islam. The prescribed daily act of collective worship is in practice mainly Christian in character, but a school's administration can choose also an Islamic character in schools with a majority of Muslim pupils. Similarly they may observe

---

10   See also the teaching curricula etc. of the IRPA available online at: http://irpa.at.tf/ (accessed 27 August 2006).
11   This cooperation and dependency on al-Azhar in the teachings of the IRPA can according to Kiefer (2005) only be appropriate as a transitional solution.

the Islamic religious festivals and emphasis on Islam in the syllabi (e.g. Schreiner, 2000; OSI, 2002, 2005; Mabud, 2002).

Besides the general religious education, which is compulsory – although parents have the right to withdraw their children under some circumstances – schools may offer public exam courses on religion and some of these courses can be done entirely on Islam as well as on another religions. For example under the exam system of Oxford, Cambridge and Revised Specimen Assessment examination board the General Certificate of Secondary Education (GCSE) syllabus 1931 full course and the short course syllabus 1031, both being on Religion, Philosophy and Ethics, can be done entirely on Islam as well as on Christianity, Judaism and Hinduism (Mabud, 2002).

There are independent Islamic schools not funded by the state in England and the UK in general (over 100 such schools in the UK in 2004), which do not have to follow the National Curriculum. The Islamic religious education given in these schools is generally denominational but different from school to school. These schools and their approach to religious education have often been criticised of fostering segregation of Muslims in society and they are up until today very controversial (Hussain, 2004). These schools have also often been criticised by the Office for Standards in Education (OFSTED) for different but also pedagogical reasons. Only ca. 3% of the Muslim pupils attended this kind of school in 2004 (OSI, 2005).

In 2004 there were only 5 state-funded Muslim schools (compared to 4,716 state-funded Church of England schools; 2,110 Catholic; 32 Jewish; 28 Methodist; 1 Seventh Day Adventist; 1 Sikh; 1 Greek Orthodox; and a number of joint-faith schools), which means that less then 0.5% of the Muslim pupils are educated in these schools. They are allowed to have their own religious education syllabus if they are voluntary aided but have to follow the National Curriculum. The waiting lists for these schools are very long and they seem to be of great symbolic values for many Muslims in the UK (OSI, 2005).

Islam in France

In France there is no proper Islamic religious education in public schools. Teaching about religions in general, (i.e. also Islam) started to be introduced beginning with 1989, when the curricula for history and geography were changed. In 1996 some study of Islam was specially introduced. In 2002 Regis Debray recommended the introduction of the study of religions in public schools across a range of subjects like history, geography or philosophy (see also Schreiner, 2000, 2005).

Only two private Islamic schools exist at present in France, where Islamic religious education is given, one in Lille and one near Paris. Only a number of ca. 100 pupils attended these schools in 2005 (CG, 2006). Since 1992 the private European Institute of Human Sciences (Institut Européen des Sciences Humaines[12]) started courses for imams and religious educators in an Islamic theological training institute in Saint-Léger-de Fougeret. A second institute was opened in 2000 near Paris in Saint-Denis. These insti-

---

12   See the information on the homepage of the institute at: http://www.iesh.org (accessed 9 September 2006).

tutes get financial support from Arab States. The training is designed for 6 years but also shorter courses are offered and the teaching seems to be of a more conservative Sunni understanding (OSI, 2002).

Islam in Religious Education in Germany

In Germany mainly the federal states (*Bundesländer*) are responsible for education. According to article 7 of the German constitution (*Grundgesetz*) the entire education system, (i.e. also religious education) is under state supervision (exception regarding religious education are according to article 141 of the constitution of the federal states of Berlin and Bremen). Furthermore religious education is in general an 'ordinary school subject' to be taught in accordance with the principles of the respective religious community, which implies that religious education is confessional in general. It is a compulsory subject with a possibility for the pupils to opt out. The religious community is generally responsible for the content of the teachings, the textbooks, the recognition and certification of the teachers etc. The state finances the teachers, has to care for the provision of religious education of each legally recognised religious community and takes care that the teachings are according to the constitution and follow the school laws.[13]

Since no Islamic Organisation is generally legally recognised at the state level as a religious community, due to sharp criteria regarding the organisation of a religious community to be recognised legally as such, the state does not have the obligation to provide Islamic religious education as an 'ordinary school subject'. So up to this day there is no regular Islamic religious education in Germany according to article 7 of the constitution, the Islamic religious education introduced in Berlin being, due to the special situation of Berlin, not a regular and compulsory but a kind of free and private education (Kiefer, 2005). Nevertheless,, several approaches to integrate Islam in the educational curricula are in place and several Islamic organisations are aiming and trying to be legally recognised as religious community.

Subsequently the main approaches in Bavaria, Berlin, Bremen, Hamburg and North Rhine-Westphalia are sketched. Models to introduce Islam in the educational curricula are also in place or planed also in other federal states like Lower Saxony, Baden-Württemberg, Brandenburg etc. The models are in general similar to those followed in Bavaria and North Rhine-Westphalia. Only one private Islamic school exists is Germany. It is a primary school in Berlin.

Bavaria

The attempt to integrate Islam in the school curricula in Bavaria started in the mid eighties. Since the school year 1987/1988 the subject 'Islamic Religious Instruction for Turkish Pupils of Islamic Belief' (IRITPIB) (Islamische Religiöse Unterweisung für Türkische Schüler Muslimischen Glaubens) was introduced. This subject is given in Turkish

---

13   See the Article of Thorsten Knauth in this book for more information with regard to the general legal framework concerning religious education in Germany.

by Turkish teachers trained in Turkey who in general only come to Bavaria for a limited period of 5 years. The subject is free of choice and not compulsory for the classes 1 to 9. For the IRITPIB there are actually, according to the understanding of the Ministry of Education in Bavaria, no agreed 'syllabuses' (*Lehrpläne*), but only accepted guidelines, which follow the syllabuses set by the Turkish Ministry of Education and Cultural Affairs in Turkey and integrate issues reflecting the specific situation of Muslims in Western Europe. The books used in the classes are Turkish schoolbooks; the teachers are supervised by the Ministry of Education in Bavaria (see Kiefer, 2005; Müller, 2005).

The problems with this approach are, according to Müller (2005), language problems between teachers and pupils, the teachers' lack of understanding regarding German culture and the specific problems faced by pupils in Germany, their different approach to teaching, teaching methods and their relatively poor understanding of religious pedagogy. Even if it may be true that the IRITPIB gives pupils an insight into Turkish culture, which might be important for a better understanding of their own origin, as Müller (2005) claims, this approach is not appropriate for integrating pupils with Turkish background in Germany and today this should be a main goal due to the fact, that most of these pupils will not leave for Turkey, which might have been controversial in the mid eighties, when the IRITPIB was introduced, but it is not anymore today (Kiefer, 2005).

Beginning with the school year 2001/2002 a pilot project in initially 5 schools was started to teach a subject called 'Islamic Religious Instruction in German' (IRIG) (Islamische Religiöse Unterweisung in deutscher Sprache). In the school year 2004/2005 already 21 schools were part of the project. IRIG was only introduced in school where IRITPIB as well as Ethics is taught, so that a comparative study about the preferences of pupils etc. could be carried out (see Müller, 2005). The syllabuses for IRIG followed first the guidelines for IRITPIB but because this turned inappropriate own syllabuses were designed. The teachers for IRIG have different backgrounds, generally without a religious pedagogical training.

About 44% of the Muslim pupils in the schools of the pilot project chose IRIG, 27% IRITPIB and 29% chose Ethic. Out of Muslim pupils with a migration background from Turkey ca. 38% chose IRIG, 36% IRITPIB, 26% Ethic, very few pupils (2 out of 743) chose protestant religious education. Out of the other Muslim pupils ca. 58% chose IRIG, 3% IRITPIB, 39% Ethics, again very few chose protestant religious education (3 out of 288). Generally the valuation of IRIG was positive (Müller, 2005).

Beginning with the school year 2003/2004 another pilot project in a school in Erlangen was started with the subject 'Islamic education' (IE) (Islamunterricht), which was this time set up in cooperation with a local Islamic organisation. IE is confessional, aiming to be more like education into Islam. IRIG and IRITPIB are regarded to be rather education about Islam.

The University of Erlangen first introduced in 2002 a visiting professorship for Islamic Religious Teaching (Islamische Religionslehre). In 2006 a chair for Islamic Religious Teaching together with an Interdisciplinary Centre for Islamic Religious Teaching (Interdisziplinäres Zentrum für Islamische Religionslehre) (IZIR) was established, which carries out the training of teachers of Islamic religion. The training is analogous to the training in Protestant and Catholic Religious Teaching. For the general subjects like education, general didactics, and history of religions, etc. included in the curriculum, the students attend the general courses offered by the respective Faculties. The special subjects like Arabic, Quranic sciences, prophetic traditions (hadith), the biography of the Prophet (sira), Islamic theology, mysticism, ethics and Islamic law etc. are given partly in cooperation with the Faculty of law and of Islamic sciences.[14]

Berlin

In Berlin the religious education lies solely in the responsibility of the respective religious community, which provides the books, the syllabuses, the training of the teachers etc. and it is only a voluntary subject. The state has to provide the premises and subsidizes the salaries of the teachers. After a long lawsuit with the government, which started in 1980, the Islamic Federation in Berlin (IFB) (*Islamische Föderation in Berlin*) was in 1998 the first Islamic Organisation to be given the right to teach Islamic religious education in public schools as a free subject according to the law in Berlin.

In 2000 also, the Culture Center of the Anatolic Alevis (CCAA) (Kulturzentrum Anatolischer Aleviten) applied for legal recognition as a religious community and the right to give religious education, a syllabus for religious education in primary schools was also advanced, which was set up in cooperation with the Alevi Community (in) Germany (ACG) (Alevitische Gemeinde Deutschland). The application was allowed in 2002 and since the school year 2002/2003 the CCAA is responsible for Alevi religious education in Berlin (see Kiefer, 2005).

The Alevism can actually be regarded as a branch of Shia Islam. Due to a range of specific beliefs regarding prophethood, revelation, relation between God and men, the image of men (Menschenbild), appreciation of ritual etc. they are sometimes regarded as not being Muslims, which is actually misleading but this appreciation was in the past responsible for pogroms and massacres on Alevis. Anyway, the self-understanding of the Alevis, according to the statements of the AGD, sees Alevism as being a branch of Islam and the World Muslim League, actually a more or less conservative Islamic organisation, regards Alevis as Muslims (see Spuler-Stegemann, 2003). None-the-less significant differences to the general teachings of Sunni Islam and also other Shia Schools, the fact that the Alevi understanding of Islam is widely neglected in the teachings of the IFB and the clear and homogeneous organisational structure of the Alevis, a significant fact with respect to the legally recognition as a religious community, have led to the recognition of the CCAA as a distinct religious community in Berlin, not represented by the IFB. The AGD attempts to achieve this also in other federal states (see Spuler-Stegemann, 2003).

Actually the IFB gives Islamic religious education courses in 37 primary schools; these are attended by ca. 4,300 pupils, the CCAA gives Alevi religious education in 10 primary schools; these are attended by ca. 110 pupils (SB, 2006). This numbers are disillusioning if we bear in mind that ca. 200,000 Muslims live in Berlin, most of them with Turkish background, out of whom more than 20% are Alevis. Only a very little percent-

---

14   See the general information on the homepage of the IZIR: http://www.izir.uni-erlangen.de/ (accessed 27 August 2006).

age of Muslim pupils in general and an even smaller percentage of Alevi Muslim pupils attend Islamic Alevi religious education.

Bremen

The religious education in Bremen lies with the state according to article 141 of the constitution. The general subject, called 'education in biblical history', is interdenominational and mainly designed as education *about* religion and not *into* religion. Since the school year 2003/2004 there has been a small scale pilot project in one school to teach 'science of Islam' (*Islamkunde*), a subject which is again understood to be education about Islam and not into Islam, children can choose irrespective of their own confession which subject they want (see Schreiner, 2000; Kaufmann, 2003; Kiefer, 2005).

Hamburg

In Hamburg the Catholic Church decided not to introduce Catholic religious education in public schools. Subsequently a model of *religious education for all* developed, were Islamic contents are taught, which are set up in cooperation with the Schura-Hamburg, an umbrella organisation of over 80% of the Islamic associations and bodies in Hamburg (see Schreiner, 2000; Kiefer, 2005). This approach seems to be widely accepted by the Islamic organisations in Hamburg, although controversial in the general discussions in Germany especially as a model for all federal states, so that when the mayor of Hamburg attempted to set up preparations to introduce confessional Islamic religious education the Schura-Hamburg officially protested, and the plans were given up. Anyhow this model can be seen from different points of view as an appropriate solution, at least for Hamburg, where over 100 registered religious communities and at least 10 Islamic denominations are in place (see Özdil, 1999).

Since the end of the 1990s there are attempts from different sides to set up an 'Academy of World Religions' in Hamburg, with one of the chairs being in Islamic Theology (see Knauth and Weiße, 2002). In 2006 the Interdisciplinary Centre 'World Religions in Dialogue' was founded, with the aim of promoting the establishment of such an Academy. Lectures, seminars and workshops for students are planed for the next semester along with the implementation of master and postgraduate courses in the near future.[15]

North Rhine-Westphalia

In North Rhine-Westphalia (NRW), the federal state with the most Muslims and Muslim pupils (actually ca. 260,000 Muslim pupils), the debates about the introduction of a school subject dealing with the Islamic religion started back in the seventies. First the subject *'Islamic Teaching' in the Context of Additional Native Language Education'* (ITCANLE) for Turkish pupils was introduced. The subject was taught by the teachers of

---

15   See the information of the homepage of the Centre at: http://www.zwid.uni-hamburg.de (accessed 7 September 2006).

Turkish language in Turkish. In 1986 a syllabus for the primary school – the first 4 classes – was published. A general Suni understanding of Islam was presented. The syllabus was produced by a commission consisting of Muslim teachers and Muslim and Non-Muslim scientists in cooperation with the Universities of Istanbul, Ankara, Konya and al-Azhar in Cairo. Between 1986 and 1989 a further education training program for teachers wanting to teach the subject was established. Ca. 600 teachers participated in the program. In 1990 books covering the syllabus for the primary school in Turkish were published. In 1991 syllabuses for the classes 5 and 6 were published, followed in 1996 by the syllabuses for the classes 7–10 (Gebauer, 2002; Pfaff, 2004; Kiefer, 2005).

Exact data regarding the participation in the ITCANLE and its valuation are not available. According to estimations ca. 50% of the Muslim pupils in the primary schools have participated in the program till 1999; the quality of teaching being heterogeneous, ranging from poor to excellent, according to Gebauer (2002).

In 1999 the subject 'Islamic Teaching' (Islamische Unterweisung) as an independent subject in German additionally to the ITCANLE was introduced in a pilot project. In 2005 the name of the subject was changed to 'Study of Islam' (SI) (Islamkunde), to emphasise that the subject is not education *into* but *about* Islam, that it is not proper 'religious education' according to article 7 of the Constitution, the responsibility lying alone with the state of NRW (whereas a proper 'religious education' has to be in the responsibility of the respective legally recognised religious community). In 2005 SI was given in ca. 110 schools, by ca. 75 teachers, the number of pupils being 7,000–8,000 (Landesinstitut für Schule, NRW, 2006). The teachers are either Islamic scientists, who then get additional pedagogical training or teachers, who taught or still teach ITCANLE. The syllabuses set up for ITCANLE were adapted for SI. This means also that mainly only a general Sunni understanding is taught. A systematic valuation does not exist but the feedback of the pupils, teachers and the schools seem to be generally positive (see Kleff, 2005; Kaddor, 2005).

In 2004 the chair 'Religion of Islam' in the new created 'Centre for Religious Studies' in the University of Münster was occupied. An MA in 'Islamic Theology and Islamic Education' is available. The curricula are somewhat similar to those of the IZIR (see above). Like in Erlangen the general subjects have to be attended in the respective faculties. Generally all law and theological Islamic schools of Sunni as well as of Shia Islam, especially those represented in Germany, are included in teachings as well as the different Islamic philosophical traditions. Due to the fact that the majority of the Muslims in Germany are Turkish and mainly Hanafi in law and Maturidi in theology, special stress is laid on teaching these schools.

Islamic Religious Education in Netherlands

The Dutch school system is a dual one and mainly oriented towards private schools, which form ca. 65% of the schools in Netherlands. Their setting-up is free to private initiative, only where there are not enough private schools the government has to establish public schools. The majority of private schools are denominational ones. Actually there are ca. 30 private Islamic schools in the Netherlands, attended by ca. 4% of the Muslim pupils (Kiefer, 2005). They are privately run but financed by the state. In these schools Islamic religious education is generally available no matter if they are primary or secondary schools. There is a controversial debate on the quality of the religious teachings as well as the quality of the general teachings in these schools and on the language of teaching, which is usually Turkish or Arabic (van de Wetering, 2001).

In the public primary schools there is, according to the law, an obligation to teach about religions. The subject 'intellectual currents' (geestelijke stromingen) is supposed to be strictly informative and to give an insight also in the main religions. Due to the separation between state and religions, Islamic religious education even in the public schools cannot be under the responsibility of the state or of the state run public schools. The schools only have to offer the possibility to choose Islamic religious education, which than takes place in the school, within the normal timetable, but is given through teachers of the Islamic organisations. The teachers have to be paid privately by the parents, the state can subsidise the salaries of these teachers but do not have to and seldom do so in practice. Because of this there is only little Islamic religious education of this kind and the teaching is often poor. In public secondary schools there is no religious education at all, not even the subject 'intellectual currents' is available (Schreiner, 2000; van de Wetering, 2001; Kiefer, 2005).

In 1997 the Islamic University of Rotterdam (IUR) was established as a result of initiatives taken by Muslims in the Netherlands. The IUR is a University funded by the state, aiming to contribute at integrating Islam in Dutch society; it has 3 faculties (Islamic science, Language and Civilisations, Islamic Arts) over 5 departments and more than 10 undergraduate and graduate programs. The curriculum is very broad and comprehensive.[16] The intention is to train: imams for mosques, moral guides for hospitals, prisons, etc., teachers of Islam (after a pedagogical training), lecturers in the mosques and/or Islamic organizations, etc.

In 2005 a BA and a MA programme in Islamic theology was set up in the Vrije Universiteit Amsterdam.[17] Lately a one-year master programme in Islamic Theology was introduced also at the University of Leiden focusing on contemporary Islam in Europe.[18]

Conclusions

The approaches to integrate Islam in the education curricula in Europe are different even if they concentrate around those presented above. And although neither a European trend nor the desire to convergence in the direction of a homogenous European model with respect to the legally constructions can be identified, one still can recognize a trend to acknowledge the importance of integrating Islam in education.

Is this due to a new awareness of the importance of religion and spirituality in general or just due to the perception that religion is important for Muslims, that it is a part of

---

16   See the homepage of the University at: http://www.islamicuniversity.nl/en/ (accessed 9 September 2006).

17   See the homepage of the University at: http://www.vu.nl/ (accessed 9 September 2006).

18   See the homepage of the programme at: http://www.postgraduate.leidenuniv.nl/programmes/ma_islamic_theology.jsp (acessed 9 September 2006).

their identity and that if one wants to integrate the people, one will have to integrate them also as Muslims, one will have to integrate Islam in Europe, to accept it as a living part, as an aspect of the culture of Europe? Maybe both are true, either from a pedagogical, or a political perspective, the question arises if one of the approaches in place or in development in Europe is more appropriate than the others to promote and to achieve a peaceful coexistence and to avoid unnecessary and painful conflicts on the arduous way lying in front of us, or if we do need different approaches to cope with the regional, national differences in Europe.

Are the differences due to legally and politically path dependencies, as it seems to be suggested for example by Hull (2005), or are they justifiable from a pedagogical point of view due to specific conditions in the respective countries, as is suggested for example by Ziebertz (2003) or Schweitzer (2006) with respect to religious education in general? Can we learn from these differences to improve the present situation? What are the key problems at present and how can we cope with them? These are only some of the question we hope to answer within the REDCo-Project along with insights into how to deal with the heterogeneity of Islam in Europe, a problem often ignored up to day.

References

Allievi, S. (2003) Sociology of a Newcomer: Muslim Migration to Italy – Religious Visibility, Cultural and Political Reactions, *Immigrants & Minorities*, 22(2–3), 141–154.

Ballard, R. (1996) Islam and the Construction of Europe, in: Shadid, W. A. R. & van Konigsveld, P. S. (Eds.) *Muslims in the Margin: Political Response to the Presence of Islam in Western Europe* (Kampen, Kok Pharos).

Bauer, T., Kaddor, L. & Strobel, K. (2003) Islamischer *Religionsunterricht: Hintergründe, Probleme, Perspektiven* (Münster, Lit-Verlag).

Baumann, U. (Ed.) (2002) *Islamischer Religionsunterricht* (Frankfurt am Main, Otto Lembeck).

Beauftragte der Bundesregierung für Migration, Flüchtlinge und Integration (BBMFI) (2005) 6. *Bericht über die Lage der Ausländerinnen und Ausländer in Deutschland* (Berlin, Bundesministerium).

Behr, H. (2005) *Curriculum Islamunterricht – Analyse von Lehrplanentwürfen für islamischen Religionsunterricht in der Grundschule*. Ein Beitrag zur Lehrplantheorie des Islamunterrichts im Kontext der praxeologischen Dimension islamisch-theologischen Denkens, Dissertation Universität Bayreuth. Available online at: http://www.izir.uni-erlangen.de/docs/IZIR_H.Behr_Dissertation_Curriculum_Islam.pdf (acessed 27 August 2006).

Bukow, W.-D. & Yildiz, E. (Eds.) *Islam und Bildung* (Opladen, Leske + Budrich).

Carens, J. H. (2000) Muslim Minorities in Contemporary Democracies: The Limitations of Liberal Toleration in: *Culture, Citizenship, and Community*, March 2000, 140–161.

CIA (2006) *The World Factbook*. Available online at: https://www.cia.gov/cia/publications/factbook/ (accessed 18 August 2006).

Cremer, J. (2006) Die Türkei und die EU – Wechselseitige Grenzüberschreitungen?, *Geschichte in Wissenschaft und Unterricht* 57 (3), S. 195–207.

Crisis Group (CG) (2006) *La France face à ses Musulmans : émeutes, jihadisme et dépolitisation*, Rappot Europe N° 172. Available online at: http://www.crisisgroup.org/library/documents/europe/172_la_france_face_a_ses_musulmans_emeutes__jihadisme_amended.pdf (accesed 26 August 2006).

Daun, H. & Arjmand, R. (2005) Education in Europe and Muslim Demands for Competitive and Moral Education, *International Review of Education*, 51(5–6),403–426.

Debray, R. (2002) *'L'enseignement du fait religieux dans l'École laïque'*. Available online at : http://www.iesr.ephe.sorbonne.fr/e_upload/pdf/debray.pdf (accesed 25 August 2006).

Denessen, E., Driessena, G. & Sleegers, P. (2005) Segregation by choice? A study of group-specific reasons for school choice, *Journal of Education Policy*, 20(3), 347–368.

Ende, W. & Steinbach, U. (Eds.) *Der Islam in der Gegenwart* (München, C. H. Beck).

Escudier, A. (Ed.) (2003) *Der Islam in Europa: der Umgang mit dem Islam in Frankreich und Deutschland* (Göttingen, Wallstein).

Gebauer, K. (2002) Religiöse Unterweisung für Schülerinnen und Schüler islamischen Glaubens in Nordrhein-Westfahlen, in: U. Baumann (Ed.) (2002) *Islamischer Religionsunterricht* (Frankfurt am Main, Otto Lembeck).

Heimbrock, H.-G. (2005) Religiöse Erziehung im wachsenden Europa. Kontextuelle Perspektiven, *Zeitschrift für Religionspädagogik*, 4(2), 4–19. Also available online at: http://www user.gwdg.de/%7Etheo-web/Theo-Web/theo-web-wissenschaft_05-2.htm (accesed 15 July 2006).

Heimbrock, H.-G., Scheilke, C., Schreiner, P. (Eds.) (2001) *Towards Religious Competence: Diversity As a Challenge for Education in Europe* (Münster, Lit-Verlag).

Heuberger, V. (Ed.) *Der Islam in Europa* (Frankfurt am Main, Peter Lang).

Hobson, P. R. & Edwards, J. S. (1999) *Religious Education in a Pluralist Society: The Key Philosophical Issues* (London, Woburn)

Hull, J. M. (2005) Religious education in Germany and England: the recent work of Hans-Georg Ziebertz, *British Journal of Religious Education*, 27(1), 5–17.

Hunter, S. T. (1998) *The future of Islam and the West: clash of civilizations or peaceful coexistence?* (Westport, Praeger).

Hunter, S. T. (Ed.) (2002) *Islam, Europe's Second Religion* (Westport, Praeger).

Hussain, A.(2004) Islamic education: why is there a need for it?, *Journal of Beliefs and Values*, 25(3), 317–323.

Islamische Glaubensgemeinschaft in Österreich (IGGÖ) (2005a) *Islamischer Religionsunterricht*. Available online at: http://www.derislam.at/islam.php?name=Themen&pa=showpage& pid=154 (accessed 27 August 2006).

Islamische Glaubensgemeinschaft in Österreich (IGGÖ) (2005b) *Mitgliedschaft in der islamischen Glaubensgemeinschaft*. Available online at: http://www.derislam.at/islam.php?name =Themen&pa=showpage&pid=2 (accessed 27 August 2006).

Janke, K. (2005) *Institutionalisierter Islam an staatlichen Hochschulen: Verfassungsfragen islamischer Lehrstühle und Fakultäten* (Frankfurt am Main, Lang).

Kaddor, L. (2005) Zur Notwendigkeit Islamischen Religionsunterrichts. Erfahrungen aus dem Schulversuch 'Islamische Unterweisung als eigenständiges Fach in deutscher Sprache in Dinslaken-Lohberg (NRW)', in: T. Bauer & T. G. Schneiders (2005): *'Kinder Abrahams': Religiöser Austausch im lebendigen Kontext* (Münster 2005, LIT-Verlag).

Karakaşoğlu-Aydın (2000) *Muslimische Religiosität und Erziehungsvorstellungen: eine empirische Untersuchung zu Orientierungen bei türkischen Lehramts- und Pädagogik-Studentinnen in Deutschland* (Frankfurt am Main, Verlag für Interkulturelle Kommunikation).

Kaufmann, H. B. (2003) *Der Religionsunterricht in Bremen – ein zukunftsfähiges Modell*. Available online at: http://www.die-bruecke.uni-bremen.de/artikel/artikel13.htm (accesed 30 August 2006).

Kiefer, M. (2005) *Islamkunde in deutscher Sprache in Nordrhein-Westfalen* (Münster, Lit-Verlag).

Kleff, S. (Ed.) (2005) *Islam im Klassenzimmer, Impulse für die Bildungsarbeit* (Hamburg, Edition Körber-Stiftung).

Knauth, T. & Weiße, W. (Eds.) (2002) *Akademie der Weltreligionen: konzeptionelle und praktische Ansätze*; Dokumentation eines Symposions am 19./20.12.2001 mit Vertreterinnen und Vertretern von Weltreligionen in Hamburg und Mitgliedern der Universität Hamburg (Hamburg, Univ. Hamburg).

Landesinstitut für Schule, NRW (LISNRW) (2006) *Islamkunde in Nordrheinwestfalen, Einige Infos, Stand 01. März 2006.* Available online at: http://www.learn-line.nrw.de/angebote/svislam/download/islamkunde.pdf (accesed 15 July 2006).

Liederman L.M. (2000) Pluralism in Education: the display of Islamic affiliation in French and British schools, *Islam and Christian-Muslim Relations*, 11(1), 105–117.

Lienemann, W. & Reuter, H.-R. (Ed.) (2005) *Das Recht der Religionsgemeinschaften in Mittel-, Ost- und Südeuropa* (Baden-Baden, Nomos).

Lovat, T. (2005) Educating about Islam and Learning about Self: an Approach for our Times, *Religious Education*, 100(1), 38–51.

Mabud, A. (2002) The Teaching of Islam in British Schools, in: U. Baumann (Ed.) (2002) *Islamischer Religionsunterricht* (Frankfurt am Main, Otto Lembeck).

Makdisi, G. (1981) *The Rise of Colleges, Institutions of Learning in Islam and the West* (New York, Columbia University Press).

Malik, J. (Ed.) (2004) *Muslims in Europe: from the margin to the centre* (Münster, Lit-Verlag).

Maréchal, B., Allievi, S., Dassetto, F. & Nielsen, J. S. (2003) *Muslims in the enlarged Europ – Religion and Society* (Leiden, Brill).

Marranci, G. (2004) Multiculturalism, Islam and the clash of civilisations theory: rethinking Islamophobia, *Culture and Religion*, 5(1), 105–117.

McLoughlin, S. (2005) Mosques and the Public Space: Conflict and Cooperation in Bradford, *Journal of Ethnic and Migration Studies*, 31(6), 1045–1066.

Müller, I. (2005) *Islamische Religiöse Unterweisung in deutscher Sprache – Ergebnisse der wissenschaftlichen Begleitung*, Erarbeitet im Auftrag des Bayerischen Staatsministeriums für Unterricht und Kultus (München, Staatsinstitut für Schulqualität und Bildungsforschung). Also available online at: http://www.isb.bayern.de/isb/download.asp?DownloadFileID=4dc817c2cc725c40e4ad2142du2ccb92 (accessed 27 August 2006).

Nielsen, J. S. (1992) *Muslims in Western Europe* (Edinburgh, Edinburgh University Press).

Nielsen, J. S. (1999) *Towards a European Islam* (New York, St. Martin's Press).

Open Society Institute (OSI) (2002) *Monitoring the EU accession process: minority protection* (Budapest, Central European University Press). Also available online at: http://www.eumap.org/reports/2002/eu/ (accesed 15 July 2006).

Open Society Institute (OSI) (2005) *Muslims in the UK: Policies for Engaged Citizens* (Budapest, Central European University Press). Also available online at: http://www.eumap.org/topics/minority/reports/britishmuslims/ (accesed 15 July 2006).

Özdil, A.-Ö. (1999) *Aktuelle Debatten zum Islamunterricht in Deutschland: Religionsunterricht – religiöse Unterweisung für Muslime – Islamkunde* (Hamburg, EB-Verlag).

Panjwani, F. (2004) The Islamic in Islamic education: Assessing the discourse, *Current Issues in Comparative Education*, Vol. 7(1), 19–29. Also available online at: http://www.tc.columbia.edu/cice/Archives/7.1/71panjawani.pdf (accesed 30 August 2006).

84   Dan-Paul Jozsa

Panjwani, F. (2005) Agreed Syllabi and Un-Agreed Values: Religious Education and Missed Opportunities for Fostering Social Cohesion, *British Journal of Educational Studies*, 53(3),
pp. 375–393.

Parliamentary Assembly of the Council of Europe (PACE) (1991) *Recommendation 1661 (1991)
on the contribution of the Islamic civilisation to European culture*. Available online at:
http://assembly.coe.int/main.asp?Link=/documents/adoptedtext/ta91/erec1162.htm (accesed 27 August 2006).

Parliamentary Assembly of the Council of Europe (PACE) (2005) *Recommendation 1720 (2005)
'Education and Religion'*. Available online at: http://assembly.coe.int/Main.asp?link=/
Documents/AdoptedText/ta05/EREC1720.htm (accessed 27 August 2006).

Pew Global Attitudes Project (PGAP) (2006a) *The Great Divide: How Westerners and Muslims
View Each Other*. Available online at: http://pewglobal.org/reports/pdf/253.pdf (accesed
15 July 2006).

Pew Global Attitudes Project (PGAP) (2006b) *Muslims in Europe: Economic Worries Top Concerns About Religious and Cultural Identity*. Available online at: http://pewglobal.org/
reports/pdf/254.pdf (accesed 15 July 2006).

Rath, J., Penninx, R., Groenendjk, K. & Meyer, A. (2001) *Western Europe and its Islam* (Leiden,
Brill).

Riedel, S. (2005) *Muslime in der Europäischen Union – Nationale Integrationskonzepte im Vergleich*. Available online at: http://www.swp-berlin.org/common/get_document.php?id
=1256 (accesed 15 July 2006).

Schaible, T. (2004) Islamischer Religionsunterricht in Österreich und die Aktuelle Situation in
Bayern, in: T. Bauer, L. Kaddor & K. Strobel (2003) *Islamischer Religionsunterricht:
Hintergründe, Probleme, Perspektiven* (Münster, Lit-Verlag).

Schreiner, P. (2004) *Religiöse Bildung ist unbestritten: Religionsunterricht in Europa. Wie bleibt
er zukunftsfähig?*, *Religionsunterricht intern*, 33(2), 2–4. Also available online at: http://ci-
muenster.de/pdfs/themen/Europa_RU-Zukunftsfaehig.pdf (accesed 15 July 2006).

Schreiner, P. (2005) *Religious Education in Europe*. Available online at: http://resources.eun.
org/etwinning/europa2.pdf (accessed 15 July 2006).

Schreiner, P. (2006) *Zur Situation des Religionsunterrichtes – Ein Blick auf Europa*, Referat Bad
Boll Tagung: Ein Ja zur religiöser Bildung. Available online at: http://ci-muenster.de/
webseiten/themen/europa/europa4.pdf (accesed 10 August 2006).

Schreiner, P. (Ed.) (2000) *Religious Education in Europe, A collection of basic information about
RE in European countries* (Münster, ICCS and Comenius-Institut).

Schweitzer, F. (2006) Let the captives speak for themselves! More dialogue between religious
education in England and Germany, *British Journal of Religious Education*, 28(2), 141–
151.

Senat von Berlin (SB) (2006) *Drucksache 15/13408 Kleine Anfrage 15. Wahlperiode des Ab-
geordneten Özcan Mutlu (Bündnis 90/Die Grünen) vom 30. März 2006 (Eingang beim Ab-
geordnetenhaus am 04. April 2006) und Antwort Islamischer Religionsunterricht im Schul-
jahr 2005/2006*. Available online at: http://www.aleviyol.com/yolalevi/index2.php?option
=com_content&do_pdf=1&id=213 (acessed 8 September 2006).

Shadid, W. A. R. & van Konigsveld, P. S. (Eds.) (1996) *Muslims in the Margin: Political Response to the Presence of Islam in Western Europe* (Kampen, Kok Pharos).

Shadid, W. A. R. & van Konigsveld, P.S. (Eds.) (2002) *Religious Freedom and the Neutrality of
State: The Position of Islam in the European Union* (Leuven, Peeters).

Shah, T. S. & Toft, M. D. (2006) Why God is Winning, *Foreign Policy*, July–August, 39–43.
Also available online at: http://www.foreignpolicy.com/story/cms.php?story_id=3493&
page=1 (accessed 28 August 2006)

Siegele, A. (1990) *Die Einführung eines islamischen Religionsunterrichtes an deutschen Schulen: Probleme, Unterrichtsansätze, Perspektiven* (Frankfurt am Main, Verlag für Interkulturelle Kommunikation).

Spuler-Stegemann (1998) *Muslime in Deutschland: Nebeneinander oder Miteinander?* (Freiburg, Herder).

Spuler-Stegemann, U. (2002) *Muslime in Deutschland: Informationen und Klärungen* (Freiburg im Breisgau, Herder).

Spuler-Stegemann, U. (2003) *Ist die Alevitische Gemeinde Deutschland e.V. eine Religionsgemeinschaft?,* Religionswissenschaftliches Gutachten erstattet dem Ministerium für Schule, Jugend und Kinder des Landes NRW. Available online at: http://www.aleviyol. com/yolalevi/index2.php?option=com_content&do_pdf=1&id=213 (accessed 6 August 2006).

Spuler-Stegemann, U. (Ed.) (2004) *Feindbild Christentum im Islam: eine Bestandsaufnahme* (Freiburg, Herder).

Talip, K. (2004) The making of Turkish-Muslim diaspora in Britain: religious collective identity in a multicultural public sphere, *Journal of Muslim Minority Affairs*, 24(2), 243–258.

Tworuschka, U. (1986) *Der Islam in den Schulbüchern der Bundesrepublik Deutschland – Analyse der evangelischen Religionsbücher zum Thema Islam* (Braunschweig, Georg-Eckert-Institut für Internationale Schulbuchforschung).

U.S. Department of State (USDS) (2005) *The International Religious Freedom report.* Available online at: http://www.state.gov/g/drl/rls/irf/2005/ (accessed 26 August 2006).

van de Wetering, S. (2001) Der Islam im niederländischen Schulwesen, in: Baumann, U. (Ed.) (2002) *Islamischer Religionsunterricht* (Frankfurt am Main, Otto Lembeck).

Vöcking, H. (1988) *Der Islam in den Schulbüchern der Bundesrepublik Deutschland – Analyse der katholischen Religionsbücher zum Thema Islam* (Braunschweig, Georg-Eckert-Institut für Internationale Schulbuchforschung).

Wardak, A. (2002) The mosque and Social Control in Edinburgh's Muslim Community, *Culture and Religion*, 3(2), 201–219.

Watt, W. M., Welch, A. T. & Schröder, C. M. (1980) *Der Islam, Band 1: Mohammed und die Frühzeit, islamisches Recht, religiöses Leben* (Stuttgart, Kohlhammer).

Weiße, W. (2002) 'Akademie der Weltreligionen' an der Universität Hamburg: Vorüberlegungen und Perspektiven, in: Knauth, T. & Weiße, W. (Eds.) (2002) *Akademie der Weltreligionen: konzeptionelle und praktische Ansätze (Hamburg),* Also available online at: http://www2. erzwiss.uni-hamburg.de/personal/weisse/AkademiederWeltreligionen.pdf (accesed 30 August 2006).

Ziebertz, H. G. (2003) *Religious Education in a Plural, Western Society: Problems and Challenges* (Münster, Lit-Verlag).

Jean-Paul Willaime

Teaching Religious Issues in French Public Schools

From Abstentionist *Laïcité* to a Return of Religion to Public Education

Before dealing with the relationship between school and religion and the teaching of religious issues in French public schools, it might be useful to give an outline of the religious landscape of France in 2006. France (population: sixty-three million) is still a Catholic country with a secular culture, but its religious spectrum has become much more diversified compared with the situation at the end of the Second World War. Roman Catholicism, although still the religion of the majority of French people, is not as strong as it used to be. In 2006, only sixty-five per cent of French people declared themselves Roman Catholics (IFOP Survey, newspaper *La Croix*, July 2006) compared with ninety per cent in the late 1950s and seventy-five per cent in 1987. France is no longer 'the eldest daughter of the Church' (as it used to be called), not only because a majority of French people have distanced themselves from the institutional Church, but also because today French Catholics represent no more than five per cent of baptised Catholics in the world, so that France can no longer claim to be the world's first Catholic country, or even to belong to the group at the top of the list. In short, through a variety of causes, in terms of numbers the French Catholic majority does not carry as much weight as before.

Still in terms of numbers, the second strongest religion in France is Islam: around four million Muslims, half of them with French nationality; that is from six per cent of the French population. The French Muslim community is quantitatively by far the most important in Europe. It meets with specific problems, due to the still heavy memory of the colonization and decolonization and to the fact that many of its members belong to unfavoured social categories. The next group are the Protestants (around one million and two hundred thousand), from the Reformed Church in the main, but with a significant growth of Evangelical and Pentecostal Protestants. Then come the Jews (estimated around six hundred thousand). Among European countries, France has the largest Muslim community, as well as the largest Jewish community (apart from Russia). But Buddhism is also present with about four hundreds thousand followers. Among religious minorities of over one hundred thousand followers, the Eastern Orthodox Church (three hundred thousand) and the Jehovah's Witnesses (one hundred and forty thousand) also deserve to be mentioned. Naturally, you also find in France a whole range of religious groups and movements labelled as 'cults' or 'new religious movements' (the use of such definitions being, of course, problematic).

France can be defined either as a Catholic country with a secular culture or as a secular country with a Catholic culture. This is due to the fact that in France the Catholic and secular worlds are closely intermingled (both on the institutional and cultural levels), owing to the development of complex relationships between institutional Catholicism and cultural Catholicism on the one hand, and the secularization of institutions and a certain cultural secularization (the secularization of practices and representations) on the other.

The first article of the French Constitution (1958) defined France as 'an indivisible, secular (*laïque*), democratic and social Republic, securing equality before the law for all its citizens without distinction of origin, race or religion'; a Republic which 'respects all beliefs'. The law on the separation of the Churches and the State, adopted in December 1905, remains the base of all relations between religions and State in France. This law applies to all the French 'départements', but with some exceptions: the 'départements' of Bas-Rhin, Haut-Rhin and Moselle (Alsace and a part of Lorraine), the oversea department of Guyane and the French overseas territories called 'Territoires et collectivités d'Outre-Mer'. The law of 1905, in its first article, 'ensures the conscience freedom' and 'guaranties the free exercise of the cult' (in the French juridical language, cult always means religion), in the unique limits of a democratic 'public order'. The second article of the law of 1905 states that 'the Republic does not recognize or subsidize any religion, nor does it pay the ministers of any religion'. The principle of no subsidizing contains some exceptions. Paragraph 2 of the above mentioned article 2 says that the State shall provide for the expenses of chaplaincies: 'there will be the possibility of including in the public budget the expenses related to services of chaplaincy and aimed at furthering the free exercise of religious practice in public institutions such as secondary and primary schools, hospitals, asylums and prisons'. Moreover, article 19 of the law of 1905 states that, 'the sums allocated for the repairing of historical monuments are not considered as subsidies'. The law of 13 April 1908 adds a new sub-paragraph to article 13 of the 1905 law: 'The State, the 'départements' and the local authorities will be free to meet the expenses for the upkeep and the conservation of the religious buildings of which they are the lawful owners'.

It is not easy to give a definition of 'laïcité', an almost untranslatable French word which means, considering the background of an historical conflict between the French State and the Catholic Church, that the State is neutral in religious matters and the public services are non-religious. But the State guarantees the free exercise of religious worship and the organisation of religious institutions in creating for them an associative structure adapted to their goals: 'les associations cultuelles'. In the tradition of 'gallicanisme' (the old alliance in the past between the French king and the French clergy with the aim of limiting the power of the Holy See), if the State is neutral, it therefore remains interested in controlling religious institutions and activities, which often are considered with distrust. In a recent report of the General Commissary's Office of the Plan entitled *Religions and Social Integration*, the French singularity of relationships to religious matters is well defined: 'When, in a general way in Europe, a secularization takes place (progressive loss of the social relevancy of the religious factor) without conflict, the politics in France has tried to reduce the social importance of religion as an institution. Out of this fact, the demand of the State in the religious regulation (on the sects, on Islam) is very strong, while a certain conflict persists on these subjects'[1]; 'France keeps a certain suspicion toward

---

1   General Commissariat of Plan, 'Religion and social integration' (by Cécile Jolly) Cahiers of plan no 8, July 2005, p. 11.

religions, a greater attention toward the confinement risk of the souls that they can conceal and a strong opposition to the religious but also ethnic visibility'[2].

Certain singularities characterize France in the sphere of State/religions/society relationships: 1) A greater sense of conflict and confrontation in Church/State relationships than at any time since the French Revolution and during XIX and XX centuries, the question of the place and role of religion in our country has been central and has given rise to deep and lasting cleavages; 2) The strongly ideological character of philosophical and political conceptions which are critical toward religion (free thought, rationalisms, Marxisms, Freemasonries). 3) The more strongly insisted affirmation of the State supremacy and its authority on the civil society, the tradition of an emancipatory and perspicacious State which plays a centralizing and at the same time a homogenizing role. 4) The strong silence to the public expression of religious groups, the privatization of religious matters being more accentuated in France than elsewhere in Europe. Even if people in other countries find certain of these dimensions to one degree or other, the French distinctiveness, according to us, lies in the importance they have had in the socio-historical configuration of our country. It is what makes that in France more than elsewhere. What is related to religion and to its public management is a particularly sensitive point of the opinion which gives rise to militant mobilizations and has a politico-philosophical and historical worldwide shape which often astonishes foreign observers. Charles Renouvier, the great inspirer of the Republican Party, a Kantian philosopher, wrote in the 1870s: 'The state is the hearth of the collectivity, it takes care of souls as well as of Churches, but on a more universal ground.'[3] This conception, veritable cultural infrastructure of the State/ Religious relationships in France, remains subjacent to many present reactions, even if obvious evolutions take place.

I have used the phrase 'secularization of laïcité' to underline the fact that laïcité no longer functions as an alternative system to religion, but rather as a regulating principle for the pluralism of both the religious and non-religious convictions existing in civil society. Paradoxically, if French laïcité is losing momentum, it is precisely because it has won. It is, however, very largely because of this 'victory' that the religious question is re-emerging once again, on both an individual and social level. In France as elsewhere, ultra-modernity inquires about the place and role of religious faith. It is equally clear that France reacts to this new situation in accordance with its particular history and characteristics. Hence the complexity of the present situation: on the one hand, French exceptionalism is beginning to dissolve in terms of both individual and institutional behaviour, but on the other Gallicanism and a particular tradition of state management with respect to religious and cultural differences continues to resonate in France.

Until World War II, the French approach to religion was marked by 'la guerre des deux France', the Catholic and the secular. By this I mean the social and political conflict that surrounded the place and the role of religion in society – above all the relationship between the Catholic Church and the French state, between religion and the school system. Secular authorities have, as a result, been suspicious of religion, which has been

---

2   Ibid, p. 33.
3   Charles Renouvier 'D'où vient l'importance actuelle de la pensee laique?' Critique philosophique, 1870 p. 100.

relegated to the private sphere (a question of personal opinion and worship). Since 1945, however, militant *laïcité* has gradually given way to what we might call management *laïcité*. The former was associated with anticlericalism and became a "negative" form of neutrality towards religion – its goal being to free itself from the controls of the clergy, in order to promote 'reason' and democracy. The latter offers a rather different formulation. Jean Baubérot (1990) has defined this evolution as 'a pact for a new *laïcité*', through which *laïcité* defines itself more as a framework regulating the pluralism of worldviews than as a counter-system imposing its control on religion. The process can be described as the secularization of *laïcité*. The politico-patriotic form of civic behaviour promoted by the victorious Republic has given way to the politico-ethical civic ideals of a Republic which has become the manager of a pluralist democracy. The spiritual and moral forces present in the country are invited to work together to maintain and to transmit a democratic ethos, and to define ethical codes in various fields (notably in biology and genetics). A 'good-tempered separation (between religion and the state)', a 'benevolent or positive neutrality (of the state towards religion)' and 'a pact for a new *laïcité*' are all expressions which confirm the current evolution towards a form of *laïcité*, which is less aggressive towards religion and which seeks to find a place and a role in society for religious facts. One reason why such an evolution has become possible lies in the effective decline of religious institutions in society. It is equally clear, however, that the traditional distrust of religion undoubtedly continues in France. In recent years, this distrust and more militant forms of *laïcité* have been reactivated by three things – concerns about cults and the practices of new religious movements, the head-scarf affair in schools, and growing evidence of religious extremism in world events. None of these events however prevent a new interest for teaching about religions in public schools.

The Separation of Church and School: Towards Abstentionist *Laïcité*

In France, the separation of church and school predates the separation of church and state of 1905. The law on obligatory primary schooling of 28 March 1882 effectively ended the provisions of the Falloux Act of 1850 which gave 'the religious ministries the right to inspect, supervise and direct private and public primary schools'. The schools were thus free of any religious tutelage. The law stipulates in Article 2: 'Public primary schools shall close one day out of the week other than Sunday in order to allow parents, if they so wish, to give their children religious instruction outside of school premises'. Thus, while enshrining the separation of school and church, the law respected the religious freedom of families and made possible its exercise in the context of the school week. 'Moral and religious instruction' was replaced by 'moral and civic instruction', and though it retained 'duties before God' on its programme, not being designed to be anti- but merely non-religious, this subject inaugurated a secular moral education clearly distinguished from religious instruction. By expunging the reference to 'duties before God' during the reorganisation of the primary school system in 1923, secular moral instruction entirely abandoned all religious reference other than by inference or allusion. The separation of church and school was complete, not only from the established religions, but also from general religious sentiment.

Jean Baubérot notes that 'although 'duties before God' were included in courses of moral education until 1923, the teachers mentioned the highly conflict-charged issue of religion as little as possible. In secondary education, boarding-school lycées permitted chaplains, but their general evolution paralleled that in primary education: Without ignoring religion, it was largely sidelined, as evidenced by the tendency to replace patristic texts with Cicero in Latin classes.' (Baubérot, 1990, p. 149)

In a similar vein, Pierre Ognier writes that at the end of the 19th century, as far as religion was concerned 'it is no longer touched upon by teachers. Why look for trouble with the parish priest on such a touchy issue when, thanks to Solidarism, you could avoid this thorny issues by following the fashion of the time?' (Ognier, 1994, p. 122).[4]

Although secular morality initially owed much to a spiritual inspiration without any hostility to religion, more positivist attitudes and sentiments later came to exert great influence. The importance accorded to the natural sciences as the foundation of all knowledge, including morals, contributed greatly to the ejection of religion from the scholastic world. To the science of that era, God remained unprovable and religious sentiment 'is an irrational attitude whose invocation risks infringing on the conscience of some students'. Indeed, numerous Socialist or atheist teachers 'thought themselves deficient in their civic and professional duty to teach truth if they did not free the spirits of their charges from the 'formidable error' of belief in the notion of God' (quoted by Pierre Ognier, 1994, p. 138).

Some teachers were even convinced that the new scientific world-view would of necessity lead to officially taught atheism (Ognier, 1994, p. 138). In 1901, the newly constituted 'amicales d'instituteurs' (primary school teachers' associations) together with the French Educational League (in its 21st Congress in Caen in August of that year), called for the removal of 'duties before God' from the programme for moral education.

Yet the French Educational League went further. According to Pierre Ognier (1994, p. 139), it proposed 'that to replace the entirely expunged reference to religion in official educational programme, 'it was to be substituted , in the programmes of state secondary schools, by education in universal history of religions''. This suggestion was taken up by two Radical and Radical Socialist party congresses in 1902 and 1903. The League restated it in its Congress of 1904". Ferdinand Buisson, Head of the department of primary education from 1879 to 1896 and editor of a famous Dictionary of Pedagogics (1878–1887) moved in the same direction when he spoke out in 1908, 'for the teaching of religious history ... in the programmes for 'lycées', secondary and upper primary schools.' (Baubérot, 1999, p. 150).

For all the positive reception they found in pedagogical writings, these suggestions never were realised. When the curricula for secondary schools were rewritten in 1905, all mention of references to God and 'life after death' were expunged, but they were not re-

---

4   Pierre Ognier here refers to to the 'Solidarism' of Pierre Bourgeois which was intended to replace religion as an ultimate foundation of morality on a "scientific" basis. The sociology of Durkheim was to play a similar role, contributing to the complete separation of lay morality from its religious dimension. On laical morality, see Bauberot (1997).

placed by any but a minimal education in religious history. 'It is indeed the case' writes P. Ognier (1994, p. 138), 'that the serious conflict between the Republican state and the Catholic church between 1901 and 1905 did nothing to inspire the Council members to tackle this burning question.' The matter was not carried through, and it took the Educational League until 1982 to once again champion the idea of introducing better information on religions into school curricula (on the occasion of its General Assembly that year in Montpellier).

The Return of Religion to Public Schools:
Towards a *Laïcité* of Understanding

During the late 1980s, numerous voices in France restated the question of religion at school. Had the secular school establishment not finally resolved the issue by leaving religious matters at the family's disposition while rendering the school and its educators free from all religious authority? In many ways that was true, but the question was asked under entirely different circumstances than it had been in the era when *laïcité* was first established. It did not constitute a challenge to the secular principle but rather gave tangible proof to its success. At issue, after all, was not the introduction of religious instruction but the question of drawing all the consequences of the fact that 'knowledge of religious cultures is necessary for an understanding of our societies past and present, their artistic and literary heritage, their legal and political systems.' (Report by Recteur Philippe Joutard on the teaching of history, geography and social sciences, 1989). Through press reports and opinion polls, an international colloquium at Besancon in 1991 (Actes du colloque international de Besançon, 1992), one on teaching the religious dimension of cultural history held at the Ecole du Louvre in Paris in 1996 (Ministère de la Culture, Ministère de l'Education Nationale, de l'Enseignement Supérieur et de la Recherche, 1997), a national interdisciplinary seminar on teaching religious facts organised in November 2002 by the Department of School Education by order of the Inspectors-General of National Education, the Association of History and Geography Teachers[5], and through numerous initiatives and courses (Hervieu-Leger, 1990; Boesplug and Martini, 1999), public opinion, above all that of teachers, was drawn towards the fact that the school, while remaining devoted to *laïcité*, needed to take account of religious cultures in its curricula.[6] This is to say that this had not been happening already, especially in history courses. But it was once more stressed forcefully how important it was to more completely take account of these cultures, with some going so far as to propose the introduction of a dedicated subject of religious-historical education as surveys of the religious ignorance of both students and teachers multiplied. Thus the debate: How, why, in view of who, by whom, and for whom can the school, should it think it necessary, take account of religious culture? – the debate involves all manner of expectations both of schools and

---

5   See the articles by that organisation in: Historiens et Géographes N° 341 (October 1993) and
     N°343 (March–April 1994).
     An overview of the French debate can be found in Boespflug, Dunand and Willaime (1996), as
     well as in Willaime (1998) and Estivalèzes (2005).

religions now (Willaime, 1995). Although it has not yet led to the creation of a new subject and teaching body dedicated to religious history, René Nouailhat (Nouailhat, 2000) points out that 'a new emphasis on religious facts appeared in the curricula of history and literature after 1996' in France. Another indication of this new interest is the creation of a collection on, 'History of Religions' edited by the Centre for Pedagogical Research and Documentation in Besancon (affiliated with the Education Department) and the publisher *éditions du Cerf*, designed to give secondary school teachers information material and teaching tools collected and redacted by university professors and allowing them to address the subject in class.[7] [8]

Consequences of the Debray Report

By charging Régis Debray to take a look after 'the teaching or religious facts in laical schools' on 3 December 2001, Minister of National Education Jack Lang recognised that 'a genuinely and comfortably laical school' had to allow each student to acquire 'an understanding of the world', which required teachers to take account of 'religions as important and, to a large degree, determining elements in the history of humanity, be it as factors of peace and modernity or of discord, mortal conflict and regression' (Debray, 2002, p. 9-10). It was in the aftermath of 9/11 that the overwhelming necessity for an initiative to bring the school closer to religious facts came home to Mr Lang. Hence the urgency of one passage, so well phrased by Régis Debray: 'from a *laïcité* of ignorance (in which religion does not concern us) towards a *laïcité* of understanding (where understanding becomes our duty)' (Debray, 2002, p. 43). To effect this, the Debray report proposed a number of measures concerning both the curriculum and the training of secondary school teachers at university and on the job. It is noted that in Alsace-Lorraine, where a Catholic, Protestant or Jewish religious instruction is institutionalised in public schools, this class has been transformed, with the approval of the regional education authorities, into part of a larger framework of values and citzenship education (Willaime, 2000). This development shows, though in the context of a specific region, the kind of agreement that public authorities may reach with the churches to enshrine their positive contribution to education in the fields of basic values and democratic social order.

An early consequence of the Debray Report was the holding of a national interdisciplinary seminar by the Department of School Instruction of the Ministry of National Education aimed at the Inspectors General and Regional of National Education of the different disciplines concerned (philosophy, history/geography, literature, languages and creative arts). This seminar, including about three-hundred participants, was held in Paris on 5-7 November 2002. Its proceedings have been published under the title 'L'enseigne-

---

7   These are: Nouailhat (1990);Clevenot (1991), Leveque and L'Huillier (1992); Ferjani (1996); Willaime and Cusenier (1998). See also: Boulade, Kohler, Montsarrat, Peter, Rolin and Weben (1998); Nouailhat and Joncheray (1999).

8   See les Actes du colloque international de Besançon (1992); Ministère de la Culture, Ministère de l'Education Nationale, de l'Enseignement Supérieur et de la Recherche (1997); Hervieu-Léger (1990); Boespflug and Martini (1999); Boespflug, Dunand and Willaime (1996); Willaime (1998).

ment du fait religieux' (Actes de la DESCO, 2003). In a message to the participants, President Jacques Chirac stressed that instruction about religion favoured a spirit of tolerance and education towards mutual respect:

'In today's world, tolerance and *laïcité* can have no better foundation than knowledge of and respect for the other. It is a retreat to oneself and ignorance that nourish prejudice and separatism. To strengthen understanding of religions, to improve the teaching on religious and related matters at our schools and universities, to follow the manifestations of faith in history, in arts, and in each culture, all of these will reinforce the spirit of tolerance in our young fellow citizens and give them the basis to respect each other more fully.' (Actes de la DESCO, 2003, p. 9)

Xavier Darcos, the Delegate Minister for School Education, opened the conference by outlining three major axes of instruction about religion:

'Above all, religious education comes down to understanding the specific language that allows us to define and understand its sign system, to understand, eventually, a system of framing the world. It also gives young people access to uncountable masterpieces of human civilisation, and finally, instruction about religion enables them to understand the role that the religious plays in the modern world.' (Actes de la DESCO, 2003, p.11).

We can thus characterise three main avenues of approach: 1) an education in the symbolic language of religion; 2) a contribution to the understanding of and insight into cultural heritage; 3) a contribution to civic education. All of this, as the minister clarified, must be effected in the context of a 'descriptive and understanding', yet 'critical and reasoned' approach. Instruction about religion, like all forms of education, must 'support the fundamental values of the Republican school' (Actes de la DESCO, 2003, p. 12). However, as Dominique Borne stressed in his concluding remarks to the conference, an exclusively historical approach to instruction about religion can be dangerous: 'It risks emptying religious fact of its topicality, considering it exclusively with a kind of nostalgia for 'the world which we have lost'' (Actes de la DESCO, 2003, p. 369). Moreover, he emphasised, such an approach runs the risk of not allowing an adequate place for Islam, which would limit its ability to take proper account of the importance of this faith in the contemporary religious landscape in France and beyond.

This seminar made acceptable the use of the term 'religious fact' (fait religieux) and reaffirmed the choice of not establishing a dedicated subject 'study of religions' but rather to address religious issues in existing school subjects. This decision, already supported by the conclusions of a colloquium in Besançon in 1991, obviously has important consequences. It effectively reduces the study of religious facts to a relatively minor position among the other school subjects. The history of human societies, literature, arts, languages and civilisations all have plenty of dimensions beyond the religious. In this perspective, the goal is to emphasise how religious facts are interwoven into societies and their developments and must be understood in this context. That does not mean reducing instruction about religion to the study of the social and cultural effects of religions: to fully understand a religious theme in a painting or literary work, one must immerse oneself in all the subtleties of theological thought. Furthermore, by speaking of 'religious facts' rather than 'religions', emphasis is placed on the fact that religion is more than mere opinion. 'No one may be inconvenienced on grounds of their opinions, including religious ones, as long as their expression does not infringe upon legally established public order', reads the relevant article of the Declaration of 1789. There has since been a tendency in France to reduce religion to the status of private, individual opinion, forgetting that, with religion, you have, on the one hand, a set of deeply ingrained beliefs capable of forcefully mobilising believers and, on the other hand, collectively organised convictions expressed through a number of visible forms such as monuments, texts, assemblies, actions etc. There are religious facts because there are individual men and women who live their religions, there are religious organisations and institutions, there are works, written, pictorial and architectural traces, in short, texts and rituals, representations and attitudes, works and conducts. Though the public school may not know whether God exists, it knows and must know that there are individuals and groups who believe he does and for whom this deeply affects their individual and social existence. The choice of the Debray Report is to begin with the texts and works in which the religious manifests itself and thence to ascend to its meaning. As Dominique Borne, head of the Inspectorate General, stated in his conclusion to the seminar:

> 'Studying texts and works always means going from form to meaning', a meaning which 'can not be reduced to a unanimous, reasoned statement.' (Actes de la DESCO, 2003, p. 368).

Paradoxically enough we find that the previous division of educational labour in which all matters religious were excluded from the school was insufficiently laical. Including religious fact within public education means including it into the sphere of knowledge and critical examination, the sphere of collective deliberation, it means religious citizenship. Religions are too important a social factor to allow them to be monopolised by clergy and religious communities. By entering into the public, and above all, the scholastic, context, religious faith enters 'into a context of maturity and *laïcité*' (Actes de la DESCO, 2003, p. 369), a new age of *laïcité* and a sign of its ultimate success.

Leading to the creation of a European Institute for the Study of Religion (I.E.S.R.) within the Ecole Pratique des Hautes Etudes – a great seat of higher learning famous for its department of religious studies where such great minds as Sylvain Lévi, Marcel Mauss, Georges Dumézil, Claude Levi-Strauss , Gabriel Le Bras and Lucien Febvre were active – the Debray Report represents a significant and major advance. It is striking that in our country, where the scientific, secular and multidisciplinary study of religious fact is so highly developed at institutes of higher learning, many universities and the C.N.R.S., such a gap should exist between higher education on the one hand and primary and secondary on the other. The mission of the I.E.S.R. is to bridge that gap.

The I.E.S.R. is dedicated to the formulation of frameworks and approaches for the National Education Department, to theoretical reflection, and to excellence in research on religious issues. It forthrightly and understandably addresses the epistemological, methodological, social, political and pedagogical problems arising from any approach to religious faith. The decision to name this Institute 'European' is entirely fortunate: it expresses the founders' willingness to integrate theoretical and practical insights gained in other European countries into French instruction about religion. In this matter – as in many other – the practices and reflections in this country must be augmented by those from abroad. It is also likely to be the best way of gaining a European response to the French solution that is emerging today. With this view, two initiatives have been taken: on the one hand the formation of a European academic council involving numerous specialists on religious matters (historians, sociologists, jurists et al..) and on the other hand, the development of a programme to enquire into the state of religious education in Europe.

At the same time, the I.E.S.R. combines regional centres (Lille, Rennes, Strasbourg, Lyon, Aix-en-Provence/Marseilles and Toulouse) in order to mobilise local academic resources and be able to influence teaching in the various regions on the spot. It is equally charged with 'working out adequate pedagogical tools (on paper or CD-ROM) and to contribute to an improved evaluation of existing publications on the educational market' (9th recommendation of the Debray Report). Another recommendation of the report – the fifth – is as important, though more modest. It concerns the introduction of a module on 'the philosophy of *laïcité* and instruction about religion' at teacher training colleges (Instituts Universitaires de Formation des Maîtres, IUFM). This obligatory module covering more than ten hours per year during the second year of study, 'entrusted to university professors of philosophy, literature, or history of that college, depending on the personnel resources available, who are trained for the purpose' has now been introduced at several colleges. This initiative is very important inasmuch as it amounts to the institutionalisation in teacher training of a course dedicated to instruction about religion and *laïcité*. Yet one cannot help but note the limited nature of the undertaking, given the small number of hours allotted.

Though the I.E.S.R. devotes a large part of its activities to supporting the Ministry of National Education, it also works to aid other ministries (such as Foreign Affairs and Culture). Thus, a colloquium on 'Religion and Politics in Asia' was organised in October 2003 in cooperation with the Ministry of Foreign Affairs, the proceedings of which are being published (Lagerwey, 2006). Also in 2003, the Institut Universitaire de Formation des Maîtres (teacher training college) of Alsace organised a national autumn school dedicated to the interdisciplinary study of 'Religion and Modernity' at Guebwiller (Haut-Rhin). This meeting was attended by many teachers from all over France (Actes de la DESCO, 2004). Other projects are under development. All these unertakings render more accessible current academic research into the religious realm while at the same time demonstrating its usefulness and its contribution towards the understanding of societies and their development.

The Challenges

Reactions to the Reception of the Debray Report

By returning to the question of religion at school, the Debray Report and the reactions it elicited have revived both fears and questions: Fears by militant laicals and freemasons that religious education might return to state schools, and fears by religious people that a historical and cultural approach to faith might reduce the religious to a heritage whose vestiges are studied without paying sufficient attention to the fact that religions are living realities mobilising millions around the world to action.

In its October 2003 issue, the journal 'Sciences et Vie' caught confessional approaches 'in flagrante delicto' in history books used in French public schools. The article accuses the history books of mixing faith and knowledge by not distinguishing between historically proven facts and beliefs. The question of how to approach religious fact at school, and of the manner of discussing it (the use of quotation marks and indirect style such as 'Adherents of this religion believe that, or say that...') has been studied by several authors in France as well as in other countries. An academic approach to religious fact needs an agreed-upon vocabulary and an appropriate language of its own. It has become obvious that, in the French context, some parties are especially keen to denounce all approaches that may appear, by using euphemism or disguising facts, to be either apologistic or proselytising. But must we, therefore, move towards a strictly positivist curriculum limited to verifiable facts and beholden to the latest archeological and historical hypotheses, at the risk of turning those into dogma? That would mean forgetting the important fact that a religion is always a living, symbolic universe which manifests and is manifested daily through believing individuals and communities.

While reacting positively to the Debray Report (to be published), Jean-Robert Armogathe in a stimulating essay incisively addresses the question whether an 'objective' religious education is possible at all (Armogathe, to be published). It is, he contends, from the point of view of the teacher who, whatever his convictions, is bound to present religious facts 'without proselytising or denigrating'. It is also possible with regard to the object of study itself as 'an important part of religious fact offers itself to an objective approach: these are the texts, events and personalities which may be given to study and learn'. He emphasises that an 'objective' curriculum is especially well possible at the international level as 'a consensus among historians regarding the *quaestiones disputatae* in the history of the church exists" and that, where differences exist, these are mainly differences between confessions, „like those among academic schools'. But, as Jean-Robert Armogathe rightly points out, an 'objective' religious education must not only take account of the cultural dimension or the liturgy which allows students to understand the calendar of religious festivals. It must also take an active interest in theology: 'Presenting a Virgin by Vladimir, a Trinity by Rublev, or a Nativity by La Tour without speaking of the Incarnation would be missing out on a profound structure of our imaginary in relation to motherhood and family relations.' An 'objective' religious education can no longer ignore the living faith of the believers:

> 'The mere 'factual' description does not take adequate account of religion which, after all, does not consist of an assembly of beliefs and rites, but begins with the faith of the believers. It would be a grave error to believe to be able to give an objective education by merely describing facts without ever attempting to present the way these teachings are integrated into the lives of the faithful. (...) It is essential for such a course to consider religious life. Without judgement, and with benevolence, the attitudes of believers, their piety and 'spirituality' must be taken in and presented. A comparative approach must play a central role here: pilgrimage, sacrifice, vows, prayer, monastic life and social morality are common themes among the great religions that allow a presentation of religious life without favouring a particular faith.' (Armogathe, to be published).

While the reception of the Debray Report was very positive in both the religious and secular milieu, reactions were more hesitant and distrustful among the representatives of an aggressively anti-religious *laïcité* and among religious traditionalists.

The Contribution of the Religious Dimension to Civic Education

Speaking of instruction about religion at school implies that this education must subscribe to the educational mission appropriate to the school as a whole. This dedication is
of fundamental importance; we are not talking of introducing any kind of rupture in the
school's ethos. In other words, if we take it as a given that the school not only transmits
knowledge, but equally contributes to the formation of a deontology of intellectual conduct, including objectivity, procedures of verification and applying proof, free examination, and critical reasoning; if we take into account the fact that the school is also a national institution which culturally and socially integrates students from different social
backgrounds and educates them in civic virtues, then it is legitimate to ask how an instruction about religion can contribute to citizenship education.

The cultural dimension of knowledge transmission is assured by the simple fact that
instruction about religion offers key knowledge and insight that contributes to a better
understanding of cultural heritage, texts and works, in short, the entirety of cultures past
and present. Yet the subject is more important than that. Actually, the introduction to the
historical method – with its criticism of sources, interpretations, transmissions and evolutions – applied to religious facts is in itself an important contribution to citizenship education. Why? Because it means entering religions into a space of collective examination,
to consider it outside of its individual and collective demands for credence, in other
words, learning to speak of one's own religion as though it was someone else's. The need
to speak of religion in front of a diverse audience, the inability to appeal to the conniv-
ance of co-religionists, the necessity to objectify and explain the worlds of representations and attitudes proper to a given religion, alone constitute a position that marries religious belief to citizenship in a pluralist democracy. It enforces the recognition from the
start that the religious worldview under discussion is not an all-encompassing symbolic
structure for all society – even if it is the majority religion – but one orientation among
many. Such an approach must inevitably clash with all religious self-descriptions that re-
fuse a historical perspective. In other words, the fact that religion is treated in school
means we must enter into conflict with all fundamentalists and especially with all understandings of religion that insist on forcibly applying their own norms to the whole of society.

There is more. By treating religious facts in school, we interfere, if indirectly, with the
religious education of all students, whether they are in conscious receipt of one or not.
For those that are receiving one, this critical and informed approach contributes to some
degree – at the very least by creating a complete schizophrenic split between what happens at school and what happens at church – to developing the religious conscience of
one or the other in a more reflective and critical direction. Even though that is certainly
not the intended aim of instruction about religion in school, the fact remains that merely
treating religion in school constitutes interference – willing or not – with religious education in general. Thus, the school treatment of religions also teaches religious citizenship,
that is to say, the affirmation of personal autonomy and the capacity to freely examine religious matters like all others. People who have received instruction about religion in
school are less easily assigned to this or that orthodoxy and have a greater proclivity to

criticise religious authority. The school approach helps the democratic ethos to penetrate into the world of religions. In particular, it gives students the tools to resist fundamentalisms and, more generally, all authoritarian impositions of orthodoxy. But instruction about religion at school not only has consequences for students who receive religious education instruction out of school. It also affects those who receive no such education. In this case the scholastic approach may strengthen some in their convictions that religions are not worth the trouble of adhering to one, or it might – however far from its stated intentions and goals this may be – awaken the interest of some in a religious path.

Another aspect of the contribution of instruction about religion to civic education is its effect on the integration of individuals into a given political collective. School instruction does not take place within a cultural vacuum, it takes place within a given society with its specific history and the cultural and religious characteristics bound up with it. If students learn about world history and geography, if they are brought into contact with literatures from various languages, still they are especially affected by the history, geography, arts and literature of a specific country – that in which they live. Must we, under the pretext of a non-confessional curriculum, systematically practise comparativistic approaches to religion and conclude that all faiths deserve equal treatment in terms of school hours dedicated to them? Some think so. They prefer the curriculum to be as remote as possible from the majoritarian religious choices of the country it is taught in, in order to render it more objective and the better to guarantee its non-confessional nature. But it is hard to see why we cannot, in the realm of religion, apply the same orientation common in other fields, that is, accord a certain privileged position to national culture and history. Societies are more than aggregates of individuals; they have a symbolic consistency tied to their history and the traditions that have made them into what they are. By placing particular emphasis on the majority religious world-view which has shaped the history, culture and manners of the country it is given in, instruction about religion can contribute to civic education. Taken out of context the subject would be contrary to the goals of school education in its entirety. The attention paid to the context, on the other hand, strengthens its contribution to the development of citizenship. Such a course is dedicated to a national education programme. It takes place in a public school, in a given location, with a given history and cultural identity. It is, in other words, perfectly defensible for such a curriculum in France to devote more time to Christianity than, say, Buddhism.

The European Challenge

Enlarging our focus to encompass all of Europe can, from a French point of view, give rise to questions and worries (Willaime, 2004; Willaime and Mathieu, 2005). After all, doesn't instruction about religion in the majority of European countries take place in the context of a dedicated subject developed in cooperation between religious and academic authorities? And does that not make the French approach – a laical instruction about religion without creating a specific subject – outdated and misplaced compared to the rest of the continent? We do not think so, for a variety of reasons. First of all, because there is no reason to believe that any kind of European model can prevail in this area, given that the relationship between church and state and thus the state of religious education are invariably specific to each country and its historical, political and religious character. Therefore the principle of subsidiarity, laid out by the European Union in the 11th Annex to the Treaty of Amsterdam, respects the status accorded to religious and non-confessional philosophical organisations according to national law. Secondly, because the arrangements for religious education made in other European countries are not static but evolve under the pressure of secularisation and increasing religious diversity. And finally, because Europe, contrary to the impression gained by a superficial study, is more laical than one would think. That is why the French solution which is now in the process of emerging can expect a positive and interested response in other European Union member states and, possibly, in countries aspiring to membership now or in future. It is not the *laïcité* of understanding, brought about through the Joutard colloquium and the Debray Report, which risks a rebuff from Europe, but an abstentionist and paralysed *laïcité* that, in the eyes of our European partners, will appear suspicious and outdated.

Between a process of internal secularisation in religious education curricula in various European countries on the one hand and the opening of the question of introducing religious culture to schools in France on the other, there is a certain degree of convergence emerging from very different historical and legal contexts. Characterised by a long-standing secularisation process and suffused with the spirit of cultural secularism, European countries face the same challenges: a growing number of Muslim school students, the threats posed to respect for civil liberties by certain religious groups, the religious ignorance of students, demands for direction and ethical guidance, and the education towards citizenship in culturally diverse societies. In all nations of Europe, be it the Northern European Protestant countries or the southern Catholic ones, we can see that the challenges of secularisation and social pluralisation are the same and that each country is trying to formulate a response based on the foundations of its specific history and situation. Whatever their legal frameworks, all European countries are facing the question of how to approach religious faith respecting the freedom of conscience of students and their families while at the same time educating them towards freedom of thought and a critical stance. The question is, then, how to integrate these different orientations into the school without diminishing its laical stance or its educative mission. In France it is the very success of *laïcité*, the maturity of the system, that allows it to open itself calmly to the question of instruction about religion in a laical school.

References

Actes du colloque international de Besançon 20–21 novembre 1991 (1992) *Enseigner l'histoire des religions dans une démarche laïque. Représentations – Perspectives – Organisation des apprentissages* (Besançon, CNDP/CRDP de Franche-Comté).

Actes de la DESCO (2003) *L'enseignement du fait religieux* (Paris, Scérén/CRDP Académie de Versailles).

Actes de la DESCO (2004) *Religions et modernité, Actes de l'université d'automne de Guebwiller, 27–30 octobre 2003* (sous la direction de Jean-Marie Husser) (Paris, CRDP Académie de Versailles).

Armogathe, J.-R. (to be published) Dieu à l'école sans Dieu. L'enseignement des religions à l'école publique, *Revue des Deux Mondes*.

Baubérot, J. (1990) *Vers un nouveau pacte laïque?* (Paris, Seuil).

Baubérot, J. (1997) *La morale laïque contre l'ordre moral* (Paris, Seuil).

Boespflug, F. & Martini, E. (1999) *S'initier aux religions* (Paris, Cerf).

Boespflug, F., Dunand F. & Willaime J.-P. (1996) *Pour une mémoire des religions* (Paris, La Découverte).

Boulade G., Kohler J., Montsarrat V., Peter L., Rolin P. & Weben V. (1998) *Pour lire les textes bibliques. Collège et lycée* (Paris, CRDP de l'Académie de Créteil)

Clevenot M. (1991) *Les religions dans le monde actuel* (Besançon, CRDP de Franche-Comté).

Debray, R. (1992) *L'enseignement du fait religieux dans l'école laïque*, Rapport au ministre de l'Education Nationale, Préface de Jack Lang (Paris, Odile Jacob).

Estivalèzes, M. (2005) *Les religions dans l'enseignement laïque* (Paris, Puf).

Ferjani M.-C. (1996) *Les voies de l'islam. Approche laïque des faits islamiques* (Besançon, CRDP de Franche-Comté).

Hervieu-Leger, D. (Ed.) (1990) *La religion au Lycée. Conférences au lycée Buffon 1989–1990* (Paris, Cerf).

Lagerwey, J. (Ed.) (2006) *Religion et politique en Asie. Histoire et actualité* (Paris, les Indes Savantes).

Leveque P. & L'Huillier M.-C. (1992) *La création des dieux de Lascaux à Rome* (Besançon, CRDP de Franche-Comté).

Ministère de la Culture, Ministère de l'Education Nationale, de l'Enseignement Supérieur et de la Recherche (1997) *Forme et sens. Colloque sur la formation à la dimension religieuse du patrimoine culturel. Ecole du Louvre* (Paris, La Documentation Française).

Nouailhat R. (1990) *La genèse du christianisme de Jérusalem à Chalcédoine* (Besançon, CRDP de Franche-Comté).

Nouailhat R. & Joncheray J. (1999) *Enseigner les religions au collège et au lycée. 24 séquences pédagogiques* (Paris-Besançon, les éditions de l'Atelier/CRDP de Franche-Comté).

Nouailhat, R. (2000) *Le christianisme à l'école*, La Pensée, 123–135

Ognier, P. (1994) La laïcité scolaire dans son histoire (1880-1945), in: Y. Lequin (Ed.) *Histoire de la laïcité* (Besançon, CRDP de Franche-Comté), 71–275.

Willaime, J.-P. (1995) Ecole et religions. Représentations et attentes in: F. Messner (Ed.) *La culture religieuse à l'école* (Paris, Cerf) 17–35.

Willaime, J.-P. (1998) Ecole et religions : une nouvelle donne?, *Revue Française de Pédagogie*, 125, 7–20.

Willaime, J.-P. (Ed.) & Cusenier D. (1998) *Protestantisme* (Besançon, CRDP de Franche-Comté).

Willaime, J.-P. (2000) L'enseignement religieux à l'école publique dans l'Est de la France : une tradition entre déliquescence et recomposition, *Social Compass*, 47 (3), 383–395

Willaime, Jean-Paul (2004) *Europe et religions. Les défis du XXIe siècle* (Paris, Fayard).

Willaime, J.-P. (Ed.) & Mathieu S. (2005) *Des maîtres et des dieux. Ecoles et religions en Europe* (Paris, Belin).

Gunther Dietz

Invisibilizing or Ethnicizing Religious Diversity?

The Transition of Religious Education Towards Pluralism in Contemporary Spain[1]

Introduction

In September 2004, during a United Nations General Assembly speech, the Spanish prime minister José Luis Rodríguez Zapatero launched the vision of an 'Alliance of Civilizations', a bridge between cultures, nations and religions which would avoid the all too self-fulfilling prophecy of an imminent 'clash of civilizations' (Huntington, 1996). As his invitation to join this new alliance was immediately and positively echoed by his Turkish counterpart, Rajip Erdogan, Spanish and other European media quickly identified a strange new coalition, between a 'Socialist' and an 'Islamist' head of government, between two marginal corners of Europe and between two Mediterranean regions which share a similarly hybrid, Muslim and Christian heritage.

This 'Alliance of Civilizations', which has survived since then more as an effort of diplomatic goodwill, basically between the European Union and the League of Arab States, has paradoxically not unleashed new visions, concepts or solutions in the Spanish domestic debate about Muslim-Christian, Moroccan-Spanish, migrant-native relations.[2] After the end of the Franco dictatorship in 1975, which had explicitly exploited the Christian-Castilian nexus through its ideology of 'national Catholicism', the step-by-step secularization of the Spanish state coincided with a process of increasing religious pluralization: apart from Muslim immigrants and converts, both the important immigration of EU and Latin American citizens and the recent, but massive conversion to Pentecostalism by the Spanish gitano (Roma) community has strengthened the formerly rather non-existent presence of Protestant Churches.

Nevertheless, this religious diversity has not been appropriately perceived nor accepted by mainstream public opinion institutions or state institutions. The Catholic Church has successfully resisted a complete secularization of the Spanish educational system – maintaining a de facto monopoly on religious instruction inside public schools and running a huge majority of state-subsidized private schools. Accordingly, non-Catholic religious instruction, which is recognized and protected by the Spanish Constitution as well as by the 'quasi-concordat' agreements signed between 1992 and 1996 with the Spanish Muslim, Protestant and Jewish communities, in practice has not existed until very lately.

1   I gratefully acknowledge the decisive collaboration of the Granada REDCo team members Eva González Barea, Iman Kluza, Latifa Mehdi, F. Javier Rosón Lorente, Francisca Ruiz Garzón and Julia Vollmer in the drafting of this chapter, which is based on their extensive bibliographical research.
2   Cf. its recently launched official web site: www.unaoc.org/ (accessed September 13, 2006).

Since the 9/11 attacks and particularly since the March 11th Madrid bombings, however, two processes are perceivable in Spanish public opinion and politics vis-à-vis the Muslim communities. On the one hand, pre-existing islamophobic and arabophobic tendencies regarding the 'return of Islam' are becoming more explicit; on the other hand, there is also a growing conviction that religious pluralism is here to stay and that accordingly Muslims have to be integrated through a 'Hispanization' or 'Europeanization' of Islam. In this context, Islamic religious instruction is now being officially promoted and implemented through pilot-projects. Therefore, religious education is currently a key issue in the domestic debates both on pending educational reforms, in particular, and on pluralism and multiculturalism inside Spanish society, in general.

In the following, after a brief sketch of the historical legacy of 'national Catholicism' in its impact on state-church relations, the current situation regarding Catholic and non-Catholic religious communities and institutions, their legal framework as well as their inter-relations since the transition period towards democracy are analyzed. Secondly, the profound transformations which are completely reshaping contemporary Spanish society through generational changes, immigration and the increasing pluralization and diversification of civil society are illustrated with cases from the Protestant and Muslim communities as well as from mainstream society's frequently islamophobic fears and reactions. In the third part, the slow and rather recent process of de-monopolization of Catholic religious education is highlighted with regard to the step-by-step institutionalization and implementation of non-Catholic confessional religious instruction inside Spanish public schools. As will be shown in detail, claims made by Muslim, Protestant and – to less extent – Jewish community, representatives have only been answered adequately by state and regional educational policy makers after the 9/11 and March 11th attacks. This current political background finally illustrates the pending tasks of reforming and plainly recognizing religious as well as inter-religious education not as a concession to 'pacify Muslims', but as an educational achievement and as a right of any Spanish citizen of whatever belief.

The Legacy of National Catholicism

Religious education in contemporary Spain is still heavily shaped by two long lasting traditions: firstly, the self-perception of Spanish society as being homogeneous in religious terms, and, secondly, the close interrelation and frequent overlapping between the Catholic Church as an institution and the Spanish nation state as another institution. Both traditions are deeply rooted in historical continuities, whose consequences for present-day societal and educational reforms will be described in the following.

Historical Continuities in Religious Homogenization Policies

Although often invisibilized, continuities in state formation policies, as well as in identity politics, are implicitly and 'covertly' maintained. Since 1492, state and church have been knit together through their institutional merger and their 'nationalizing' endeavours. The end of the *reconquista* symbolizes the often-cited, prototypical and pioneering attempt at creating the first European nation-state based on the principles of territorial, linguistic, ethnic, religious and ideological homogeneity, a – failed – attempt which is first implemented through the forced conversion of ethnic and religious minorities such as *moriscos* (Muslims living under Catholic rule) and *sefardíes* (Spanish Jews) and which later leads to the expulsion of the visibly persisting members of these minorities. Simultaneously, other ethnic groups such as the *gitano* (Spanish Roma) communities are either forced to sedentarize and to 'hispanicize' or excluded towards rural and marginal areas. The publication – precisely in 1492! – of the *Gramática de la lengua castellana*, the first 'vernacular', non-Latin grammar, by Antonio de Nebrija, who dedicates his work to the 'Catholic Kings', illustrates not only the self-confidence Castilian Spanish as an emerging 'national language', but also the confluence of linguistic and ethno-religious 'markers' of national identity.[3]

Accordingly, since the end of the fifteenth century, the actors of political and religious unification and homogenization of the country have been closely collaborating in their effort to persecute minorities, heterodoxy, and dissidence. These 'state-church mergers' are present in the sadly famous Estatutos de Limpieza de Sangre, a public law established in the mid 16th century with the purpose of screening everybody's genealogy in order to neatly distinguish between 'pure-breed' castellanos viejos and supposedly convert and 'impure' nuevos castellanos, whose loyalty to the Crown and to Spanish unity is called into question and scrutinized. Both in the Spanish mainland and in the American colonies, these 'caste statutes' are applied by the state, but are controlled by the Holy Inquisition. In order to obtain a civil servant status, these procedures of ethno-racial-religious profiling are used even until 1834![4]

These joint state-church policies of distinguishing, stigmatizing and excluding large parts of the population have decisively contributed to the maintenance of two main features of Spanish society, which are still strongly present even throughout the twentieth century: on the one hand, these distinctions end up dualizing society in 'castes' of included vs. excluded, 'orthodox' vs. 'heterodox' Spaniards – a dualization which heavily reappears in the Spanish Civil War (Vilar, 2000) –; and, on the other hand, these persistent dualizations constantly mix up linguistic, ethnic, religious and racialized phenotype criteria in order to establish a discrete frontier between the 'authentic' and the 'false', between the Catholic Castilian 'proper' and the Moorish or Sephardic or Protestant or 'Erasmist' or all too French (afrancesado) 'other' – that is, between 'us' and 'them'. As a consequence, religious differences and diversities, as they are perceived in Spain, are not 'just' about religion or about confessional differences, but about ethnicity: about the nation-state and its mainstream ethno-religious element, national Catholicism.

Accordingly, the 1936 coup d'État by a group of disloyal, anti-Republican generals based above all in the north African Spanish colonies and led by Francisco Franco, is presented in subsequent historiography as a 'Crusade' aimed at re-establishing the essence of 'authentic', 'true' Spanish-ness. This Catholic-cum-Castilian authenticity had supposedly been distorted not just by 'left-wing' governments, by 'Marxists' and

---

3   Cf. Stallaert (1998), Álvarez-Junco (2002) and Manzano Moreno & Pérez Garzón (2002).
4   For an illuminating comparison between these nationalist inquisitorial practices and the German Nazi ideology, cf. Stallaert (2006).

'laicists', but by a 'Jewish-Masonic' conspiracy against the holy institutions of the unified state and the unified church. Republican cultural and educational policies were therefore an early target of the dictatorship's 're-Catholization' and 'purification' procedures'
(Gervilla Castillo, 1990).

Already in October 1936, an officially promoted meeting of an *ad hoc* created Catholic
parents' association, the *Confederación Católica de Padres de Familia*, declared that
from now on 'all teaching has to be Catholic' (Gervilla Castillo, 1990, p. 132). From this
moment on, throughout the Franco dictatorship, the omnipresence of the Catholic Church
and its monopoly of power in cultural, educational and 'ideological' affairs will be re-
established after the short interim period of the Republic. Since 1936, Spain is officially
defined again as a 'confessional state'.[5]

In the educational sphere, the state's confessionalism is implemented through two decisive legal measures:

* The first legal corpus developed by the Franco regime on educational issues, the 1945
  Ley de Educación Primaria, is a high level 'basic law' on primary education which
  systematically transfers public educational functions to the Catholic Church and its
  dependencies and applies church law where formerly state law regulated Spanish
  schools (Gervilla Castillo, 1990).

* More comprehensively then, in 1953, the Franco regime, which now in the midst of
  the Cold War is internationally recognized, signs an all encompassing and far reaching Concordat with the Vatican; among many other issues that, taken together, now
  officially establish 'national Catholicism' (Linz, 1993), this Concordat introduces
  Catholic religious education as a compulsory and central subject throughout all levels
  and ages, which has to be taught both in public and in private schools throughout the
  country (Gervilla Castillo, 1990; Fernández Almenara, 2003).

The close interrelation and cross-breeding of religious and secular, church and state institutions, organizations and civil servants resulting from this alliance between the Vatican
and the heavily centralized Spanish nation-state has been coined by some authors as a
'clerical fascism' or 'total religion' type of regime.[6] In the educational field, the regime
emphasizes religious and theological homogeneity as a means to eradicate not only anti-
clerical positions shown by formerly Republican sectors of Spanish society, but also di-
vergent regionalist and localist religious and institutional traditions, as those illustrated
by the Basque and Catalan dioceses, which since the end of the nineteenth century have
been often showing support for Catalan and Basque regionalist/nationalist movements.
Therefore, during the dictatorship, i.e. from 1936 until 1975, one of the central missions
of religious instruction in schools was the development of a unified and universally
taught 'national *catequismo*' (Fernández Almenara, 2003). The resulting religious textbooks expressed a very conservative, even reactionary and completely theocentric view
of men, of creation, of gender roles, of attitudes towards religious as well as secular authorities. Not only religious education, but the whole school instruction was based on
'obedience, sacrifice, intolerance and transcendence' (Gervilla Castillo, 1990, 476).

---

5   Laboa (1981) analyzes the nuances in state-church relations, as expressed in different Spanish
     constitutions.
6   Cf. Giner & Sarasa (1993), Díaz Salazar (1993a) and Sádaba et al. (1994).

The position of the Catholic Church was so central throughout the dictatorship that even change and reform had to be unleashed from within the church itself. The transition towards first, slight reforms of the educational system and of religious education as part of this system starts in the context of the Second Vatican Council. Not only proposed reforms inside the church hierarchy, but also relations towards contemporary society start to be debated inside church institutions and organizations (Fernández Almenara, 2003). Slowly, but constantly, certain groups inside the church such as the Hermanos Obreros de Acción Católica (HOAC) become internal incubators for dissidence and resistance against the Franco regime. Since the end of the sixties, a distinctively 'social Catholicism' emerges, which disagrees – sometimes openly, but mostly in a hidden way- with official, 'political Catholicism' (Cuenca Toribio, 2003). This trend coincides with broader changes in Spanish society; under the influence of increased mobility, emigration and mass tourism, processes of secularization as well as individualization start exerting considerable pressure on a petrified, national Catholic regime.

Transition Towards Democracy: Transition Towards Diversity? Church-State-Relations Today

Despite these societal changes, a very broad and diverse range of Catholic institutions, organizations, fraternities and lay associations persists, whose strength as a 'moral power' does not disappear with the death of Franco in 1975 and with the beginnings of the period of 'transition towards democracy' (Montero, 1993). Thus, an ever more visible tension appears between the political and the 'religious transition' (Díaz Salazar, 1993a) towards democracy. Since the mid seventies until the beginning of the nineties, Spanish society undergoes a vibrant, accelerated and profound process of institutional democratization, social pluralization and 'Europeanization', which succeeds in effectively (re-) integrating the country in the whole of European democratic societies.

On the other hand, however, the Catholic Church is simultaneously and increasingly faced with the necessity of de-institutionalizing itself (Díaz Salazar, 1993a); the former 'total religion' now has to develop a new role inside society, but separate from the state structures. This de-institutionalization, which also implies redefining the cultural and moral role of Catholicism in an individualized and pluralized Spanish society (Giner & Sarasa, 1993), is not completely accomplished until today. The Catholic Church retains certain privileges of a quasi-state monopoly, while, on the other hand, not completely 'arriving' in Spanish civil society (Linz, 1993).

The resulting ambiguity in contemporary state-church relations, which has a strong impact on religious education, as will be shown below, is already inherent in Spain's post-dictatorship constitutional design. The 1978 Spanish Constitution, generally praised as an outstanding symbol of the consensual, peaceful and inclusive character of the transition process, defines the Spanish state as neither completely laicist nor completely confessional. In an attempt at bridging the historical divisions between national Catholic and anti-clerical traditions, article 16 of the Constitution obliges the state to (1) guarantee religious freedom, (2) 'consider' the majority religious belief of Spanish society and (3) actively co-operate with the existing religious communities (Constitución Española, 1991; Gómez Movellán, 1999).

The Catholic Church does not only hold the privilege of being the only religious community which is explicitly mentioned in the Constitution; it is also the first and, for several years, the only denomination which succeeds in defining, developing and specifying its rights vis-à-vis the Spanish state through an official agreement. The 1979 Concordat between Spain and the Vatican, which replaces the 1953 Francoist one, includes a series of detailed agreements on legal, economic, cultural and educational aspects of state-church relations, which have been slowly negotiated throughout three years, i.e. parallel and simultaneous with the elaboration of the Spanish Constitution.[7]

On the basis of this Concordat, and particularly of the cultural and educational agreement – Acuerdo entre el Estado Español y la Santa Sede sobre Enseñanza y Asuntos Culturales, signed in January and ratified in December 1979 –, the Catholic Church maintains a legal position which situates it beyond Spanish domestic law. This privileged situation still appears in several public debates on religion in society and in education, where Catholic Church representatives argue that they are not subject to national law, but to an international treaty. Since the end of the seventies and beginning of the eighties, this ambiguity is particularly visible in the issue of the state funding of the Catholic Church (Gómez Movellán, 1999). During – again – a 'transitory' period, the Spanish central state agrees to completely finance all expenses of the church, while the church is obliged to seek self-financing mechanisms as soon as possible.

When even in 1988 the Catholic Church, stuck in the tradition of close state-church cooperation, still had not developed any alternatives to state funding, the Socialist government implemented a further 'transitory' solution: from that year on, and until the church develops mechanisms for obtaining funding through its members and fellow believers, the Spanish state will transfer 0.5% of the yearly collected income tax to the Catholic Church. As this would contradict the non-confessional character of the Spanish state, the government is forced to introduce an option, according to which each tax payer may decide if her/his 0.5% of income tax is delivered either to the Catholic Church or to – sometimes secular, but often religious – non-governmental organizations (Dietz & El-Shohoumi, 2005).

This mechanism, on the one hand, introduced a 'non-church' alternative, originally designed for non-Catholic taxpayers, while, on the other hand, avoided asking each Catholic to either pay directly or indirectly for their church membership or to renounce their church membership – an option which has been fiercely resisted by the Catholic Church itself. Nevertheless, paradoxically it is only a third of all tax payers who nowadays agree in dedicating their respective percentage to the church, although there are supposed to be at least 90% of Catholics among all taxpayers.[8] Consequently, the financial crisis of the Catholic Church has not been resolved. Church representatives are therefore continuously claiming an increase in the income tax percentage to be transferred to

---

7   For details, cf. Acuerdo entre el Estado Español y la Santa Sede (1979), Laboa (1981) and Gómez Movellán (1999).

8   There are no official figures on denominational membership in Spain, so data and percentages on religious affiliations are based on estimates.

them. As a result, and in order to avoid complete bankruptcy and to maintain the church's services, since the signing of the Concordat the Spanish state has stepped in and – apart from the 0.5% of income tax transfers – directly subsidizes the Catholic Church with an annual increase of approximately 2%. Only in 2005, the state has subsidized the payment of 69 bishops' and about 20.000 clergymen's salaries with 11.789.140 euro per month, i.e. 141.5 million Euro per year, which are directly transferred to the Spanish Episcopal Conference (El País, 05–10–2004 and 26–11–2005). Apart from this amount, which is only destined for salaries, the state also transfers payments for church-run services such as private and subsidized schools (cf. below), salaries for teachers of religious education (cf. below), military chaplaincy and for the conservation of religious heritage.

According to several legal experts, this current practice of financing the church is not backed by the Spanish Constitution, as it contradicts the secular and neutral definition of the Spanish state, it blurs the boundaries between the state and the church and it discriminates against other religious communities, thus violating constitutional principles of equality. Periodically, debates appear in public opinion about the issue of the financing of the Catholic Church; in 2005, a Plataforma Ciudadana por una Sociedad Laica openly claims that the only way to assure equality and non-discrimination of religious beliefs would consist in re-negotiating the Concordat, which is always invoked by church representatives when reminding the state of its financial obligations with the Spanish society's 'majority belief' (Gómez Movellán, 1999).

Multiculturalism *a la Española*

These increasing legal, political and institutional debates on the status of Catholicism in Spain reflect two different, but closely intertwined phenomena which are currently transforming Spanish society: both a growing detachment of ever more Catholic Spaniards from their church and growing numbers of non-Catholic immigrants challenge the *de facto* monopoly of the Catholic Church. According to several opinion polls,[9] a huge majority of Catholics persists, but two different trends are particularly illustrative: On the one hand, due to demographic changes and to immigration, the absolute as well as relative number of Catholics is constantly decreasing in the last years; whereas in 1978 there were still 90% of Catholics, in 2005 the number decreased to 80%.[10] On the other hand, in these opinion polls ever more Catholic Spaniards, and above all young people, express a growing distance towards the church as an institution, to its representatives and its moral guidelines, particularly on sexuality, contraception, homosexuality and marriage.

---

9   For details, cf. the monthly 'barometers' published by the governmental Centro de Investigaciones Sociológicas, which are similar to the 'Eurobarometers', at: http://www.cis.es (accessed September 13, 2006).
10   These are estimations based on the above cited polls; in Spain, no official data are gathered on membership in religious communities.

Nature and Degree of Multiculturalism

This trend, which weakens the Catholic Church from within Spanish majority society, is indirectly fostered by immigration-induced religious pluralization (Amérigo Cuervo-Arango, 1995). Due to the remarkable increase in its immigrant population that Spain has experienced during the last years, it has been widely claimed that this country has changed from being a classical country of emigration to becoming a country of immigration.[11] During the eighties and nineties of the past century, Spain has experienced – like other southern European countries – decreasing emigration while becoming a place of destination for immigrants. This 'uneasy transition' (Cornelius, 2004) reflects a highly heterogeneous migration pattern, made up of Spanish 'return migrants' – Spanish 'guest workers' who migrated to western and northern Europe and who did not succeed in definitively integrating into their host society tend to re-migrate to their regions of origin once they retire, sometimes alone, but often together with their children, who settle down in a country which the second generation only knows from short holiday trips (Ruiz Garzón, 2001) –, European retirement migrants – often 'trans-migrants' (Pries 1999), many of whom spend half of the year in their country of origin and half of it on the Canary or Baleares Islands or on the southern Spanish Mediterranean shores (Fernández Cordón et al., 1993) –, non-EU immigrants, who are increasingly choosing Spain not any longer as a mere transit route – often due to post-colonial links that still exist between the Spanish peninsula and its formerly dependant Latin American as well as North African territories, and, finally, a growingly diversified immigration from Eastern European and from other non-EU countries, who often choose Spain either for temporary work or as a 'port of entrance' not only to Spain, but to the EU Schengen territory as a whole (Cornelius, 2004).

According to different sources, the non-EU population living in Spain is estimated around 2.5 million people, including both documented and undocumented, mere residents and people with a working-permit. These immigrants are mostly coming from North Africa – especially Morocco and Algeria –, from Latin America – in particular, Peru, the Dominican Republic and Colombia –, Asia – basically from China and the Philippines –, South Africa – particularly from Senegal and Nigeria. Meanwhile, immigration from certain countries is rapidly increasing, such as in the case of Ecuador,[12] China or Eastern European countries such as Romania, Poland and the Ukraine. Most of them, above all Maghrébien migrants, have been shifting from choosing Spain as a mere transit route on their way towards France or Belgium, to settling down more permanently in their northern Mediterranean neighbour country. The most outstanding feature of this immigration model consists of its very recent nature; as migrants are just settling down in the last years, this 'age effect' means that demographically the immigrant groups are made up of predominantly young people.

---

11   Cf. Izquierdo (1992, 1996) and Cornelius (2004).
12   The case of Ecuador is very representative for this changing demographic trend of replacing 'classical' countries of origin, as this country, formerly of nearly no significance as a region of origin, in the last three years it has become the second most important provider of immigrants in Spain (Cornelius 2004).

There are two basic elements which shape the demographic and social profile of immigration to Spain. On the one hand, although the percentage of immigrant population in the country remains low, its composition is highly heterogeneous and noteworthy differences appear between nationalities regarding gender, skills, migratory projects and degrees and types of labour market integration. On the other hand, the geographical distribution of their settlement over the country is very diverse and their labour market integration is limited to a reduced number of sectors, which show a rapid tendency towards segmentation. The foreign workers are demanded for those labour niches where there are insufficient local workers; this is, for those domains of work that nobody wants – because of economic and/or social reasons or labour conditions. Consequently, the immigrants have to work in those degraded niches like agriculture, construction, manufacturing, domestic services or in the broader service sector; i.e. in immigrant enclaves in the secondary labour market which are characterized by its unstable and short-term employment, high workers' rotation, low salary and its nearly total lack of ascending mobility. In addition, most of these jobs are inserted into the shadow economy, with almost no labour inspections, where all too often exploitation and abuses occur. In consequence, the integration of foreign workers into these occupations contributes even more to their stigmatization as a marginal group, working at the margins of the labour market in some specific geographic areas: the legal category of 'foreigner' is thus complemented by the connotation of marginality and inferiority.

Religious Pluralization: Immigration and Conversion

Until very recently, as a result of the above stated long lasting tradition of state and church induced homogenization, non-Catholic religious communities nearly did not exist at all in Spanish mainland society. And although Protestant, Jewish and Muslim communities slowly started to (re) settle down in several Spanish cities since the seventies, they were not visible until the nineties. The most 'invisible' of all is still the Jewish community. It is currently made up of approximately 30.000 members, whose activities in cities such as Toledo, Girona, Ceuta and Melilla are focused on the reconstruction, re-opening and re-vitalization of their respective local synagogues (Gómez Movellán, 1999; El País, 26–04–2005).

Protestant communities, on the other hand, were only perceived as 'foreigners' or 'tourists', although conversion to different Evangelical groups started early in the seventies. Today, there are approximately 2.200 Protestant congregations existing in Spain, 1.970 of whom are members of an umbrella organisation, the Federación de Entidades Religiosas Evangélicas de España (FEREDE). The first generation of Protestants which was perceived as 'different' was not made up of Protestant immigrants – northern and central European immigrants are still not perceived as inmigrantes, but as extranjeros, as long-term 'residential tourists' –, but of Spanish Roma. Already in 1958, the Iglesia de Filadelfía Pentecostal Church initiated missionary as well as grassroots charity and welfare activities particularly in deprived urban Roma settlements, which appeared in this period due to rural-urban migration towards Madrid, Barcelona and other growing Spanish cities. Starting from Balaguer in Catalonia, the Pentecostal Church quickly expanded to other gitano neighbourhoods, promising and promoting Roma upward mobility through 'modern values' such as an individual work and savings ethos, responsibility not towards a huge kin group, but to one's nuclear family, access to formal education and training also for Roma women, the reluctance to participate in all too expensive kin and/or communal fiestas and the active rejection of alcohol and drugs (Gómez Movellán, 1999; Cantón Delgado, 2004).

Nowadays, it is estimated that at least 150.000 of the approximately 350.000 Spanish Protestants are of Roma origin. Apart from these Spanish converts, immigration has rapidly promoted the diffusion of Protestant congregations throughout the country. Strikingly, it is not immigration from historically Protestant regions of the world which promotes Protestantism in Spain, but the immigration of individuals and families who come from Catholic regions, above all in South America, but who have converted to different kinds of Evangelical faith before migrating. Therefore, these groups – there are estimated to be around 800.000 non-Spanish Protestants living in the country (El País, 26–04–2005) – have quickly joined Spanish Protestants, as they not only share post-colonial links, but also similar conversion biographies, which frequently are related to their social and geographical mobility.

Although these immigrant as well as native Protestant communities are currently the most successful non-Catholic congregations with regard to their internal organization, their broader claims and their access to religious education (cf. below), the most important, most visibilized and most stigmatized communities in contemporary Spain are the Muslim ones. According to unofficial estimations, based above all on the predominant 'religion of origin' of mainly Moroccan and Algerian immigrant populations, approximately 700.000 people may identify themselves as Muslims.[13] As to their regional distribution and as a result of the main immigration areas of Moroccans, the Muslim population of Spain is concentrated in the urban centres of the Madrid and Catalonia autonomous communities (López García, 1996). Nevertheless, Andalusia is emerging as a third focus of Muslim population. In this latter case, Spanish converts to Islam are an increasingly important sector of the overall Muslim population (Dietz & El-Shohoumi, 2005; Rosón Lorente, 2005).

The two different factors analyzed above, the recent nature of immigration to Spain as well as the rather novel trend towards the religious pluralization of the country's majority society, determine the situation of Muslim communities in Spain. On the one hand, after the slow beginning of family regrouping, immigrant communities, made up of mainly Moroccan foreign workers have been appearing in recent years. Such groups rarely identify themselves in public as distinctively Muslim communities, but as foreign workers' associations in labour contexts and/or as parents' associations in school environments. On the other hand, above all in Andalusia, the growing group of Spanish converts has started to build up a tiny but publicly significant minority of Muslim intellectuals who are overtly challenging the implicitly Catholic common sense of the Spanish and/or Andalusian host society (cf. Dietz & El-Shohoumi, 2005).

---

13   Again, these figures are rouge estimates, as no official data are available. Cf. Abumalham (ed., 1995), Gómez Movellán (1999), Moreras (1999), Lacomba Vázquez (2001) and Sánchez Nogales (2004).

Internally, immigrants from Muslim countries such as Morocco, Algeria, Senegal and Bangladesh do not form homogeneous communities either in social or economic or in religious terms. A wide scope of attitudes towards Islam in the migratory situation persists, ranging from those immigrants who – once they left their officially Muslim country of origin – reject Islam as a source of belief and of community cohesion to those who identify with Islam only in cultural and/or geographical terms until those who rediscover, adapt and reinterpret their religious belief in the diaspora situation. These heterogeneous attitudes of 'negative', 'cultural' and 'religious' identification with Islam (Lacomba Vázquez, 2001) diversify and enrich the religious landscape of Islam in Spain, but end up weakening the organizational strength of Muslim associations and representations vis-à-vis the Spanish state and society (cf. below).

Apart from these internal differences among Muslim immigrants, the main distinction that still divides Muslims in Spain and particularly in Andalusia is that between migrants from Muslim societies of origin, on the one hand, and Muslim converts, on the other hand. The converts are mostly of Catholic background and are either Spaniards or incomers from other Western countries who are 'in search of Islam' and its legacy of tolerance, as symbolized by the 'myth of Al-Andalus'. Since the eighties, cities such as Granada and Córdoba, and inside these cities above all their historically Muslim or Muslim-Jewish neighbourhoods become 'poles of attraction' for conversion-related north-south migration. Most converts implicitly distance themselves from the North African immigrants by distinguishing two kinds of Islam: the culturally and geographically rooted 'traditional' Islam and the 'universal belief system', shared by the transnational umma of all fellow-Muslims (cf. Allievi & Nielsen, 2003). Accordingly, convert communities may be locally rather small, but they are integrated into transnational networks of fellow-converts who share the same schools of interpretation and sometimes also the same religious 'leaders'. While Muslim migrants tend to identify themselves in ethnic or national terms – e.g. as Moroccans or as Amazigh (Berbers) – the converts turn to the umma as their broader identity 'horizon' (Dietz, 2004; Dietz & El-Shohoumi, 2005).

As a consequence of this process of enclosure and community building, many migrant Muslims completely lack relations with the converts. When asked about their relation to the local host society, most of the migrants express a strong general desire to deepen their interaction with the non-Muslim local population in the neighbourhood, at school, at the workplace or during leisure activities. Only those who have to cope with serious Spanish language difficulties feel that they are completely isolated from their local surroundings. By contrast, those young Moroccans from urban middle- and upper-class backgrounds who study at southern Spanish Universities – most of them choose the University of Granada, due to its historical ties to the educational system of the former Spanish protectorate of northern Morocco – are the ones who feel best integrated. They enjoy the openness of Spanish youth and try to participate in their leisure activities (cf. González Barea, 2003).

Finally, apart from these 'immigrated' and 'convert' Muslim communities, a historically rooted, third group is formed by 'nationalized Muslims' (Hernando de Larramendi, 2001), i.e. native Muslim inhabitants of Ceuta and Melilla, the Spanish enclave cities in northern Morocco. Reflecting old colonial practices, only the Spanish Catholic inhabitants of these cities, most of them related to the important military bases located in both cities, were considered fully 'Spanish citizens'. The Muslim communities – in their majority ethnically Arabic in the case of Ceuta and Amazigh in the case of Melilla – as well as the Jewish and Hindu ones[14] had been denied citizenship rights until the end of the eighties, when they were finally 'nationalized' as Spanish citizens (López García & del Olmo Vicén, 1995; Planet Contreras, 1998). Non-Catholic communities are nowadays visible and vitally present in both cities, their main religious feasts – such as Ramadan and Yom Kippur – are officially recognized, but they are still discriminated against and often excluded from Spanish neighbourhoods and institutions (Planet Contreras, 1998).

The End of the Catholic Monopoly

These demographic changes, which pluralize the 'religious landscape' of the country, will force the Spanish state to reconsider its privileged treatment of the Catholic Church and its relationship to non-Catholic denominations. Until the eighties, open discrimination against these denominations and communities persisted; not only the Constitution itself, but several laws and decrees distinguish between 'the Church' and 'any other religious minorities'. For example, the 1980 Law on Religious Freedom (*Ley Orgánica de Libertad Religiosa*) makes this distinction by only mentioning these 'religious minorities' as objects of governmental treatment, while it simultaneously invisibilizes the main religious force, the Catholic Church itself (Díaz Salazar, 1993a, 1993b).

Nevertheless, at the beginning of the nineties the governing Socialist Party admit and acknowledged this discrimination and is hesitantly starting to recognize all 'religions with notorio arraigo', religions which are visibly rooted in the country. (Amérigo Cuervo-Arango, 1995). This change of attitude, induced mainly by the analyzed trends in immigration and conversion, unleashes a process of 'de-monopolization' of the Catholic Church (Moreras, 2005). Since 1992, a series of high-level 'Agreements' are being negotiated and signed between the Spanish state, on the one hand, and the Muslim, Protestant and Jewish umbrella federations, on the other hand. These 'quasi-Concordats' include wide ranging provisions and concessions in economic, cultural and educational terms, which attempt to equal the privileges included in the 1979 Concordat signed with the Vatican and which are therefore nationally and internationally praised by different religious communities (Mantecón Sancho, 2001).

Despite international recognition, the main challenge faced by the 'minority religious communities' consists in the implementation of these rather far reaching agreements. As will be detailed below for the case of the educational competences, the Protestant and Jewish federations succeed – in different degrees – in forcing governmental institutions to apply these agreements step by step, basically by financing parts of their community activities. The 1992 Acuerdo de Cooperación del Estado Español con la Comunidad Islámica de España is *de facto* not being applied at all (Acuerdo de cooperación, 1992; Mantecón Sancho, 2001). Officially, the Spanish government justifies this blockade atti-

---

14   For example, according to unofficial estimates, apart from about 40.000 Catholics, in Melilla there are approximately 25.000 Muslims, more than 1.000 Jews and about 100 Hindus historically settled in the city (Planet Contreras 1998).

tude with a lack of a representative counterpart who can transfer and impose any high-ranking decision to the diverse range of local mosques and Muslim communities.[15] In fact, and in contrast to the Jewish and Protestant federations, the so-called 'Muslim Community of Spain', who acted as a signatory in the 1992 agreements, is a loose coalition of the two main Muslim federations acting in Spain: the Federación Española de Entidades Religiosas Islámicas (FEERI) and the Unión de Comunidades Islámicas de España (UCIE). Both umbrella organizations differ from each other with regard to their internal organizational structure – degree of autonomy of local communities –, to the percentage of mainly convert vs. mainly immigrant member communities as well as to the presence of only Sunni or of also Shia Muslims among its local member communities. Consequently, the Muslim Community of Spain as its joint 'superfederation' (Catalá Rubio, 2001) is rather weak both in relation to its member federations and local communities and vis-à-vis the Spanish central and regional governments, their main counterparts for negotiating claims, competences and resources (Jiménez-Aybar, 2004).

This organizational weakness and the resulting low pressure exerted by the Muslim federations against the Spanish state are, however, not the only reasons why it is precisely the agreements signed with the largest religious minority which are not implemented at all. Immediately after the signing of the agreements, a Conservative government replaced the original politicians who acted as signatories, and the new state representatives, who overtly reveal their proximity not only to the Catholic Church, but even to such 'fundamentalist' Catholic lay organizations as Opus Dei and the Legionarios de Cristo, consider these agreements as an obsolete legacy from the former administration. Since the middle of the nineties, this official attitude of 'deaf ears' against Muslim claims-making is shared by many regional and local government levels, who are in charge of authorizing the construction of mosques and prayer rooms, the concession of burial sites inside municipal cemeteries, the hiring of religious education teachers (cf. below), the recognition of Islamic health practices in public hospitals and the recognition of Muslim wedding practices.[16]

Rising Islamophobia and Persistent Discrimination

Obviously such discriminatory attitudes towards Muslim religious beliefs and practices are not limited to state, regional or local politicians. Anti-Islamic and anti-*moro*, anti-'Moorish' attitudes reflecting the combination of ethnic, religious and nationalist dimensions of discrimination prevail amongst large sectors of the Spanish general public. These attitudes in fact are deeply-rooted and can be interpreted in one sense as nothing less than historically transmitted stigmatisations of 'the other'. As Stallaert (1998) shows in detail, since 1492 the Spanish nation-state project has been founded on a mixture of ethnically-based 'arabophobia' and religiously motivated 'islamophobia'.[17] Despite the important

---

15 Cf. Catalá Rubio (2001), Mantecón Sancho (2001), Ciáurriz (2004).
16 For details on these conflicts cf. Moreras (1999, 2004), Hernando de Larramendi (2001), Sánchez Nogales (2004), Dietz & El-Shohoumi (2005) and Rosón Lorente (2005).
17 The notion of 'islamophobia' has been introduced in the nineties in the United Kingdom in the broader context of the so-called 'race-relations' policy as a particular term to highlight the dis-

efforts not only of democratizing, but also of decentralizing and federalizing the Spanish nation-state, this long lasting 'identity politics' of the centralized Spanish state is still observable in the ethnographic present (Dietz & El-Shohoumi, 2005). The Catalan novelist Juan Goytisolo recalls how these xenophobic *topoi* are reinforced by the Spanish colonial heritage as well as by the use General Franco made of Moroccan mercenary troops in order to fight the Second Republic:[18]

> 'The instinctive aversion towards the `Moor´, fed throughout decades by the bad memories of our hateful and stupid colonial endeavours and by the use the Franquistas made during the Civil War of 1936–39 of miserable mercenaries from the Rif, is an illness which is rather extended even among those who declare themselves as leftists' Goytisolo 1978, p. 123).[19]

A major quantitative study, conducted under the auspices of the Spanish Ministry of Labour and Social Affairs (ASEP, 1998), for the first time tried to break down the diverse elements which make up anti-immigration attitudes in Spain. On the basis of these statistical data, collected through the scaling of 'positive', 'negative' and 'indifferent' opinions about certain minorities – using different nationalities, ethnic minorities such as the *gitanos*, racialized terms such as *negros* and religious classifications such as *judíos* and *musulmanes* –, it was possible to detect processes of deeply-rooted and historically transmitted stigmatizations of 'the other'. Despite the variations observed in the study according to the educational level of the Spanish interviewees, the degree of contact they maintain with minority populations, among other indicators, these stigmatization processes reflect a shared, implicit ethno-religious hierarchy of common 'others'. In this hierarchy, the lowest position is still ascribed to the Spanish Roma community, followed by a generalized negative attitude towards people of Arabic origin and/or Muslims,[20] a label which is ranked worse than the opinion about 'immigrants' in general.

Since the 9/11 attacks, and particularly since the March 11th 2004 Madrid bombings, this islamophobia-cum-arabophobia re-appears openly in the media – where supposed Al-Qaida sleepers or network units are suspected of existing in nearly every Muslim immigrant community in Spain – and in the opinion polls – the post-9/11 opinion polls, published through the above cited monthly barometers by the Centro de Investigaciones Sociológicas, show a dramatic increase in anti-immigrant attitudes.[21] The historically rooted fear of the re-conquered, then expelled and afterwards colonized 'other' is discursively channelled through the combination and overlapping of the rather different issues of external security, internal security and criminality, and migration control (Agrela Romero & Gil Araujo, 2005).

---

tinctively western legacy of religious discrimination against people of Muslim belief and/or origin (Runnymede Trust 1997, Halliday 1999).

18   Details on this colonial heritage and its impact on Spanish perceptions of Morocco and of Muslims in general are provided by De Madariaga (2001), El Harras (2001) and Hernando de Madariaga 2001).

19   Translation is mine.

20   Unfortunately, the mentioned study fails to adequately distinguish ethnic and religious classifications, i.e. by asking the interviewees to rank árabes y musulmanes as one minority group (ASEP 1998:23).

21   Cf. http://www.cis.es (accessed September 13, 2006); these polls reflect an increasing concern with 'immigration as a threat' and not as a matter-of-fact, as it had been usually perceived by the majority of the Spanish population, well accustomed on their own to migratory experiences.

Unfortunately, religious authorities of the Catholic Church are not taking a strong and explicit stand against these discriminatory attitudes. On the contrary, they often – willingly or not – contribute to a negative image of Islam. According to a recent opinion poll, conducted among Catholic clergymen, an overall 47% of Catholic priests and nuns consider Muslims to be generically 'fanatics' (Ideal 6–10–2001). These attitudes make inter-religious initiatives rather awkward and nearly impossible. A recent conflict illustrates these obstacles for dialogue: in March 2002, a group of Muslim women attending the Third International Congress of Muslim Women in Córdoba, spontaneously prayed inside the ancient Córdoba Mosque, which since the reconquista has been the property of the Catholic Church and within which the Cathedral of Córdoba has been built. After this prayer, the governing Cabildo Catedralicio formally prohibited any Muslim from praying in the mosque-church. This 'unusual' prohibition was even confirmed from higher ranks when in March 2004 the Vatican Council for Inter-Religious Dialogue denied the Muslims' right to pray in the mosque because – as stated in the Vatican document – 'they have to accept history without trying to take revenge' (El País, 12–3–2004).

Apart from these conflicts, which only occur in the case of Muslims, there are certain practices which still reveal the old monopoly of the Catholic Church. Although all non-Catholic denominations are nowadays recognized as legally equal with regard to Catholicism, official discrimination of non-Catholics is an ongoing problem: the 0.5% income tax dedicated to either the Catholic Church or non-governmental organizations, which apparently will be increased up to 0.7% in 2007, is not transferred to non-Catholic denominations,[22] special restrictions are applied by local authorities for the public exercise of non-Catholic religious rites, access to public space and urban land is often obstructed for non-Catholic religious infrastructure, and religious education is not accessible for the majority of Muslim, Jewish and Protestant pupils.

Religious Education in Spain: Aims and Debates

Into this societal framework of mainstream secularization, Catholic de-monopolization, a rampant pluralization of minority communities and an insufficient recognition of religious diversity, inter-religious affairs are increasingly shaping the debate on the present and future of religious education, as well. Since the end of the dictatorship, the educational sphere in general has been a central 'battleground' between conservative and progressive, Catholic and secular, traditionalist and liberal politicians. Large domains of primary and secondary education have been quickly, but profoundly reformed and 'Europeanized' after the transition to democracy – not only with regard to content and curriculum, but also in relation to the functioning of the 'educational community' of the school, its relation to the neighbourhood, the participation of the parents' association and the role of the formerly very authoritarian teacher (Fernández Almenara, 2001).

On the other hand, certain features have persisted since the Franco regime. It is particularly the development of a mixed, three-folded school system which reflects the

---

22   The new Spanish government just recently promised to 'try to' include non-Catholic 'religious minorities' in the 2006 income tax transfer scheme, which will be functioning in 2007.

deeply rooted tradition of transferring educational competences to the Catholic Church. Even after decades of reforms and debates, three different school types persist: (1) escuelas públicas, public schools which are originally owned and run by the central state, but which in ever more regions are now transferred to the autonomous communities' governments, (2) escuelas concertadas, private schools which are mostly owned and run by Church institutions, congregations or orders, but which are nearly completely subsidized by the state or the region, and (3) escuelas privadas, completely private schools owned by co-operatives or by private enterprises, which are not subsidized by any public resources and which tend to respond to special demands such as alternative pedagogies, internationally recognized grades or bilingual curricula.

While these latter, completely private schools only reach a tiny minority of pupils, about 1.7 million pupils attend subsidized Catholic schools, representing approximately 25,5% of all Spanish pupils attending compulsory educational levels. 91% of these schools are owned by members of the Federación Española de Religiosos de la Enseñanza (FERE), which transfers the school administration to another church-run entrepreneurial organization, called Educación y Gestión (EyG), which administers 2.158 schools, employs approximately 60.000 teachers and attends 1.169.000 pupils in both primary and secondary education (Rodríguez Sanmartín, 1988; Gómez Movellán, 1999).

It is mostly the Spanish middle and upper class parents who send their children to these schools, which are generally not considered of better 'teaching quality' (Fernández Enguita, 1990); in interviews conducted in southern Spain, the main reasons mentioned by parents for choosing these schools are always the same: that they are supposed to be 'better equipped' and that they are more selective and socially more homogeneous than public schools. The strong presence of the Catholic Church is, however, not limited to its educational engagement through their own schools. As many teachers of public schools have been educated themselves in Catholic schools and/or have been once trained as teachers in church-run pedagogical Escuelas de Magisterio, they tend to be very receptive and tolerant towards Catholic elements of 'moral and value education' in public schools. Consequently, even public schools show an overt presence of Catholic religious symbols, liturgical traditions, practices and feasts.

This continuity with the omnipresence of Catholicism during the dictatorship, which until very recently has only been apparent to non-Catholics, is increasingly being perceived and criticized by secular actors such as the Socialist Party, teacher unions and non-Catholic parents' associations. Subsequent debates, mainly emphasizing above all the presence of the crucifix in the classroom, have been among more or less secularized Catholic actors. Surprisingly, non-Catholic parents or their religious communities have been rather silent about this issue; only in October 2003, the oldest Muslim federation UCIRI for the first time dared to question the presence of Catholic symbols in public schools.

Religious Education in Public Schools

Reflecting the slow 'transition' towards de-monopolizing the position of the Catholic Church in public schools, the subject of religious education has been reformed step by step through each new educational reform (Gasol et al., 1997; Llerena Baizán & Llerena Maestre, 2002). Since the beginning of the Civil War in 1936 and until 1977 religious education, understood only as Catholic RE, has been a compulsory and main subject of instruction during the primary, secondary and pre-university (*bachillerato*) levels (Rodríguez Sanmartín, 1988).

The legal situation changes with the 1978 Spanish Constitution. As mentioned above, its article 16 guarantees religious freedom, which makes compulsory religious instruction unconstitutional; on the other hand, article 27 of the same Constitution emphasizes the right of all parents 'to obtain for their children a religious and moral instruction which be coherent with their own convictions' (Constitución Española, 1991). Although the parents' right to obtain RE for their children literally does not imply necessarily nor automatically that it has to be delivered in public schools (Laboa, 1981), de facto it has ever since been interpreted as a state obligation. This interpretation is consistent with the Church's educational privileges, as included in the 1979 Concordat (cf. below).

From 1977 until 1980, there was no law or regulation on the issue of religious instruction at school. Thus, RE just continued to be taught as in pre-Constitution times, with the only exception that it was not enforced any longer for those pupils whose parents opted against it. In response to criticism by secular parents, the 1980 Ley Orgánica del Estatuto de los Centros Escolares for the first time – and only for secondary education – introduces an official alternative for RE. The first detailed official decree regulating RE was issued in 1994, after the farthest reaching educational reform was started by the Socialist government, through its all encompassing 1990 Ley de Ordenación General del Sistema Educativo (LOGSE). The 1994 decree, which includes all dispositions mentioned in the 1979 Concordat, but none of the state obligations resulting from the 1992 Agreements with the other denominations (Bescansa & Esteban, 1999), turns RE into a subject which is compulsorily offered by any public school, but which also includes a secular alternative subject. While RE is considered an 'official subject', whose grades accordingly count in the same way as those of other subjects, the alternative does not count at all. Since then, both teachers and pupils have interpreted this alternative activity as 'guided leisure time' or as 'homework support'.

Since this reform process of the nineties, politicians, Church authorities, teacher unions and parents' associations continuously debate the problematic aspects of the position of RE in public schools (Comisión Episcopal de Enseñanza y Catequesis, 2005): the concrete conditions and ways of integrating RE into the overall curriculum, the subject's equal or unequal treatment in relation to other subjects, its numerical impact on the grade average and the role, choice and payment of the RE teachers. Despite these debates, which will be detailed with regard to Catholic and Islamic RE below, from a formal point of view RE is today taught during 105 hours per year, which means 1,5 hours per week, from the first grade of primary education until the first grade of post-secondary (bachillerato) education, i.e. for 6 until 17 year old pupils (Salas Ximelis & Gevaert & Giannatelli, 1993; Bescansa & Esteban, 1999).

Currently, the legal situation of the subject is again being reformed and counter-reformed. Through its Ley Orgánica de la Calidad de la Educación (LOCE), the outgoing Conservative government had tried to fulfil its promise towards the Catholic Church to strengthen the position of RE by abolishing the non-religious alternative and by plainly integrating two alternative subjects into the core curriculum: both the confessional subject of Religión (católica) and the non-confessional subject of Hecho religioso, conceived as an introduction to the history of religion (Llerena Baizán & Llerena Maestre, 2002; Esteban Garces, 2003). Nevertheless, the landslide victory of the Socialists in the elections held in the shadow of the March 11th Madrid bombings paralyzed this reform, which is now being substituted by a new Ley Orgánica de Educación (LOE). It maintains the current practice of RE, but – for the first time – explicitly states that RE will be taught 'in compliance with all signed Agreements', not only with the 1979 Concordat. Furthermore, the distinction between a confessional and a non-confessional subject of RE is adopted from the Conservative draft regulation, but is supplemented by a third subject, Citizenship Education, which will be compulsory during one year in primary and two years in secondary education.

Catholic Religious Education

Since the transition period towards democracy, in the debate on the secularization and de-monopolization of the school system the Catholic Church, as represented by the Spanish Conference of Bishops' Commission for Education and Catechesis, has fiercely defended its presence in the public school as well as its right to maintain private Catholic schools subsidized by the Spanish state.[23] In subsidized Catholic schools, i.e. in approximately one third of all Spanish schools, the church succeeds in maintaining its pre-constitutional denominational monopoly (Rodríguez Sanmartín, 1988): RE, which is chosen by 99% of all pupils, is only offered for Catholics, while non-Catholics tend to be rejected or discouraged to apply for admission. Although this practice – as well as the ongoing rejection of female applicants in traditional 'boys' schools' and vice versa – is unconstitutional, the lack of explicit anti-discrimination legislation make it very difficult for parents to sue the Catholic school for this exclusive behaviour. As an – obviously intended – side effect of this rejection of immigrant and other minority students, subsidized Catholic schools thus succeed in preserving their pupils' homogeneity not only in terms of social background, but also in terms of culture and religion.

Apart from its privileged position in subsidized private education, the Catholic Church is nevertheless also very concerned about its presence in public schools, as well. In order to justify its quasi-monopoly in RE as offered and taught in public schools, church representatives, pedagogues and theologians not only allege confessional, 'pastoral arguments' – the necessity to build in school the basic religious knowledge through faith-based RE before moving towards out of school, parish based catechesis. These reasons are complemented by 'sociological arguments' (Fernández Almenara, 2003), according to which Catholicism is still the one and only 'majority belief' which encompasses Spanish society and the only religion which is explicitly mentioned in the Constitution.

---

23 For details on this debate, cf. Rodríguez Sanmartín (1988), Gasol et al. (1997), Comisión Episcopal de Enseñanza y Catequesis (2001, 2005) and Llerena Baizán & Llerena Maestre (coords., 2002).

In public schools, Catholic RE is plainly and autonomously designed, organised and offered by the Spanish Conference of Bishops' Commission for Education and Catechesis (Comisión Episcopal de Enseñanza y Catequesis, 2001). Catholic RE is still chosen by a huge majority of pupils, but the percentage of involvement is constantly diminishing during the later years: in primary education, it has decreased from 81% to 75% of all pupils, and in secondary education, Catholic RE only reaches 53% of all pupils (El País, 15–11–2004).

The content and teaching methods of Catholic RE have not been affected by the subsequent educational reforms. Since 1992, on the basis of a document elaborated by the Bishops' Commission for Education and accepted without any modification by the Spanish Ministry of Education, Catholic RE is taught in the whole country according to the same curriculum and following very similar, officially approved text books (Gasol et al., 1997; Rodríguez Sanmartín, 1988). Emphasis is placed on the comprehensive knowledge of the Old and New Testament, but particularly of Church traditions, liturgy and rites. For example, in primary education, the core topics include 'the relation between God and man in life and in nature', 'the relation between God and man in the history of the people of God', 'the relation between God and man through Jesus Christ, our Lord', 'the relation between God and man in the life of our community (the Church)', 'the relation between God and man through the prayer and the rite of our Church', 'the relation between God and man through our behaviour as believers' and 'the relation between God and man through culture and the arts' (Comisión Episcopal de Enseñanza y Catequesis, 2001). Inter-religious contents are not included in the official curriculum, but are often addressed by teachers on their own.

RE contents are not publicly debated at all. In contrast, the most delicate and often polemical aspect of Catholic RE is the teacher in charge of this subject. Following regulations included in the 1979 Concordat and confirmed in specific decrees in 1994 and 1998, the Spanish state pays the approximately 17.000 RE teachers' salaries – spending about 600 million euro per year for their payment –, but neither the central state's nor the region's school authorities may interfere in any aspect of the selection, hiring and supervision of RE teachers, are appointed entirely by the Commission for Education and Catechesis.

As Rodríguez Sanmartín (1988) pinpoints, two weaknesses shape their particular condition between their church authorities and their secular colleagues inside the public schools in which they work. Firstly, their training is highly precarious and often debated; since 1868, when all Faculties of Theology were excluded from the Spanish public university system, training in theology and in religious education is only provided by private, church-run universities and seminaries. As a reaction to this lack of training opportunities, the Catholic Church accepts as RE teachers university graduates from any B.A. studies, which have to be three year programmes (Diplomatura) in the case of future primary school RE teachers and four year programmes (Licenciatura) for secondary level RE teachers. Additionally, prospective RE teachers have to obtain a Declaración Eclesiástica de Idoneidad, a kind of Missio Canonica which certifies supplementary training in Catholic theology and religious education, and have to pass an individual interview with representatives of the Episcopal Commission for Education, about the congruity between the church's teaching and their personal life style, values and moral behaviour (Comisión Episcopal de Enseñanza y Catequesis 2001, Fernández Almenara 2001).

Defensively re-acting to secularization processes taking place inside Spanish society – and particularly to the increasing gap between the majority's governing norms and values, on the one hand, and the official Catholic stance on traditional family and gender values, on the other hand, in the past decade the mentioned Church Commission for Education has started suspending those RE teachers who in their own private lives do not comply any longer with Catholic morality. Sheltered by a 1998 decree, which excludes RE teachers from the legal provisions of collective bargaining, the Church now has the possibility of removing all those teachers who get divorced, who marry a divorced couple, who express sympathy with homosexuality and who, through any other means express opinions or claims – such constitutional rights as the right to go on strike or the right to collective bargaining – which are contrary to the official Catholic positions.

As a reaction, a minority of about 2.000 Catholic RE teachers founded the Federación Estatal de Profesores de Enseñanza Religiosa (FEPER), an interest group that acts as a quasi-teacher union in order to defend RE teachers who are attacked by the Catholic hierarchy. Since the late nineties, this organization has struggled for the application of Spanish labour laws also for the contracting of RE teachers; they are backed not only by current Spanish legislation, but also by the EU directives 1999/70 and 2000/78 on the implementation of equality and stability at the work place. Nevertheless, the Spanish government always argues that the 1979 Concordat, which allows the Church's 'hire and fire' policy, has a more binding nature than domestic law.

Non-Catholic Religious Education

Although the 1992 Agreements *de iure* acknowledge the same rights and privileges of designing, organising and teaching RE in public schools to Jewish, Protestant and Muslim religious communities throughout the country, *de facto* these rights have not been comprehensively fulfilled for these non-Catholic denominations. Thus, the constitutional right of parents to obtain religious instruction for their children is currently only applied in the case of Catholic families. Reacting to the former government's unwillingness to put into practice the Agreements, to transfer the necessary resources to contract teachers and to adapt the school infrastructure to these new necessities, the 'religious minorities' have adopted rather different strategies and solutions.

In the case of the Jewish communities, the Spanish state has not contracted nor financed a single RE teacher. Therefore, the Federación de Comunidades Judías de España has reached a different solution, now asking the Spanish state for direct financial transfers to its federation in order to organize Jewish religious instruction not inside public schools, but inside their own synagogues (El País, 15–11–2004).

Protestant denominations have been facing the same governmental resistance, but pressure has been exerted more successfully by FEREDE, the Protestant federation. As a result of official negotiations, since 2004 90 RE teachers have been hired, who are currently teaching approximately 5.900 pupils. Apart from the Catholic Church, the Protestant federation is the only religious organisation which has already established institutional mechanisms for training their own RE teachers. As public universities do not admit theological and RE training, FEREDE has founded its own, privately run Centro de Formación del Profesorado de Enseñanza Evangélica (El País, 15–11–2004). Contents of Protestant RE have been officially standardized and approved through the same mechanism as the Catholic ones; in primary education, for instance, the core curriculum includes 'The Bible: God's word', 'Jesus Christ: the only mediator and an example to follow', 'Gods' people', 'The world created by God', 'the family', and 'God loves us' (Comisión Episcopal de Enseñanza y Catequesis, 2001).

Finally, the largest 'religious minority' is still the least present in religious education taught in public schools. Apart from the organizational difficulties undergone by the competition between the two mentioned umbrella federations in their struggle for representing 'Spanish Islam', suspicion and rejection by national as well as regional school authorities against the admission of Islamic RE in public schools has been the main reason for this ongoing discrimination. According to article 10 of the 1992 Agreement, Islamic religious instruction has to be offered by both public and subsidized private schools throughout the country. The only exception admitted is when the inclusion of Islamic RE would 'enter into contradiction with the school's ideas'; this refers to Catholic schools, which are therefore excluded from the overall obligation to offer Islamic instruction.[24]

Echoing this far reaching right of Muslim parents to obtain Islamic RE in public schools for their children, already back in 1995 an official curriculum has been agreed upon by the two federations FEERI and UCIRI, which is presented to, and approved by, the Spanish Ministry of Education. Based on a cognitive approach, similar to the one which is still predominant in Catholic RE teaching, the core curriculum of Islamic RE is divided – for primary as well as for secondary and Bachillerato levels – into three main content areas: 'knowledge of God', 'the revelation' and 'the Prophet'. As a last step, in 1996 an agreement was signed by the two federations as well as by the Spanish state which regulates the details of incorporating incorporate Islamic RE teachers into public schools, a regulation which is very similar to the one ruling the Catholic teachers.

However, neither the 1992 agreement nor the 1995 curriculum nor the 1996 regulations have been even partially applied even now. Only on a small number of occasions, and reflecting local pressure, have there been pilot projects approved and implemented in a selected number of schools.[25] For example, in Málaga fifteen RE teachers were admitted by the regional school authorities, who taught Islamic RE for about 500 pupils in different local schools. As the ministry did not, however, agree to contract the teachers, they have been hired by charities and have been chosen by the Mosque of Fuengirola, whose imam has a reputation of being rather 'orthodox' and polemical in questions of gender relations. Therefore, several parents' complained about alleged obligations of their

---

24   Cf. Acuerdo de cooperación (1992); the exemption for Catholic schools is often justified by 'conflicts of interest' which would arise between the Catholic nature of the school and the Islamic instruction offered; this argument is rather contradictory, as Spanish Catholic schools already look back to a long colonial tradition of school instruction in Morocco, where both Catholic and Islamic instruction have been offered without any conflicts of interest (Salas Larrizabal 1992).

25   Cf. Martí (2001), Lorenzo & Peña Timón (2004) and Moreras (2005).

daughters to wear the headscarf in school; although the RE teachers who supposedly had forced them to wear the headscarf rejected these complaints, this internal conflict was used by the school authority to immediately cancel the whole project.

Another attempt at introducing Islamic RE in public schools was started in a primary school in the Arabic Albayzín neighbourhood in Granada (Dietz & El-Shohoumi, 2005). Some years ago, a group of convert parents from Granada and its surroundings decided to develop another pilot project through which Islamic religious instruction and Arabic language classes would be jointly offered as an RE alternative for the Muslim pupils, who would be 'co-educated' with the non-Muslim pupils in all other subjects. Apart from the RE classes, Islamic dietary prescriptions would be respected in an alternative lunch menu. After a very brief first exploratory phase, during which a Spanish convert teacher was in charge of the Islamic instruction and the Arabic language classes, the project was suddenly cancelled by the Andalusian Regional Ministry of Education. The motives expressed above all by the Catholic parents for protesting against the project, lay in the fear that this multi-religious school would attract too many Muslim pupils from other neighbourhoods, which would then run the risk of 'ghettoisation' – a fear shared by the educational authorities, who also argued that they perceived this parent-initiated project as a partisan attempt of one single Muslim convert group of gaining control of the public school in the neighbourhood. Paradoxically, this project seems to have been cancelled because there were suddenly 'too many' Muslim pupils, while in all other schools Islamic RE is refused because there are 'too few' Muslim pupils attending them.[26]

Not only in Granada, but also in other localities which have experienced these 'pitfalls' and disappointments with pilot projects, parents often 'opt out' of public school Islamic instruction. Alternative ways of Islamic RE are emerging; for example, in Catalonia already about 60% of all prayer rooms offer Quranic instruction classes, and in Granada parents have tried to create a privately run madraza. These attempts, however, often lack continuity, as teaching is organized voluntarily by younger students whose level of pedagogical training and didactical experiences is still rather low. There is currently now a strong and explicit movement struggling for privatizing Islamic RE (Dietz & El-Shohoumi, 2005; Moreras, 2005).

In public schools, the most far reaching experience with Islamic RE has been developed in the Spanish enclaves in northern Africa, Ceuta and Melilla.[27] In these cities nearly half of all pupils are Muslims, and – reflecting the above mentioned colonial legacy of exclusion and segregation still perceivable in both cities – a much higher percentage of them faces problems of school failure than in the case of Catholic pupils: 72% of them fail when changing from primary to secondary education (only 15% in the case of non-Muslims), and only 7% of Muslim pupils reaches the Bachillerato or A-level.

In this demographically and socially polarized context, the local school authorities had to concede much earlier equal treatment to the Muslim religious communities. Islamic instruction was accordingly introduced for the first time in 1996; this first pilot project

---

26   The impact of this early, but failed project on current efforts to diversify religious instruction in Granada schools will be further analyzed in our local REDCo field work.

27   Cf. Planet Contreras (1998); reflecting these experiences, one of our two local REDCo projects will be carried out in Melilla schools and neighbourhoods.

failed, however, as the local Muslim communities of Melilla did not agree on the list of selected RE teachers (Moreras, 2005). In Ceuta, the first Islamic RE classes were introduced in January 1999, but – contrary to the Catholic RE classes – were relegated to an extra-school afternoon timetable, where they were scarcely attended by the pupils and soon cancelled by the school authorities. Finally, in both cities more regular Islamic RE classes started in 2002, when the Spanish state contracted 20 teachers; 12 of them offered Islamic RE in diverse schools in Melilla and 8 of them did the same in Ceuta (Moreras, 2005).

Since 2002, both Muslim federations ask for a further hiring of another eighty teachers in order to expand the coverage to other Spanish cities, but each year the Spanish Ministry of Education rejects their claims with the same argument: there are too few Muslim pupils per classroom in order to make the contracting of larger numbers of Islamic teachers 'feasible'. According to data presented by the UCIRI federation in 2002, approximately 42.000 Muslim pupils are thereby excluded from their constitutional rights. Although the governmental argument contradicts both the 1992 Agreements and the Spanish Constitution – where parents' and pupils' rights are not subject to 'minimum numbers' –, in the post 9/11 situation the federations prefer not to sue the government in order to avoid further conflicts and tensions with an ever more Islamophobic public opinion.

Sadly, the situation only changed after the March 11th bombings in Madrid. Rapidly and dramatically, the perception of Muslims worsens in public opinions, but high ranking policy makers now have to admit that they, 'just did not care about the Muslims' before. As several press reports suspiciously question the origin of the financial resources the Muslim communities obtain in order to build mosques, pay for imams and/or maintain madrazas (Islamic schools), the Muslim representatives take up the unfulfilled agreements again, arguing that they would not need to look for 'obscure' sources elsewhere if the Spanish state complied with its legal obligations (Moreras, 2005).

The new Spanish government suddenly perceives the discrimination suffered by Muslim communities with regard to the agreements. Immediately, a novel, state-run Fundación Pluralismo y Convivencia has been created with the one and only aim to channel financial resources to the minority religions.[28] Compared to the funding practice of the Catholic Church, however, the support for the non-Catholic religions still faces restrictions: the amount of financial resources is limited to only three million euros – whereas the Catholic Church obtains 141,46 million euros annually for similar issues –, and the religious communities are – contrary to the Catholic Church – not free to use these resources, as they are to be channelled through specific cultural, educational and social integration projects which have to be applied for explicitly.

As a first measure taken by the foundation, the central government quickly promised to contract 74 Islamic RE teachers, who were supposed to start teaching in selected primary schools in Madrid, Catalonia and Andalusia in the 2005–2006 school year. But as post March 11th public concern diminishes, the number is again being reduced, and finally only 17 new teachers have been hired – together with the twenty teachers already

---

28   Cf. their official web site: http://www.pluralismoyconvivencia.com/ (accessed September 13, 2006).

serving in Ceuta and Melilla schools –, mostly in Andalusia. This measure is completely insufficient, as now there are already about 100.000 Muslim pupils who are excluded from RE (El País, 15–11–2004; Moreras, 2005).

As the official criterion is maintained, that there have to be at least ten pupils per school in order to authorize Islamic RE for the respective school, the newly contracted teachers are forced to constantly travel around different schools, which they attend more or less simultaneously. Following a proposal elaborated by the UCIRI federation, the new Islamic RE teachers are now selected according to the following criteria: they have to hold a Spanish university degree (normally a B.A.), to take a course on Spanish constitutional and legal system, to be fluent in Spanish and to be proposed to the Spanish Ministry of Education by the Comisión Islámica de España, the joint unit of the two umbrella federations. The fact that it is the central state and not the regional Ministry of Education which hires the Islamic teachers is highly confusing in the decentralized Spanish educational system, as it seems to re-centralize at least this aspect of religious education.

Despite all of these shortcomings, since September 2005, Islamic RE is finally being offered in certain public primary schools in Andalusia, Madrid and Catalonia for those pupils whose parents are interested. Classes are taught during normal school hours, not in the afternoon, and teachers are urged to apply the 1996 common core curriculum. The language of instruction is Spanish, while Arabic is used for those contents which are directly related to the Quran.

Perspectives

Despite its scarce lived experience with religious pluralism as well as with diversified religious education, the Spanish situation offers a range of opportunities for the future development of dialogical and inclusive alternatives of religious and inter-religious education.

Possibilities of RE for a Contribution to Dialogue in School and Society

First and foremost, both the 1978 constitutional design and the agreements signed with all relevant religious communities present in Spain provide a point of departure for the recognition of religious diversity and for its active and equal inclusion into public school curricula. The trends towards pluralizing and secularizing Spanish society will finally force the different levels of the Spanish state and of the autonomous communities to abolish the last privileges the Catholic Church still holds.

On the other hand, there is a strong tradition of both anti-clericalism and French-inspired laicism,[29] which stems from the Enlightenment period and which has been strengthened during the Second Republic under the intellectual influence of Fernando de los Ríos (Díaz Salazar, 1993a). Nevertheless, the gradual character of the transition towards democracy has contributed to weaken again, since the eighties, the historical claims made by this intellectual tradition. As currently no Conservative nor Socialist

---

29   Cf. Willaime's contribution on France in this volume.

government will be able to exclude Catholic RE from the public school, Islamic, Protestant and Jewish RE will finally also obtain their place inside the Spanish school system. And hopefully this process of de-monopolization currently prevailing in the broader context of state-church relations will create the societal conditions for better inter-relating the teaching of the different beliefs and confessions inside school. Even if today no inter-religious variant of RE is being taught either in public or in private schools, the increasing, migration-induced importance of religious diversity and inter-religious relations in society as a whole will end up opening confessional RE towards inter-faith alternatives or complements, as our local REDCo projects currently carried out in the cities of Granada and Melilla will hopefully be able to prove.

The Challenge of Ethnicized Hierarchies

These potentially positive features of the current situation of incipient RE in Spain, however, contrast sharply with a serious risk, which does not stem from the educational system *per se*, but from the above analyzed, persistent phenomenon of islamophobia-cum-arabophobia. The transition towards democracy has not plainly included a transition towards diversity which justly recognizes and deals with the problem of deeply rooted and therefore silenced and invisibilized perceptions of alterity. As illustrated above, the Spanish nation is originally based on the forced assimilation or expulsion of ethnic, linguistic and religious 'otherness', but the contemporary generation of educators and policy makers has not come to terms with this past.

Although the legacy of Al Andalus is frequently praised as a model for intercultural and inter-religious relations, the historical destruction of this plural society is not thematized in its impact on contemporary Spanish national identity politics. Therefore, continuities in the perception of alterity are neither addressed nor deconstructed. The long lasting tendency to blur complex, diverse and never completely discrete and dichotomic ethnic, national, linguistic and religious and phenotypical distinctions into a sharp cut distinction between 'us' and 'them' still contributes to 'essentialize' and over-represent the historical other (Muslim, Moor, Arab etc.), while at the same time silencing the (Catholic-cum-Castilian) 'subtext' of Spanish national identity.[30]

A 'double dichotomy' results from these blurred and overlapping distinctions: firstly, the dichotomy of 'oriental' religiosity versus 'Western' secularism; secondly, the dichotomy of Christian-Castilian versus Muslim-Arab ethno-religious categories. As Spanish state representatives and educators frequently state, the 'return of Islam' to the Iberian peninsula challenges the process of secularisation which the Spanish state and society are currently undergoing. In this perspective, a fundamental contradiction is perceived and postulated between an all-encompassing, comprehensive world-view – formerly national Catholicism, nowadays Islam – on the one hand, and Western meta-religious laicism, on the other. This dichotomic view, however, is constantly challenged and contradicted by the 'ancient rivalry' of Spanish national identity politics: the supposed antagonism be-

---

30   Cf. López García & del Olmo Vicén (1995), Dietz (2004) and Rosón Lorente (2005).

tween Islam, perceived as 'Arab' or 'Moorish', on the one hand, and Catholicism, on the other hand, identified with the predominantly Castilian ethnicity.

The resulting ethnic, intercultural and/or inter-religious conflicts have a negative impact particularly on the still emerging Muslim communities. If not treated in a shared and inter-religious setting, these artificial, but efficient dichotomies will continue to ethnicize these communities in a way that will in the long run transform Islam into an ethnic marker. To counter these dangerous tendencies, a historically self-aware, cross-confessional and intercultural approach to teaching religion and religious diversity will necessarily contribute to the pending task of jointly constructing a modern, plural and inclusive 'new Al Andalus'. Only by educationally, culturally and religiously reappraising the country's legacy of pluralism not as an obstacle, but as a particular resource, will Spanish society be able to build solid bridges for the much invoked, but seldom practiced 'Alliance of Civilizations'.

References

Abumalham, M. (Ed.) (1995) *Comunidades islámicas en Europa* (Madrid, Trotta).

[Acuerdo de cooperación] (1992) *Acuerdo de cooperación del estado Español con la Comisión Islámica de España* (Ley 26/1992, de 10 de noviembre, B.O.E., November 12, 1992).

[Acuerdo entre el Estado Español y la Santa Sede] (1979) Acuerdo entre el Estado Español y la Santa Sede sobre Enseñanza y Asuntos Culturales. (Firmado el 3 de enero de 1979 y en vigor desde el 4 de diciembre de 1979), in: Comisión Episcopal de Enseñanza y Catequesis (ed., 2001), *Documentación jurídica, académica y pastoral, sobre la enseñanza religiosa escolar y sus profesores: 1990–2000* (Madrid, Edice), 17–21.

Agrela, B. & Araujo, S. G. (2005) Constructing Otherness: The Management of Migration and Diversity in the Spanish Context. *Migration: European Journal of International Migration and Ethnic Relations*, Vol. 43/44/45, 9–33

Allievi, S. & J. S. Nielsen (eds., 2003) *Muslim Networks and Transnational Communities in and across Europe* (Leiden, Brill).

Álvarez-Junco, J. (2002) The Formation of Spanish Identity and its Adaptation to the Age of Nations. *History and Memory* 14/ 1–2, 13–36.

Amérigo Cuervo-Arango, F. (1995) Breve apunte histórico de la relación Estado-confesiones religiosas en España, in: M. Abumalham (Ed.), *Comunidades islámicas en Europa* (Madrid, Trotta), 161–162.

ASEP [Análisis Sociológicos, Económinos y Políticos, S.A.] (1998) *Actitudes hacia los inmigrantes* (Madrid, Ministerio de Trabajo y Asuntos Sociales – Observatorio Permanente de la Inmigración).

Bescansa, M. J. & Esteban, C. (1999) *El área de religión en la LOGSE: Andalucía* (Madrid, PPC).

Cantón Delgado, M. (2004) *Gitanos pentecostales : una mirada antropológica a la Iglesia Filadelfia en Andalucía* (Sevilla, Signatura).

Catalá Rubio, S (2001) La inscripción de las Comunidades Musulmanas en el Registro de Entidades Religiosas, in: J.M. Martí & S. Catalá Rubio (coords.), *El Islam en España: historia, pensamiento, religión y derecho* (Cuenca, Universidad de Castilla-La Mancha), 125–134.

Ciáurriz, M. J. (2004) La situación jurídica de las comunidades islámicas en España, in: A. Motilla (Ed.), *Los musulmanes en España: Libertad religiosa e identidad cultural* (Madrid, Trotta), 23–64.

Comisión Episcopal de Enseñanza y Catequesis (2001) *Documentación jurídica, académica y pastoral, sobre la enseñanza religiosa escolar y sus profesores: 1990–2000* (Madrid, Edice).

Comisión Episcopal de Enseñanza y Catequesis (2005) *50 preguntas a la enseñanza de la religión católica en la escuela: todo lo que debe saber sobre la enseñanza de la religión católica en la escuela* (Madrid, Edice).

[Constitución Española] (1991) Constitución Española, in: Editorial Arguval (Ed.), *Declaración Universal de los Derechos Humanos – Constitución Española – Estatuto Autonómico de Andalucía* (Málaga, Arguval), 17–105.

Cornelius, W. A. (2004) Spain: the uneasy transition from labor exporter to labor importer, in: W.A. Cornelius/T. Tsuda/P.L. Martin/J.F. Hollifield (eds.), *Controlling Immigration: a global perspective* (Stanford CA, Stanford University Press), 387–429.

Cuenca Toribio, J. M. (2003) *Catolicismo social y político en la España contemporánea (1870–2000)* (Madrid, Unión Editorial).

De Madariaga, M. R. (2001) La imagen de Marruecos y la interpretación de la historia en el sistema educativo español, in: G. Martín-Muñoz (dir.), *Aprender a conocerse: percepciones sociales y culturales entre España y Marruecos* (Madrid, Fundación Repsol-YPF), 117–150.

Díaz Salazar, R. (1993a) La transición religiosa de los españoles, in: R. Díaz Salazar & S. Giner (comps.), *Religión y sociedad en España* (Madrid, Centro de Investigaciones Sociológicas), 93–173.

Díaz Salazar, R (1993b) La institución eclesial en la sociedad civil española, in: R. Díaz Salazar & S. Giner (comps.), *Religión y sociedad en España* (Madrid, Centro de Investigaciones Sociológicas), 283–331.

Dietz, G. (2004) Frontier Hybridisation or Culture Clash? Transnational migrant communities and sub-national identity politics, in Andalusia, Spain'. *Journal of Ethnic and Migration Studies*, 30/6, 1087–112.

Dietz, G. & El-Shohoumi, N. (2005) *Muslim Women in Southern Spain: Stepdaughters of Al-Andalus* (La Jolla, CA, University of California at San Diego – Center for Comparative Immigration Studies).

El Harrus, M. (2001) La inmigración marroqui en España: percepciones desde dentro y fuera, in: G. Martín-Muñoz (dir.), *Aprender a conocerse: percepciones sociales y culturales entre España y Marruecos* (Madrid, Fundación Repsol-YPF), 55–66.

Esteban Garces, C. (2003) *Enseñanza de la religión y ley de calidad* (Madrid, PPC).

Fernández Almenara, M. G. (2001) *El profesor de religión católica en la escuela española: un estudio de su perfil docente* (Granada, Grupo Editorial Universitario).

Fernández Almenara, M. G. (2003) *La enseñanza de la religión católica en la escuela pública española: evaluación por los docentes* (Madrid, Dykinson).

Fernández Cordón, J. A. et al. (1993) *Informe sobre extranjeros de tercera edad en España* (Madrid, Instituto d Demografía).

Fernández Enguita, M. (1990) *Juntos pero no revueltos: ensayos en torno a la reforma de la educación* (Madrid, Visor)

Gasol, R. et al. (1997) *La enseñanza religiosa escolar* (Barcelona, Edebé).

Gervilla Castillo, E. (1990) *La escuela del nacional-catolicismo: ideología y educación religiosa* (Granada, Impredisur).

Giner, S. & Sarasa, S. (1993) Religión y modernidad en España, in: R. Díaz Salazar & S. Giner (comps.), *Religión y sociedad en España* (Madrid, Centro de Investigaciones Sociológicas), 51–91.

Gómez Movellán, A. (1999) *La iglesia católica y otras religiones en la España de hoy: un ensayo político* (Madrid, Ediciones Vosa).

González Barea, E. (2003) *El proceso migratorio de los/as estudiantes marroquíes a la Universidad de Granada: ¿hacia una comunidad transnacional?* (Ph.D. thesis, Universidad de Granada).

Goytisolo, J. (1978) 'Judíos, moros, negros, gitanos y demás gente de mal vivir...', in: J. Goytisolo, *Libertad, libertad, libertad* (Barcelona, Seix Barral), 119–125.

Halliday, F. (1999) 'Islamophobia' Reconsidered. *Ethnic and Racial Studies* 22 no.5, 892–902.

Hernando de Larramendi, M. (2001) Imágenes del Islam en la España de hoy, in: J.M. Martí & S. Catalá Rubio (coords.), *El Islam en España: historia, pensamiento, religión y derecho* (Cuenca, Universidad de Castilla-La Mancha), 63–73.

Huntington, S. P. (1996) *The Clash of Civilizations and the Remaking of the World Order* (New York, Simon & Schuster).

Izquierdo, A. (1992) *La inmigración en España 1980–1990* (Madrid, Trotta).

Izquierdo, A. (1996) *La inmigración inesperada: la población extranjera en España (1991–1995)* (Madrid, Trotta).

Jiménez-Aybar, I. (2004) *El islam en España: aspectos institucionales de su estatuto jurídico* (Pamplona, Navarra Gráfica Ediciones).

Laboa, J. M. (1981) *Iglesia y religión en las constituciones españolas* (Madrid, Encuentro).

Lacomba Vázquez, J. (2001) *El Islam inmigrado: transformaciones y adaptaciones de las prácticas culturales y religiosas* (Madrid, Ministerio de Educación, Cultura y Deporte).

Linz, J. J. (1993) Religión y política en España, in: R. Díaz Salazar & S. Giner (comps.), *Religión y sociedad en España* (Madrid, Centro de Investigaciones Sociológicas), 1–49.

Llerena Baizán, L. & Llerena Maestre, J. E. (coords., 2002) *La calidad educativa, compromiso de la educación cristiana: III Congreso Andaluz de la Educación Católica* (Granada, Consejo Interdiocesano para la Educación Católica en Andalucía).

López García, B. (1996) *Atlas de la inmigración magrebí en España* (Madrid, Universidad Autónoma de Madrid – Taller de Estudios Internacionales Mediterráneos).

López García, B. & del Olmo Vicén, N. (1995) Islam e inmigración: el islam en la formación de grupos étnicos en España, in: M. Abumalham (Ed.), *Comunidades islámicas en Europa* (Madrid, Trotta), 257–276.

Lorenzo, Paloma & Peña Timón, M. T. (2004) La enseñanza religiosa islámica, in: A. Motilla (Ed.), *Los musulmanes en España: Libertad religiosa e identidad cultural* (Madrid, Trotta), 249–267.

Mantecón Sancho, J. (2001) El Acuerdo de Cooperación con la Comisión Islámica de España, in: J.M. Martí & S. Catalá Rubio (coords.), *El Islam en España: historia, pensamiento, religión y derecho* (Cuenca, Universidad de Castilla-La Mancha), 111–123.

Manzano Moreno, E. & Pérez Garzón, J. S. (2002) A Difficult Nation?,' *History and Memory* 14/1–2, 259–286.

Martí, J. M. (2001) La enseñanza de la religión islámica en los centros públicos docentes, in: J.M. Martí & S. Catalá Rubio (coords.), *El Islam en España: historia, pensamiento, religión y derecho* (Cuenca, Universidad de Castilla-La Mancha), 135–161.

Montero, J. R. (1993) Las dimensiones de la secularización: religiosidad y preferencias políticas en España, in: R. Díaz Salazar & S. Giner (comps.), *Religión y sociedad en España* (Madrid, Centro de Investigaciones Sociológicas), 175–241.

Moreras, J. (1999) *Musulmanes en Barcelona: espacios y dinámicas comunitarias* (Barcelona, CIDOB).

Moreras, J. (2004) *Predicar en tierra ajena: los roles asumidos por los imames en el contexto migratorio* (Ms, paper presented at the '4° Congreso sobre la inmigración en España, Ciudadanía y participación'). Girona.

Moreras, J. (2005) La situation de l'enseignement musulman en Espagne, in: Jean-Paul Willaime (Ed.), *Des Maîtres et des Dieux: écoles et religions en Europe* (Paris, Belin), 165–179.

Planet Contreras, A. I. (1998) *Melilla y Ceuta espacios-frontera hispano-marroquíes* (Melilla, UNED).

Pries, L. (1999) New Migration in Transnational Spaces, in: L. Pries (Ed.), *Migration and Transnational Social Spaces* (Aldershot, Ashgate), 1–35.

Rodríguez Sanmartín, Á. (1988) *La presencia de la iglesia católica en el sistema educativo español, según las bases legales (1953–1980)* (Ph.D. thesis, Universidad Complutense de Madrid).

Rosón Lorente, F. J. (2005) Tariq's Return? Muslimophobia, muslimophilia and the formation of ethnicized religious communities in southern Spain. *Migration: European Journal of International Migration and Ethnic Relations*, Vol. 43/44/45, 87–95.

Ruiz Garzón, F. (2001) *De la primera a la segunda generación: identidad, cultura y mundo de vida de los emigrantes españoles en Hamburgo, Alemania* (Granada, Asociación Granadina de Emigrantes Retornados).

Runnymede Trust (1997) *Islamophobia: a challenge for us all* (London, Runnymede Trust).

Sádaba, J. et al. (1994) *La influencia de la religión en la sociedad española* (Madrid, Ediciones Libertarias).

Salas Larrazabal, R. (1992) *El protectorado de España en Marruecos* (Madrid, MAPFRE).

Salas Ximelis, Antonio/Joseph Gevaert/Roberto Giannatelli (1993) *Didáctica de la enseñanza de la religión: orientaciones generales* (Madrid, CCS).

Sánchez Nogales, J.L. (2004) *El Islam entre nosotros* (Madrid, Biblioteca de Autores Cristianos).

Stallaert, C. (1998) *Etnogénesis y etnicidad en España: una aproximación histórico-antropológica al casticismo* (Barcelona, Proyecto A).

Stallaert, C. (2006) *Ni una gota de sangre impura: la España inquisitorial y la Alemania nazi cara a cara* (Barcelona, Círculo de Lectores).

Vilar, P. (2000) *La guerra civil española* (Barcelona, Crítica).

Fedor Kozyrev and Vladimir Fedorov

Religion and Education in Russia

Historical Roots, Cultural Context and Recent Developments

Whether or not Russia is recognised as a part of Europe (Federov, 2004) its contemporary culture is quite evidently rooted in a common European cultural and religious heritage. Taking this into account, one might expect that the new global challenges facing Russia today will bring to life the same social, cultural and scientific developments as in the West and that that would result in growing partnerships and mutual understandings with European states.

The new Russia is a state that quite recently – just fifteen years ago – proclaimed the abolition of the predominantly atheistic Communist ideology. When the dream of a Socialist Empire proved a failure and the USSR brotherhood of fifteen national republics collapsed, the country found itself in severe crisis. The disintegration of the USSR, far from removing the inter-ethnic strains within Russia, has, for several reasons, made the situation worse. The first was the rapid increase in immigration from former USSR republics and Asian countries. Powerful separatist movements (e.g. Chechnya) and the criminal redistribution of property, related to ethnically-based gangs, contributed to the deterioration of the social climate, resulting in serious ethnic/religious clashes and terrorist acts. Racism, xenophobia, intolerance and violence along ethnic and religious lines became serious obstacles to Russia's progress towards the community of democratic European states.

Secondly, a retrospective step back from the chaos of the 1990s to the totalitarianism of the 1920s–1950s, or even further back – to the absolutism of the 19th and 18th centuries – would reveal other historical reasons why now, at the end of the cold war, Russian society finds it difficult from time to time to enter into the new European discourse. It is hardly reasonable to talk about some special 'Russian' system of values as if it were different from a European one but, nonetheless, perception and interpretation of reality do depend upon life experiences, so that whenever social norms and ideals are considered, a kind of collective, historical apperception should be taken into account as a factor of consciousness. In order to promote dialogue and to prevent conflicts the religious dimension of this apperception is surely worth study.

The participation of Russia in the REDCO European project entails at least three developmental trends. First, any comparison of the Russian situation with those of other countries would enrich the palette of contexts and create opportunities to better understand what is really common in uniting European societies. It is not only that Russia has experienced the longest totalitarian experience in modern Europe but also that it has had the longest period of peaceful co-existence between Christians and Moslems within one state. That peculiar characteristic of modern Russian history could well become a source of new theoretical discoveries and practical suggestions relevant to the REDCO project's main findings.

Secondly, the project can make a solid input into the process of European integration through bringing Russian and European scientific discourses closer to each other. The task does not seem too ambitious since the project proposes to include, not only an exchange of information, but also a joint, purposeful search for new forms, approaches and international standards of scientific cooperation and communication.

Thirdly, and finally, it can give an impulse for innovative activity within the Russian educational system. Whatever might be the answer to the main question formulated in the title of the project, the way towards it promises to be instructive and to provide new knowledge, new vision and new inspiration towards improving the state of the Arts.

Demographic and Ethno-Confessional Situation

Russia, with its population of about 145 millions citizens, remains geographically the biggest country in the world and one of the most multicultural and multi-ethnic societies. Ethnic Russians constitute 83% of the population, while the remaining 17% represent 160 ethnic groups, speaking more than 100 different languages and dialects. The biggest ethnic groups after Russians are Tatars (4%), Ukrainians (3%), Bashkires and Chuvashes (each more than 1%). In addition there exists a range of smaller ethnic minorities, some of which are represented by no more than a few hundred people.[1]

The latest history of Russian demography is highly dramatic. In 1900 a great Russian chemist Dmitry Mendeleev, after studying demographic dynamics in Russia, made a scientific prognosis, according to which by the year 2000 the Russian population should be about 600 millions. The terrible cataclysms of the 20th century significantly revised his calculations. According to the scientifically approved statistics something between 16 and 21 million citizens of the Russian Empire were killed during the First World and Civil wars. In addition between 4 to 12 million citizens emigrated during the 'Big Exodus' of 1918–1921. The losses of population caused by collectivization and state repressions during the decade 1920–30 are estimated at about 10 million. Then came the Second World War, which, according to official statistics, resulted in a further loss of 27 million lives but several researchers talk about 40 million. The indirect losses of population connected with such factors as gender unbalance, adversity, social instability, decrease of health and mass frustration made an even greater contribution to the devastation of Russia. A more stable natural growth of population during post-war period came to a stop in 1992, since when the population has been decreasing.

The situation has been slightly counterbalanced by increasing immigration. From 1989 to 2002 some 5 million people left Russia while 11 million came in, only half of whom are ethnic Russians. As a result, the recent growth of immigration has become a factor of growing multiculturalism in Russia.

---

1   'Krugosvet' encyclopedia – http://www.krugosvet.ru/articles/123/1012332/1012332a1.htm (accessed 20 September 2006).

More than 70 religious denominations are now registered in the Russian Federation. Although there are no exact statistics that break down the population by denomination, the Russian Orthodox Church undoubtedly plays the most significant part in the religious life of the country. Among 22,513 religious organizations registered by the end of 2005, 12,214 groups belong to this denomination.[2] According to the International Religious Freedom Report 2005 released by the Bureau of Democracy, Human Rights, and Labor (USA), available information suggests slightly more than half of the residents consider themselves Russian Orthodox Christians.[3] N. Mitrokhin's data (Mitrokhin, 2004, p. 38) point to 59% self-proclaimed Orthodox. Some other sources give higher figures up to 65–70% for Orthodox believers in Russia (Fedorov, 1999, p. 334; Metlik, 2004, p. 38). The Orthodox tradition of baptizing children just after birth and the absence of confirmation, makes the confessional identification and self-identification especially difficult, since a rather numerous group of people baptized as Orthodox but not active presently in parish life may give different answers to a question about their identity.

The second largest religious group in Russia is Muslim; 3,668 Muslim organizations were registered by the May 2004 and somewhat about a thousand remain unregistered. Islam is one of the oldest religions here. Some historians claim that it came to the lands of Central Russia even before Christianity. The majority of Muslims are formed as traditionally Muslim ethnic groups living in the Volga-Urals region – which includes Tatarstan and Bashkortostan – and the North Caucasus. The average readings of poles show that 4–6% of Russia population call themselves Muslims (Filatov & Lunkin, 2005).

By most estimates, Protestants constitute the third largest group of believers. Nowadays in spite of the official habit of addressing Catholic and Lutheran churches as the most 'traditional' among non-Orthodox Christian denominations, it is charismatic Christian groups and movements that constitute the biggest and most rapidly growing part of Russian Protestantism.1,558 Pentecostal communities are registered in Russia – a really impressive figure when compared with the 255 Roman Catholic and 228 Lutheran organizations registered. There are data showing that the biggest increases in Protestant population are to be found in several Siberian and Far East regions (Schipkov, 1998). As these lands served for centuries as places of exile for Russian sectarians, this geographical trend does not justify treating the growth of Protestantism and new charismatic movements as a mere ideological import from the West.

There are three large ethnic Buddhist groups in Buryatia, Tuva, and Kalmykia, which constitute about 1% of the Russian population.

An estimated 600,000 to 1 million Jews remained in Russia (0,5% of the population) after the large-scale emigrations over the last 2 decades. According to the IRF Report cited above, the Jewish community has undergone a major institutional revival since the fall of the Soviet Union. In the past five years, the number of organized Jewish communities in the country has increased from 87 to over 200.

Pagan, pantheistic and nature-based religions such as Shamanism are practised traditionally by a good number of ethnic minorities located in several regions, both in the European (Mariel, Chuvashia etc.) and the Asian (Yakutia, Chukotka etc.) parts of Rus-

---

2   http://www.religare.ru/article32687.htm (accessed 20 September 2006).
3   http://www.state.gov/g/drl/rls/irf (accessed 20 September 2006).

sia. A relatively small but active number of ethnic Russians participate in so-called new-pagan movements, associated as a rule either with ecological or nationalistic ideologies.

Statistical data based on either questioning or indirect proofs, such as the number of registered organizations, patterns of ethnic structure and so on, are questioned and suspected today by a number of scientists (Filatov & Lunkin, 2005).

Cultural and Socio-Political Background

History of Church-State Relations

The history of Christianity in Russia goes alongside the history of the state. According to a wide-spread legend it was the Apostle Andrew who brought the Gospel to the pagans living in the lands between Kiev and Veliky Novgorod. But the first historical witnesses of Christians in Russia date from the 10th century.

Orthodox Christianity (Orthodoxy) is often defined in Russia as a state-shaping and culture-shaping religion. This social mission of the Church was evident, for instance, during so-called Troubled Time at the beginning of the 17th century when Moscow was occupied by Polish troops. In 2005 the State Duma banished the official holiday of 7th November devoted to the Revolution of 1917 and established instead the official holiday of 4th November devoted to the liberation of Moscow from Polish capture in 1612. As the political activity of Patriarch Germogen and the miracle of Kazanskaya Mother of God were a big part of the story, this recent change of celebrations clearly indicates the shift of orientations in contemporary Russian politics, state ideology and cultural life.

There have been several turning points in the history of Church-State relations. The first is connected with the Florence Treaty between the Greek Orthodox Church and the Vatican (1439) followed by the fall of Constantinople (1453). Being interpreted as the apostasy of Greek Orthodox Church and a divine retribution, the sequence caused profound changes in the Russian Church both on mental and organizational levels. Russians began to recognize their church as the only heir of the Orthodox faith and the successor of the holy Empire. It was the birth of the theocratic idea of 'Moscow the Third Rome' ever significant since that time in Russian spirituality and the beginning of what a distinguished Russian theologian Alexander Schmemann called the historiosophical lure of Russian thought (Schmemann, 2005).

Among the most significant events of the end of 15th century a theological dispute (and a real political struggle) between a group of 'zavolzhskie startsy' (or 'nestjazhately') and the devotees of Joseph Volotsky should be mentioned. The first, being devoted to the old Eastern ascetic tradition, nurtured an ideal of Church as a community of the poor in spirit as well as in everyday life, deliberately distancing themselves from power and social activities. The second stood for the socially active and powerful Church taking part in civil life through charity and involvement in state affairs. As a consequence of the victory of the 'party of Joseph', ROC became a big landowner and a serious actor in Russian politics. Some Russian theologians and historians regard it as a great spiritual tragedy, others treat it as a historical chance for liberalization of Russia through creating the bipolar (Pope-Caesar) political system as it had occurred in the West. However, the opportunity was not realized and the establishment of the absolutism of the Moscow tsar in the middle of 16th century opened a long story of the subjugation of the church by the state and the long list of Russian martyrs, among whom the Metropolitan Philip, strangled in 1569 by the body-guard of John the Terrible, is fairly considered as a founder of the tradition of Church intercession for people persecuted by state.

The Great Schism of the 17th century, which indeed, as suggested by Alexander Pushkin, should be considered as a big religious war, was another tragedy of the Russian church, which is still on-going to the present day. Supported by the state, the Orthodox hierarchy, for the first time in its history, initiated mass executions in the name of Christian faith. On the part of Patriarch Nikon it was not only a struggle for the purity of the faith but also for the power and independence of the hierarchy that underlay his reforms. He lost the game, being overthrown by Tsar Alexey. On the part of the old-believers it was also a matter of power that underlay their resistance. According to Georges Florovsky, 'the topic of schism was not "the old belief" but the Kingdom', in which the Tsar and the Church people rather than the hierarchy were considered to be the main possessors of power (Florovsky, 1937, p. 67–68). Russian schism put an end to the Moscow dream of Holy Kingdom and came, according to Alexander Schmemann, as a retribution for anti-historian and utopian Russian theological thought (Schmemann, 1977). But the dream did not disappear completely and, mixed up with the old resentments and consequences of the Great Schism, played its role in the success of a Communist utopia.

January 1st, 1700 was the beginning of a new era for Russia with a new 'New Year' celebration, a new chronological system counting the years from Christ, and social reforms turning upside down all sectors of public and civil life. Peter the Great, in his truly titanic efforts to make Russia a European country, could hardly rely on the support of the church. 'Antichrist' became the common nickname of the young Tsar, with clergy taking an active part in his political opposition. As the result of Peter's radical secularization policy the rest of Church independence was withdrawn. The Institute of Patriarch was abolished and substituted by the institute of Synod with a lay state service bureaucrat (ober-procuror) at its head. The Church was recognized as no more than a unit in the overall mechanism of the Empire and all its affairs were to be controlled by state. As to the spiritual leadership, 'The Spiritual Regulation' (1721) explicitly delivered it to the Emperor, calling him the Bishop of Bishops and announcing his supreme power over all powers, lay and cleric (Florovsky, 1937, p. 87). From that time clergy became a 'frightened caste' (ibid, 89) of Russian society, pushed out to the periphery of public life, poor and isolated from the 'high' secular culture. This isolation produced a split between the 'secular' and the 'spiritual' cultures that were largely responsible for the future dramatic history of the Russian Empire.

A new chapter in Church-State relations began with the revolutions of February and October 1917. It was not only a story of Church devastation and abasement. It was also a story of courage and glory, a story of more than 2000 saint martyrs canonized by the Church Council of 2000 and of innumerable confessors who saved the Orthodox faith and transmitted tradition through the severe atheistic campaigns of Lenin, the early Stalin and Khrushchev times. It was also a story of the revival of Church independence that began in October 1917 with the restoration of the Patriarchate and the election of Patriarch

Tikhon and is continuing now since the principle of the separation of Church and State was reaffirmed by the new Russian Constitution (1993). After a long time of being an institution of 'state religion' and a much shorter time of being a marginal 'survival of the past' doomed to die out, the Russian Orthodox Church now finds itself in a quite new situation, that calls for a search for new ways of participating in civil life and partnership with the state and civil institutions.

Education in Russia

There are plenty of archaeological data proving a wide-spread literacy in Medieval Russia before the Tatar yoke. The most famous educational centre was organized by Yaroslav the Wise in the first half of the 11th century at the Sophia Cathedral in Kiev. It included a grammar school for clergy and translators, a big library and a court school for nobilities. Russian chronicles, graphities on the wall of Saint Sophia and European Medieval literature, provide evidence that youngsters from the royal families of Sweden, England, Hungary and Poland were educated at the Yaroslav court.

During the period of Moscow reign (15th – 17th cc.) family education evidently dominated over schooling. Hagiography, spiritual instructions by holy fathers and the famous Domostroy with its three parts devoted to religious regulations, piety in family life and economy of housing, were among the most popular readings.

Western enlightenment was brought to Russia, together with the radical secularization of civil and cultural life, by Peter the Great. While accepting in general the design offered by Western scholars (with Georg Leibnitz among them), according to which the Russian system of education should be a copy of the German one, the Russian Emperor made one exception concerning religion. He separated theology from academic science. Religious ('spiritual') educational institutions (parish and monastery schools, theological seminaries and academies) and civil schools (mostly of military and engineering profile with so called 'numeral' mathematic schools as a preliminary phase) were subordinated to different state structures. Clergy became an isolated caste. It was forbidden for the clergy "brood" to enter civil schools. They had only two options: to learn in seminaries to become priests or to become soldiers for 25 years. The first theological departments began to appear in Russian universities several years ago.

The segregation of church (spiritual) and civil (secular) cultures became a powerful factor shaping Russian spirituality and mentality. Though basic religious education was not left outside the curricula of civil schools (see below), the isolation of clergy from the new developments in science and education led to a widening gap between the 'high culture' of upper class and the traditional 'Orthodox way of life' that began to be associated more and more with the commitment to Russian antiquity and with the rejection of the 'Western way' of scientific and social development.

At first, Russian professional pedagogues, like Ivan Betskoy (1704–1795), the son of a Russian diplomat in Sweden, got their education abroad or they were foreigners like Yankovich de Merievo (1741–1814), an Austrian Serb invited by Catherine II to organize the system of schooling. It is usual to identify Konstantin Ushinsky (1824–1870) as the founder of the Russian academic tradition of pedagogy, although he refers in his works to other distinguished Russian scholars dealing with pedagogical matters. An article, "The issues of life", (1856) written by the famous Russian surgeon Nikolay Pirogov (1810–1881) and obviously inspired by 'Emile', is among pedagogical masterpieces of that time, reviewed by Ushinsky. It was not only an explicit accent on national factors in education and a well-grounded criticism of authoritative western pedagogues (such as Karl Schmidt) that made Ushinsky the first original Russian theorist of pedagogy. He was probably the first Russian educator who began to treat pedagogy not merely as an art of teaching but as an autonomous sphere of scientific investigation. He was the first to achieve an integral vision of goals and methodological standards of pedagogy contextualized in Russian discourse. 'If pedagogy wants to bring up a human being in all respects, it must first study him in all respects' (Ushinsky, 1988, V. 5, p. 15). That is how he sets out his main unfinished work, 'The Human as an Object of Education: An experiment in pedagogical anthropology'. Trying to describe the educational process in physiological terms, he never tended to bracket out or reduce to physiology the spiritual dimension of human nature and personality.

The development of pedagogy in the 19th century gave the impulse for exuberant innovative activity. The earliest private school for peasants' children, based on the ideas of Rousseau, was opened as early as in 1805 on the estate of Duke Izmaylov, near Moscow (Piskunov, 2005). The famous Lev Tolstoy was also the author of one of the non-traditional pedagogical systems based on the principle of pedagogical anarchism (Zenkovsky, 1996a) and tested by him for several years at his estate Yasnaya Polyana.

In the 20th century socially oriented pedagogical systems and concepts such as that of the labour school (G. Kerschensteiner), social pedagogy (R. Natorp) or learning-through-practicing approach (J. Dewey), became very popular among Russian pedagogues. Supported by the Soviet government and enriched theoretically with the doctrine of collective learning (Lev Vygotsky) this movement gave fruits in successful educational practice of such outstanding and talented teachers as Stanislav Shatsky (1878–1934) or Anton Makarenko (1888–1939). Although some other movements, for instance pedology promoted by Pavel Blonsky (1884–1941), were labelled 'capitalistic' and demolished, education continued among the most advanced sectors of the socialist market throughout the Soviet period.

Multiculturalism

Multiculturalism in Russia grew gradually throughout its history, along with the expansion of the territory of the Russian state. The original national unity of Russia, based on the power of Viking rulers, Orthodox faith and Cyrillic script, did not manage (and throughout the major period of its history actually had no such intention) to result in ethnic unity. That is why there is a difference in the meaning of the word 'Russian' as it is used outside and inside Russia. For Russians it is the term traditionally indicating ethnic identity, and, as to the national and cultural identities, alternatives are employed, such as, 'a citizen of Russia', 'a Russian-speaking', or 'Rossiyanin'. (This last being a linguistic innovation coined at Yeltsin times when Russia reappeared again as a separate state.)

A famous Russian Medieval chronologist, Nestor, reckons that about fifteen non-Slav peoples were living on the territory of future Russia at the time when the Vikings came. After the active colonization of the Volga basin and then of the Northern and the Eastern (Siberia) territories in the 15th – 17th centuries the number of these, mostly presented by peoples of Mongolian race, increased significantly.

The transformation of Moscow Russia into the Russian empire, after the victory in the Northern war under Peter the Great (1721), opened a new level of multiculturalism. From that time Russia began to incorporate not only native tribes but already civilized nations as well. During the expansion to the West in the 18th century, Baltic lands (Estonia, Latvia and some others) were taken from Sweden and made a part of the Russian Empire. In the 19th century a group of Middle Asian and Caucasus countries, that formerly belonged to the Arab Caliphate, joined the Russian Empire. This process, being accompanied by a half-century long war on the Northern Caucasus with the Chechens, caused growing ethnic tensions that initiated in turn the state policy of the forcible 'russification' at the end of the 19th century. This short-sighted policy awakened one of the main motive powers resulting in the Russian revolution.

The Russian Orthodox Church was always an active agent in the expansion of Russian cultural as well as political influences. And it is largely responsible for the nature of Russian multiculturalism. It settled in new lands but not in the same way as the Roman Catholic Church did. J. Stamoolis in his "Eastern Orthodox Mission Theology Today", claims that the accent on the translation of the Bible, the conduct of worship in native languages and the ordination of natives as Church ministers, were the main distinctive features of Eastern Christian mission inherited by the Russian Church from the Greeks (Stamoolis, 1986). Indeed, for dozens of ethnicities living in Russia, Cyrillic became their first script but it did not prevent them from reading both Gospel and Liturgy in their own language. Alongside persecutions of pagan priests and wizards, Church dissidents and schism activists, the history of Russian Christian mission exhibits a lot of examples of respect toward cultural diversity and of truly enlightening activity and self-denying charity and care carried among ethnic minorities by distinguished missionaries like Stephan Permsky in the fourteenth or Makary Glukharev in the nineteenth centuries. A rather high level of inclusiveness of Russian national identity, fostered by both State and Church, provided Russian culture with a strong assimilative potential. Ethnic subcultures, formed before the 'Empire phase' of Russian history, rarely show a tendency of relating to the dominating 'Big Russian culture' as contra-cultures.

With the establishment of the communist regime in Russia the ideal of internationalism became a part of state ideology. Practically, it proved to be no less destructive than all the other social ideals imposed by communists, for the consistent discrediting of the value of ethnic identity was furnished with aspersions and persecutions. Many famous Russian artists, scientists and pedagogues (Ushinsky included) were condemned as nationalists. These policies began to change under Stalin whose plan to exploit all aspects of patriotism, religious and ethnic included, contributed significantly to both the victory over fascists in the World war II and his popularity among broad segments of Russian society remaining until today. Nonetheless, internationalism never ceased to be a clause in communist dogma and in the late 70s the leader of the Communist Party, Leonid

Brezhnev proclaimed that a new social body had appeared in the world, namely 'the So-viet people'. Partly it was true, for the melting pot of the Soviet Empire really produced a new type of mentality common for all citizens regardless of their ethnicity (Homo So-vieticus was its code name widely spread among intellectuals of that time). But as a reac-tion to the subservience of ethnic identities, a burst of nationalist and racist movements occurred throughout post-Soviet territories and Russia was not an exception. Today these kinds of movement are among the most dangerous challenges for civil peace and public order throughout Russia. Immigrants from Middle Asia and the Caucasus, foreign stu-dents from Africa and Asia and Jews most often become victims of extremists. Referring recently to these extremists with their motto, 'Russia for Russians (meaning ethnic Rus-sians)' President Putin called them in a live TV broadcast (18 December 2003) either fools or provocateurs and reminded them that if their ideology was to get public support, other suggestions would appear in response, such as 'Tartarstan for Tartars' and Russia would be torn into pieces.

So multiculturalism cannot be called a new challenge for Russia because it arrived here very early, has deep historical roots, and, indeed, constitutes the very nature of the Russian State. Nevertheless, it is hardly possible to speak about harmony achieved in the sphere of intercultural and inter-ethnical relations. The problems at stake are connected with the reconceptualisation of Russian national identity after the collapse of the Soviet Union. What is it to be Russian, or to belong to Russia in a cultural sense? How does the desired unity of Russian cultural space correspond to ethnical and confessional diversity? Related to these questions are the vital decisions and options of Russian politics, both in home and international affairs. Openness toward globalization, including the readiness to increase the level of cultural diversity caused by growing immigration, is one of the burn-ing issues of public debates. There is also a special problem of Russia-Belorussia-Ukraine relations. The majority of Russians treat the separation of these three former parts of Russia (Velikorossia, Belorussia and Malorossia) as a historical mistake or artifi-cial separation caused by the 'defeat of Russia' in the cold war. The availability of cul-tural justification for this separation is still questioned within different segments of Rus-sian society. For many Russians this separation remains the most painful point of na-tional and ethnic consciousness.

Inter-Religious and Inter-Confessional Issues

In the Russian empire, ethnic and confessional issues were very close-knit, since confes-sional identity was treated by state power as ethnically derived. It means that one could make a good personal career being a German Lutheran or Tartar Muslim, but if an ethnic Russian were to convert to Islam or Lutheranism, he would immediately become *persona non grata*. The Code of the Russian Empire (1832) put religions into a strict hierarchical order. Orthodoxy or 'The Christian Orthodox Catholic Faith of Eastern Confession' was declared 'primary and dominating' (Article 40). The Emperor was obliged by law to keep and guard Orthodoxy. The conversion of Orthodox believers into other confessions was considered a crime.

Other Christian confessions (Catholic, Lutheran, Reformed, Anglican, Armenian) were tolerated and partly supported by the state as 'foreign' beliefs. They were forbidden to proselytize Russian Orthodox believers, but they were not restricted in pastoral care for non-Russian ethnic groups, rather numerous in Western parts of Empire. Moreover tsars often donated to the construction and restoration of church buildings, and the ministry of the churches possessed all the privileges of state-supported ethnic elites. Because of the large number of Lutherans among high-ranked military officers, scientists and specialists in industry, during the 18th and 19th centuries Lutheranism enjoyed the highest level of privileges after state supported Orthodoxy.

Islam was not supported by the State and for a long time Muslims were seen as a target for Christian mission. It was Catherine II who granted religious freedom to Muslims, including the rights to build mosques and to open confessional schools. In 1787, by her special order, the Koran was published in Russia for the first time. There is a well grounded opinion that Catherine's decision was made under the pressure of the severe and extremely dangerous Pugachevian revolt in which Muslims of the Volga basin played a leading part. In the 19th century Muslims became a respectful part of Russian society, with a large number of rich families and high-positioned nobility.

Relations with Jews became a subject of regulation after Poland, with the largest European Jewish *diaspora,* became a part of the Russian Empire. Catherine II refused to grant full civil rights to Jews, explaining the decision in explicitly religious terms. The line for settlement was drawn that forbade Jews to live in big cities. They were the only confessional group restricted by law from being employed as civil servants (Bendin, 2003, p. 105). The discriminative regime was eased after the liberating reforms of 1861 and fully abolished in 1905.

Remarkably, the old-believers who were in fact the most 'orthodox' part of Orthodoxy and whose faith was finally recognized as 'equally-salvatory' by the ROC Council of 1917, had been discriminated against for a long time, more roughly than any other confession including Jews and pantheists. They possessed no right for public witness of their faith and their marriages had no official status. The State began to register marriages of the 'schismatics' only after 1874 and it was the first case of civil (non-religious) marriages in Russia. Only the position of non-permitted sects or cults (khlysty, subbotniki, skoptsy etc.), blamed for inhuman perversions and persecuted by law, ranked lower among religious groups.

Religious pluralism, while tolerated as an aspect of multiculturalism, was never welcomed or theologically justified by the Russian Orthodox Church. The idea or dream of Holy Russia, united by one faith and acting as one religious body, was always a great temptation for Russian thought stuck to a holistic or 'totalitarian' stance (Berdyaev, 1992). It fitted quite well to the model of church-culture relations described by R. Niebuhr as, 'Christ within culture' (Niebuhr, 1951), but it was obviously in dissonance with the liberal value of individual rights and with any notion of relativism. As a result the idea of freedom of conscience and belief had a tricky history in Russia.

In 1902 a famous Religious-Philosophic dispute between intelligentsia and the Orthodox hierarchy started in St. Petersburg. Freedom of conscience was its main topic. Participants articulating the, 'church position' insisted that the concept of freedom of conscience should be recognized as a contradiction in terms. How can a judge (conscience) be free from the law? – asked Bishop Nikanor. What else is legitimization of this freedom if not a right for spiritual illness? – asked archimandrite Antonin Granovsky (Polovinkin, 2005). This kind of argumentation is still explicitly developed in recently adopted Church documents such as the Social Doctrine of ROC (2000) as well as in the messages of Orthodox hierarchs. Among them is the report of Metropolitan Cyrill for the 10th 'World Russian National Council' (2006) in which he questions the 'Western' value of moral autonomy and calls for the use of external criteria in morality for the correction of conscience corrupted by sin.

The Manifest of 17 October 1905 granted the freedom of conscience to citizens of the Russian Empire. But it was only for a very short time of less than 15 years that they actually could freely confess and express religious beliefs. Communism became a new state-supported and dominating quasi-religion, much less tolerant toward pluralism of beliefs than the Russian monarchy. During this time of new martyrdom the ROC shared misery with all other religious communities and the history of GULAG is full of amazing stories of inter-religious brotherhood and cooperation.

With the establishment of a new political order in Russia after the collapse of Communism, inter-religious cooperation acquired an official dimension. On December 23, 1998 the Inter-religious Council of Russia was established to promote the co-operation of four major (principal) religions – Christianity, Islam, Judaism and Buddhism, presented in the Council by the Russian Orthodox Church, the Council of Muftis of Russia, the Federation of Jewish Communities of Russia and the Buddhist Traditional Sangha in Russia.[4] In the course of this partnership between state and religious organizations several attempts were made to amend the Federal Law "On Freedom of Conscience and Religious Associations" so that it could give legal privileges for so called 'traditional' religions and discriminate against religious minorities. These attempts failed after facing rigid public opposition and loud criticisms on the part of human rights organizations.[5]

Today, besides the structures with official representation, a number of informal initiatives associated with non-governmental organizations are active in Russia, facilitating inter-religious cooperation in the field of education on an international level. St. Petersburg is a prominent centre of inter-religious activity of that kind. It can be explained by the history of the city: the northern capital of the Russian Empire was destined to be 'a window cut into Europe'. Now there are the Interchurch Partnership "Apostolic City – Nevskaya Perspectiva", the World Council of Churches (WCC) office for coordinating ecumenical theological education in Eastern and Central Europe and the office of the Association of the Religion and Theology Educators in Eastern and Central Europe (ARTE) that retain the traditions of religious tolerance and openness in this 'most European' city of Russia.

The basis for Christians' participation in inter-religious dialogue should obviously be prepared within Christian ecumenism. Unfortunately the ecumenical situation in Russia

---

4   See official site of the organization: http://www.m-s-r.ru (accessed 30 September 2006).
5   See the Moscow Helsinki Group website: http://www.mhg.ru/english/1FCD037 (accessed 30 September 2006).

is poor and even worse than some 30 years ago. It is usual to hear from many people that ecumenism is the worst heresy of the 20th century.

In the 1990s there was an explosion of anti-ecumenism in several churches and the ecumenical situation seemed to be in a sharp crisis. A considerable portion of clergy and laity criticised the Church authorities for participation in WCC and CEC and pressed the authorities to withdraw from these organizations.

Although the overall situation remains today anti-ecumenical there are some signs showing that the crisis can be pass over. For instance, in comparison with the Eighth Assembly of the WCC held in Harare in 1998, the number of Orthodox participants in 2006 in Porto-Alegre was significantly larger. In 1998 the Moscow Patriarchate was represented by a delegation of three people headed by a monk priest. To the assembly in 2006 it sent a delegation of 21 persons headed by a bishop.

The main obstacle for ecumenical thinking among Orthodox believers is a lack of tolerance within the tradition. A tendency to search for enemies, heretics, 'not Orthodox enough', is very characteristic of today's post-communist religious life in Russia. Awakening to the awareness of Orthodoxy as a rich diversity rather than uniformity, as an open way for the Church to live between akribeia and oikonomia is a main opportunity for ecumenical development in Russia.

Religious Education in Russia

Historical Context

During the early periods of Russian history when the Church was considered to be an irreplaceable curator of education, reading sacred texts was both the main content and the main goal of schooling. After Peter's reforms divided education into two trends, religious education became a prerogative of a spiritual trend, targeted to the professional training of clergy, while in the schools of a secular trend, learning religion was either withdrawn or substituted by learning courtesy, Western languages and 'noble arts' such as horse riding and fencing. This radical change made a solid contribution into a stable Russian prejudice, associating the 'Western' with a secular and even antireligious stance.

However, with the establishment of a system of universal popular education in Russia under Catherine II, catechesis returned to school as a 'fourth R' of grammar and remained there until 1917. The, 'Design of popular education in all sciences' made up for Russia by the famous French philosopher Denis Diderot, included recommendations to teach about the existence of God and about two essences in Christ. As the author professed, 'the inclusion of religious subjects was made as a concession to the Empress's will' (Ahayan et al., 2005, p. 126). Following educational reforms (1802–1804, 1826, 1860–1868, 1871–1872) greatly changed the system of general and higher professional education, affecting the structure of educational system, the ratio of its elements and trends, the subordination and administrative aspects and the level of autonomy of educational institutions and leading principles of schooling. But the attestation for religious subject called, "God's Law" invariably occupied the first line in the state certificates of general education.

By the end of 19th century two trends of the educational system were presented at the primary level by Church parochial and grammar schools, subordinated to Synod and supported by parishes and dioceses, on one hand, and the 'town schools,' founded and supported either by government or by civil local communities (zemstva) on the other. The ratio of the two was 50:50. Religious subjects occupied about 40% of parochial schools curricula and included, besides "God's Law", training in Church choral groups and in Church-Slavonic reading. The main goal of these schools was defined by State Regulation (1902) as, 'the dissemination of education in the spirit of the Orthodox faith and church'. Civil primary schools divided curriculum time between, 'God's Law', grammar, arithmetic, geometry and basics of history, geography and natural science. According to the Regulation of 1872 their goal was, 'to provide children of all classes with the essentials of mental and religious-moral education' (Piskunov, 2005).

The most typical school at secondary level was the classical gymnasium, training elites to enter universities and to occupy positions in the state service. 'God's Law' was usually taught twice a week and made up about 8% of classes.

As for the universities, the tradition of offering students, 'God's Law' as an obligatory subject, was established by the oldest – Moscow University. Nevertheless, the idea was not supported by all universities, and attempts to enforce it in the1830s caused a resistance from the professoriate, especially in the 'non-Orthodox' parts of the empire (Tartu, Kazan).

Regarding the content of RE, the, "God's Law" subject, normally included three big parts: Bible; Church Canon and Catechesis (Dernov, 1913, p. 55). The first part was usually called in Russia, 'The Sacred History" and the selected narratives from the Old and New Testament were used as the main didactical sources for it. Basic knowledge about liturgy, fasts and celebrations was the core element of the second part. Catechesis had the objective of teaching Church doctrine, to explain religious truths and to inspire pupils with piety. It was based mainly upon three doctrinal sources: Credo, Lord prayer and Decalogue (ibid, p. 76). Besides classes the participation in weekly Church worship was considered to be an important element of RE. It was usual to underline, in methodological guidelines, that the aim of the subject is not so much to give abstract knowledge as to contribute to moral and religious growth and perfection (ibid, p. 48). That is why a specific Russian term, 'spiritual & moral education' was often used instead of RE.

In the late 19th – early 20th centuries "God's Law" and the whole enterprise of spiritual education undoubtedly become the most frequent target for public and professional criticism. A reminiscence by Vasily Rozanov, an outstanding philosopher, pedagogue and journalist, who wrote on church topics at that time, is quite typical and indicative,

'During eight years of gymnasium studies we learned catechesis, liturgics, the history of Russian Church, the "Sacred History of Old Testament" by Rudakov and the "Sacred History of New Testament" by him as well. But I never read Gospel and Bible, and the only thing I knew to distinguish between them was that Gospel is small and Bible is huge and heavy. I want to say and I want to complain at last that at the so called "God's Law" we were taught everything but a word of God and the word of God seemed to be in quarantine for all that time [...] And the second fact I know that we finished our course all being fierce atheists and my first religious feeling was awakened only at the University [...] under the impression of talented lectures on the world history' (Rozanov, 1995, p. 77).

No better was the situation in the 'spiritual' trend of the educational system – that is in the parochial schools, theological ('spiritual') seminaries and academies. The official reports of the diocesan bishops written in 1905 and published 100 years later contained extremely negative evaluations. The low level of pedagogical skills of the professorship, the lack of elaborated methodology in Seminaries and the unwillingness to sponsor primary parochial schools were the items of most frequent criticisms. Some reports were explicitly pessimistic. The Volyn (Ukraine) Bishop Antony (Khrapovitsky), who later became the leader of the Russian Orthodox Church Abroad, confessed that he had to agree with 'one respectful archbishop' in his opinion that our theological school can't be reformed. 'It must be dispersed and destroyed, the basements of seminaries and academies must be blown up and the new institutions instead must be created on new places, and filled up with new people' (Comments…, 2004, V. 1, p. 726).

A revolutionary mood shared by bishops with all other segments of Russian society was a justified reaction to the corrosion in the educational sphere caused by the perverse state politics and fairly described in a note of the Alliance of Teachers of Secondary Schools (1905): 'We are witnesses of a portentous moment of the collapse of the secondary school. It was shielded from every aspect of life, but life burst into the school and threw the youth, mostly the boys, onto streets under Cossack lashes. It imposed Orthodoxy but having brought it forth in heavy forms of government formalism, cultivated religious indifferentism…' (Pinkevich, 2001). Pre-revolutionary RE failed to fulfil its tasks more obviously than any other part of school education.

Pedagogical Trends and Innovations.

Ideas of European Enlightenment came early to Russia through the personal contacts of the royal family and nobility. Under the rule of Catherine II the main actors of the movements were members of Masonic lodges, such as Ivan Lopuchin (1756–1816), Alexander Kutuzov (–1790), Nikolay Novikov (1744–1818) and Alexander Radischev (1749–1802). It seems a paradox, but G. Florovsky described Masonic movements in terms of the 'return of the Russian soul to itself', 'gathering of the spirit' after the alienation caused by the absolutism of the state and by scholasticism having no roots in Russian spirituality (Florovsky, 1937). It was a 'school of humanism' as the other famous Church historian and pedagogue Vasily Zenkovsky defined (Zenkovsky, 1991, 1.1, p. 106). It was an attempt to cultivate in Russia the romantic ideal of Shoeneseele – Beautiful Soul.

This pedagogical trend, accentuating mysticism and personal piety, was supported by Alexander I. The Ministry of Education, established in Russia in 1802, was fused in 1817 with Synod, 'in order to make Christian piety the basement of true enlightenment' (Piskunov, 2005, p. 343). The leading position of Alexander I in the Holy Alliance of European monarchies, demanded attention to interchurch relations in education. By one of his special orders, it was strictly forbidden to extol Orthodoxy over the other Christian confessions – a fact without precedent in Russian history. At this time the Russian Biblical Society translated the Bible into Russian. This event had the most important effect for the religious enlightenment of Russia. The other significant outcome of Alexander's educational policy was Lyceum organized almost literally under the wing of the Emperor, for its students learned and lived in a specially erected building communicating with the Emperor's palace. Alumni of the Lyceum, with Pushkin among them, formed a new Russian cultural elite. Commitment of this elite to the value of 'inward Christianity', deliberately nurtured at that time, became a significant factor of the humanization and europeanization of Russia. At the same time an impulse for innovative activity in religious pedagogy was given. Demonstrative is the Charter of the St. Petersburg Academy (1814), prepared by the metropolitan Filaret and claiming to establish an educational system 'on the authentic pedagogical base'. It was noted there especially that, 'the good method of teaching lies in promoting students' own mental power and activity' (Florovsky, 1937, p. 145–147).

In the course of the counter-reforms of 1824–26, the Biblical Society was closed, the new catechism by Metropolitan Filaret written in Russian (instead of traditional Church-Slavonic) was withdrawn, translated Bible editions were burnt and RE became an instrument to foster loyalty in accordance with the new priorities of state policy generated by the futile liberating revolt of the nobility in 1825. In 1834 Minister of Education Sergey Uvarov proclaimed a formula "Orthodoxy – Autocracy – Nationality" that became a *credo* of reactionary policy in culture and education. The rejection of the Western way of social development and, as a consequence hostility towards all kinds of liberalism, the search for the "authentic Russian way" and the promotion of spiritual exclusiveness based on the 'only true faith' became the main components of ideology. Nurturing loyalty to the state and commitment to traditional national values became the main task for RE.

What was remarkable was the argumentation of the leaders of counter-reformation, archimandrite Foty and admiral Alexander Shishkov. From Foty's point of view a Biblical society, as well as other 'secret societies', had only one task – to destroy Orthodoxy: 'The enemies planned to induce somewhat Biblical religion, to make a mixture of faiths and to reduce the Orthodox Christian faith' (Florovsky, 1937, p. 153). Shishkov openly argued not only against the translation of Holy Scripture into Russian ('It would be indecent to read Lord Prayer in a vulgar language') but also against the dissemination of the Bible among people, for this could produce in his eyes only, 'heresy and schisms'. He was sure that people couldn't be allowed to have Scripture at home, for that would disgrace the Scripture: 'It would lie about on the floor under a bench' (ibid, p. 163). Within this frame of reference a liberal education, oriented toward the ideal of personal autonomy, became impossible and inadmissible.

The story was repeated after the liberating reforms of Alexander II in the 1860s. This time it was a powerful chief of Synod, Konstantin Pobedonostsev (1827–1907) who was at the head of the reactionary movement in the1880s. Religious Education 'in the orthodox spirit', allowing, 'to keep people in strict subservience to the order of public life', was a key element in the complex of measures he offered to prevent democratic revolution and to save the monarchy in Russia. 'Defeat of personality' – that is how an outstanding Russian pedagogue Vasily Stoyunin (1826–1888) defined a main feature of Russian psychology fostered by state education. A similar judgment was made recently by E. Bondarevskaya and S. Kulnevich in their teacher-training book "Pedagogy"(1999):

"Pedagogical tradition in Russia have been founded not on what learners demanded from education for the development of their personality but on what state demanded from learners to pursue national interests" (p. 126).

The submission of Church to State made it impossible to develop an alternative educational strategy from a theological background and within the clerical domain. Moreover, as the loyalty toward church became tightly interlinked with the loyalty toward reactionary political ideology, the progressive part of society found it morally impossible to obey the hierarchy. The spiritual opposition between intelligentsia and church made Russian Orthodoxy even more conservative and hostile to liberal ideals. Nikolay Berdyaev maintained that church people <...> recognized inhumanity as an essential element of the church's official doctrine' and witnessed that the word 'humanism' was used among Orthodox emigrants negatively 'almost as an invective' (Berdyaev, 1997). The definition of 'ideology of humanism' as one, 'proclaiming the authentic value of human being and thus confronting the spiritual guidelines of Christianity' in the first post-Soviet Orthodox manual for general schools developed under the guidance of church-affiliated structures (Borodina, 2002), the regular calls for struggle with the idea of anthropocentrism and liberal standards articulated at high levels of hierarchy, clearly show that this tendency is not still overcome.[6]

Being aware of the real situation, the majority of leading Russian pedagogues always advocated the emancipation of school from church. Ushinsky wrote that "after the school ceased to be an instrument of religious propaganda and began to evolve in accordance with the demands of civil life... clergy began to hinder its development more than to assist it" (Ushinsky, 1988, 1, p. 254). According to Stoyunin, 'the contemporary school can't be satisfied with what the representatives of the Church are able to offer. It elaborated its own ideal without them, and can't fall away, no matter how strong is the pressure from the side of those who have no idea about the reasonable preconditions of school functioning' (Stoyunin, 1991, p. 189). Ushinsky grounded his opinion in the 'caste character' of confessional education that inevitably put forward the 'group interests' of clergy. Stoyunin derived the destructive role of clergy from the economic factors, namely from the absence of a fixed salary for priests and their habit of earning money from special 'ordered worships' (treby) directed to the practical needs of parishioners. Thus clergy were financially interested in supporting superstitions and deliberately prevented enlightenment. Rare examples of successful educational practice based on traditional Orthodox values, such as the famous school in village Tatevo near Smolensk organized and managed by pedagogue Sergey Rachinsky (1833–1902), did not meet proper public and professional recognition, partly because they met recognition on the part of Pobedonostsev and the state.

Most of the critics of confessionalism in education were not against RE per se. On the contrary, Ushinsky following Pestalozzi and other great German pedagogues projected a national school based on Christian faith and Christian values: 'If we don't make religion a focus of humane education, it is only because it should be at the head of it' (Ushinsky,

---

6   See for instance the report of bishop Feofan at Moscow Christmas Conference 2006 at: www.pravoslavie.ru/cgi-bin/jurnal.cgi?item=1r600r060208173422 (accessed 30 September 2006).

1988, 2, p. 432). Censorship and the political status of Orthodoxy did not allow him to develop explicitly the idea of non-confessional RE, but many fragments of his writings and public speeches reveal it pretty well. Only after the admission of civil freedoms in 1905 could the proposals to develop RE on educational non-confessional grounds appear in pedagogical literature. Peter Kapterev (1849–1922) in his 'Pedagogical process' (first published in 1905) states in a categorical form that, 'the claims of the Church (such as unshakable dogmatic beliefs and distrust of natural science) as well as the claims of the state are absolutely alien to the nature of pedagogical process'. He states also that, 'it is necessary to educate a human being as a creature provided with a religious conscience though it does not imply at all that we need to incorporate confessional claims into the pedagogical process' (Kapterev, 1982, p. 210). He pronounces some very advanced ideas about RE, for instance that religiosity can be expressed not only in confessional forms: "Undoubtedly there could be, and there are, higher forms of religious life than church-belonging and consequently religion can be present in new forms within the educational process' (ibid, p. 267). He foresees an RE that accentuates essential similarities between religions and reveals the unity of human religious consciousness. He advises teachers to put Bible stories into a modern context and to improvise with them in order to awaken a vivid emotional experience of religion in students.

Konstantin Ventzel with his group, 'Free education', advocated a more radical, inno-vative approach. Being the author of one of the first Declarations on the Rights of the Child (1917) he consistently extended his pedocentric principles to the field of RE: "In the domain of religion a child should be guaranteed full freedom of development even more than in any other aspect of life" (Borisovich & Boguslavsky, 1999, p. 188). Ventzel claimed that the only justifiable assumption for the theory of free education should be, "the fact of the existence of a religious problem but not a definite method of its resolu-tion" (ibid). Since children of even pre-school age already have living experience that in-evitably leads to religious feeling, these experiences, and not external religious ideas, should be used as grounds for religious development. Moreover, "the religious develop-ment of a child should be a result of his own authentic creativity" (ibid, p. 190).

One can find challenging innovative ideas in the lecture, "On the methods of religious upbringing" delivered by religious philosopher Alexey Losev (1893–1988) at Nizny Novgorod State University in 1921 (Losev, 1993). Losev regards religion as a phenome-non belonging predominantly to the domain of personal experience and therefore abhor-ent of any fixed frames. He formulates the 'principle of creative fluidity of religious ex-perience' and sees the main task of RE to be that of, 'widening personal religious experi-ence' that should help students, 'to plunge into various kinds of religious insights' and 'to feel themselves branches on the tree of global human history and religion'.

Archpriest Vasily Zenkovsky (1881–1962) is a unique figure in the history of Russian emigration, for he managed to combine deep studies in history, philosophy and theology with vigorous missionary activity and professional concern in pedagogy. Although he can be identified in some sense as a confessionalist educator, his fundamental pedagogi-cal works published in post-Soviet Russia are highly appreciated among academic schol-ars. His observations and conceptual findings in the psychology of religious and sexual individual development, implying pedagogical recommendations for RE, are of special interest. While working on the theological justification for pedagogy he broke the limits of confessionalism and looked for new ways of church-school relationships. He dreamt of a, 'new school awestruck with Christian principles from inside, not from outside, guided by the spirit of the Church, not by its power' (Zenkovsky, 1996b, p. 25).

It is impossible to review briefly the enormous resources for the methodology of RE embedded in the works of the other representatives of the Russian religious Renaissance of the 20th century, concerning issues of literature and art (V. Rozanov, D. Merezhkovsky, Vyach. Ivanov, M. Bakhtin, and others), philosophy and theology (S. Bulgakov, N. Berdyaev, P. Florensky, S. Frank, N. Lossky, I. Ilyin and others). It could be mentioned only that the last work by Ivan Ilyin (1883–1954), the 'Axioms of religious experience', (Ilyin, 1993) offers a brilliant philosophic generalization of the nature of re-ligion based on a phenomenological approach and is full of extremely important peda-gogical conclusions. Alongside with the comprehensive culture-centric pedagogical sys-tem elaborated by Sergey Hessen (1887–1950) in his 'Basics of Pedagogy: An Introduc-tion to Practical Philosophy' (Hessen, 1995) and other works mentioned earlier, it constitutes a solid theoretical base for the authentic development of non-confessional re-ligious education in Russia.

State-of-the-Art

The main factors that make the Russian situation with RE specific and distinct from the situation in the West, are the almost 90-years rupture of pedagogical tradition of school RE and the experience of quasi-religious communist totalitarianism. More remote his-torical factors such as the split between spiritual and civil trends in education, the opposi-tion of the intelligentsia to clergy and the submission of education to state interests, con-tribute to the current situation as well.

Until the very collapse of the Soviet regime, manuals for Soviet teachers mentioned the nurturing of confirmed atheists as among the main tasks of Soviet school (Maryenko, 1984). After 1988 the situation began to change and since that time religious communi-ties have begun to open their own schools and send their representatives to the state edu-cational institutions mostly with missionary and charity tasks in mind. The Federal Law on Education (1992) forbade religious organizations to act within state and municipal educational institutions and all levels of administration (chapter 1). It also proclaimed the secular nature of education in state and municipal educational institutions as a principal of national policy in education (chapter 2). Regulations concerning confessional educa-tion were included in the Federal Law on Freedom of Conscience and Religious Organi-zations (1997). According to it, religious communities were allowed not only to organize confessional schools but also to give confessional RE in state schools 'outside the curric-ula' and under certain reasonable conditions (chapter 5).

Despite the availabilities provided by law, religious classes and religious schools did not become a normal element of the educational system in post-Soviet Russia. As to the network of confessional educational institutions, the main obstacle for its development is the lack of financial support from the state. In violation of the Law on Education the ex-penses of secondary level institutions for providing general education are not covered by the state and it makes them non-competitive with state and municipal schools. As to the intrusion of religious subjects and topics into the curricula of state schools, attempts were made several times but they met with loud protests from a part of Russian society and caused heavy debates accompanied by denunciations and criminal investigations.

Two conflicting positions are usually in the focus of public debates. One is linked with defending the 'secular principle' and with referring to the Russian Constitution and to the historical choice of France and the U.S. The other is linked with promoting the expansion of Church influence in education and with referring to the neglect of moral aspects in contemporary schools, to the national traditions and to the 'common European' (mainly German) educational practice. Two examples are given below to show how conflicting are the positions. 'It is necessary to return to Orthodoxy as a public, if not a state, ideology', that is how the bishop of Stavropol and Vladikavkaz diocese Feofan started his already mentioned report at the annual Christmas Educational Conference in Moscow (2006). According to him, 'the intrusion of elements of religious education into the secular education' should be targeted at, 'the formation of standards of life and the system of values that determine individual modes of behaviour and makes the Christian motivation essential for personal acts and decisions'. Conversion to the 'Orthodox way of life' by means of RE seems to him a strategy not in contradiction with the secular principle of education. The St. Petersburg newspaper, "Chas pick" presents the opposite point of view. A short appeal to public opinion signed by eight members of the Russian Academy of Science was published there in November 2002. A short quotation from it: "Collaboration of school and Church ... threaten to lead our country to full cultural degradation and collapse of all infrastructure of science and education".[7]

The choice between two strategies targeted to either strict secularism of school or schooling based on 'Orthodox ideology' has remained the main topic of public and professional debates about RE for the last 15 years. Problems of religious minorities remain at the periphery of public interest while leaders of the communities participate in the main debate on different sides. There were several statements in support of a confessional model of RE in Russia coming from Roman-Catholic clergy, some Protestant denominations and leaders of Jewish communities. Muslims are more inclined to promote neutral scientific approaches for school studies of religion.

Three main obstacles to the development of school RE in Russia derive from the historical factors mentioned above. These are:

- extreme politicisation of religious issues,
- low standards of civil conduct, and
- a lack of elaborated contemporary educational theory and methodology dealing with religion in a secular environment.

It is not surprising that after the decades of living in a totalitarian system parents are often afraid that some kind of new ideological control may enter schools under the guise of RE and children may once again be told in an authoritarian way what is permitted and what is not. This kind of distrust naturally leads to resistance among professional pedagogues against the inclusion of religious education in Russian school programmes. Abso-

---

7   Chas Pick, 46 (252), p. 11.

lutism of consciousness, nurtured by means of 'pedagogical demonology' (Bondarevskaya & Kulnevich, 1999, p. 162) in which the global Evil (capitalism) was struggling against the global Good (communism), significantly adds to it being projected now to the sphere of religion and helping citizens of post-Soviet Russia to find malicious secret plans of enemies behind any initiative in RE. Religion in Russian history was either the collaborator with the state or its rival. There was no real experience of free partnership between church and state. A long enforced isolation of Russian science from the opportunity to study foreign experience of that kind, contributes today to the common confidence according to which religion can appear in an educational context only in the form of ideology.

There are serious problems with juridical aspects implicated in RE issues on the conceptual level. The term 'religious education' is usually perceived as a synonym for 'induction into religion' or Christian nurture, and this confusion puts a substantial obstacle on the way of developing non-confessional educational models. Sometimes definitions borrowed from Soviet reference literature are found in both academic works and legislative acts where religious education is defined as the preparation for ministers of religion. Very obviously, while using such definitions, it is very easy to set forth arguments against admitting RE into school.

The same is true with the concept of the secular which is the most significant one, since in fact the whole regulation in the sphere of RE is hung legally on the only notion of, 'secular nature of education' in the second chapter of the Law on Education. Secularists try to fix the meaning according to which 'the secular' designates space totally free from religion. Their opponents, those who want religion to be taught in school, frequently use the word 'secular' as an antonym of 'clerical' and make on this ground alarming statements like one in the open letter to the Ministry of Education dated 21 January1999 and signed by Moscow Patriarch Alexey, the President of the Russian Academy of Education N. Nikandrov, academic Y. Osipov and rector of Moscow University V. Sadovnichy: "the declaration of the secular nature of education [...] means only that the state school is not dependant upon Church either administratively or financially and does not put forward a task of training clergy". This definition obviously opens doors for the legitimatisation of 'Orthodox ideology' as a principle of state education. Another example of juridical challenges is an official letter of Ministry of Education (4 June1999) interpreting a clause 5.4 of the Federal Law on freedom of conscience (which allows religious communities to teach religion in secular schools under certain conditions) as a clause forbidding teaching religion by anybody except for religious communities. This misinterpretation of the law was obviously inspired by the will of some officials to restore pre-Revolutionary status of Church in state schools not on legal grounds but by means of purely administrative tools.

A recent publication in this field – a monograph by Igor Ponkin on the concepts of secular state and secular education (Ponkin, 2003) makes the situation a little bit better. The book is not free from political prejudices that result in some strange statements and assessments. For example, according to the typology elaborated by the author of the book, only three states in the modern world do not meet criteria of, 'the secular state'. These are Vatican, North Korea and 'partly' USA (p. 175). Nevertheless, it provides readers with a wide review of diverse concepts and criteria of, 'the secular' in the modern juridical practice all over the world and contains a professional criticism on a series of misinterpretations of law in Russia including the Minister's letter cited above.

Definite progress has taken place during the last five or six years in the field of pedagogical research concerning problems of religion in education as this topic is gradually being recognized by official pedagogy to be an object of academic investigation. 'Orthodox Pedagogy' by Evgeny Shestun (2001), 'Religious Culture in the Content of Education' by Lyudmila Kharisova (2002a), 'Religion and education in public school' by Igor Metlik (2004) and 'Religious education in public school' by Fedor Kozyrev (2005) are the most significant monographs regarding the theoretical problems of RE. A good number of didactical manuals and materials, schoolbooks and handbooks for teachers have been published during these years too. Mostly they are for teaching Orthodoxy or Orthodox culture. But among them there is also a manual for teaching Islam at school by L. Kharisova (2002b).

The increase of interest toward a religious topic on the part of pedagogues was obviously stimulated by the plan of the Ministry of Education to include the subject, "Orthodox Culture" (OC) into curricula for general education schools and by the release of the official letter on that (dated 22 October 2002) with the attachment "The Draft Content of Education on the Subject, 'Orthodox Culture'". The project itself can be regarded as a decisive, positive step on the way of reanimation and innovation of RE practice in Russian schools. It is important in at least three respects. First, it is a precedent legitimising a non-confessional approach to RE in the system of Russian general education. The document defines the subject as 'culturological' in approach and affirms that, 'the most significant for the organization of study of OC is the principle of the secular nature of education'. Secondly, the document proclaims some important guiding principles that can be applied for the study of any religious subject on non-confessional premises. Thirdly, the project carves a middle way between the two extremes proposed by secularists and confessionalists and makes it in a way most relevant to national pedagogical tradition. Culture-centrism, innate to Russian pedagogical thought and explicit in the works of both Russian classics (K. Ushinsky, S. Hessen) and modern theorists (see: Gusinsky & Turchaninova, 2002, p. 97–99; Bordovskaya & Rean, 2004, p. 62; Bondarevskaya & Kulnevich, 1999, p. 162) may be recognized in a Russian historical context as the most appropriate if not the only alternative to state-centrism. A 'culturological study' of religion may prove to be a promising approach that can enrich the pedagogy of RE as ethnography and anthropology have enriched the phenomenological study of religion.

As the issues concerning RE are regulated predominantly at a regional and local level, the real situation with the OC in schools vary significantly over the territory of Russia. There are places such as St. Petersburg where, 'the secular model' is strictly maintained within primary and secondary school. Several hours for the study of 'Bible topics' in the course of literature classes and a few topics in history classes provide the only opportunity for teachers to touch upon religious matters within programs. Some other regional authorities, on the contrary, show a tendency to enforce Orthodox teaching. For instance, the regional 'Program of Religious and Moral Education in state schools of the Voronezh region' was adopted in 2001. It defines religious and moral education as, "an influx of knowledge shaping students' moral beliefs on the basis of the spiritual traditions of our country – that is on the base of Orthodoxy". Voronezh, Kursk, Smolensk, Kaliningrad, Kemerovo regions were among the first regions where OC was included into the curricula of secondary schools. ITAR Tass stated, in 2004, that about 615 of the 877 schools in Kursk were teaching OC. Informational agencies of the Moscow Patriarchy reported that teaching 'the Basics of Orthodox Culture' (as the subject is usually called), will be obligatory as from 1st September 2006 in all secondary schools in Belgorod and Kaluga.[8] The same strategy has been approved by the Parliament of the Vladimir region. Federal officials have confirmed the obligatory status of OC in the school curricula of two regions (Belgorod and Bryansk).[9] The new Minister of Culture, Andrey Sokolov, ascertained that the practice of teaching OC is rapidly spreading and running ahead of legal decisions.[10] OC is taught by ordinary educators after they have got a special qualification at the pedagogical courses that are organized, usually by dioceses of the ROC in cooperation with the state network of institutes for post-diploma improvement of professional pedagogical qualifications. Since theology was included in 1994 in the list of officially admitted profiles of professional education, theological faculties have been opened in the state universities of Vladivostok, Omsk, Barnaul, Ekaterinburg, Ryazan Tula and Belgorod.[11] These are also planned to become centres for providing professional qualification for school religious educators.

As only about half of society manifests a positive attitude toward the reanimation of a religious element of general education, hot debates with strong political implications continue. As an example, a public debate between Igor Ponkin and Nikolay Mitrokhin should be mentioned. In January 2005 N. Mitrokhin the chief of the Institute for Civil Analysis presented his report 'Clericalization of Education in Russia' in which he claimed that 'the activities of ROC in the field of school education […] lead to the institutional split of pedagogic community between devotees of modern and traditional ideologies, is an attempt to de-modernise the younger generation and, moreover, may lead to unexpected consequences in the future' (Mitrokhin, 2005, p. 75). In a response, I. Ponkin incriminated Mitrokhin's professional incompetence and, 'tendentious anti-church hysteria that is fatally out of date and meets with no understanding even among liberals'.[12] In the context of these kind of debates the slow movement toward public consensus, compromise settlements and moderate reasonable approaches to RE begins to show the first signs of possible future success. The new Minister of Education Andrey Fursenko's plan to introduce in September 2006 in state schools of Moscow a subject entitled 'History of Religion' and including teaching about the history of the main world religions, may be regarded as one of these signs.

It is quite probable that in the near future the idea of intercultural RE will get official support at federal level. The principles and priorities of Russian state educational policy

8   www.prokimen.ru (accessed 30 September 2006).
9   NG-Religii, 4.10.2006 – http://religion.ng.ru/facts/2006-10-04/1_uchebniki.html (accessed 30 September 2006).
10   www.religare.ru (accessed 01 October 2006).
11   http://vos.1september.ru/articlef.php?ID=200200307.
12   Information analytical portal 'State and Religion' http://www.state-religion.ru/cgi-bin/cms/show.cgi?in=104021101164628&id=205072619220545 (accessed 26 July 2005).

as they are indicated in basic official documents such as the National Doctrine of Education in Russian Federation (2000) or the Concept of Modernization of Russian Education, until 2010 (2002), exhibit a will to coordinate a national strategy of development towards a process of European integration. 'The widening of the scales of intercultural communication' is mentioned in the Concept of Modernization (chapter 1.1) as a factor that puts forward the task of fostering tolerance, up-to-date thinking and communicability among youth. In addition to it, preventing international terrorism and extremism with intolerance at their roots, also becomes one of the priorities of Russian state policy.

Conclusion

After the end of the Communist era religion has got a chance to become a constitutive element of Russian general education as it had been before the revolution. Yet there are historical factors at work that have made this process much more difficult and problematic than in some other parts of the post-Soviet world (such as Poland or Romania). They are:

- multi-ethnicity and the polyconfessionalism of Russian society,
- strong positions of secularism and anticlericalism deeply grounded in history,
- caste isolation of clergy and consequently:
- split of national culture into church ('spiritual') and secular subcultures,
- isolation of theology from university science,
- sharp opposition of hierarchy and intelligentsia,
- negative experience of confessional religious education subordinated to the interests of the state,
- lack of scientific and pedagogical research in the field of RE,
- lack of experience of partnership between state and religious organizations based on the principles of democratic freedoms and plurality.

Due to these factors as well as to the syndrome of post-totalitarianism, common to all East European countries, the issues of RE have strong political connotations and divide society on the principle of pro et contra. In this situation the increasing role of RE in schools can easily become either a contribution to dialogue or a factor of conflict. Nevertheless, the present insufficient level of religious literacy, tolerance and skills for intercultural communication, demonstrated by the alumni of state schools, consolidate the opponents on the basis of a conviction that schools should pay more attention to religious issues. The challenge of terrorism has contributed significantly to this conviction during last five years. Since, in most cases, terrorist acts were committed by young people, who acquired faith in its fanatical and extremist interpretation, it has become evident that society needs some form of education that fosters citizens in another system of religious values. Hence the search for the preferable strategies of introducing religion into school education was recognized as one of the urgent tasks for Russian educators and scientists, school ministry and officials and representatives of religious communities. The REDCO project goes precisely in line with this search and brings an international perspective with it.

According to the description of the Russian context given above in this chapter, it will be reasonable to focus the research of a Russian team on the problem of compatibility of the freedom of conscience with religious commitments. Russian schools and educational institutions would be a good place to see how the society, sticking formerly to the state religious and quasi-religious ideologies, but exposed now to globalization and to the demands of an international community for a certain level of democracy and pluralism, faces up to these new challenges and how different confessional and educational backgrounds help or hinder managing with them. We believe also that the different sectors of Russian social practices and especially education will benefit from this inquiry by opening a new resource for self-criticism and widening the horizon of future development.

References

Ахаян Т.К., Свиридова И.А., Смирнова В.В. (2005) *История образования в России.* – СПб.: Изд. РГПУ им. А.И. Герцена [Ahayan T.K., Sviridova I.A., Smirnova V.V. *The History of Education in Russia* (St. Petersburg, Herzen RGPU)].

Антология педагогической мысли Древней Руси и Русского государства XIУ-XУ11 в.в. (1985) – M. [Anthology on Pedagogical Thought of Ancient Russia and Russian State XIV –XVII cc. (Moscow)].

Бендин А.М. (2003) Религиозная толерантность в Российской империи как этнообразующий и консолидирующий фактор (вторая половина XIX – начало XX вв.)/*Кафоликия: сб. научных статей* /под. ред. А.В. Данилова. – Минск: Тесей. – C.96–108 [Bendin A.M. Religious Tolerance in Russian Empire as an Ethno-genetic and Consolidating Factor (second half of XIX – beginning of XX cc.), in: Danilov A.V. (Ed.) *Catholicia: collection of scientific articles* (Minsk, Tesey)].

Бердяев Н. (1992) Русская идея: основные проблемы русской мысли XIX века и начала XX века//Мыслители русского зарубежья. – СПб, «Наука». – C.37–260 [Berdyaev N. *Russian Idea: Basic Problems of Russian Thought in XIX – beginning of XX century, in: Russian Thinkers Abroad* (St. Peterscburg, Nauka)]

Бердяев Н.А. [1936] (1997) Ответ протоиерею Сергию Четверикову/Антифон – № 1. – C. 7–10 [Berdyaev N.A. A Response to Archpriest Sergey Chetverikov, *Antifon*, 1, 7–10].

Бондаревская Е.В., Кульневич С.В. (1999) *Педагогика: личность в гуманистических теориях и системах воспитания.* – M. – Ростов-на-Дону [Bondarevskaya E.V., Kulnevich S.V. Pedagogy: *Personality in humanistic theories and educational systems* (Moscow: Rostov-na-Donu)].

Бордовская Н.В., Реан А.А. (2004) *Педагогика.* – СПб.: Питер [Bordovskaya N.V., Rean A.A. Pedagogy (St. Petersburg, Peter)].

Вентцель (1999)/Сост. и авт. предисл. Г. Б. Борисович, М. В. Богуславский – M.: Изд. дом Шалвы Амонашвили [Borisovich G.B., Boguslavsky M.V. (Eds.) *Ventzel* (Moscow, Publishing House of Shalva Amonashvili)].

Бородина А.В. (2002) *Основы православной культуры.* Учебное пособие для основной и старшей ступеней общеобразовательных школ, лицеев, гимназий. – M.: Издательский дом «Покров», [Borodina A. *The Basics of Orthodox Culture: textbook for secondary and high school* (Moscow, Pokrov)].

Отзывы епархиальных архиереев по вопросу о церковной реформе в 2 частях (2004). – M.: Изд. Крутицкого подворья [Comments of Diocese Archbishops on Church Reform (Moscow, Krutitskoye Podvorye), Vol. 1, 2].

Дернов А.А., прот (1913) Методика Закона Божия. Чтения по Закону Божиему об истинно-христианском воспитании. Изд. 3-е.– СПб: Издание Я. Башмакова и Ко. [Dernov A.A.

God's Law Didactics. Lectures on the true Christian upbringing for God's Law classes (third ed.) (St. Petersburg, Bashmakov &Co)].

Православная миссия сегодня (1999)/составитель В. Федоров, прот. – СПб.: Апостольский город [Fedorov V (Ed.) *Eastern Orthodox Mission Today* (St. Petersburg, Apostolic City)].

Fedorov V. (2004) Russia: Europe or not? *Concilium*, 2

Филатов С., Лункин Р. (2005) Статистика российской религиозности: магия цифр и неоднозначная реальность //Социологические исследования. – № 6. – С. 35–45 [Filatov S., Lunkin R. Statistics on Russian religiosity: magic of figures and vague reality – *Sociological Research*, 6, 35–45].

Флоровский Г., прот. (1937) *Пути русского богословия*. – Париж [Florovsky G. *Ways of Russian Theology* (Paris)].

Гусинский Э.Н., Турчанинова Ю.И. (2000) *Введение в философию образования*. – М.: Логос [Gusinsky E.N., Turchaninova J.I. *Introduction to Philosophy of Education* (Moscow, Logos)].

Гессен С.И. [1923] (1995) Основы педагогики. Введение в прикладную философию – М., Школа-Пресс [Hessen S. *The Basics of Pedagogy: An Introduction to Practical Philosophy* (Moscow, Shkola-Press)].

Ильин И.А. [1953] (1993) *Аксиомы религиозного опыта*. – М.: Рарогъ [Ilyin I. *Axioms of religious experience* (Moscow, Rarogue)].

Институт гражданского анализа (2005) *Доклад «Клерикализация образования в России»* (подготовлен Н. Митрохиным) – М.: ИИФ «Спрос» КонфОП [Institute for Civil Analysis *Clericalization of Education in Russia*: report, given by N. Mitrokhin (Moscow, IIF "Spros")].

Каптерев П.Ф. (1982) *Избранные педагогические сочинения*/Под ред. А.М. Арсеньева. – М.: Педагогика [Kapterev P. *Selected pedagogical works*, ed. by A.M. Arsenyev (Moscow, Pedagogika)].

Харисова Л.А. (2002a) Религиозная культура в содержании образования. – М.: Просвещение [Kharisova L.A. Religious Culture in the Content of Education (Moscow, Prosveschenije)].

Харисова Л.А. (2002b) *Ислам: Духовно-нравственное обучение школьников*: Конспекты занятий. – М.: ВЛАДОС [Kharisova L.A. *Islam: Spiritual and Moral Teaching for Schoolchildren* (synopsis) (Moscow,Vlados)].

Козырев Ф.Н. (2005) Религиозное образование в светской школе. Теория и международный опыт в отечественной перспективе. – СПб: Апостольский город [Kozyrev F.N. Religious Education in Public Schools: Theory and international experience in Russian perspective (St. Petersburg, Apostolic City)].

Лосев А.Ф. (1993) О методах религиозного воспитания //*Вестник русского христианского движения*. – № 167 (1). – С. 63–87 [Losev A.F. On the methods of religious upbringing, *Vestnik RChD*, 167 (1)].

Примерное содержание воспитания школьников (1984) /Под ред. И. С. Марьенко. – М. [Maryenko I.S. (Ed.) Draft content of school education (Moscow)].

Метлик И.В. (2004) Религия и образование в светской школе. – М.: «Планета–2000» [Metlik I. V. *Religion and Education in Public Schools* (Moscow, Planeta–2000)].

Митрохин Н. (2004*) Русская православная церковь*: Современное состояние и актуальные проблемы. – М.: Новое литературное обозрение [Mitrokhin N. Russian Orthodox Church: *State of arts and relevant problems* (Moscow: NLO)].

Модзалевский, Л.Н. [1866] (2000) Очерк истории воспитания и обучения с древнейших до наших времен. Соч. в 2-х тт. (СПб, Алетейя) [Modzalevsky L. N. Essay on the History of Education and Didactics from Ancient Times until Today (St.Petersburg, Aleteya)].

Niebuhr Richard (1951) *Christ and Culture* (New York, Harper & Row).

Пинкевич В.К. (2001) Церковь и государственная политика в отношении образования в конце XIX – начале XX в./Государство, религия, церковь в России и за рубежом. Информационно-аналитический бюллетень №3 (27) – Москва: Изд-во РАГС. – С.69–78 [Pinkevich V.K. Church and State Politics in Education at the end of XIX- beginning of XX cc., in: State, Religion Church in Russia and Abroad: The informational-analytic bulletin, 3 (27), (Moscow,RAGS).

История педагогики и образования. От зарождения воспитания в первобытном обществе до конца XX в.: Учеб. пособие/Под. ред. А.И. Пискунова (2005). – М.: ТЦ Сфера [Piskunov A.I. (Ed.) The History of Pedagogy and Education from the Origin in Primitive Society till the End of XX c. (Moscow, Sphera)].

Записки Петербургских Религиозно-философских собраний 1901–1903 / Под общ. ред. С.М. Половинкина [1906] (2005) – М.: Республика [Polovinkin S.M. (Ed.) Proceedings of St. Petersburg Religious-Philosophic Assemblies of 1901–1903 (Moscow, Respublika)].

Понкин И.В. (2003) Правовые основы светскости государства и образования. – М.: Про-Пресс [Ponkin I.V. Legal Basics of Secularity of State and Education (Moscow, Pro-Press)].

Розанов В.В. [1901] (1995) Слово Божие в нашем ученьи //*Около церковных стен. Собр. соч.* /Под общ. ред. А.Н. Николюкина. – М.: Республика [Rozanov V.V. Word of God in Our Studies, in: A.N. Nikoljukin (Ed.) Nearby Church walls. Collected works (Moscow, Respublika)].

Щипков А. (1998) *Во что верит Россия. Религиозные процессы в постперестроечной России* (курс лекций) – СПб.: Изд. РХГИ [Schipkov A. What Russia believes: Religious processes in post-perestroyka Russia (course of lectures) (St. Petersburg, Russia Christian Institute for Humanities)].

Schmemann A. (1977) *The Historical Road of Eastern Orthodoxy*, Lydia Kesich, tr. (Crestwood, NY, St. Vladimir's Seminary Press).

Александр Шмеман, прот (2005). Дневники 1973–1983. –М.: Русский путь [Schmemann A. *Diary 1973–1983* (Moscow, Russky Put')].

Евгений Шестун, прот. (2001) *Православная педагогика.* – М.: Православная педагогика [Shestun E. *Orthodox Pedagogy* (Moscow, Pravoslavnaya pedagogika)].

Stamoolis J. (1986) *Eastern Orthodox Mission Theology Today* (Maryknoll, N.Y.).

Стоюнин В.Я. [1892] (1991) *Избранные педагогические сочинения.* – М.: Педагогика [Stoyunin V. *Selected pedagogical works* (Moscow, Pedagogika)].

Ушинский К.Д. (1988) //*Педагогические сочинения* в 6-и тт. – М.: Педагогика [Ushinsky K.D. Pedagogical Works (in 6 Volumes). (Moscow, Pedagoguika)].

Зеньковский В. В. [1948] (1991) История русской философии. – Л.: Эго [Zenkovsky V. *The History of Russian Philosophy* (Leningrad, Ego)].

Зеньковский В.В. (1996a) *Педагогика.* – М.: Православный Свято-Тихоновский богословский институт [Zenkovsky V. *Pedagogy* (Moscow, Orthodox Saint-Tikhon Theological Academy)].

Зеньковский, В.В. [1934] (1996b) Проблемы воспитания в свете христианской антропологии (М., Школа-пресс) [Zenkovsky, V. Problems of Formation in the Light of Christian Anthropology (Moscow, Shkola-Press)].

Pille Valk

Religious Education in Estonia[1]

Introduction

Estonia is a small country (45 227 km^2) of 1.35 million people situated on the Eastern coast of the Baltic Sea. The collapse of the Soviet totalitarian regime, the re-establishment of independence, accession to the European Union – these are the milestones of Estonian history during the last twenty years. It has been a time of tremendous changes. After fifty years behind the 'Iron Curtain', Estonians have found themselves in a pluralistic global world. After the years of a 'monotheistic' atheistic ideology experienced for more than two generations, Estonians face a multi-religious world. These changes also comprise religious dynamics in society. During the last twenty years religious interest and activity have undergone a rapid rise followed by a steep fall. In the days of the re-establishment of national independence, when the church was the most trusted institution in society, the popularity of the church increased dramatically. More recently, however, church attendance and membership numbers have fallen significantly and the popularity of the church has been replaced by critical caution, shaped by personal disappointments for many people. This *exodus syndrome* background creates a challenging context for Religious Education (RE) – the school subject that has generated the most passionate debates in educational discussions during the last decade. No doubt the analyses of developments within RE in this context can contribute several colourful supplements to the general scene of RE in Europe and thus, point to issues that need closer inspection, in particular those concerning the main topic of the REDCo project – namely, how can RE contribute to the dialogue and handling of the conflicts between different religions and world views.

The following disquisition begins with a historical preamble to acquaint readers with traditions of RE in Estonia and aims to present in outline some significant factors from the totalitarian, Soviet occupation period. It is hoped that the following description of today's cultural and religious landscape and an outline of state and church relationships will set the stage for a closer look at the current developments of RE in Estonia. This part of the chapter outlines the main trends in the development of the subject and the formation of the legislative framework for it. To complete the picture there follow some comments regarding RE debates in the media. The third part of the chapter is dedicated to the search for a the suitable model of RE for Estonian public schools. Here a contextual approach to define the basis for RE and for a new RE syllabus is introduced. Finally, I will expand upon some research outcomes to present some feedback 'from the field'.

1   The article presents a part of research funded by Estonian Research Foundation grant 5839.

Historical Tradition and the Socio-Political Background of RE

Traditions of RE in Estonia

The history of RE in Estonia is as old as the history of Estonian schooling. Shortly after Estonia – the land dedicated to the Virgin Mary – was conquered by the German and Danish crusaders at the beginning of the 13th century, cathedral, monastic and Latin schools were founded in different towns. Religious instruction made up the core of the studies in these schools to the extent that without it the system would be incomprehensible. . Wider access to education became available for Estonians after the end of the 17th century, when the network of public schools started to expand. To some extent one can say that the public school itself was a child of the Lutheran Church, developed from the idea that every Christian had be able to read the Bible. The formation of Estonian national identity and the national awakening movement in the middle of the 19th century took place in a Christian environment. Up to the end of the 1930s an absolute majority of Estonians belonged to the church. According to the census in 1934, 78% of Estonians identified themselves as Lutherans, 19% of the population belonged to the Orthodox Church. The percentage of non-believers in society was 0.7%. (Eesti Statistika, 1935, p. 126).

RE encountered the first serious challenges in the late 1910s and early 1920s. The Constitution of the newborn Republic of Estonia stipulated the separation of the state and the church as well as of the church and the school. With the formation of a new national school system, heated debates broke out about the place of RE in the school. An inner crisis in the methodology of teaching the subject and strong left-wing influences in first the Asutav Kogu (Constituent Assembly) and then the Riigikogu (Parliament) of Estonia must be mentioned as the background of these debates. Most of the MPs aimed at removing the subject from the school curriculum. After a series of stormy discussions, RE was excluded from primary schools in May 1920. It was preserved in secondary schools as a voluntary subject (Valk, 1997, pp. 22–24).

The decision of Parliament did not coincide with the will of the people. More than 88,000 signatures were collected by supporters of RE for the change of the Primary Schools Act. In the subsequent referendum of 1923 – incidentally, the first referendum in Estonian history – 72% voted for the reintroduction of RE (Eesti Statistika, 1923, pp. 32–33). Thus the subject was again included in the school curricula. However, its status was now different – optional for pupils and teachers but obligatory for schools. In any event, RE required a significant reform.

Great progress in the theory and methodology of RE teaching can be observed between 1920 and 1940. Two people must be mentioned in connection with the reformed RE, both of whom were theologians: Peeter Põld, the first professor of pedagogy of Estonian descent, and Johan Kõpp, the first Estonian professor of Practical Theology and future archbishop of the Lutheran Church. The new approaches took into consideration the psychological peculiarities of pupils and put a stronger emphasis on the child. The aim of RE was to give first-hand knowledge of Christianity and other world religions (particularly at the secondary high- school level) and to support the pupils' moral development. The new methodology pursued the aim of building bridges between the subject of RE and the daily life and world of the pupil.

The nature of RE was subjected to the greatest changes. RE at school was no longer viewed as a 'branch of the church'. The reformed RE was defined as a non-confessional subject. J. Kõpp repeatedly defended the viewpoint that RE should not be turned into a tool of indoctrination with the aim of raising church members (Valk, 1997, p. 85). This marks a clear distinction between RE in school and catechisms in church, without, however, precluding co-operation between schools and churches. Many pastors continued to work as RE teachers (especially at the high school level) and were involved in drawing up the curricula and textbooks for RE.

In the syllabus for RE the aims of the subject were stated in the following way:

1. RE aims to be a means of supporting pupils' moral development into responsible and mature persons.
2. RE is an important factor in insuring the continuity of national culture.
3. RE was required to introduce Christianity as a way of living that could shape people's entire lives, creating the basis for social justice.
4. In interaction with other subjects taught in school, RE aims to enrich pupils' knowledge and spiritual growth.
5. It is necessary to introduce outstanding personalities from Biblical stories, from church history and from world religions as possible examples that can support pupils' personal growth.
6. The questions of the relationships between religion and science must be openly discussed in RE lessons.

Close attention was paid to the personality of the RE teacher. It was found that s/he should be a Christian, a person with a high degree of sensibility, whose role was to accompany and supportively guide pupils' development. S/he must be able to find a creative and personal way of teaching (Valk, 2000b, p. 98).

The most significant distinction of the reformed RE was the fact that in subsequent years the classes of voluntary RE were attended by almost all pupils, among whom the subject enjoyed an average or even higher-than-average popularity (Valk, 1997, pp. 120-123).

Shadows of the Soviet Past

It is impossible to understand the current developments of religiosity and attitudes regarding religious issues in Estonian society as well the debates around RE, without a closer look at the years of Soviet times in Estonia.

The normal development of the Church and RE was broken by the Soviet occupation that began in 1940. Religious Education was banned in schools.[2] Under Soviet occupation, atheistic ideology was enforced in Estonia. By means of repressive measures, the Church and Christian faith were banned from social life, Church property was confis-

2   Riigi Teataja [State Herald], 1940/102, Art. 1011.

cated, and the Theological Faculty at Tartu University was closed. In the 1970s, fewer than 10% of the population openly admitted to being Christians.

Official communist ideology saw religion as, 'the opium of the people', serving the interests of exploiters and meant to coerce working people to obedience. Everything connected with religion was sentenced to be abolished from Soviet society. All youth organisations were forbidden as well all children's and youth work performed by churches (Raid, 1978, p. 136). A notable increase in the organization of atheistic propaganda began in the end of 1950s. Courses in atheism became a compulsory part of university education in the 1960s (Valk, 2000a, pp. 78–93). Atheist education at schools explained religion as being a relic, something old-fashioned and stupid, meant only for old women and having no place in the modern and scientific world. Careful censorship withdrew all the positive influences of Christianity, Church, and other religions from the discourses on culture and history. Almost all people over 35 (the generation of the pupils' parents and also teachers!) have experienced the influence of such strong atheistic education.

An important task was to avoid all possible contacts of children and young people with believers. A systematic and persevering atheistic campaign of enlightenment, supported by the totalitarian regime, made much progress in Estonia, and the Church was pressed into a 'ghetto-situation'. This development can be illustrated by the fall in the membership of the Estonian Evangelic Lutheran Church. Its 874,026 members formed 78,8% of the Estonian population in 1934: in 1986 EELC had 48 590 members which made up only about 3% of the population (Veem, 1988, p. 348; Eesti A & O, 1993, p. 94). Also remarkable were the changes in the percentage of church rites. If we compare the figures of 1933 and 1975, the tendencies are quite clear: the percentage of children baptised fell from 77% to 11%; of church weddings from 78% to 2,8%; of funerals from 97% to 37% (ibid).

As a result religion was shifted into a very deep private sphere. Most of the people were distanced from the church. For them church was not a normal part of everyday life and religion became a distant memory of an alien past. It was widely accepted that to be educated meant to be unreligious. Peoples' knowledge about religion increasingly contained many prejudicial assumptions, often totally lacking in objective facts. To some extent the features are similar to the Russian situation, described in the previous chapter of this book.

Present Context

Cultural and Religious Landscape in Estonia

Estonia is not a culturally homogeneous country. People from more than 100 nationalities live here. Data from the year 2005[3] chart the picture of the different nationalities living in Estonia as the following: Estonians make up 2/3 of the total population of The Estonian Republic. The second largest group are Russians (26%), followed by Ukrainians (2%), Byelorussians and Finns (both 1%).

---

3   URL: http://pub.stat.ee (accessed 18 October 2006).

Regionally the composition of different nationalities varies remarkably. In Ida-Virumaa, the industrial region in North-East of Estonia, the percentage of Russian speaking population is almost 80%. In the capital, Tallinn, more than 1/3 of inhabitants are Russians. By contrast, on the Estonian islands, Russians make up only 1% of the population.

The significance of today's situation becomes more obvious if we compare it with the situation before Soviet occupation. Prior to World War II Estonians made up 88,2% and Russians 8,2% of population.[4] One of the reasons behind these changes is the national policy of Soviet authorities through its support for migration into the occupied territories. Although the tensions between Estonians and Russian minority members are not as sharp as they were in the later years of the Soviet period, the problem has remained. Surveys conducted during recent years have demonstrated permanent distrust among native Estonians regarding Russian politics, and the involvement in this by the local Russian minority. (Vihalem & Lauristin, 1997, p. 282–283). Vihalem and Lauristin resume:

> 'Even when small nations like Estonians have their own states, the small nation remains vulnerable to the political and cultural expansionism of big nations, especially, if they have enclaves of these big nations on their own territory. The crucial problem is whether the Russian minority, which in the near past represented "a big brother", has developed an identity of its own, embedded in the given territorial-historical environment which they share with the majority, or whether this Russian minority still represents, not only for others but also for themselves, "mother Russia" and her collective interests' (ibid.).

Above all, the issue of majority-minority relationships in Estonia needs attention also from the viewpoint of RE. Here the researches in the framework of the REDCo project can provide new data. Thus, it is also necessary to carry out surveys in Russian speaking schools in Estonia. It might bring forward interesting comparisons, especially with similar surveys in Russia.

Estonia has not jet experienced a wave of new immigrants. But on the other hand – open borders in the European Union have provided, for many Estonians, possibilities of work abroad, where the issues of cultural and religious diversity are much more a part of everyday life than at home.

Today's religious landscape in Estonia is pluralistic. During the last ten years, the decade of societal transformation, the religious interest and activity of Estonians have undergone a rapid rise followed by a steep fall. In the days of the re-establishment of national independence, when the church was the most trusted institution in society, (Kui kristlik on Eestimaa?, 1997, p. 43), the popularity of the church shot up. The popularity of the church peaked in 1992. Today, we see that the enthusiasm has fallen (Valk, 2003b, p. 112–113).

According to the last census from 2000, 29% of the Estonian population identified themselves as believers (Census, 2000). The following table gives a general overview about the main religious groups.

---

4   URL: http://www.estonica.org/est/lugu.html (accessed 1 December 2006).

Table 1: Religious landscape in today's Estonia (persons aged 15 and above)

Lutherans	152 000 (14%)
Orthodox	144 000 (13%)
Baptists	6 000
Roman-Catholics	6 000
Jehovah Witnesses	4 000
Pentecostals	2 600
Old Believers	2 500
Adventists	1 500
Muslims	1 400
Taara- or Earth Believers (New pagan movement)	1 000
Atheists	69 000 (6%)
People without religious affiliation	382 000 (34%)
Missing data	343 000 (31%)
Total	1 121 600

There are some significant differences in the religious landscape, when coming down to the local context. 30% of the Orthodox people live in the North-East part of Estonia, where almost every third person is an Orthodox and only one of twenty belongs to the Lutheran church. The majority of Russian Old Believers (82%) are concentrated in the villages on the coast of the Peipsi Lake where their predecessors have lived already for centuries. In the South-East part of Estonia, in historical Setomaa, the Orthodox Church has made a deep cultural impact in people's lives throughout the last millennium. Estonian Muslims are mostly descendants of Tatars who came to Estonia on the 18th century.

Different sociological studies paint a picture of the attitudes of the Estonians towards issues related to religion and faith. In this area, it is difficult to draw final conclusions due to the lack of a representative, broad-sample study. Rather, all the conclusions on religious attitudes are attempts to form a mosaic picture out of scattered pieces.

One of the most debated and referenced studies on the subject is a query called, 'Of Life, Faith and Faith Life' (Hansen, 2000) held by the Estonian Council of Churches, the Estonian Bible Society and the Estonian Evangelisation Alliance in 1995 and 2000 (2,910 and 1,092 respondents, respectively). It appears from the query that the percentage of the official membership of Christian churches does not necessarily reflect people's attitude towards Christianity, namely, that the share of those favourably disposed towards Christianity is greater than the share of those registered as members of a particular church. It is also interesting to draw attention to the differences in the attitudes between Estonians and Russians. The question, 'Regardless of whether you have joined a church or not, do you consider yourself...' received the responses presented in Table 2:

Table 2: Attitudes towards Christianity among the Estonians and the Russians in 1995 and 2000 (Hansen, 2000)

Regardless of whether you have joined a church or not, do you consider yourself ...	Estonians (%)		Russians (%)	
	1995	2000	1995	2000
a convinced Christian	9	11	25	35
well disposed to Christianity	51	47	50	44
indifferent to Christianity	32	32	22	19
well disposed to atheism	6	8	2	1.2
a convinced atheist	2	2.2	1	1.4

Thus, more than a half of the respondents claimed to be believers or well disposed towards Christianity. Conspicuous differences between Estonians and Russians regarding their attitudes towards Christianity (correspondingly 58% and 79%) are remarkable. The phenomenon of 'believing without belonging' seems to be the case with many Estonians. The findings from H. Heino's query (conducted in 1992 and 1998), according to which 40% of the Estonians considered themselves Lutherans (Liiman, 2001), support the statement. If we compare this percentage with the number of people connected officially with the EELC (204 602 in 1992 and 174 349 in 1998, in each year constituting 13% of population), we see that the difference is not inconsiderable. Many people seem to view formal connection with the church as part of national identity. The considerably higher rate of Christians among the Russians could be interpreted in a similar way – the Orthodox Church might play a notable role in the identity of this minority group.

However, a favourable disposition towards Christianity does not necessarily coincide with Christian activity. From the query, 'Of Life, Faith and Faith Life' for 2000, the following characteristics of religious practice can be set forth.

Table 3: Religious practice among the Estonians and the Russians in Estonia 2000 (Hansen, 2000)

Statements about religious practice	Estonians (%)	Russians (%)
I never go to church	32	43
I go to church once or twice a year	49	33
I go to church every week	3	5
I never pray	45	34
I pray every day	16	30
I never read the Bible	41	44
I read the Bible every day	3	4

Considering the relatively broad backing for Christianity on the one hand and the small official church membership and low activity in religious practice on the other, it appears that many people have not translated their religious attitudes into action.

In the area of religion, Estonia holds a very specific place among the other European countries. It is probably one of the most secularized countries in Europe. The investigation of European values, performed in 1999/2000 (Halman et al, 2005) indicated that people in Estonia are most conspicuous with regard to their alienation from traditional religion. Here the percentage of non-members of the church was the highest – at about 75% (ibid, p. 72).

The Eurobarometer survey, 'Social Values, Science and Technology', conducted at the beginning of 2005 adds some eloquent details to the mosaic. One of the questions in the query dealt with the nature of religious beliefs. In Estonia less than one in five declares that they believe in God (16%). By contrast, more than one in two Estonians (54%) believes there is some sort of spirit or life force. At the same time, more than half of all EU citizens believe there is a God (52%) and more than a quarter (27%) believe there is some sort of spirit or life force (Eurobarometer 225, p. 9).

In her study of the religious dynamics in Estonian society during the second half of the 20th century, L. Altnurme concludes: 'We already have a developing third generation, most of whom have no knowledge that would help them understand the meaning of many works of literature, music and art in the context of centuries-old traditions. They also do not possess the knowledge they would need to help them communicate adequately with the representatives of other religions and understand them in today's pluralistic cultural situation and globalized world, be they in the same neighbourhood or on the other side of the globe. The lack of religious education has condemned the religious development of the human being, even though human beings have a native ability and need for this. And although people nowadays also have religious experiences, they are largely unable to express and interpret them' (Altnurme, 2006, p. 306).

No doubt, the context described above brings into the open many challenges for developing RE in schools belonging to such a transient society.

Summing up the main consequences for RE rising from Estonian cultural and religious landscape, one can point on the following issues:

1. RE has to take into consideration the cultural diversity within the country.
2. The question of how RE can contribute to the growth of mutual understanding between Estonian and Russian communities has to be worked through. These aspects need to be reflected also in the RE syllabus.
3. A remarkably high percentage of Estonian people are alienated from the traditional forms of religion and from the Church.
4. A lack of basic knowledge about religions and widespread religious illiteracy raise problems of communication both, for fruitful discussions about RE in the society, and for the teaching of RE.

State and Church Relationships

According to the Constitution of the Republic of Estonia, accepted on the referendum in 1992:

> § 12: Everyone is equal before the law. No one shall be discriminated against on the basis of /.../religion /.../grounds. The incitement of national, racial, religious or political hatred, violence or discrimination shall, by law, be prohibited and punishable.

> § 40: Everyone has freedom of conscience, religion and thought. Everyone may freely belong to churches and religious societies. There is no state church. Everyone has the freedom to exercise his or her religion, both alone and in community with others, in public or in private, unless this is detrimental to public order, health or morals.[5]

These statements do not forbid cooperation between the state and churches in different areas, RE included.

Fruitful contacts between government officials and the Lutheran Church led to the formation of the joint commission in 1995. In the co-operation agreement RE is mentioned as one of the fields where parties are interested in co-operating.[6] RE is also mentioned in the protocol of joint interests, signed in 2002 between the Estonian Council of Churches and the Estonian Government.[7] Both, EELC and ECC have formulated their official positions regarding RE. In these documents RE is acknowledged as a subject in which dialogue and understanding may be developed between different worldviews, while fundamentalism, discrimination and intolerance may be resisted. Clauses point to the importance of RE in identity building, moral development and in preparing pupils for life in a pluralistic, globalized world. It is agreed that RE in school cannot be seen as proselytizing and, in developing RE, a wider dialogue with different groups in society and between representatives of different religions, is needed. The ECC has organised round-table discussions on the issues of RE, bringing together, Church leaders, representatives from the Ministries of Education, Internal Affairs and Theological High Schools.

Representatives of the Churches are involved in the work of the RE council by the State Examination and Qualification centre. This council deals with RE syllabus developments, teaching-learning resources, and serves as a link between RE teachers and High Schools, who train teachers for the subject.

In fact, it can be said that churches have been the main spokespersons and supporters for developing RE. For one thing, much of the work that has been done in developing RE has been possible thanks to them, although it is the ECC's financial support which has helped to work out teaching-learning resources for RE classes. The churches have also organised several surveys on RE. But on the other hand, this situation has created public accusations regarding RE of being, as it were, 'a branch of the Church', and thus, not suitable for schools.

---

5   URL: Constitution of the Republic of Estonia. http://www.legaltext.ee/text/en/X0000.htm. (accessed 18 October 2006).

6   URL: http://www.eelk.ee/konsistoorium.php (accessed 18 October 2006).

7   URL: http://www.ekn.ee/dokumendid/vv_ekn_yhishuvi_17.10.02.pdf (accessed 18 October 2006).

RE in Current-day Estonian Schools

After setting the scene up to this point, let me now turn more concretely to the developments of RE in today's Estonia.

The period of revival time during the late 1980s brought about new possibilities for teaching RE again in Estonian schools. The first RE lessons, initiated by some school headmasters, were held in 1989/90. It was a period of great expectations, religious activity and hopes. Many schools were interested in the new subject and at the beginning of the 1990s RE was taught in approximately 100 schools, most of which (70) were primary schools (Valk, 2000a, p. 85).[8] The beginning was promising. But very soon the problems began to occur. The first challenge RE had to face was the lack of experience of teaching the subject. Several teachers who went to school had only very limited experiences from, work in church Sunday Schools (also a new thing for most of them!). Some schools invited local pastors to teach RE. But many pastors did not have pedagogical experiences. This situation has been made more complicated also by some negative experiences. When schools became open to RE, many eager people, without pedagogical experience and professional skills rushed to teach it. Unfortunately however, individual failures have been exaggerated and generalized.

RE teacher training was begun in 1989/1999 by the Theological Institute of the Lutheran Church in the form of distance learning. Important help was provided by the Finnish Lutheran Church. At the beginning of the 1990s four groups of Estonians were given the possibility of studying theology and RE didactics in Finland. Among them were also several teachers, who began teaching RE in schools. When the first graduates completed their studies in the re-opened Faculty of Theology in Tartu University in 1995, it became possible to start also with an RE teacher training program in the University. RE teacher training programs were also developed in denominational theological Seminars (Valk & Lehtsaar, 2003, p. 104–106).

With regard to teaching-learning resources one can best describe the situation in the beginning of 1990 as *in the beginning there a teacher and her/his word.* It was typical, that resources for teaching RE consisted of the teacher's own Bible and perhaps one book of Bible stories for the whole class. The first great assistance came again from the Finnish Lutheran Church and teachers of RE. With money, collected there, four RE textbooks for Gymnasium students were translated and published in 1990–1991. As a sign of the times they could be published only as books for confirmation studies. Regardless of this status, the books became widely used in schools. Of great help for primary RE teachers was the translation, from the Finnish, of the RE teacher's manual, 'The Good Shepherd', organised by the Sunday School Union of the Lutheran Church. The first original textbooks for RE appeared at the end of 1990s. Bible and Church History textbooks were written by Toomas Jürgenstein, one of the first graduates of the Faculty of Theology, working at the time as an RE teacher in one of the best Estonian gymnasiums.

The first syllabuses for RE were worked out in 1991 and 1993. Regarding the approach, the syllabus from 1997 follows the same line. It is not surprising that Finnish in-

---

8   Total number of schools in these years was around 750.

fluences were recognisable in all of them. The syllabuses saw RE as a subject which is taught through all the school grades. Among the topics Christianity was granted the major attention. In reality these syllabuses were not suitable for use in schools. First, only a very few schools found it possible to organise RE classes for all grades. Thus teachers had to work out their own syllabuses, taking into consideration different situations in different schools. As a result it became more and more complicated to prepare suitable resources for RE classes and to follow common standards in teaching the subject. Secondly, the strong emphasise on Christianity began to arouse critical public concerns. Critical attitudes gained more voice with the fall in popularity of the Church.

Today RE is taught in approximately 60 Estonian schools out of more than 600, mostly in primary classes and in Gymnasia. School headmasters have argued about this marginal status of RE, pointing to the low interest of pupils, a shortage of time and the lack of competent teachers (Valk, 2003a, p. 239–252). It is hard to get the entire picture about the spread of RE in our schools because the subject is often taught under different names and in different forms. It is not an exaggeration to say that even the Ministry of Education and Research has no complete picture of it. Anyway, it became clearer year by year, that the optimism of the early 1990s about common agreement in society to participate in Christian RE did not correspond to reality.

Legislative Framework

The development of the legal status of RE has been quite complicated and accompanied by a lack of clearly founded concepts of the subject and, the religious dynamics in society. The possibility of teaching RE was mentioned for the first time in the 'Act Regarding the Bases of Contemporary Administration of Estonia' that was carried out by the Supreme Council of Estonian Soviet Socialist Republic (ENSV Ülemnõukogu) on the 16.05.1990. The Act proclaimed religious freedom as well as the right to get and to give Religious Instruction ('usuõpetus').[9] A circular of the Ministry of Education, dated 08.03.1991, gave some concrete instructions regarding the organisation of RE classes. Here the term, 'Ecumenical Religious Education' ('usundiõpetus')[10] was used. Schools were recommended to organize RE classes according to the request of pupils and parents when there are competent teachers available. Only teachers, who had passed basic training in Theology and had a certificate from the attestation commission of the Ministry of Education, were accepted to teach RE. The Act of Education, accepted by Parliament in

---

9   Act About the Bases of Contemporary Administration of Estonia [Seadus Eesti valitsemise ajutise korra alustest] on the 16.05.1990. URL: https://www.riigiteataja.ee/ert/act.jsp?id=24030 (accessed 18 October 2006).

10   The Estonian name for the subject RE needs some comments because it has created lots of discussion, often evincing misunderstandings. 'Usuõpetus' (word by word translation 'faith instruction') is the traditional name of the subject in the Estonian language. Unfortunately, the common wide-spread interpretation of the term sees it as narrow Christian instruction ('learning religion'). 'Usundiõpetus' (which might be translated as 'religious education') is often mixed up with the old term. In current discourse the use of the term 'religiooniõpetus' is recommended, especially in the context when speaking about the subject taught on the bases of the new RE syllabus (2003).

1992, determined that the teaching and learning RE is voluntary. Though the first version of the Act of the Basic School and Gymnasium, passed by the Parliament in 1993, did not say anything about RE, this Act, after the supplement, made in 1999, is the main legislative Act regulating the organisation of RE. According to this Act, RE ('usuõpetus') is defined as a non-confessional and optional subject. A new supplement was also made about the obligations of the schools – schools are obliged to organize RE classes when there are 15 pupils interested in this subject per school stage.[11] The last official document dealing with RE is the circular of the Minister of Education from the 17.08.1999 that gives concrete instructions to the schools. Schools were recommended to find possibilities of introducing both the subject and teachers to pupils and parents. There are currently (2006) discussions going on in the Parliamentary Commission of Culture regarding changing the name of the subject in legislative documents. The proposal to clarify obligations on the schools in organizing RE classes lies also on the table. 17 Members of Parliament made a proposal to solve the above mentioned problems and also to make RE a compulsory subject in Gymnasia in October 2006. After the first round of negotiations with Ministries the proposal was rejected.

To conclude the list of legislative documents connected with RE, one has to mention the official requirements for teachers' professional standards that were inaugurated in 2000. According to these standards all teachers have to pass both subject and pedagogical training, equivalent to the 300 ETCE credit points.

Summing up this development process of the legislative framework for RE we can draw out the following main points:

1. RE is a non-confessional optional subject. Learning RE is voluntary. In the primary classes parents decide on the participation of their children in RE lessons; older pupils make decision by themselves.

2. Schools are obliged to organize RE classes on the demands of pupils or their parents. It is suggested that parents and pupils should be informed about the aims and nature of RE and be introduced to the teacher before they can make their decision

3. There is no alternative subject to RE for the pupils who don't attend RE classes to get knowledge about world religions and ethics.

4. For RE teachers, both theological as well pedagogical, training is needed.

At the same time several problems can be pointed to. Concrete instructions for schools, given by Ministry of Education circulars, can be considered as only recommendations. Unfortunately the development of RE has been influenced also by personal attitudes of different Ministries of Education. If a person who is positive towards RE holds the post, he has paid attention for concrete steps to organize it. If a Minister's viewpoint is different, it will shape the attitudes of other officials as well. It means that insufficiency of higher-level legislative documents leaves several aspects in organizing RE open. How and when to find out interested pupils? Who has concrete responsibility to do it? How can schools guarantee RE classes when there are not enough teachers? What are the obligations of schools in finding RE teachers? How is the status of RE as a voluntary subject

---

11   There are 4 stages in Estonian School system: I stage grades 1.–3.; II stage grades 4.–6.; III stage grades 7.–9.; IV stage (Gymnasium) grades 10.–12.

to be interpreted? Who is responsible for developing RE curricula? A lot of confusion is connected also to the different use and common interpretation of the name of the subject. 'Usuõpetus' and 'Usundiõpetus' are often understood as narrow Christian Instruction. More neutral 'Religiooniõpetus' is not officially mentioned in legislative documents.

As a result, in real school life, it is often headmasters who decide whether RE will be taught in their schools or not. Thus, the state of RE often depends on their personal attitudes and initiative. One has to mention one more detail – the majority of current teachers and principals belong to the generation whose education was influenced by the strong atheistic paradigm of Soviet educational system. Often it means both lack of knowledge and prejudice on religious questions.

Thus it is not very surprising that the issues of RE meet cool acceptance also in the Ministry of Education and Research where its official position is to give preference for spreading topics about religion among different school subjects (Literature, History, etc) instead of having RE as a separate subject in the curriculum.[12]

Religion and RE in the Media – A Hot Topic

Developments in RE during the last 15 years have been accompanied by sharp and passionate debates. RE has been probably one of the most vividly discussed educational questions in the public media (Valk, 1999; 2006). The longest debate took place in the spring and summer of 2003, when it was a daily topic in all the main newspapers and internet chat sites for 10 weeks. One demonstration was even organised by people who were against RE. The event was also presented in the TV evening news program Thus, everybody could see that the demonstration had about ten to fifteen participants (Valk, 2006a, p. 141). Debate began when the daily newspaper 'Postimees' published on the front page an article about RE and averted (actually without any grounds) that RE would become a compulsory school subject in 2007. A closer look at the debates in DELFI, one of the most well-known Internet portals in Estonia, offers some insights into the scope of these discussions.

DELFI[13] launched a special rubric of columns to raise discussion on topical current affairs in February 2000. Columns on religious topics were published weekly. The following table offers an overview of the number of comments sent to DELFI columns during a period of eighteen months (2003 – June 2004). The data has been collected from the portal's archive. Table 6 presents a number of columns on religious and all other topics (N), the means and medians of the numbers of comments given to the columns, the minimum and maximum numbers of comments.

---

12   According guidances were given to the working groups who prepared the new National Curriculum in Spring 2006.

13   URL for DELFI: http://www.delfi.ee (accessed 18 October 2006).

Table 6: Comments on DELFI columns January 2003–June 2004

Topics	N	Mean	Median	min/max
Religious topics	75	2 318	2 239	537/8 165
All other topics	541	118	78	2/976

This data shows clearly that religion has been by far the most popular discussion topic in DELFI. The difference in the number of comments is about 20 times (!). The constant high attention to religious topics is also evident from the fact that the mean (2,318) and median (2,239) of this variable are quite close. The maximum number of comments was written during four days in the column, 'Evolution or Creation' (published in 19 June 2003).

Reading these comments, one recognises that a remarkable majority of them are critical, and sometimes even sacrilegious.

The main critical statements could be grouped into the following series:

1. **Religion and violence**: The spread of Christianity is strongly connected with violence (the crusades, inquisition, witch trials etc). The history of Christianity is permeated with violence. In other words Christians preach love and goodness, but the ways of reaching this are violent.
2. **Religion and Science are in conflict**. Christianity is full of contradictions. Religion obstructs the development of science.
3. **Religion and legislation**: RE is a violation of human rights. The church tries to increase its membership unfairly by using RE.
4. **Religion and morality**: Christianity creates hypocrisy. Religion has nothing to do with morality.
5. **Religion and personal life**: Religion is a way to escape from real life – it is *'the opium of the people'*. It is only for weak people. Religion obstructs the free development of the individual. The Church prohibits doubts and nonconformity.

It is interesting to note that all of these statements were among the truisms of the atheistic propaganda widely promoted during the years of the Soviet occupation.

In spite of this dominantly critical picture in anonymous Internet sites, there is some evidence that the general attitudes in society are more balanced and positive (Valk, 2006, pp. 166–186). In the context of the current article it is worth pointing out the results of the poll carried out among the students of humanities in Tartu University in 2004. The general aim for this poll was to gather empirical data about the influence of Religious Studies upon students' positions regarding religion. The questionnaire with several statements about religion was completed by students twice – before and after the studies about Christianity (accordingly 276 and 324 respondents). The analyses of the data brought forward the following results (ibid):

The rate of disagreement rose about the following statements:

1. The history of Christianity is soaked through with violence;
2. Religious canons demand unconditional obedience;
3. Religion obstructs the development of Science;
4. Religion obstructs the free development of people;

5. Science liberates people from religious trammels.
6. The positions of Christianity clash with contemporary Science.

The rate of agreement rose about the following statements:
1. Every human being believes in something.
2. Believers are morally better people than others.

Thus, there might be some hope that RE can contribute to more balanced positions regarding religious issues and can also offer some help against slighting religious prejudice.

But what use might there be from analysing hundreds of thousands of comments on religious topics on the Internet? I found that such debates help to identify important topics for RE – where the most burning questions and problems are, which argumentation is used, where the prejudices show up and where there are signs of 'missing files' in knowledge.

Contextual Approach to RE

Model of Contextual Analyses

Problems around the developments of RE in Estonia in all their complexity are a serious challenge. How to find bases for the subject, how to find some starting points, how to choose learning contents, how to set up aims for studies, how to overcame prejudges regarding the subject etc, etc. Altogether, in other words – there is a need for a clear well grounded concept of contemporary RE, which is suitable for the public schools in a very secularised society like Estonia and which is spellbinding in order to motivate pupils to participate in the classes of the optional subject (if the school timetable is very intensive already).

Working on the concept of RE adjusted to a concrete situation, I have suggested a model of a contextual approach to RE that offers a complex model on how to determine the basis for RE in any particular society.

To be meaningful, RE must be targeted. It has to address pupils' specific needs and expectations, deal with pupils' questions and problems and take into consideration the particular society in which it is taught. This constitutes the context of the instruction. Thus, I argue that context should be an important ingredient of RE. In developing the concept of the contextuality of RE, I draw on the ideas presented by Finnish colleague K.Tamminen (1982). The term 'context' here refers to the social and cultural environment in which RE is conducted. For analytical purposes, it is possible to distinguish between different aspects of this context.

Figure 1: Model for Contextual Approach to Determine the Bases for RE

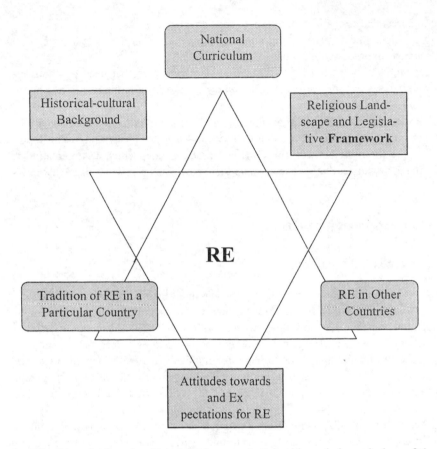

1. **The historical and cultural background** – provides a balanced view of the impact of religions on the historical and cultural development of society.
2. **The religious landscape and legislative framework** – charts the role and influence of various denominations and religions represented in society; legislation related to religious issues must also be taken into consideration.
3. **Attitudes towards and expectations for RE** – acknowledges peoples' expectations, fears, prejudices, etc.
4. **The traditions of RE in a particular country** – helps to learn from positive and, especially, from negative experiences.
5. **The developments in and experiences of RE in other countries** – emphasises the importance of creative contemplation of the experiences of others.
6. **RE, the national curriculum and the challenges that education must face in today's world** – acknowledges the confluences and aims of education in general and RE in particular.

The outcomes of the analyses of the various aspects help to identify the emphasis of, and the main problems related to, RE and choose suitable teaching methods – to create the research-based foundation for RE (Valk, 2002).

RE Syllabus

Recent versions of the RE syllabus[14] are worked out on the bases of the contextual analyses. Basic principles of the teaching of the subject state that RE must be taught in accordance with the respect towards Human rights, and the freedom of religion and consciousness. It is stated that RE could not be used for proselytising. RE is seen as a sphere in which dialogue and understanding may be developed between different worldviews while fundamentalism, discrimination and intolerance should be resisted. RE is contextualised also with the contributions of moral and value education. Taking into consideration the deep impact of religions in culture – literature, music, and art etc. – it is noted that knowledge about religions is a necessary precondition to understanding the world's cultural heritage.

The following are listed as the main targets of RE:

1. The provision of knowledge about different religions, worldviews and cultures is a means towards religious literacy that in turn offers a key to understanding cultural heritage.
2. The development of an open identity, i.e. that pupils know their own culture and also get to know others, so as to create the bases for mutual understanding and tolerance.
3. The development of religious literacy as a precondition to dialogue, in order to help overcome national and religious conflicts.
4. Acknowledgement and evaluation of spiritual values.
5. The development of critical attitudes towards mass culture and consumerism.
6. The development of social and ecological awareness and responsibility.
7. To support pupils' moral development.
8. The development of the skills necessary for acknowledged and responsible choices and the development of one's own worldview.

Developing the RE syllabus in the situation, where some schools offer RE only in the first grades, some only in gymnasium, and where there are very few schools with RE in all of the grades, is a complicated issue. At the moment the problem is solved in the way that the syllabus contains more fixed 'core courses' and 'optional courses'. The system is described in figure 2.

---

14   URL: http://www.religiooniopetus.ee (accessed 18 October 2006).

Figure 2: Structure of the syllabus ('Unity in Diversity' model)

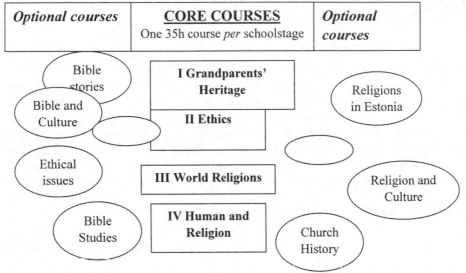

Core courses have more detailed and determined content, but the teacher and the pupils themselves might still design 20% of its content. It opens up the possibility of taking pupils' problems and local context more into consideration. In designing optional courses teachers have more freedom. Basic principles and main targets of the subject form a frame for the course, but the concrete content is for teachers and pupils to decide about. As is indicated with the empty circles on the scheme, the list of possible optional courses is not closed.

Some Feedback from Surveys

To test the eligibility of the concept of the RE described above, I conducted two researches in 2004–2005. The first one was connected to the pilot project of the new RE syllabus that was tested in 16 schools. The research had two target groups – upper secondary school students and the parents of the primary school pupils whose children participated in RE classes.

Let's take a look at the results from the upper secondary school students. Questions about the religious affiliation of students gave the following picture: 92% of students had no connection to any religious community. On the other hand, 25% of them said that religion is important to them. For 9% of respondents religion was very important. 59% of them agreed on the usefulness of RE classes, two thirds said that things learned in RE lessons have been useful in other school subjects as well. In media debates RE is often blamed for brainwashing. Students did not share this accusation – only 5% of them agreed with the statement that, 'sometimes they have felt that the teacher is pressing his/her opinions upon pupils'. Students were asked to evaluate different topics for RE

classes on the Likert scale (1= not interested at all, ... 5 = very interested). The following tables present the Top –10 and Bottom–10 of these interests.

Table 7: Top–10 of students favourite topics for RE

Topics	Average evaluation
Love	4,18
Different ways to interpret the world	4,05
Meaning of life	4,0
Sexuality	3,99
World Religions	3,95
Happiness	3,94
Destiny	3,94
Natural and supernatural	3,88
Relationships between religions	3,85
Is there afterlife?	3,84

Table 8: Bottom–10 of topics for RE

Topics	Average evaluation
Church and congregational life	2,32
Mission	2,34
Christian churches in the world	2,44
Jesus and his life	2,47
Estonian Church History	2,49
Bible stories	2,51
General Church History	2,54
Bible studies	2,58
Christian festivals	2,61
Prayer and praying	2,62

These outcomes show the students as, 'real children of the secularised society' where the
attraction to traditional religious institutions is almost missing. It is quite obvious that the
model of classical confessional RE will not match this context, especially for the optional
subject. I don't want to say that traditional objectives of RE are totally, 'out of time', but
it is quite clear that if we want students to discover the richness of the Christian tradition,
we have to find a starting point, where we will meet the interests and questions of our
pupils. It also demands creativity to find suitable teaching methods and a re-thinking of
learning objectives from the perspective of students. However, the results confirmed the
choice of RE topics in the new RE syllabus – all the main themes gained average evaluation over 3 points.

The inquiry among the primary school pupils' parents (N=187), carried out in spring 2004, lightened their positions about the subject. Answers to the question 'Why did you send your children to RE classes?' were as follows:

- To broaden my child's outlook; It is a normal part of education; It helps to understand different cultures;
- RE teaches us to see things from different perspectives.
- The child was interested in RE.
- It is a means of moral and spiritual education.
- So they may learn something that I missed in my school.

It is interesting to note also that parents did not agree with the main accusation from the media debates where RE is accused of brainwashing and proselytising.

The Social and Marketing Research Company, SaarPoll conducted the second piece of research in 2004–2005. The sample contained 618 upper secondary school students from 23 schools; half of them had started to study RE, the other half not. The research had two rounds – first questionnaires were fulfilled in the autumn and the survey was repeated in the spring. The main aim of the research was to chart the attitudes of the students regarding RE and religion in general, and to find out whether or not RE makes a difference in students' positions regarding religious questions and especially tolerance?

Students with church backgrounds made up 4% of the sample. The question 'How important is religion to you?' got the following replies – 2% for 'very important', 10% for 'quite important', 37% for 'generally not important', 29% for 'not important at all' and 22% for 'I don't know'. The similarity of these percentages with the Pilot-project research is remarkable. The students who studied RE described the classes as mainly positive: 73% found RE interesting, 77% confirmed that they feel getting wiser by participating in RE classes. 83% said that teacher introduced different religions objectively and with respect. Teachers' respect of students and friendliness was evaluated very highly (96%). 88% said that teachers encouraged students to ask questions and present their positions. Although the deeper analyses of the results of this study is in progress, especially concerning the changes of the positions, it is possible to say that, during this short period, between two rounds of questionnaires (6 months) the attitudes of students, who studied RE, changed positively towards tolerance and higher moral standards (Saar, 2005). The survey confirmed strongly that RE is not a brainwashing. It is a subject that should deserve much more attention and support.

Conclusion

The summing up comes out of the previous overview of the developments of RE in Estonia and one can point to the following issues:

1. Although one can mention a considerable degree of high-level agreement about the necessity of RE in society as a whole, RE is still taught in few schools
2. Deep influences of the totalitarian Soviet system and atheistic ideology have left many Estonians without the literacy in religious issues necessary to manage in the contemporary multi-religious and pluralistic world.

3. Weak orientation in world religions and different world views might create problems with the quarantine on observing religious freedom in society. This freedom needs to be based on religious literacy. An optional, marginal subject cannot create the necessary requirements for this issue.

4. One of the main problems obstructing RE in schools arises from the insufficiency of legal documents and the possibility of interpreting them in different ways. RE is defined as an optional subject. On the one hand schools are obliged to organise RE classes, but on the other hand there are insufficient possibilities for fulfilling this law (lack of teachers and free lessons in school timetable etc).

Today's changing world creates new challenges for RE. In a secularised society, where religious traditions lose more and more adherents, RE has the task of 'bridge-builder' – to help pupils to find access to the rich heritage of religious traditions. In the plural global world simple indoctrination or introduction into particular religious tradition is not enough for schools in many cases. Concrete models of RE need to be developed from the concrete context, taking seriously into consideration the questions and problems of pupils. Co-operation in the REDCo project offers fruitful possibilities for such analyses. Hopefully the model of contextual analyses, presented in this current article, can serve here as one of the examples for finding new fresh perspectives for this, 'little subject with the great aims'.

References

Altnurme, L. (2006) *Kristlusest oma usuni* (Tartu, Tartu Ülikooli kirjastus).

Eesti A & O [Estonia from A to Ω] (1993). (Tallinn, Eesti Entsüklopeediakirjastus).

Eesti Statistika [Estonian Statistics] (1923), (Tallinn, Riigi Statistika Keskbüroo).

Eesti Statistika [Estonian Statistics] (1935), (Tallinn, Riigi Statistika Keskbüroo).

Eesti Vabariigi Haridusseadus [Act of Education if the Estonian Republic]. Riigi Teataja 1992,12, 192.

Eurobarometer 225 'Social values, Science & Techniology'. Report. URL: http://europa.eu.int/comm/public_opinion/archives/ebs/ebs_225_report_en.pdf. (accessed 30 August 2006).

Halman, L., Luijkx, R. & Zundert van, M. (2005) *Atlas of European Values* (Koninklijke Brill NV and Tilburg University).

Hansen, H. (2000) *Religioonisotsioloogilise küsitluse 'Elust, usust ja usuelust II' tulemused* (Tallinn).

Kui kristlik on Eestimaa? [How Christian is Estonia?] (1997) (Tallinn, Eesti Evangelisatsiooni Allianss).

Liiman, R. (2001) *Usklikkus muutuvas Eesti ühiskonnas* (Tartu).

Raid, L. (1978) *Vabamõtlejate ringidest massilise ateismini. Marksistlik ateism Eestis aastatel 1900–1965* (Tallinn, Eesti Raamat).

Riigi Teataja [State Herald] (1940), 102, Art. 1011.

Riigi Teataja [State Herald] I 2000, 87, 575.

Riigi Teataja [State Herald] I 2002, 107, 640.

Riigi Teataja [State Herald] I 2002, 105, 626.

Saar, A. (2005) *Religiooniõpetuse kvalitatiivuuring*. Materials for the presentation about the results of the poll among upper secondary school students. (Tallinn, SaarPoll, manuscript).

Tamminen. K. (1982) *Kuidas õpetan usuõpetust?* (Tallinn).

Valk, P. (1997) *Ühest heledast laigust Eesti kooli ajaloos* (Tallinn, Logos).

Valk, P. (1999) About Some Atttudes Towards the Church and Religion in nowadays Estonia. in: Kulmar. T. ja Dietrich, M. (Eds.) *Religionen in der sich ändernden Welt* (Münster)147–156.

Valk, P. (2000a) From Soviet Atheism to National Identity – a Specific Background for Religious Education in Estonia, *Panorama*, 78–93.

Valk, P. (2000b) Johan Kõpp ja kooli usuõpetus, in: R. Altnurme (ed.). *Johan Kõpp 125* (Tartu, Eesti Kirikuloo Selts), 58–70.

Valk, P. (2002) *Eesti kooli religiooniõpetuse kontseptsioon* (Tartu, Tartu Ülikooli kirjastus).

Valk, P. & Lehtsaar, T. (2003) Developments of Practical Theology in Today's Estonia. International, *Journal of Practical Theology* 7 (1), 101–130.

Valk, P (2003a) Religious Education Through the Eyes of Pupils, Teachers and Headmasters, in: Dietrich, M. & Kulmar, T. (Eds.) *Die Bedeutung der Religion für Gesellschaften in der Vergangenheit und Gegenwart,* FRAG, Band 36. (Münster, Ugarit-Verlag), 239–252.

Valk, P. (2006) Churches and European Integration. A Challenge for Religious Educaiton in the Post-Social Context. *Kirchliche Zeitgeschichte* 19,1, 166–186.

Valk, P. (2006a) Is There Something More Than Crusades, Iquisition and *Opium of People?* Gutmane, S. (Ed.) *Zinatniskie Raksti 1. Proceedings 1 of the Latvian Christian Academy* (Latvias Kristiga akademija), 141 – 158.

Veem, K. (1988) *Eesti Vaba Rahvakirik* (Stockholm, Eesti Vaimulik Raamat).

Vihalemm, T., Lauristin, M. (1997) Cultural Adjustment to the Changing Societal Enviroment: The Case of Russians in Estonia, in: Lauristin, M., Vihalemm, P., Rosengren, K. E. Weibull, L. (Eds.) *Return to the Western World. Cultural and Political Perspectives on the Estonian Post-Communist transition.* (Tartu University Press), 279–298.

Robert Jackson and Kevin O'Grady

Religions and Education in England

Social Plurality, Civil Religion and Religious Education Pedagogy

Introduction

In England, religious groups have been involved since the nineteenth century in partnership with the state in the provision of schools and the curriculum subject of religious education. Institutionally, the Church of England holds a privileged place as the established church. Changes in society have led to more equality within education between religious traditions, initially for the Roman Catholic and Jewish communities and more recently for other traditions.

These changes included increasing secularisation in the 1960s and 1970s; and the pluralisation of society, mainly through migration. Britain has had long experience of migration and settlement of peoples, especially from former colonies in South Asia, Africa and the Caribbean. In the light of the 2001 census data, considered together with figures on regular church attendance, Britain might be described as a society combining various kinds of Christian, secular and multifaith elements.[1]

With regard to accommodating religious diversity in schools, some schools now provide prayer spaces and dietary diversity. Occasionally the wish to take pupils out of school, for visits to ancestral family homes, for example, has been seen as a problem in the press. Problems have arisen in locations where local demography has determined that some schools in poor areas have an almost entirely white population, while nearby schools have a predominantly Muslim population of South Asian origin.[2] The issue of wearing distinctive religious symbols in schools is discussed in a separate section below.

The educational structures and arrangements that produce syllabuses for religious education have evolved from those of earlier times. In the fully state-funded schools in

---

1   The 2001 UK census was the first to include a question (optional) about religious affiliation, which respondents could choose to complete [http://www.statistics.gov.uk/cci/nugget.asp?id=954]. 71.8 per cent of respondents identified themselves as Christian, 2.8 per cent Muslim, 1 per cent Hindu, 0.6 per cent Sikh, 0.5 per cent Jewish, 0.3 per cent Buddhist and 0.3 per cent 'any other religion'. 15.1 per cent identified themselves as having no religion and 7.8 per cent did not state their religion. The figures raise interesting questions about religious identity since, in the case of Christianity, for example, only around 7 per cent of the population attended church during 2005 [http://www.christian -research.org.uk/res.htm]. Note that the census question was phrased slightly differently in N. Ireland, England & Wales, and Scotland. For good discussions of many issues relating to religion and the census, see Voas & Bruce (2004) and Weller (2004).
2   Fuelled by the attentions of extreme right wing pressure groups, riots took place in some northern English towns and cities in 2001 in which white and Asian (mainly Muslim) young men came into conflict. Religious organisations, especially national and local inter-faith groups, take great pains to alleviate such tensions.

England and Wales, religious education aims to foster knowledge and understanding of Christianity and the other main religions represented in British society, and also to help pupils to form their own views and opinions on religious matters.[3] In certain types of mainly state-funded religious schools, however, it should be noted that religious education continues to be a form of religious instruction or formation.

Syllabuses for religious education (the name of the subject is often abbreviated to RE) in community schools in England are drafted at local level by a conference including four committees: representatives of teachers; the Church of England; other denominations and religions; and local politicians.[4] Conferences can co-opt further members (for example humanists and members of minority religious groups represented in the locality). Thus the interests of professional educators, religious bodies and politicians come together at a local level in determining syllabus content. There is also a trend towards a national pattern for the subject (see below on the National Framework for Religious Education).

Different pedagogical approaches to teaching religious education have been developed by researchers and curriculum developers. Some of these have influenced initial and in-service teacher education and particular curriculum materials (Grimmitt 2000b). For example, the interpretive approach, developed at the University of Warwick, aims to help children and young people to find their own positions within the key debates about religious plurality (Jackson, 1997, 2004, 2005, 2006, forthcoming). Drawing on methodological ideas from social anthropology and other sources, it recognizes the inner diversity, fuzzy edgedness and contested nature of religious traditions as well as the complexity of cultural expression and change from social and individual perspectives. Individuals are seen as unique, but the group tied nature of religion is recognized, as is the role of the wider religious traditions in providing identity markers and reference points. Pedagogically, the approach develops skills of interpretation and provides opportunities for critical reflection in which pupils make a constructive critique of the material studied at a distance, re-assess their understanding of their own way of life in the light of their studies and review their own methods of learning.

The Warwick RE Project is a curriculum development project that applies the interpretive approach, converting ethnographic source material into resources for use by children in class (e.g. Barratt, 1994 a, b and c; Jackson, Barratt & Everington, 1994; Mercier, 1996; Wayne et al., 1996). In designing experimental curriculum materials to help teachers and pupils to use this approach, the project team drew on ethnographic research on children related to different religious communities and groups in Britain, and on theory from the social sciences, literary criticism, religious studies and other sources (Jackson, 1997, Chapter 5, 2006; forthcoming). The intention was to provide a methodology that was epistemologically open and, within the limits of using books as learning resources, conversational in tone. The framework for teaching and learning encouraged sensitive

---

3   Many University and University College Departments of Education provide specialist courses in religious education for students training to teach in secondary schools. Short courses for students training to teach in primary schools are also offered as part of general teacher training. Students on any of these courses may be of any religion or none.

4   Fully state funded schools that do not have a religious character, since 1998, have been called community schools (formerly, county schools). Voluntary schools are schools, funded wholly or partially by the state, that retain a connection with their founding religious group.

and skilful interpretation, opportunities for constructive criticism (including pupils' re-flections on their own use of interpretive methods), and reflection by students on what they had studied. The interpretive approach has been adapted by others, to meet particular classroom needs and is in the process of development through the REDCo project.

Separate from religious education is the daily act of collective worship. In county schools from 1944, this had to be a form of non-denominational Christian worship. Since 1988, acts of collective worship have to be 'wholly or mainly of a broadly Christian character', a rather vague requirement that allows schools much latitude in interpretation. In 2004, the Chief Inspector of Schools expressed his reservations about daily collective worship, noting the many cases of non-compliance with the law found by school inspectors (Bell, 2004).

Religious Education

The Legal Framework

In the state-funded Board schools set up as a result of the 1870 Education Act, Boards could opt for Bible teaching without denominational instruction, in accordance with the so-called Cowper-Temple clause which stated: 'No religious catechism or religious formulary which is distinctive of any particular denomination shall be taught in the school'. This clause influences the legislation to this day. The Act also included a conscience clause by means of which parents could withdraw their children from religious instruction.

The 1944 Act made mandatory the use, by fully state-funded schools, of Agreed Syllabuses for Religious Instruction. Each English Local Education Authority (LEA) had to convene a Syllabus Conference consisting of four committees. Two represented religious constituencies: the Church of England and 'other denominations'. In practice 'other denominations' meant 'other Protestant Christian denominations', since the Roman Catholics confined their energies to their own schools, and no other religion was considered. It was not until the 1970s that some LEAs liberally interpreted the Act as allowing representatives of non-Christian religions on to the 'other denominations' panel. Between the publication of the City of Birmingham Agreed Syllabus in 1975, and the 1988 Education Reform Act, many new syllabuses included a significant amount of work on religions other than Christianity in addition to studies of the Christian tradition, reflecting both the social changes in Britain resulting partly from immigration, and the rise of a globally oriented Religious Studies as a secular subject in institutions of higher education.

The 1988 Legislation

Changes to religious education brought about by the 1988 Education Reform Act have to be seen against the background of the Conservative Government's introduction of a national curriculum, with compulsory core and foundation subjects. Some commentators saw the decision to maintain local arrangements for designing syllabuses of religious education as showing the Government's lack of concern for the subject. However, the

Secretary of State for Education believed that enforcement of the 1944 requirements, with RE as part of the basic curriculum (the national curriculum plus RE) – the entitlement of all pupils in state funded schools – was sufficient to guarantee its status, and to satisfy lobbyists, such as Church bodies (Copley, 1997, p. 135–6). Nevertheless, the churches would much rather have had a settlement which included religious education as part of the national curriculum, but retaining local determination with regard to the detailed content of syllabuses (Copley, 1997, p. 137–8). In retrospect, it has been observed that many schools concentrated on the core and then the foundation subjects of the national curriculum in the years immediately after 1988, to the detriment of RE. The National Framework for Religious Education (see below) is, in part, an attempt to focus attention on the subject at a national level.

The 1988 Education Reform Act retained many features of the 1944 Act (provision, withdrawal and Agreed Syllabuses), but introduced changes which strengthened RE's place in the curriculum and acknowledged some recent developments in the subject. A significant change was the use of 'religious education' to replace the term 'religious instruction' with its suggestion of deliberate transmission of religious beliefs. The subject now had to justify its aims and processes on general educational grounds.

Recognising the need for different interest groups to have a say in the production of syllabuses, and for local circumstances to be considered, the arrangements for producing Agreed Syllabuses were retained in a modified form. For the first time in law, representatives of faiths other than Christianity were 'officially' given a place on Agreed Syllabus Conferences, on what used to be the 'other denominations' committee. Also, Standing Advisory Councils on Religious Education (SACREs) now had to be set up (post 1944 they were optional) with functions that include monitoring the use of Agreed Syllabuses and the power to require an LEA to set up a Conference to review the locally Agreed Syllabus. SACREs have a composition which parallels that of Agreed Syllabus Conferences, and they can co-opt extra members.

Because of its position outside the national curriculum, religious education stayed out of nationally agreed assessment arrangements and did not become a foundation subject. The Department of Education and Science's non-statutory guidance stated that Agreed Syllabus Conferences could decide to include assessment arrangements in syllabuses that paralleled those established in national curriculum subjects.

The Reform Act requires that any new Agreed Syllabus 'shall reflect the fact that religious traditions in Great Britain are in the main Christian, whilst taking account of the teaching and practices of the other principal religions represented in Great Britain' (UK Parliament, 1988, Section 8.3). This says nothing about instruction in Christianity, and the Act specifically prohibits indoctrinatory teaching. New Agreed Syllabuses needed both to give proper attention to the study of Christianity and, regardless of their location in the country, had also to give attention to the other major religions represented in Britain; this was no longer an option for Local Authorities.

The Education Reform Act also sets religious education in the context of the whole curriculum of maintained schools which 'must be balanced and broadly based' and must promote 'the spiritual, moral, cultural, mental and physical development of pupils at the school and of society...' (UK Parliament, 1988, 1 (2) para 2). Religious education then, as well as being broad, balanced and open, should not simply be a study of religions but, like the rest of the curriculum, should relate to the experience of pupils in such a way that it contributes to their personal development.[5]

A disturbing feature of the debate about religious education during the passage of the Education Reform Bill through Parliament was the lack of attention by politicians to the research and thinking done about religious education since the early 1960s. The debate in 1988 was often reduced to a crude wrangling over whether the content of RE should be 'Christian' or a multi-faith 'mish mash' (Alves, 1991). One effect was to produce a spate of statements from certain politicians supporting a form of religio-cultural exclusiveness, demanding the teaching of confessional Christianity as a means to preserving 'British culture' and ordering society morally (Jackson, 2004, Chapter 2).

Quite apart from the dismay felt by RE professionals that a vital area of the curriculum should be used as a theological and political football, the debate obscured the real crisis for religious education in England and Wales, namely the chronic shortage of resources in terms of staffing, training and materials identified by successive surveys (REC, 1988; see also REC 1990) and inspection reports (Orchard, 1991; OFSTED, 1994, 1995).

The most positive feature of the 1988 legislation, although a compromise, was that it confirmed the educational nature of RE and ensured that all the principal religions in Britain would be studied as part of the programme of all students in fully state-funded schools.

National initiatives: The Model Syllabuses and the National Framework for Religious Education

In 1994, two model syllabuses were published by the School Curriculum and Assessment Authority (SCAA), including material on six religions in Britain (Christianity, Judaism, Islam, Hinduism, Buddhism and Sikhism) and produced in consultation with members of faith communities.[6] The two models (SCAA, 1994a, b) were non-statutory; they were for the use of Agreed Syllabus Conferences, who could choose to ignore them or could edit or borrow from them. The process of producing the model syllabuses was dictated by very tight deadlines prescribed by politicians. Thus there were weaknesses in the ways members of faith groups were selected and consulted, and in the limited number of models produced by SCAA.

The model syllabuses had some influence (OFSTED, 1997), with some LEA Agreed Syllabus Conferences using them creatively. The key achievement of the exercise was the involvement of different faith groups at national level, but the way in which the tradi-

---

5   Schools are free to choose their own textbooks for religious education. There is no requirement by the state or the local authority that particular texts should be used.
6   Humanism was not included on the grounds that there had been an earlier court ruling (not in the context of RE) that it was not a religion. Many SACREs and AS conferences have co-opted humanist members or have ensured a humanist presence on the committee including representatives of teachers.

tions are represented in the models tends to the essentialist and raises some serious issues of interpretation (Everington, 1996; Jackson, 1997).

Further work took place at national level in 2003–2004. The Department for Education and Skills commissioned the Qualifications and Curriculum Authority to produce a new national framework for religious education, for use by Agreed Syllabus Conferences and others. The framework, which is non-statutory, was completed in draft, following consultation with faith communities and professional RE associations, and sent out for public consultation. The final version of the document was published in October 2004 (DfES & QCA, 2004). This framework, which has received the approval of all the professional associations and faith communities (Gates 2005a), aims to clarify standards in religious education, promote high quality teaching and learning, and recognize the important contribution of the subject to pupils' spiritual, moral, social and cultural development by supporting local SACREs and local Agreed Syllabus Conferences. The Framework is intended to ensure that local syllabuses meet the needs of pupils, and to facilitate the development of more national support materials for RE. It is also intended to increase public understanding of religious education by providing clear guidance on what is covered in the subject. The framework also explicitly permits the study of non-religious philosophies such as humanism, in addition to the religions, and explains how religious education can contribute to intercultural understanding and citizenship education. The structure of the framework closely follows that of national curriculum requirements. A further development possibly could be the introduction of a national syllabus, with RE becoming part of the national curriculum; such a move, however, would require further legislation. Although the law and national framework see RE as a separate curriculum subject, it is expected to contribute to pupils' spiritual, moral, social and cultural development and is regarded as an important contributor to citizenship education (Jackson, 2003, 2004, Chapter 8).

Since the publication of the National Framework, the Religious Education Council of England and Wales, representing professional organisations and faith communities, has lobbied for the development of a national strategy for the subject based on the National Framework.[7] The strategy includes improving the quality of the religious education taught in maintained community and faith schools (a drive for extending and improving initial and in-service training of teachers – including non-specialists – is envisaged), encouraging those responsible for RE in faith-based voluntary aided schools, academies and independent schools to consult and use the National Framework for Religious Education in planning their RE syllabuses, and encouraging schools generally to strengthen an inclusive approach to the subject, by developing links with faith communities in their local areas. Funding from the Department for Education and Skills has been provided to take the proposals forward.

---

7   The strategy was published at the end of September 2005. See http://www.religiouseducation council.org/index.php?option=com_content&task=view&id=34&Itemid=89 (accessed 27 November 2006).

State-Funded Religious Schools

History

The existence of state-funded religious schools acknowledges institutionally an element of plurality in England. About a quarter of all state-funded schools in England and Wales are schools with some kind of religious orientation.

The close collaboration between Church and state in education in England goes back to the 1870 Education Act. The 1902 Education Act established the 'Dual system' of partnership between the state and the churches in providing a national system of education. The 1944 Act clarified this system, by distinguishing different types of maintained (i.e. state funded) schools. County schools were entirely publicly funded and had no Church appointed governors. Voluntary schools, originally funded by religious bodies, went into voluntary partnership with the state.

They were of three types: Aided, Controlled and Special Agreement.[8] In voluntary schools controlled by the state, the church was still able to provide a minority of governors but made no financial contribution. The RE syllabus was provided by the LEA. In schools aided by the state, the religious body retained more influence and contributed towards the cost of buildings and their maintenance. These Voluntary Aided schools (Church of England, Roman Catholic, some other Christian schools and, significantly, a few Jewish schools[9]) had a majority of governors appointed by the sponsoring religious body. Since 1988, Voluntary Aided schools, like all other maintained schools, have had to follow the national curriculum. However, they have continued to teach religious education and to have collective worship according to the religious tradition represented in the school, although many governing bodies of Church of England Aided schools, following advice from their Diocesan Education Authorities, are using the local agreed syllabus.

The fact that some Jewish Voluntary Aided schools were established in 1944 has lent weight to the argument that other non-Christian religious bodies should apply for certain independent schools to be granted Voluntary Aided status. There was an unsuccessful attempt to establish a Hindu Voluntary Aided comprehensive school in London in the 1970s. Several Muslim independent schools attempted, again without success, to obtain Voluntary Aided status during the 1980s and 1990s.

Another possible route to state funding for independent religious schools was introduced in the 1993 Education Act (UK Parliament, 1993). Groups of parents, charities, religious bodies etc could apply directly to the Department for Education to establish their own schools. However, the strict financial and demand led criteria imposed by the incoming Secretary of State, Gillian Shepherd, kept independent evangelical Christian schools and Muslim schools out of the state system (Walford, 2000).

---

8   Special Agreement Schools had curriculum arrangements close to those of Aided schools.
9   There were some Jewish schools with public grants even before1870 (Gates 2005b).

Law and Policy since 1997

Radical changes have been effected since 1997. In addition to the Labour Government's stated aim of achieving fairness and good community relations, evidence (from Ofsted statistics) of higher attainment and a stronger sense of community in some religious schools, an increased demand from parents and lobbying from pressure groups have all contributed to this more pluralistic view of the state school system. Some independent faith-based schools, including the Islamia school in Brent, were brought into the state system.

In 1998 the School Standards and Framework Act introduced the concept of 'religious character' and modified the range of types of school receiving state funding (UK Parliament, 1998). There are now four categories of school within the state system: Community (formerly County schools); Foundation; Voluntary Aided and Voluntary Controlled. All Community schools must use the local agreed syllabus as a basis for religious education and may not have a religious character. Schools within the other categories may have a 'religious character'. Most, but not all, Voluntary Aided and Voluntary Controlled schools and some Foundation schools have a religious character. All schools with a religious character can have collective worship that is distinctive of the religious body concerned. Only Voluntary Aided schools can have 'denominational' religious education. Voluntary Controlled and Foundation schools with a religious character have to use the local agreed syllabus, except in the case of children whose parents have specifically requested 'denominational' religious education. A school may have a religious character of more than one religion or denomination.[10] All schools with a religious character must have an ethos statement. This statement becomes part of the Instrument of Government

---

10   There are nearly 7000 state funded schools in England with a religious character (the overwhelming majority being primary schools). The following figures are based on Department for Education and Employment statistics published in January 1999 and the Religious Character Order of September 1999. The figures in the first column represent the total number of primary schools with a religious character within each listed category while the second column gives total numbers, including secondary schools.

Roman Catholic (RC)	1771	2108
RC/CE	3	11
Church of England (CE)	4531	4717
CE/Methodist	28	29
CE/URC	2	2
CE/Free Church	1	1
CE/Christian	0	1
Methodist	27	27
United Reformed Church	1	1
Congregational	1	1
Christian	13	32
Society of Friends	1	1
Seventh Day Adventist	1	1
Jewish	25	30
Muslim	2	2
Sikh	1	2
Total	6408	6966

The first Greek Orthodox Voluntary Aided school opened later, in 2000.

for the school, and the governors are responsible for deriving a mission statement or set of aims for the school from it. In effect, a wider range of religious schools has been incorporated into the state system, partly for reasons of fairness and partly because such schools are recognised as potentially having certain qualities that might be more difficult to develop in some Community schools.[11]

The expansion of state funded Jewish education (very much at the primary level) should be seen against a background of assimilation (the Chief Rabbi's 1994 book is entitled *Will We Have Jewish Grandchildren?* [Sacks, 1994]), while the expansion of Church of England secondary provision should be seen in the context of falling church attendances and the belief that Church schools are an important instrument for the Church's mission (Archbishop's Council, 2001).

The 1998 School Standards and Framework Act also introduced school organisation committees, one of whose roles is to make decisions at the local level about proposals for new faith based schools. They are composed of five groups, including Anglican and Roman Catholic groups (and, in some circumstances, there may be a sixth group representing other local interests).

Estelle Morris, the Secretary of State for Education and Skills at the time, in her speech in the debate in the House of Commons on admissions to faith based schools, stated emphatically that the responsibility for approving or rejecting applications lay with these local committees and not with government: 'the Government do not intend centrally to create, authorise or designate more faith schools' (Morris, 2002).

The Education Act 2006 (at the time of writing awaiting royal assent) will abolish school organisation committees. Under the new system, Local Authorities will propose, opening, closing or changing the status of schools. Objections would lead to proposals being referred to a Schools' Adjudicator. Until the new system is in place, school organisation committees will continue to complete any schemes in the pipeline.

Current thinking in the Labour Government (2006) strongly supports the incorporation of more independent schools within the state system, including more faith-based schools, and radical and controversial plans to change the character of the state system, giving considerably more autonomy to individual schools, are due for implementation.[12] However, in an attempt to ensure that state funded faith-based schools are inclusive of children from different backgrounds, the Government considered requiring new faith schools to make 25 per cent of places available to pupils from backgrounds other than that of the school's religious affiliation. This proposal was vehemently resisted, especially by the Catholic Church and by the Jewish community, and was withdrawn by the Government (October 2006).

---

11   As an example of its confidence in the ability of religious bodies to make schools work in difficult social settings, the Government, in March 2000, announced its intention to develop Inner City Academies (later called 'Academies') catering for children of all abilities. A few of these are sponsored by Church related bodies. Further information is at URL: http://www.standards. dfes.gov.uk/academies/what_are_academies (accessed 16 July 2006).

12   The proposals have been toned down to some extent, and the Education and Inspections Bill has now been approved by Parliament (October 2006) and will become the Education and Inspections Act (2006), following Royal Assent.

Religious Symbols and the Debate about 'Multiculturalism'

Although there were some individual disputes over the wearing of religious symbols in schools some years ago (the Sikh turban for example), a tradition has developed in which it is normal, for example, for girls from some Muslim families to wear the hijab ('head scarf'), or for boys from some Sikh families to wear a top knot (tying up uncut hair) or a turban.[13] Until recently, there had not been any serious problems with regard to the wearing of religious symbols, and cases of conflict over dress in schools were rare. However, there has been a change in climate in relation to some forms of Islamic dress in recent times, as illustrated by two cases.

In the first, a female Muslim student at a secondary school in Luton took the school to court, on the basis of the Human Rights Act, following the school's refusal to allow her to wear a jilbab – full length traditional dress, covering the body, but not the face. The case went to the Court of Appeal which judged that the school had denied her the right to express her religion. However, this judgement was overturned by judges at the House of Lords (in March 2006) who found that the school had 'taken immense pains to devise a uniform policy which respected Muslim beliefs' and had done so 'in an inclusive, unthreatening and uncompetitive way'. They noted that the school's rules on dress were acceptable to mainstream Muslim opinion. The student moved to another local school where she was permitted to wear the jilbab.

The second case needs to be seen against the background of an apparent hardening of attitudes towards multiculturalism in general, and towards Muslims in Britain in particular, by members of the Government. In a speech launching a Commission on Integration and Cohesion, Ruth Kelly, the Secretary of State for Communities and Local Government, suggested that 'multiculturalism' may well be a source of social division. The speech includes the following passage:

> '... there are white Britons who do not feel comfortable with change. They see the shops and restaurants in their town centres changing. They see their neighbourhoods becoming more diverse. Detached from the benefits of those changes, they begin to believe the stories about ethnic minorities getting special treatment, and to develop a resentment, a sense of grievance. The issues become a catalyst for a debate about who we are and what we are as a country. About what it means to live in a town where the faces you see on the way to the supermarket have changed and may be constantly changing. I believe this is why we have moved from a period of uniform consensus on the value of multiculturalism, to one where we can encourage that debate by questioning whether it is encouraging separateness.'[14]

The speech was presented as initiating an important public debate.[15] However, within a short time, some Government Ministers were questioning the value and limits of multi-

---

13   See Jones and Welengama (2000) for an account of a successful legal appeal in 1983 against a ruling that an independent school could require Gurinder Singh Mandla to remove his turban and cut his hair as a condition of admission as a pupil.

14   The speech was delivered on 24th August 2006. The full text was accessed at http://www.guardian.co.uk/religion/Story/0,,1857368,00.html on 27 October 2006.

15   Kelly's ideas on 'multiculturalism' are closely related to those of Trevor Phillips, Chair of the Commission for Racial Equality, and she refers directly to Phillips in the speech.

culturalism, contrasting 'multiculturalism' and 'integration'. The opinion of Kelly takes a simplistic view of cultures as separate and bounded entities and ignores years of research and scholarship on different meanings and uses of the terms 'multicultural' and 'multiculturalism' (eg Baumann 1999; Jackson 2004; May 1999; Modood, Triandafyllidou & Zapata-Barrero 2006; Parekh 2000; Rattansi 1999, Runnymede Trust 2000). Ideas of 'critical multiculturalism' (May 1999) or 'reflexive multiculturalism' (Rattansi 1999), as presented in academic discourse, are totally compatible with a diverse but integrated society. The false polarization of 'multiculturalism' and 'integration' was widely interpreted, especially in influential segments of the media, as a statement of governmental disapproval towards difference within society and as an appeal for cultural assimilation, rather than integration. However, on December 8th 2006, the Prime Minister, Tony Blair, clarified his own views on multiculturalism and integration, giving a much more measured view, affirming Britain as a multicultural society, whilst emphasising the vital importance of integration.

> '… multicultural Britain was never supposed to be a celebration of division; but of diversity. The purpose was to allow people to live harmoniously together, despite their difference; not to make their difference an encouragement to discord. The values that nurtured it were those of solidarity, of coming together, of peaceful co-existence. The right to be in a multicultural society was always implicitly balanced by a duty to integrate, to be part of Britain, to be British and Asian, British and black, British and white … So it is not that we need to dispense with multicultural Britain. On the contrary we should continue celebrating it. But we need – in the face of the challenge to our values – to re-assert also the duty to integrate, to stress what we hold in common and to say: these are the shared boundaries within which we all are obliged to live, precisely in order to preserve our right to our own different faiths, races and creeds. We must respect both our right to differ and the duty to express any difference in a way fully consistent with the values that bind us together.' (http://www.number10.gov.uk/output/Page10563.asp).

The second case should be considered against the background of the debate about 'multiculturalism' during the latter months of 2006. A Muslim female bilingual support worker was suspended from her post at a primary school in Dewsbury, after she insisted on wearing a niqab (veil covering all the face except the eyes) in lessons. She was asked to remove the veil after pupils said they found it difficult to understand her during English language lessons. The support worker refused and was suspended (September 2006). After her suspension, she brought a test case under the Employment Equality (Religion or Belief) Regulations 2004. The tribunal found she had not been directly or indirectly discriminated against on religious grounds, but did find she had been subjected to conduct which created an intimidating, hostile, degrading, humiliating or offensive environment for her, and she was awarded damages for 'injury to her feelings' (*Daily Telegraph* 20 October 2006). Before the tribunal arrived at its findings, a senior Government Minister and former Foreign Secretary, Jack Straw, expressed his own discomfort at meeting women in his own constituency surgery who wore the niqab, stating that 'wearing the full veil was bound to make better, positive relations between the two communities more difficult'. The words of the politicians have, on the whole, been carefully expressed. However, the clearly changing view of some senior politicians towards cultural difference was taken by elements of the press as a licence to generate conflict. In the case of the niqab debate, for example, the *Daily Express* reported the story in a lurid way, and then conducted a readers' poll on whether the niqab should be outlawed in schools. Un-surprisingly 99 per cent of those who completed the poll said that it should.[16] Whether intended or not, the perceived shift in policy legitimized certain forms of racism in parts of the media.

The debate about the niqab was widely reported in the media, and various points of view were expressed. The Muslim Council of Britain, a national association whose aims include promoting co-operation, consensus and unity on Muslim affairs in the UK, issued a moderate joint statement.[17] This includes the view that 'the veil, irrespective of its spe-cific juristic rulings, is an Islamic practice…'. There is an appeal for Muslims 'to show solidarity against criticising the veil or any other Islamic practice', but also 'to avoid seeking to capitalise on this debate in order to further political or personal interests'. Women who customarily wear the veil 'in the work-place or in educational premises' are advised to avoid disputes with their employers, since these would likely lead to further bad publicity and the possible imposition of compulsory dress codes in the work place and elsewhere. The Council expresses understanding towards 'those who may find the veil a barrier to communication', but it is claimed that 'the level of discomfort caused is insignificant', particularly when compared to discomfort resulting from other 'less widely condemned practices such as sexual promiscuity, nudity and alcohol consumption by other segments of society'.

Despite the widespread media attention to the issue, the niqab is worn by a tiny minor-ity of Muslim women in Britain, who choose it for different reasons, some primarily be-cause of cultural tradition (often relatively recent migrants, from Somalia or Yemen for example), others (usually younger women, with a Salafi connection) as a symbol of wor-ship and resistance to the corrupting influences of the world.[18]

Those considering the issue of the niqab seriously, including discussing it in an educa-tional context, need to separate facts from prejudices, to reflect on why the niqab awak-ens negative feelings among some people, and to analyse the issues in a calm and bal-anced way.[19]

---

16   Ban it! Daily Express, 21 October, 2006. An Ipsos MORI telephone poll shows, however, that members of the British public consider that Muslim women have a right to wear a niqab, but not in the classroom, or on television, for example. Very few respondents (14%) claimed to feel frightened or intimidated by women wearing a veil, but the majority considered wearers to be segregating themselves (61%) and are making a clear statement of separation and difference (59%). Interviews were conducted on 11th October 2006 with 1,023 British adults aged 18+; data were weighted to reflect the national population profile. [http://www.ipsos-mori.com/polls/2006/itv.shtml]

17   The full statement is at http://www.mcb.org.uk/article_detail.php?article=announcement-595 accessed 27 October 2006.

18   See, for example, A Veiled Woman's Response to the Niqab Debate http://www.islaam.ca/ fo-rum/islam-in-the-news/a-veiled-woman-s-response-to-the-niqab-debate/view.html (accessed 29 October 2006).

19   Excellent material on doing exactly that, which could be used in religious education or citizen-ship education, appeared by mid October, providing students with a range of reliable internet sites for background information on the debate, and encouraging informed discussion (Turner, 2006).

Pedagogical Trends in Religious Education

England has a rich tradition of religious education pedagogy. Much of its impetus has arisen in pedagogical studies in university departments of education or religious studies departments and in innovative local education authority agreed syllabus conferences (Copley, 1997). The key debates of this tradition can be traced back to the changes of the 1960s and 1970s described earlier. No doubt the debates have deeper roots, but their investigation is beyond our present scope. Few would argue that the pedagogical initiatives of the 1960s and 1970s have not been decisive for English religious education practice, although, as we shall see, their legacy is keenly contested. A comprehensive treatment of these initiatives cannot be offered here, but briefer remarks on selected figures should serve to illustrate some major issues.

In the early 1960s Harold Loukes was a key figure in the beginnings of a shift in English religious education's emphasis (Loukes, 1961). Loukes reported research undertaken in secondary modern schools where discussions in religious instruction lessons, as they were then called, were audio-taped and school pupils interviewed about their content. A high level of negativity towards religious instruction was evidenced. Many pupils accused teachers of marginalizing their own experiences and ideas, interpreting lessons as Christian indoctrination. Loukes' response was to recommend a problem-centred syllabus focused on relationships, responsibilities, and other issues of approaching adulthood. The principle that religious education needs to be existentially relevant has been prominent ever since Loukes. It is reflected in General Certificate of Secondary Education examination courses for the subject that are taken by a substantial majority of 14–16 year old students.[20]

Although Loukes anticipated that religious content for the subject would be drawn from the Christian tradition, whose teachings would be placed alongside students' own perspectives in a more conversational way than before, by the later 1960s the privileged position of Christianity in English religious education came under challenge. Ninian Smart's establishment of the University of Lancaster Department of Religious Studies from 1965 was a highly significant development. Smart's project was to create a multidisciplinary, open setting for the study of religion conceived as a global human phenomenon (Smart, 1958, 1968, 1973, 1977, 1986a, 1986b, 1993, 1995, 1996). The approach is associated, often, with phenomenology but care should be taken to distinguish Smart's position from later uses and misuses of the same term (O'Grady, 2005a). The methods of phenomenological agnosticism (temporarily suspending judgment on religious beliefs and practices) and structured empathy (attending carefully and sympathetically to the beliefs of others and considering whether or not these have similarities or differences with one's own) were central to Smart's university religious studies teaching and considerable literary output. He chaired directed projects designed to apply these methods in secondary (Schools Council, 1971) and primary (Schools Council 1977) school religious edu-

---

20   http://www.edexcel.org.uk/quals/gcse/rs/gcse/1483/,
      http://www.ocr.org.uk/qualifications/GCSE(ShortCourse)ReligiousStudiesB(PhilosophyandEthi
      cs).html , http://www.aqa.org.uk/qual/pdf/AQA–3062–3067–W–SP–07.pdf (all accessed 10 July
      2006).

cation, and is widely regarded as the pioneer of a world religions approach that was in-
spirational to many teachers and landmark agreed syllabuses (Birmingham, 1975; Hampshire, 1978).

Changing Aims of Religious Education

We do not hold the over-simplified view that English religious educational pedagogy
since the 1960s has been a series of footnotes to Harold Loukes and Ninian Smart. Yet,
from consideration of Loukes' and Smart's positions and recognition of their undoubted
influence, a useful explanatory idea arises: that much pedagogical debate has attempted
to integrate their emphases, broadly conceived, into a coherent set of principles and
strategies for religious education pedagogy (Grimmitt, 2000b, Chapters 1 and 2). Loukes
insists that school students' own views and experiences should take a central position in
the religious education curriculum, Smart that religious education must be an academi-
cally reputable, non-confessional and multi-faith subject of study. Our argument is that it
is clear that good religious education pedagogy has to take account of both emphases and
to hold both productively in balance and interaction.

Thus, we have a criterion to assess the different developments in English religious
education pedagogy through the 1980s and 1990s. Again, lack of space prevents comprehensive treatment of these developments (but see Grimmitt, 2000b; Jackson, 2004); we
will, rather, discuss illustrative examples that have been and continue to be influential on
practice, some more so than others. It has been part of the self-understanding of several
influential English religious education writers that they seek to undermine a phenomenological or liberal consensus associated with Smart and a 'world religions' approach,
although not all of these writers echo Loukes' call for more attention to young people's
existential concerns. An interesting contribution has been made by experientialist religious educators, for example; whilst they do not question the importance of existential
relevance in religious education, these writers are unhappy about the representation of the
nature of religion associated with world religions approaches (Hammond, et al., 1990).

For Hammond, Hay and their co-writers, religious education pedagogy must be about
more than the surface description of religious phenomena. Attempts should be made to
connect students with the inner felt reality of spiritual experience. Hammond and Hay
present a series of exercises for the classroom, including 'stilling' and meditation on the
question 'who am I?' that are designed to bring students to a more empathetic awareness
of the affective dimensions both of religion and their own selves. Hay acknowledges that
the 'new methods' have not succeeded as an alternative pedagogy (Hay, 2000). The contribution of experientialist ideas has been as a corrective to the overly descriptive tendency of some phenomenological work. However, there are serious problems with the
assumption that school students' own affective states are analogous to religious experience (O'Grady, 2003).

A movement within English religious education loosely allied to experientialism has
sought to ground pedagogy in creative arts approaches (see Miller, 2003 for an overview). Although such approaches avoid the difficulties of experientialism – there is no
assumption that students' products are analogous to religious art or proceed from or re-

flect religious experiences, students being simply invited to explore themes in artwork – further work is needed to document examples of successful classroom practice and to clarify how such activities help to build understanding of religion. These criticisms are apposite, for example, with regard to the writing of Brenda Lealman (1993, 1996), a source of potential for religious education teachers hitherto realised partially at best.

Andrew Wright's opposition to the alleged overly descriptive quality of world religions approaches has come from a different angle from that taken by the experientialists (Wright, 1993, 1996, 1997, 2000, 2003, 2004, 2006). For Wright, it is vital that liberal agendas of respect and tolerance do not obscure public debates over issues of religious truth. The main strength of Wright's position is his insistence that young people are able and entitled to participate in such debates. The aim of religious education as he sees it is to provide them with the linguistic and conceptual skill necessary for such participation – his is a religious education based on religious literacy or, as he sometimes characterises it, it is a critical religious education that mirrors the rigour of academic theology and religious studies at their best.

Wright's work has attracted criticism on several grounds. He tends, unnecessarily, to polarise experience to language (O'Grady, 2005a, b; Teece, 2005). It can be questioned whether younger students will thrive in the philosophically exacting classroom Wright envisages (Jackson, 2004, chapter 5). Like Lealman, Wright has a scarcity of proven classroom strategy or practice on which to call. However, Wright's work, like Lealman's and that of experientialism, is a corrective to some over-emphases in different approaches rather than a fully developed pedagogical approach. Wright's more recent work places him closer to what may be an emergent hermeneutically-driven consensus in English religious education pedagogy (Wright, 2004, 2006). Additionally, Wright's point that concerns for respect and tolerance should not be allowed to hide differences over truth-claims is an important one to bear in mind as we seek to explore not only dialogue but also conflict in religious education. This places high demands on teachers but these demands have to be faced. For Liam Gearon, it is important that the negative aspects of religion should be dealt with in the subject (Gearon, 2002). Gearon does not say how this should be done but it is one of the matters that our Warwick REDCo community of practice will try to address (see below).

There are also writers who have sought from radical post-modern perspectives to undermine an alleged liberal, multi faith hegemony. Clive Erricker and Jane Erricker have argued for the deconstruction of the pre-set religious education curriculum in favour of an approach centred on children's personal narratives (Erricker & Erricker, 2000). Here, intuited personal spirituality is to be protected from external impositions: authentic understanding must be constructed for children by themselves. Erricker and Erricker contribute much of value to the debate about English religious education pedagogy. Their advocacy of children's right to have agency in their own education is one that we join. Once more, however, we are inclined to value their contribution as a corrective element rather than a complete pedagogy for religious education (Jackson, 2004, Chapter 3). As already indicated, our preference with regard to religious education pedagogy is an amalgam of studies of religions and reflexive and critical elements that encourages young people to analyse and develop their own values and beliefs. Clive and Jane Erricker's work, whilst strong on the analysis of personal narratives, regards the study of religions as an imposition of artificially constructed meta-narratives. Clive Erricker's position, however, in so far as it is reflected in the recent Hampshire agreed syllabus, has been modified (Hampshire, 2004). Through an accommodation towards a more generally accepted view of religious education in English common schools, his pedagogy has also taken on a more hermeneutical cast and is essentially interpretive in its approach. Amongst other innovative local syllabuses, note should be taken of the Bradford syllabus which has very clear emphases on religion in the community, on hermeneutical learning and on student autonomy and self-development.[21] Interestingly, school age students were themselves involved in the writing of the syllabus, as a 'shadow' syllabus conference.

In the Introduction (above), some limited attention was given to the interpretive approach to religious education developed by Robert Jackson and colleagues at the University of Warwick (Jackson, 1997, 2004, 2006, forthcoming). But what is the contribution of the interpretive approach to the debate on appropriate pedagogy for religious education in the English common school? We will outline the key pedagogical principles of the approach, describe some of its practical applications in classroom-based research and give a provisional answer to this question, before anticipating some (presently embryonic) new developments. The key principles are as follows:

Representation. In religious education, religious traditions should be represented not as bounded systems but in ways that recognise their diversity and the uniqueness of each individual who is subject to many influences (e.g. from membership group, wider tradition and beyond the tradition).

Interpretation. In studying religious traditions students should not be expected to set aside their own presuppositions, but should compare their own concepts with those of others: 'the students' own perspective is an essential part of the learning process' (Jackson, 2004, p. 88).

Reflexivity. Through their studies of religious traditions students should re-assess their own ways of life; they should be constructively critical of the material they study; and they should maintain an awareness of the development of the interpretive process, reflecting on the nature of their learning.

Thus, the interpretive approach clearly conceptualises the link between religious studies and young people's personal development. There should be a reflexive, ongoing process of comparison and contrast between material from religious traditions and pupils' own ideas. Wright too perhaps comes close to this hermeneutic when he speaks of critical religious education as a series of encounters with alternative horizons (Wright, 2004, p. 177–8, see also Wright, 2006). Yet an additional strength of the interpretive approach is the presence of supportive empirical studies, whether through ethnographic research on children's religiosity (Jackson & Nesbitt, 1993; Nesbitt, 2004), action research (Jackson, 2004, p. 103ff; O'Grady, 2003, 2005b), dialogical approaches to religious education (Ipgrave, 1998, 2002, 2003; Jackson, 2004, Chapter 7) or other areas including research into religious education and special needs (Jackson, 2004, Chapter 6).

---

21   URL: http://www.ngfl.ac.uk/re/syl/contents_secondary:htm   (accessed   10   July   2006); http://www2.warwick.ac.uk/fac/soc/wie/wreru/aboutus/research_projects/current/redco/community ofpractice.doc (accessed 12 July 2006).

Debates on Religious Education and Open Questions

We cannot go so far as to say that there is a positive present consensus on the nature and aims of religious education in England. However, as we have seen, there is much focus on hermeneutics and the idea of a developmental conversation between young people and religious materials (or in dialogical approaches to religious education, between young people of different backgrounds and dispositions). Can this be viewed, retrospectively, as an accommodation of Loukes' concerns with those of Smart? Actually, it can be argued that there were already signs of this in Smart's own work, in relation to structured empathy (O'Grady, 2005a). The constructivist religious education pedagogy of Grimmitt (2000a) also has strengths to offer in this regard.

What are the questions that exercise religious educators in England in the early 21st century? We have shown how, in some ways, they are the same questions posed in the 1960s by Loukes and Smart. There is also an emerging cluster of questions around human rights and citizenship (Gearon, 2002, 2004, 2006; Hull, 1996, 1998, 2002; Jackson, 2003; Jackson & Fujiwara 2007). These questions include the issue of increasing 'cultural racism' in society (see Jackson's chapter in part one of this volume). A recent and continuing focus on intercultural education partly results from the internationalisation of English religious education research (Jackson & McKenna, 2005), and from the Government initiated debate about 'multiculturalism'. All of this ought to lead to discussion of what achievement in religious education now means. How do we now characterise a religiously educated young English person? And in the light of this question, what does successful classroom practice look like and do? How do we deal not just with dialogue but also with conflict in religious education, especially in relation to racism of various kinds?

Possibilities for Religious Education

What, given the foregoing open questions, does religious education have to offer to young people now? For these questions to remain open our answers have to be tentative. Yet we have maintained throughout the chapter that religious education should help young people to gain both a positive sense of the development of their own values and beliefs and a growing understanding of their role as citizens of a religiously plural society: the two aims should be seen as cross-cutting. How can the subject develop and grow in the future and what challenges have to be faced? What is needed is a well-documented truly hermeneutical pedagogy (or series of related pedagogies) so that these questions can be answered and development agendas set 'on the ground' of school life. Our lack is not of good theory but of detailed description of successful classroom pedagogy informed by good theory. Within the Warwick Religions and Education Research Unit, we have instituted an action research community of practice intending to address this lack.[22] Our community of practice constitutes the English strand of the REDCo project. A group of

---

22   http://www2.warwick.ac.uk/fac/soc/wie/research/wreru/aboutus/research_projects/current/
      redco/communityofpractice.doc (accessed 5 Nov 2006)

researchers is undertaking studies in different educational settings and with different age groups of children and young people, designed to investigate the power of the interpretive approach to secure the necessary pedagogical description. These studies are focusing on different aspects of religious education pedagogy (for example, philosophy for children, assessment, dialogical religious education, community cohesion and religious education, beginning teacher education).

Conclusion

Although there has been some expansion of faith based schools, the vast majority of state-funded schools continue to be community schools. The approach to religious education in state community schools in England and Wales is open and liberal, intending neither to promote nor to erode faith. It could be said that the particular approach to multiculturalism to be found in the syllabuses (rather than in current Government rhetoric) reflects the particular history of civil religion in the UK, and Britain's particular history in becoming a multicultural society (Jackson, 2004). Religious education is thus potentially an arena for dialogue between pupils from different religious and secular backgrounds. The recent debate about 'multiculturalism' and Islam, initiated by the Government, including intemperate remarks from some Ministers, together with emotive and sensationalist stories representing Muslims in parts of the media (particularly some tabloid newspapers), show the vital importance of reasoned and informed discussion – tackling the issue of representing religions, for example – that can be fostered through religious education.

   In relation to the above remarks about the importance of dialogue – and this is the argument of our chapter as a whole – the key challenge is to develop and document a truly hermeneutical religious education pedagogy. This links very closely to what we hope to achieve through the Warwick REDCo strand. We consider that the interpretive approach provides an appropriate pedagogical basis. Through our action research community of practice, we intend to illustrate the potential of the interpretive approach to draw together the different concerns of English religious educators since the 1960s, thus also addressing the need for more and better description of successful pedagogy than has been available to date. There ought to be impacts not just on classroom practice but also on teacher education and on policy.

References

Alves, C. (1991) Just a matter of words? The religious education debates in the House of Lords, *British Journal of Religious Education*, 13 (3), 168–74.

Archbishop's Council (2001) *The Way Ahead: Church of England Schools in the New Millennium* (London, Church House Publishing).

Barratt, M. (1994a) *Something to Share*, Bridges to Religions series, The Warwick RE Project (Oxford, Heinemann).

Barratt, M. (1994b) *The Buddha's Birthday*, Bridges to Religions series, The Warwick RE Project (Oxford, Heinemann).

Barratt, M. (1994c) *The Seventh Day is Shabbat*, Bridges to Religions series, The Warwick RE Project (Oxford, Heinemann).

Baumann, G. (1999) *The Multicultural Riddle: Rethinking National, Ethnic and Religious Identities* (London: Routledge).

Bell, D. (2004) *Change and Continuity: Reflections on The Butler Act, speech to commemorate the 60th anniversary of the 1944 Education Act: House of Commons, 21 April 2004*. URL: http://www.ofsted.gov.uk/publications/index/cfm?fuseaction=pubs.displayfile&id=3615& type=pdf /accessed 11 July 2006).

Birmingham (1975) *The Birmingham Agreed Syllabus for Religious Education* (Birmingham, Birmingham City Council).

Copley, T. (1997) *Teaching Religion. Fifty Years of Religious Education in England and Wales* (Exeter, Exeter University Press).

DfES & QCA (2004) *Religious Education: The non statutory national framework* (London, Qualifications and Curriculum Authority) Available online: http://www.qca.org.uk/ 6163.html.

Erricker, C. & Erricker, J. (2000) *Reconstructing Religious, Spiritual and Moral Education* (London, RoutledgeFalmer).

Everington, J. (1996) A question of authenticity: the relationship between educators and practitioners in the representation of religious traditions, *British Journal of Religious Education*, 18 (2), 69–77.

Gates, B. (2005a) Editorial, *British Journal of Religious Education*, 27(2), 99–102.

Gates, B. (2005b) Faith schools and colleges of education since 1800, in R. Gardner, J. Cairns & D. Lawton, *Faith Schools: Consensus or Conflict?* (London, RoutledgeFalmer).

Gearon, L. (2002) Human rights and religious education: Some postcolonial perspectives, *British Journal of Religious Education*, 24(2), 140–48.

Gearon, L. (2004) *Citizenship through Secondary Religious Education* (London, Routledge-Falmer).

Gearon, L. (2006) Human rights and religious education: Some postcolonial perspectives, in: M. de Souza, K. Engebretson, G. Durka, R. Jackson, A. McGrady (Eds.) *International Handbook of the Religious, Moral and Spiritual Dimensions of Education* (The Netherlands, Springer Academic Publishers), 375–385.

Grimmitt, M. (2000a) Constructivist pedagogies of religious education project: Rethinking knowledge, teaching and learning in religious education, in: M. Grimmitt (Ed.) *Pedagogies of Religious Education* (Great Wakering, McCrimmons) 207–27.

Grimmitt, M. (Ed.) (2000b) *Pedagogies of Religious Education* (Great Wakering, McCrimmons).

Hammond, J., Hay, D., Moxon, J., Netto, B., Raban, K., Straughier, G. & Williams, C. (1990) *New Methods in Religious Education: An Experiential Approach* (London, Oliver and Boyd/Longman).

Hampshire (1978) Paths to Understanding: The Hampshire Agreed Syllabus for Religious Education (Winchester, Hampshire County Council).

Hampshire (2004) *Living Difference: The Agreed Syllabus for Hampshire, Portsmouth and Southampton* (Winchester, Hampshire County Council, Portsmouth City Council and Southampton City Council).

Hay, D. (2000) The religious experience and education project: Experiential learning in religious education, in: M. Grimmitt (Ed.) *Pedagogies of Religious Education* (Great Wakering, McCrimmons) 70–87.

Hull, J. (1996) Freedom and authority in religious education, in: B. Gates (Ed.) *Freedom and Authority in Religions and Religious Education* (London, Cassell) 97–111.

Hull, J. (1998) *Utopian Whispers: Moral, Religious and Spiritual Values in Schools* (Norwich, Religious and Moral Education Press).

Hull, J. (2002) Spiritual development: Interpretations and applications, *British Journal of Religious Education*, 24 (3), 171–82.

Ipgrave, J. (1998) Issues in the delivery of religious education to Muslim pupils: Perspectives from the classroom, *British Journal of Religious Education*, 21 (3), 146–57.

Ipgrave, J. (2002) *Interfaith Encounter and Religious Understanding in an Inner City Primary School,* Unpublished PhD thesis (Coventry, University of Warwick).

Ipgrave, J. (2003) Dialogue, citizenship and religious education, in: R. Jackson, (Ed.) *International Perspectives on Citizenship, Education and Religious Diversity* (London, RoutledgeFalmer) 147–68.

Jackson, R. (1997) *Religious Education: An Interpretive Approach* (London, Hodder and Stoughton).

Jackson, R. (Ed.) (2003) *International Perspectives on Citizenship, Education and Religious Diversity* (London, RoutledgeFalmer).

Jackson, R. (2004) *Rethinking Religious Education and Plurality: Issues in Diversity and Pedagogy* (London, RoutledgeFalmer).

Jackson, R. (2005) L'approche interprétative en enseignement religieux: une pédagogie de la compréhension interculturelle, in: Fernand Ouellet (Ed.) *Quelle formation pour l'education a la religion?* (Quebec, Les Presses de l'Universite Laval).

Jackson, R. (2006) Understanding religious diversity in a plural world: The interpretive approach, in: M. de Souza, K. Engebretson, G. Durka, R. Jackson & A. McGrady (Eds.) *International Handbook of the Religious, Moral and Spiritual Dimensions of Education*, (The Netherlands, Springer Academic Publishers), 399-414.

Jackson, R. (forthcoming) *Education and Religious Diversity: The Interpretive Approach in an International Context* (Münster, Waxmann).

Jackson, R., Barratt, M. & Everington, J. (1994) *Bridges to Religions: Teacher's Resource Book*, The Warwick RE Project (Oxford, Heinemann).

Jackson, R. & Fujiwara, S. (Eds.) (2007) *Peace Education and Religious Plurality: International Perspectives* (London, Routledge).

Jackson, R. & Nesbitt, E. M. (1993) *Hindu Children in Britain* (Stoke on Trent, Trentham).

Jackson, R. & McKenna, U. (Eds.) *Intercultural Education and Religious Plurality*, Oslo Coalition Occasional Papers (1) (Oslo, Oslo Coalition on Freedom of Religion or Belief).

Jones, R. & Welengama, G. (2000) *Ethnic Minorities in English Law* (Stoke on Trent, Trentham).

Lealman, B. (1993) Drum, whalebone, & dominant x: A model for creativity, in: D. Starkings (Ed.) *Religion and the Arts in Education* (Sevenoaks, Hodder and Stoughton) 55–66.

Lealman, B. (1996) The whole vision of the child, in: R. Best (Ed.) *Education, Spirituality and the Whole Child* (London, Cassell) 40–51.

Loukes, H. (1961) *Teenage Religion* (London, SCM Press).

May, S. (Ed.) (1999) *Critical Multiculturalism: Rethinking Multicultural and Antiracist Education* (London, Falmer Press).

Mercier, C. (1996) *Muslims*, Interpreting Religions series, *The Warwick RE Project* (Oxford, Heinemann).

Miller, J. (2003) Using the visual arts in religious education: An analysis and critical evaluation, *British Journal of Religious Education*, 25 (3), 200–213.

Modood, T., Triandafyllidou, A. & Zapata-Barrero, R. (Eds.) (2006) *Multiculturalism, Muslims and Citizenship: A European Approach* (London, Routledge).

Morris, E. (2002) House of Commons, *Hansard*, 6 February, Column 898.

Nesbitt, E. (2004) *Intercultural Education: Ethnographic and Religious Approaches* (Brighton, Sussex Academic Press).

O'Grady, K. (2003) Motivation in religious education: A collaborative investigation with year eight students, *British Journal of Religious Education*, 25 (3), 214–25.

O'Grady, K. (2005a) Professor Ninian Smart, Phenomenology and Religious Education, *British Journal of Religious Education*, 27 (3), 227–38.

O'Grady, K. (2005b) Pedagogy, dialogue and truth: Intercultural education in the religious education classroom, in: R. Jackson & U. McKenna (eds.) *Intercultural Education and Religious Plurality* (Oslo, Oslo Coalition on Freedom of Religion or Belief) 25–34.

OFSTED (1994) *Religious Education and Collective Worship 1992–3* (London, Her Majesty's Stationery Office).

OFSTED (1995) *Religious Education: A Review of Inspection Findings 1993/94* (London, Her Majesty's Stationery Office).

OFSTED (1997) *The Impact of New Agreed Syllabuses on the Teaching and Learning of Religious Education* (London, Her Majesty's Stationery Office).

Orchard, S. (1991) What was wrong with religious education? An analysis of HMI Reports 1985–1988, *British Journal of Religious Education*, 14 (1), 15–21.

Parekh, B. (2000) *Rethinking Multiculturalism: Cultural Diversity and Political Theory* (Basingstoke, Macmillan).

Rattansi, A. (1999) Racism, postmodernism and reflexive multiculturalism, in: S. May (Ed.) *Critical Multiculturalism: Rethinking Multicultural and Antiracist Education* (London, Falmer Press).

REC (1988) *Religious Education: Supply of Teachers for the 1990s* (Lancaster, The Religious Education Council of England and Wales).

REC (1990) *What Conspired against RE Specialist Teacher Supply?* (Lancaster, The Religious Education Council of England and Wales).

Runnymede Trust (2000) *The Future of Multi-Ethnic Britain: The Parekh Report* (London, Profile Books).

Sacks, J. (1994) *Will We Have Jewish Grandchildren?* (London, Valentine Mitchell).

Schools Council (1971) *Working Paper 36: Religion in Secondary Schools* (London, Evans / Methuen).

Schools Council (1977) *Discovering an Approach: Religious Education in Primary Schools* (London, Macmillan Education).

School Curriculum and Assessment Authority (SCAA) (1994a) *Model Syllabuses for Religious Education: Model 1: Living Faiths Today* (London, School Curriculum and Assessment Authority).

School Curriculum and Assessment Authority (SCAA) (1994b) *Model Syllabuses for Religious Education: Model 2: Questions and Teaching* (London, School Curriculum and Assessment Authority).

Smart, N. (1958) *Reasons and Faiths* (London, Routledge and Kegan Paul).

Smart, N. (1968) *Secular Education and the Logic of Religion* (London, Faber and Faber).

Smart, N. (1973) *The Phenomenon of Religion* (London, Macmillan).

Smart, N. (1977) *Background to the Long Search* (London, British Broadcasting Corporation).

Smart, N. (1986a) The exploration of religion and education, in: D. Wiebe (Ed.) *Ninian Smart: Concept and Empathy* (London, Macmillan) 220–30.

Smart, N. (1986b) The principles and meaning of the study of religion, in: D. Wiebe (Ed.) *Ninian Smart: Concept and Empathy* (London, Macmillan) 195–206.

Smart, N. (1993) *Buddhism and Christianity: Rivals and Allies* (London, Macmillan).

Smart, N. (1995) *Worldviews: Crosscultural Explorations of Human Beliefs* (London, Prentice-Hall).

Smart, N. (1996) *Dimensions of the Sacred: An Anatomy of the World's Beliefs* (London, HarperCollins).

Teece, G. (2005) Traversing the Gap: Andrew Wright, John Hick and critical religious education, *British Journal of Religious Education*, 27(1), 29–40.

Turner, L. (2006) Take your students behind the veil, *EducationGuardian*, October 17, 7.

UK Parliament (1988) *Education Reform Act 1988* (London, HMSO).

UK Parliament (1993) *Education Act* (London, Her Majesty's Stationery Office).

UK Parliament (1998) *School Standards and Framework Act* (London, Department for Education and Employment).

Voas, D. and Bruce, S. (2004). The 2001 census and Christian identification in Britain, *Journal of Contemporary Religion* 19(1): 23–28.

Walford, G. (2000) *Policy and Politics in Education: Sponsored Grant-Maintained Schools and Religious Diversity* (Aldershot, Ashgate).

Weller, P. (2004). Identity, politics, and the future(s) of religion in the UK: The case of the religion questions in the 2001 decennial census, *Journal of Contemporary Religion* 19(1): 3-21.

Wayne, E., Everington, J., Kadodwala, D. and Nesbitt, E. (1996) *Hindus, Interpreting Religions series, The Warwick RE Project* (Oxford, Heinemann).

Wright, A. (1993) *Religious Education in the Secondary School: Prospects for Religious Literacy* (London, David Fulton).

Wright, A. (1996) Language and experience in the hermeneutics of religious understanding, *British Journal of Religious Education*, 18 (3), 166–80.

Wright, A. (1997) Mishmash, religionism and theological literacy: An appreciation and critique of Trevor Cooling's hermeneutical programme, *British Journal of Religious Education*, 19 (3), 143–56.

Wright, A. (2000) The spiritual education project: Cultivating spiritual and religious literacy through a critical pedagogy of religious education, in: M. Grimmitt (Ed.) *Pedagogies of Religious Education: Case Studies in the Research and Development of Good Pedagogic Practice in RE* (Great Wakering, McCrimmons) 170–87.

Wright, A. (2003) The contours of critical religious education: knowledge, wisdom, truth, *British Journal of Religious Education*, 25 (4), 279–91.

Wright, A. (2004) *Religion, Education and Post-Modernity* (London, RoutledgeFalmer).

Wright, A. (2006) Critical realism as a tool for the interpretation of cultural diversity in liberal religious education, in: M. de Souza, K. Engebretson, G. Durka, R. Jackson and A. McGrady (Eds.), *International Handbook of the Religious, Moral and Spiritual Dimensions of Education* (The Netherlands, Springer Academic Publishers), 333–347.

Ina ter Avest, Cok Bakker, Gerdien Bertram-Troost and Siebren Miedema

Religion and Education in the Dutch Pillarized and Post-Pillarized Educational System

Historical Background and Current Debates

Introduction

The story of religion and education in the Netherlands starts with the history of public education in state schools (Thurlings & Van Vugt 1997, p. 28). This may seem a remarkable statement and needs some clarification. At the end of the 18th century and the beginning of the 19th century, during the French occupation under the governmental responsibility of the brother of Napoleon Bonaparte, Lodewijk Napoleon, the Netherlands were then called the Batavian Republic, in which the government felt responsible for the education of all inhabitants. The educational system was centralised and education became the responsibility of the state. Also a Department of Education was established in the Netherlands, being the first department of education in Europe. The formalization of the educational policies in the Education Act of 1806 embodied the separation between state and church, but did not imply a separation of religion and state.

The relation between religion and education in state schools was embodied in the teaching of Christian ethics and in RE classes, in those days within the area of responsibility of the churches. However, according to the principles of the Batavian Republic the fear for punishment by God or by men should be replaced by a 'clear understanding of good and evil' (cf Thurlings & Van Vugt, 1997, p. 29). The 1806 law on primary education expected that all pupils should be educated in 'all social and Christian virtues', that being the task of all state schools. These schools were characterized by a climate of Christianity that goes beyond all institutionalized religion, a Christianity above religious differences.

> Education has to prioritize all social and Christian virtues, instead of giving preferential treatment to one of the churches, like the standardized Dutch language is prioritized to any of the dialects (Thurlings & Van Vugt, 1997, p. 31)

In article 140 of the 1814 Constitution – during the kingdom of King William I – this principle read as follows:

> In order to foster religion as a solid support for the State and as an enlargement of knowledge, public education in state schools (primary schools as well as secondary schools and higher education) are the Government's concern continuously. Yearly the sovereign authority reports to the General Council upon these schools' condition (Meijsen, 1976).

So, in the 19th century with the start of the Netherlands as a nation-state, there was at the state level no institutional relation in education with the church, but there was a connection between religion and education in all state schools.

State schools were financed by the government. Notwithstanding the fact that Christianity imbued state schools' education, already around 1830 some groups of parents and teachers considered this type of Christian education as incomplete because it did not aim at socialization into a church community but instead aimed at good citizenship rooted in Christian virtues and values. They critizized the fact that there was no continuity between the specific religious beliefs and practices in the families and at school. They had also serious doubts about whether the plural state schools could be an adequate means for the transmission of religious subject-matter when – as it happened in their view – a particular enlightened ethical-theological stance was dominating as a hidden religious educational curriculum. They strongly argued against any form of pluralistic public schooling – the form originally intended in the state-protestant tradition – in which all religious denominations should find their place.

As a result of this clash between certain Protestant groups and the official state policy, from 1830 onwards separated Christian schools were founded sometimes illegally and sometimes in the form of education at home, but always financed by a community of parents or by teachers themselves. Religious education in these private schools was shaped in accordance with the religious life view of the parents (cf Rietveld-van Wingerden et al., 2003).

So, after a short harmonious period in respect of the relationship between religion and (school) education a deep-seated conflict was born regarding a pluralistic versus a preferred monistic organization of religion in education. Denominational, that is Protestant and after 1864 also Roman Catholic schools, having got the same constitutional rights in 1848 and obliged to meet the gradually strengthened governmental criteria for quality of teaching and learning, started to strive for equal financial treatment for their schools. This *School Struggle* ('Schoolstrijd') ended in 1917 with the Pacification Act, and the new educational policy was stated in the Education Act from 1920.

The concept of 'pillarization' is coined to describe this religious diversity within a monocultural society (cf. extensively Lijphart, 1968). The Pacification from 1917 gave an extra, and, according to some historians, the impetus for the process of societal pillarization, that is the denominational segregation of public life in the Netherlands. It resulted in a fragmentation of almost all societal institutions and groups along denominational lines. So, the pillarization was not restricted to education alone but all of public and political life in society became organized along segregational lines: universities, political parties, trade-unions, welfare work, hospitals, elderly homes et cetera. This, what can be characterized as vertical pillarization, resulted in a synchronic societal plurality which blocked the way for value exchange, for sharing and mutual construction of values, and for encounter and dialogue between people from different pillars. The politics of pacification was, according to Lijphart, a way to accommodate religious or world view plurality within a monocultural society and it resulted in a strong separation on the basis of society between the divers denominationally split groups. Groups, each locked up in their own organizations and institutions. This dissension was at the same time combined with co-ordinated co-operation between the elites, the leaders at the top of the pillars. This kind of policy-making by the elites resulted in political passivity and indifference on the side of the majority, and in the social isolation of the divers groups. For several decades after 1917 there was a more or less peaceful and harmonious co-existence of, but at the same time a sharp division between, state and denominational schools. While state schools interpreted themselves as religiously neutral[1], denominational schools positioned themselves as religiously loaded.

However, at the beginning of the twenty-first century the equal treatment of state and private denominational schools is seriously threatened, in particular with regard to the combination of religion and education in private education. After the Dutch publicist Paul Scheffer wrote in 2000 his famous article on the multicultural society, entitled, 'The multicultural drama', more and more people threw serious doubts on the role of religion in education in the multicultural society. On the one hand people stress the importance of private denominational schools, being Christian, Jewish or Islamic schools, since pupils are deeply rooted in the respective religious philosophies of life. On the other hand it is precisely this rootedness that opponents in particular fear. The focus in this fear is on the 'new pillar' of recently founded Islamic schools, because they might hold people on to their convictions in a rigid way, leading to intolerance and fixed fanatical religious points of view.[2] Elaborating on this the more orthodox Christian schools are also drawn into the debates.

But after '9/11' the place and role of religion in society and in education is also dealt with in a completely different way. In his New Year's Address 2002 the mayor of the city of Amsterdam, Job Cohen, called on people not to underestimate the binding role of religion, and to give more attention to it in the public domain. He established his insight that, "for a long time the government in this country has not paid attention to the role of religion: the separation of church and state is deservedly well thought-of with us. But the question is whether the government, though in compliance with the doctrine of that separation, should not be a better judge of the role of this religion, just because it does play such an important role as the binding agent. If we want to keep the dialogue between each other going, then we also need to take into account the religious infrastructure. Without mosques, temples, churches and synagogues we will not succeed".

The recent public debates on the realization of religious lessons in Islamic and other denominational schools, have had among other things to deal with the fact that in 2003 the Minister of Education ordered the schools' inspectorate not to evaluate the religious lessons of denominational schools structurally, but only if there were signs that children were being influenced towards attitudes of hatred, or in cases where there were other things going wrong with these lessons. Interestingly enough the Minister of Education has recently also declared that she will prepare an amendment of the law that will make it possible for the schools' inspectorate to evaluate also the lessons in Christian religious education, Islamic religious education and humanist world views education that are given on a facultative basis *in* state schools and during school time, but which are not part of the responsibility of the state schools.

It should be clear that these developments and tendencies leave the relatively autonomous status of denominational schools untouched. It still challenges denomina-

---

1   See for a different conceptualization of the very concept of neutrality chapter 3.
2   More can be found in extenso about the position of the Islam and the different perceptions of it in chapter 4.

tional schools to speak openly about their particular school identity concept. So, they need to make clear how they want to position the religious dimension of their identity in theory as well as in practice. Such a strategy with regard to the task of the inspectorate may challenge the state schools to drop their frequently observed forced neutrality, and to make clear what value-loaded teaching and schooling in their view could mean. In short they need to show what they really mean by the new identity phrase, 'active plurality', introduced in the ninety-seventies.

Within this context of debate and with at least two lines of thought: a minority that wants to ban religion to the private sphere, and a majority that is really open for an open discussion on a renewed positioning of religion in education, Article 23 of the Constitution – the article that enacts the freedom of founding private (religious based) schools – is regularly debated. Reformulating or even the removal of this article in the democratic Dutch society is at stake.

The English version of this article of the Dutch prevailing Constitution runs as follows: Article 23 [Education]

1. Education shall be the constant concern of the Government.
2. All persons shall be free to provide education, except for the authorities' right of supervision and, with regard to forms of education designated by law, its right to examine the competence and moral integrity of teachers, to be regulated by Act of Parliament.
3. Education provided by public authorities shall be regulated by Act of Parliament, paying due respect to everyone's religion or belief.
4. The local authorities shall ensure that primary education is provided in a sufficient number of state schools in every municipality. Deviations from this provision may be permitted under rules to be established by Act of Parliament on condition that there is opportunity to receive the said form of education.
5. The standards required of schools financed either in part or in full from state funds shall be regulated by Act of Parliament, with due regard, in the case of private (denominational) schools, to the freedom to provide education according to religious or other belief.
6. The requirements for primary education shall be such that the standards both of private schools fully financed from public funds and of public-authority schools are fully guaranteed. The relevant provisions shall respect in particular the freedom of private schools to choose their teaching aids and to appoint teachers fit to their views.
7. Private primary schools that satisfy the conditions laid down by Act of Parliament shall be financed from public funds according to the same standards as state schools. The conditions, under which private secondary education and pre-university education shall receive contributions from public funds, shall be laid down by Act of Parliament.
8. The Government shall submit annual reports on the state of education to the Parliament.

The precise formulation in this form was adopted on 17 February 1983 – after several attempts in the seventies to change earlier versions. The first original formulation, however, originates from 1848 when the Constitution of the Kingdom of the Netherlands, constructed by the liberal statesmanThorbecke was accepted. A crucial difference between the versions since 1920 and those before that date, is that from 1920 on there has been equal financial support for state, as well as denominational schools, that is to say mostly religious-based schools.

From then on the financial support has been the same for state as well as for denominational schools, and this is combined with the already existing regular assessment or evaluation which has been in place since 1848, sharpened by law in 1857 and 1878, by the Ministry of Education's inspection on the quality of education. But the only exception till quite recently was that (the teaching of) religious education in denominational schools was seen as an issue which the inspection should not touch, because it is the particular responsibility of the boards of the schools, they being the proper authorities. The sections (5), (6) and (7), dealing with the freedom of education and the equal financial treatment of denominational schools, are the most important ones in respect of religion and education.

From recent newspaper headings we learn that in various ways people cope with the threatening segregation that becomes manifest in the field of education. Some look for integration by stressing the common interests of living together in the same neighbourhood. They try to restore the sociability between neighbours without even mentioning differences at the level of religiosity. Others point at schools as bearing a special responsibility for teaching children to live together despite differences in religious backgrounds or the economic positions of the parents. They promote, for example, the mixing of rich and poor children in order to stimulate the integration of indigenous and immigrant groups. As an example of this we mention the recent Gouda initiative to organize an equal distribution of immigrant (read: Muslim) children all over the town. To have state and private schools equally involved in educating both indigenous and immigrant pupils is the explicit aim. Another recent initiative points to groups of white Rotterdam and Amsterdam parents who decided to have their children educated in a so called, 'black school'. A third example of how the Dutch experiment in this field of interest is working was the founding of the first (and only) Christian-Islamic school in the Netherlands in 1989: the Juliana van Stolberg primary school in Ede. Whereas the other initiatives mentioned above reasoned from negative feelings of fear for segregation on the base of economic deprivation, the initiative of the Juliana van Stolberg school was based on the positive contribution of religion as an important aspect of the life view of each participant in the multicultural society and also in education (cf Avest ter, 2003). However, the fear for Islamisation caused a flight of white parents from this school and as a result in 2003 the Juliana van Stolberg school had to close its doors.

Describing these types of experiments, it becomes clear how complex it is to harmonize the right for private schools allowing children to be socialised in the (religious) life view of their parents, the fear for fanatical religiosity and Islamisation, the need for citizenship education of the coming generation participating in the multicultural and multireligious society, and the tension between the daily practices and the formal pillarized structure of the educational system.

cal Tradition and Socio-Political Background of
on in Education

In any discussion on the relationship between religion and education, and focusing on the situation and practices in the Netherlands, it is very important to see the complex and unique way education in that country is organised. But also how educational policy is strongly determined by the above mentioned Article 23 of the Constitution. The article proclaims the right of all people to establish a school and organise and provide education according to their own religious or pedagogically based educational theory. The resulting pillarized society and related pillarized educational system was at its heighest in the fifties and sixties of the last century. The pillarized organisations, as they were established and functioned before World War II (1940–1945), reorganised themselves immediately after the war in order to collaborate in restoration activities. In the following years social change pervaded the entire pillarized society, in particular the process of secularisation, understood as the decline of influence of (institutionalized) religion. As a consequence it seemed that the process of de-pillarization could not be stopped and seems to be irreversible. Walls between pillars were demolished which resulted in communication between people of different (religious) life-views, resulting in adaptation to the new situation, a flight into a new isolation or the reinterpretation of the familiar life view. The pillarization process shows itself in education amongst others in the heterogenisation of the so far more or less homogeneous school population, in particular in Christian schools.

At the beginning of the twentieth century, the Netherlands gave a picture of a static homogeneous monocultural society. What at first glance, though, seems to have been a homogeneous culture, on closer inspection requires a more shaded description. On the one hand Dutch society was homogeneous in the field of ethnicity, but on the other hand a certain degree of heterogeneity is discernible, as several (sub-) cultures ('pillars') existed alongside each other. The 'pillars' distinguished themselves by a difference in philosophy's of life, mostly related to confessional affiliation. Diversity occurred particularly in the area of religion, and the pillarized system was the Dutch strategy for coping with this.

During the second half of the last century the monocultural, homogeneous and 'pillarized' society has been transformed into a multicultural and multireligious society. The arrival of guest workers in the fifties already changed the scene, but the reunion with their families starting in the eighties and their permanent stay had a decisive influence on the Dutch culture. The confrontation with the other-ness of the guest workers and their other religion, the Islam, articulated the religious plurality within the Dutch society.

In Europe, at the beginning of the twenty-first century the Netherlands, together with Estonia and the Tsjech Republic, belong to the most secularised countries. While it is no longer true for sporting clubs, political parties, newspapers, etc., however, the Dutch educational system still is characterized by its 'pillarized' nature based on religious diversity. State schools account for only 25% of schools, the rest being private schools, providing education from a specific religious background or a specific pedagogical or philosophical concept. Examples of these schools are Roman Catholic, Protestant, Islamic, Jewish, Hindu, Montessori, Jenaplan, Waldorf schools and others.

What is remarkable is, that of the total number of Dutch schools, approximately 30% are Roman Catholic and roughly another 30% Protestant. Of the 15% of private schools left, several only have a specific pedagogical or philosophical background, but they also regard themselves as standing in the Christian tradition. This means that about 65% of the schools in the Netherlands are – formally speaking – Christian schools. In the last decade of the twentieth century the new 'pillar' of the Islamic schools has been added to the system, with some forty schools counting. This is a very interesting development, albeit that it is less than 1% of the total number of schools in the Netherlands. Within each 'pillar' every school has its own culture, related to its 'well-considered convictions' such as implicit or explicit opinions about 'the good life', the ideal person, the ideal child, the good society and what the transcendental or God is like. All this shapes the instruction that is offered, and gives direction to the activities of the members of the school community, be it managing activities, teaching activities or a variety of supportive activities.

In total 15% of the total Dutch school population is from a non-Western ethnic minority group (CBS, 2004); 50% of them are educated in state schools; 50% in private schools. So, a majority of the Christian schools have pupils from ethnic minorities. Most of these children have an Islamic background. The tendency towards secularisation is also reflected in both state schools and schools with a religious basis. So there are Christian schools where only 25% of the children attend church services on any regular basis (Vreeburg, 1993). Of course these data concern the overall situation. Looking more carefully to the situation in the four biggest cities of the Netherlands the situation is more urgent: 56% (Amsterdam), 59% (Rotterdam), 45% (Den Haag) and 33% (Utrecht), of the schools have more than 50% children from ethnic minority groups. In the debates they are called the 'black schools'. In Rotterdam even 39% of the schools have more than 80% ethnic minority children. (CBS, 2004, p. 100). Segregation is a serious issue then, because this tendency is stressed by a so-called 'white flight'. It is important to have this all in mind in our description of the history and the actual situation of religion and education in the Dutch context. Besides this quantitative data on Dutch education it is important to keep in mind the governmental responsibility for the quality of education at all state schools as well as at private schools, be it Christian, Islamic, or Hindu schools, or schools with a particular pedagogical point of reference for their teaching, like Montessori and Dalton schools.

The Relation between Church and State

In the actual situation of religion in education in the Dutch context the role of article 23 of the Dutch Constitution is pivotal. In this article it is stated that groups of citizens have the right to found a school according to their own religious philosophy of life. Mainly, this has resulted in the founding of private schools belonging to a particular Christian denomination. Religion is central in the characteristic aspects of these schools, or the individual school's identity. In the polity of these schools parents play a decisive role. Very often, they take part in the school's administration as well as in various committees. Participating in discussions on boards and committees, parents have the possibility to stress of their religious philosophy of life in the schools' management as well as in itines. Put in another way: private schools are 'parents' schools'.

cle 23 of the Constitution opened the possibility for Muslims to found their own Islamic schools. However, this right is subject to discussion in the first place because of the high degree of secularisation in the Netherlands and, in the second place, because of the fear for isolation of particular religious groups or, even worse in case of Islamic schools, they fear the possible tendency to stimulate the development of fundamentalism which is believed to be at the base of terrorism.

We have seen that at the beginning of the 19th century there was a separation between state and church, but not a separation between state and religion. When the dual Dutch educational system got its legal basis in the constitution of 1848 denominational schools became more and more religiously affiliated schools and state schools, schools with an all inclusive admittance policy, got characterized by their passive neutrality in respect to religion and world view. The role of the state changed during the 19th century accordingly. Due to a strict interpretation of the relation between state and church the state was expected not to have a preferential stance in religious matters and should not deal with matters of religious components whatsoever. So, even the judgement whether a denominational school should be allowed to start due to its unique religious or worldview character brought the state in a difficult situation due to the separation of state and church. The earlier mentioned recent intervention by the Minister of Education in respect to Islamic religious education and religious education on a facultative basis, is really a Gestalt switch in the state policy regarding religious matters.

The role of the churches in the relationship of religion and education and in RE has been different. Until the sixties of the 20th century a lot of denominational schools had an institutional relation with a church or particular churches. Ministers and elders very often were – in accordance with the regulations of the school – both member of the school board and the church council. After the sixties when most denominational schools became open schools (with open admittance policy in regard to pupils) there no longer was any institutional binding between the two. However, up till the present day a small percentage of so-called closed schools are still 'church schools'. But both for open denominational schools and state schools the teachers in their personal reflection on state affairs may be inspired by church leaders and their view on public affairs seen from a Christian point of view. In the same way teachers in Christian private schools may be inspired by their beliefs and values rooted in Christianity, though at the same time these teachers in the implementation of their views are not subjected to any church authority.

In contrast to the absence of institutionalized religion in private schools, it is remarkable that the church plays an active facilitating role in RE classes in state schools. There, RE-classes are given on an optional base, if parents wish their child to become familiar with the Christian ecumenical tradition. RE teachers in state schools are trained and paid by the churches.

The administration of state schools differs from that in private schools, the most remarkable aspect being the completely different relationship to the personal life view of the parents. It is not their subjective life view which is central, but the communal spirit of the philosophy of equality of each pupil's background. State schools adhere to a neutral standpoint in relationship to the religious life views of parents and children. Each child, be it a child from a Christian family, an Islamic, Hindu or secularized background, is welcomed as a person that is respected in her or his own way. Parents who wish their children to get familiar with the Christian tradition in state schools have the choice to allow their children for participation in RE classes: the executive board of the state school has to realise RE classes, 'if parents wish so for their children' (Rath et al., 1996, p. 52). Parents also may request for lessons in the humanistic tradition. In RE lessons pupils are given information on the Christian tradition as well are familiarized with stories from the Bible, symbols and rituals from Christian religion, like the traditional celebration of Christmas and Easter. The possibility for one-hour-a-week classes in different philosophies of life is part of the state schools' tradition since 1920. The church is responsible for the content as well as the payment of the RE teachers in state schools.

Half of all the Turkish and Moroccan pupils populate state schools (Karagül, 1994, p. 125). Their parents, like the Christian parents, have the right to ask for Islamic RE lessons for their children. Until now this has hardly been practiced, since the greater part of Islamic RE teachers (hodja's and imams) do not speak the Dutch language fluently, and in state schools the Dutch language is compulsory since education in state schools should be accessible for each inhabitant of the Netherlands.

An interesting question in the Dutch context for Muslims and other specific groups is how they can best participate in education and the educational system. Should a specific *Islamic school* be founded which aims at creating a homogenous Islamic educational setting, or should Muslim children attend a normal, pluralistic 'Dutch' school which can be found in every town and village, in the belief that this will create better opportunities for integrating into a pluralistic Dutch society. There are many arguments in favour and against these ideas. In this complex weighing up of arguments it is interesting to look at the facts. In 2006 there are about forty Islamic primary schools, all – as other private schools – are fully financed by the Dutch government. This is quite a small percentage (less than 1%) of the total number of primary school in the country. Analogous with this, only 4% of Dutch Muslim children attend such a specific Islamic school. The large majority attends other (non-Islamic) schools, of all types. A large number of Muslim children attend education in Christian private schools. It appears that for Muslim parents, the criteria for selecting an appropriate school for their children are rather similar to those of indigenous Dutch people. This means that other criteria such as the local reputation of the quality of the school, the accommodation within the school and its surroundings, and the distance of the school from the home are very often more important as selective criteria than the formal, confessional profile of the school. Parents have their own subjective criteria for choosing a school for their child. The state also has criteria for 'good education', criteria to which each school is subjected to, no matter if it is a state school or a private school. The only aspect of education that the state does not control nor influence is the aspect of philosophy of life. As is stated above the freedom of education in concrete daily activities refers to the classes in philosophy of life, since it is in these classes that the life view of the parents determines the content of the lessons.

f Education

eriod from the sixties to the eighties homogeneity within a specific 'pillar' was a com... on good. There was a tense and close relationship between the religious orientation of the family a child was raised in, the church the family belonged to and the school the children attended. The religious orientation of the various 'domains-of-living' was more or less similar. This was – sociologically speaking – supported by sets of life-styles and conceptions of the good that were not questioned and were shared by all those belonging to the 'pillar'. All these resulted in a rather static social context and contributed to people remaining within the family's own tradition.

In a variety of ways Christian private schools shape their Christian identity. In some schools the typical aspect of their school, characterizing it as a Christian school, is the fact that twice or three times a week RE classes are scheduled. These RE classes, though, are more or less isolated from other classes. This way is called a 'restricted' way of shaping the Christian identity in the daily activities of the school. In the same way schools and teachers could focus on the religious feasts, school-prayers and other explicitly religious issues. Contrary to this is the 'integrated' way of shaping the Christian identity, in cases where Christian virtues and values imbue the other dimensions of education, like the pedagogical and organizational dimension. The 'integrated' way is understood as resulting from a coordinated view on education in which the educational theory comprises the pedagogical and didactical as well as the organizational views in mutual relationship with the religious philosophy of life as formulated in official documents from the foundation the school belongs to.

Starting from the sixties for teachers of RE classes the arrival of Turkish and Moroccan children caused a problem for them. Not only the other language of the pupils appeared to be problematic, but even more so their socialization in a different religious tradition. Central in the debate on the multicultural society and the role of education became the otherness of the other and his human right of alterity and uniqueness. In Holland this was phrased as 'integration (in the Dutch culture) going with conservation (of the native culture)' The quest for handling alterity is the red thread in the public debate since the seventies, accumulating since the notorious events of '9/11'.

Whether the school follows a restricted or an integrated view on identity, the aim of RE classes may focus on teaching in, teaching about or teaching from religion. In the Netherlands schools in which RE classes focus on teaching in religion and socializing the pupils in knowledge, rituals and symbols of the Christian denomination the parents adhere to, are named 'witnessing schools'. Not aiming at socializing but instead, on familiarizing pupils with the knowledge and manifestations of the Christian religion and other religious traditions are called 'schools of encounter'. The concept of 'schools of encounter' has been developed as an answer to the quest for living together with 'the other', in particular the other religion that was part and parcel of the lives of pupils from Turkey and Morocco. Starting from the concept of 'love thy neighbour' space was created for the encounter with children raised in the other (Islamic) tradition. 'Dialogical schools' are those schools where in RE classes the dialogue is central in order to learn from the different religious traditions in what way in their Holy Scriptures answers are given to central issues in life, like astonishment and men's responsibility in Creation, men's suffering and death. The construction of a unique and authentic life view of each pupil is the aim of RE classes in 'dialogical schools'.

Impact of Multiculturalism and Globalisation: Teaching about World Religions

In 1985 a new law on Primary education was implemented by the Dutch Ministry of Education. Part of this law was the introduction of a new field in the school's curriculum called 'Religious and Ideological Movements'. From that moment on it became obligatory for all schools to pay attention to religions and philosophies of life, regardless whether a school had a confessional basis or a neutral one. It should be clear that this was quite a remarkable step in the Dutch educational system. Religious and ideological movements could be offered as a regular school subject as such or could be integrated into other regular school subjects like geography, history and world studies. It aims at acquainting pupils with the main world religions and discussing religious arguments, and at helping pupils gain an insight into the various systems of values and norms/standards and values in a pluralistic society. The original idea of this approach was to present religious traditions and philosophies of life in an objective way, rather than as an encyclopaedia. In an interesting discussion at the time the new law was developed, it was said it was important to avoid emphasising the actual experience of a religion or a conviction. (Braster 1996, p. 197). The subject is quite explicitly about the phenomenology of religion and philosophies of life, and is far removed from actual experiences of pupils in the classroom.

As already said, 'Religious and Ideological Movements' is a compulsory subject in every primary school. In practice this means that in Christian schools, where religion used only to be taught from a normative (Christian) point of view, it is now expected to be also taught from an objective (phenomenological) point of view. In state schools, however, where RE was never taught before, religion is a new subject. Looking at the implementation of Religious Studies in this typically Dutch context, it should be clear that there are several difficulties.

1. What is the relationship between this and other subjects and learning areas, including the relationship with the possible subject of confessional oriented Religious Education?;
2. The law expects the teacher to deal with religion in a particular way. But can it ever be treated in such an objective, cognitive way? What about the beliefs of the teacher? What about the actual and ready to hand religious experiences from a certain tradition in the children's group?
3. There are doubts about the way children perceive religion, about how it relates to their comprehension and mental grasp (cf. developmental theories and their implication for teaching religion[s]);
4. There is a lack of teaching material and textbooks to give shape to this subject in concrete teaching practice.

Although the introduction of the subject and its theoretical underpinnings has been very interesting, its position is still very vague (cf Westerman, 2001). In 1998, thirteen years after its introduction, it was found that not all schools were teaching world religions; and that where it was taught, there was no similarity in contents, didactics and the time spent on it. In addition, research has shown that in 80% of the schools, its importance is easily accepted. Both in public and confessional schools Religious and Ideological Movements is seen as meaningful (Brasters 1997, p. 297; De Jonge et al., 1999).

Pedagogical Trends

a) Interreligious Learning

Although developments on religion and education and RE as described in the previous section took place in the changing world of the nineties, they still mainly focused on mainly schools within the Roman Catholic or Protestant 'pillar'. Contrary to this inner movement we notice a development that also started in the last decade of the twentieth century that focussed on crossing boundaries between the 'pillars', the interreligious movement.

In 1994, in a sweeping statement Trees Andree, at that time holding the chair on interreligious education at the Utrecht University, pleaded for education for all children based on interreligious principles.

> Necessary is education in dialogue, respecting each individual's uniqueness, looking for communal aspects in the different life views, being conscious of equality of all humans and a common responsibility to construe new fundamentals for a true humanity in a multi-religious society. (quoted in Miedema 2006, p. 16)

In Andree's view education should care for the development of each pupil's unique (religious) identity as well as at the same time creating opportunities for the encounter with people from other religions. Not only children who are socialized in a religious tradition, but also pupils from secularized families should be welcomed in this new interreligious school and feel at ease. It is in this school that pupils are taught to build bridges between people, bridges between religions, bridges from today till tomorrow. Andree showed a special interest in the developments of the Christian-Islamic Juliana van Stolberg primary school, where teachers experimented with the type of interreligious education Andree favoured.

b) Structural Identity Consultations

After the notorious events of '9/11' schools' religious identity is on the agenda again. The trend we notice as successful in the case of discrepancy between the official identity of the school as it is formulated in official documents, and every day practice with a multicultural and multireligious classroom population, is a radical, non-deductive approach, which was presented as a radical inductive approach, practised in the SIC, the Structural Identity Consultation (Bakker & Avest ter, 2005).

Instead of interpreting the negative feelings of the persons involved as troublesome, these feelings are seen and interpreted as 'proofs' for their commitment – be it a negative involvement. The exploration of their involvement anyhow is the aim of an inductive approach in the school meeting, instead of arguing about opinions and procedures. Elementary forms of the more complex Self Confrontation Method (SCM) are used to support the teachers of the school team in exploring their personal emotional commitment to important issues related to the school's identity (Avest ter & Bakker, 2005). The Self Confrontation Method is based on the valuation theory and the theory of the Dialogical Self. (cf Hermans & Hermans-Jansen, 1995).

In this process of school-identity formation, special influences and motivating forces are ascribed to the principal of the school. To explore these influences an instrument with diagnostic and developmental characteristics, based on the SCM may be used. This exploration generates a deeper insight in the roots of his basic motivations, which results in the formulation of a 'life theme' and a normative concern, which could be interpreted as a fundamental of his professionalism. This reflection, however, gets through the level of the daily practice to the layer of valuations and basic motivations, rooted not only in the professional biography, but even more in the personal biography. Thus, it is a three-layered reflection. This radical non-deductive approach of school identity proves to be a surprising way of making educational interventions. It is interesting to notice that this type of inductive and contextual reflection by teachers is not self-evidently linked to the formal identity(-ies) of the school.

SIC and the SCM as well stimulate the understanding that decisions in the daily professional practice, but also in the official documents on the mission of the school and school ethos, are essentially normative. A leading principle is the statement that a teacher is a professional and that every professional is supposed to be trained not only in skills and techniques, but also in a deliberate decision making that is essentially normative and in which life-orientation is central. This idea of *normative professionalism* and the provocation of a three-layered reflection on it, is crucial in this radical inductive approach. It concerns identity in a broader sense (religious feasts and issues on class room behaviour are covered both) and it is inductive in its reasoning (because individual biographies and experiences are unavoidably needed in those deliberations).

Religion and Education: Aims and Debates

a) Position of Islamic Schools and Islamic Education

In 2006 confessional schools, in particular Islamic schools are under serious criticism concerning the content of RE lessons and the reputed poor general school record. Compared to the average Dutch school the children's performances in Islamic schools are falling behind. Hustinx, (1998) found that, in absolute terms it might be true that pupils' performances are slightly falling back in Islamic schools, but seen in perspective of other variables like the socio-economic background of the child, this judgement has to be revised. Moreover, the performance of these children in secondary education is even better than that of Dutch children with a similar social background.

RE lessons in Islamic schools are given by either the imam or a teacher trained in the subject of Islamic RE. During classes teachers regularly refer to the content of the RE lessons. The difference between parents and the school board on the one hand and the teaching staff and management on the other, being rarely in agreement concerning their subjective religious affiliation (parents and the schoolboard are Muslims, while the teaching staff mostly consists of Dutch Christian or secular teachers), is a serious problem in particular in Islamic schools. Concrete examples of debates on this topic are reminiscent of conflicts connected with the setting up of a new 'pillar' in the complex educational system. What is new and could possibly gain power is vulnerable at the beginning. Even if this is true and can be explained in this way, too much attention is paid to the phenomenon in media and politics. Again, what is said holds only for the few Islamic schools.[3]

b) Regauging the Religious Affiliation of a School

Secularization was, and is, defined as the decline of the impact and influence of religious institutions. Dogmatic stances, religious documents, the church as an institution and any other form of institutionalised religion is becoming less popular and is less accepted as steering principle and guideline for actual decision making and individual behaviour. In fact, talking about Christian schools threatens to become a talk about a relic of institutionalized religion. Parallel to this development in society, school as a Christian institution belonging to the Christian pillar is in trouble. An interesting observation apart from this is the growing interest in non-institutionalized religion. By means of notions like, 'informal religion', 'wild devotion', or 'spirituality' and a growing interest in, 'sense-making processes' very often this field of non-institutionalized religion is pointed at. Religious traditions still play a role in this debate, but it is by means of the individual interpretations of the religious persons involved. This is a new challenge for the debates on the religious (Christian) identity of the school, for example in the above mentioned SIC process, and the interrelation of religion and education in general.

c) Religious Education as an Examination Subject

The complete freedom to shape the relationship between religion and education in secondary education, according to the perceived school identity and to the individual professional standards of each teacher in RE, will be limited from September 2007 on. Every secondary school has the option to choose for RE as an *examination* subject. On the national level the debate is on the objectives and adequate teaching materials for this subject. The quest for adequate qualifications needed to feature a subject as a serious examination subject raises the necessary debates.

The topical picture of this set of qualifications is a complex mix of all three options mentioned earlier: teaching in, from and about religion. The tendency is that compro-

---

3   The issue whether there are Islamic schools for primary and/or secondary education is dealt with in almost all the chapters of this book. It makes it possible to compare the different situations in the countries at stake but also shows the state system as their govermental context.

mises can be found concerning the latter two. The first strategy ('to teach in religion') seems to be more complicated and is very much related to the former issue on regauging the religious affiliation of the school. The government policy allows for a certain degree of freedom to the schools (which, though, generates plenty of 'homework' for the schools).

d) Religious Education for all and Citizenship Education

Citizenship education and development for citizenship is an important issue in the political and public debate nowadays in the Netherlands. In 2005 the Dutch Minister of Education, Maria van der Hoeven, proposed a change of the Law on Secondary Education in terms of the obligation for schools to stimulate active citizenship and social cohesion. On 1 February 2006 this change became manifest in the law 'Stimulating Active Citizenship and Social Integration'. It is quite remarkable that in a flanking brochure to this law with the title *A Basis for Citizenship*, for the very first time the denomination of the schools is taken into account and also the question is raised how citizenship education and religious education are related to each other. The core concepts that are mentioned are: the recognition of different views, tolerance and openness for encounters with persons with different views and opinions.

There are fruitful possibilities now to further link religious education and citizenship education. One option might be to strengthen the view that every child and youngster in every school should be able to develop her or his personal religious identity or personhood. Religious edification could so be interpreted as an integral part of a broad concept of personal identity development. A broad concept of citizenship education then implies that religious education and development is part and parcel of citizenship education and should not form an optional or facultative element, but instead a structural and necessary element of all citizenship education.

It is widely recognized that citizenship education is the responsibility of each country's government. And if the government takes the responsibility for an inclusive concept of citizenship education seriously, it means that without any preference at the side of the government itself for a particular world view or religion each government should take the *political-pedagogical responsibility* to stimulate the policy of and practice in schools to foster religious edification as part of an integral citizenship education. Democratic citizenship and religious education definitively should be combined in schools to the field of religious citizenship education. From a societal perspective, it is desirable that children already in the embryonic society of the school, experience or are confronted by and should become acquainted with other children's religious backgrounds, ideas, experiences and practices. Seeing the impact of the religious domain on political, cultural and economic areas they can also benefit from such experiences and insights when they encounter religious 'others' in society at large. So, from a societal as well as pedagogical point of view, all schools should be obliged to foster a religious dimension to citizenship, and thereby bring about mutual respect and understanding and should stimulate the development of a the personal religious identity formation of children and youngsters in school life (cf Miedema, 2006).[4]

Conclusions

Ignorance of the content and meaning of others' religious traditions, as well as religious illiteracy shows up in the media as well as in personal encounters. This is becoming a challenge to the historical development of separated roles of church and state in the Netherlands. In former days the church's role of conserver and intermediary of the Christian tradition was emphasized, handing over to the teacher the content of the tradition and how to teach their pupils in and about this tradition. However, it is obvious that teachers need support in exploring their own questions concerning faith and religion in its relatedness to pedagogical themes as a contribution to their normative professionalism of teaching about and from religions. As we have shown above, in the Netherlands this discussion started two centuries ago and has incorporated diversity ever since, be it diversity within a particular (Christian or Humanist) tradition, or diversity between different traditions (Christianity, Islam, Humanism, Atheism). The REDCO-project being a European project may strenghthen the insights for the current situation and may show how the relationship between education and religion in past and present has been given form and content in the different participating countries of this project.

The awareness of a subject like 'RE for all'[5] is related to the consciousness that many societal debates and controversies are triggered by or even based on religious distinctions and oppositions. A deliberate tuning of religion and education, for example in religious citizenship education, with the challenge to match these subjects in an appropriate way, is a daring as well as a complicated endeavour. Daring not only because of the differences between the religious traditions concerned, but also because of the differences within these traditions, which might be a serious threat to social cohesion, in the school as well as in society. The characteristic of appreciating scatteredness, being the strength of a typical Dutch brand of social cohesion, coined 'unity in diversity' in the post-pillarized society, is at the base of the change into an adapted contemporary version.

References

Avest ter, I. (2003) *Kinderen en God, verteld in verhalen* (Zoetermeer, Boekencentrum).

Avest ter, I & Bakker, C. (2005) Religion: voice of the multi-voiced Self?, *Scriptura* (89) 283–292.

Bakker, C. & Avest ter; I.(2005) Schoolethos and its religious dimension, *Scriptura* (89), 350–362.

Braster, S. (1996) *De identiteit van het openbaar onderwijs* (Groningen, wolters-Noordhoff).

---

4   It is interesting to see the difference between the introduction of citizenship education and the relation with religion in for example England (see chapter 8) and the Netherlands.

5   Especially the Hamburg case on 'religion for all' is very insightful in this respect and shows clearly the pitfalls and possibilities of such an approach. See chapter 12 about the pros and cons of this approach.

CBS (2004) *Allochtonen in Nederland* (Den Haag, CBS).

Hermans, H.& Hermans-Jansen, E. (1995) *Self-narratives, the construction of meaning in psychotherapy* (New York, Guilford Press).

Hustinx, P.W.J. (1998) *Milieu, sekse, etniciteit en schoolloopbanen*, een onderzoek onder Nederlandse jongeren in het begin van de jaren negentig (Utrecht, proefschrift Universiteit Utrecht).

Jonge de, K., Wetering van de, S. & Bakker, C. (1999) *Proeven van Interreligieus Leren* (Utrecht, Centrum voor Interreligieus Leren, Universiteit Utrecht).

Karagül, A. (1994) *Islamitisch godsdienstonderwijs op de basisschool in Nederland* (Amsterdam, Universiteit van Amsterdam).

Lijphart, A. (1968) *The Politics of Accomodation: Pluralism and Democracy in the Netherlands* (Berkeley, University of California Press).

Meijsen, J. (1976) (Ed.) *Lager onderwijs in de spiegel der geschiedenis, 1801–1976* ('s Gravenhage, Staatsuitgerverij).

Miedema, S. (2006) 'Levensbeschouwelijk leren samenleven: een godsdienstpedagogische balans', in: S. Miedema & G.D. Bertram-Troost (Eds.), *Levensbeschouwelijk leren samenleven. Opvoeding, Identiteit & Ontmoeting* (Zoetermeer, Meinema), 7–23.

Rath, J., Penninx, R. et al. (1996) *Nederland en zijn Islam. Een ontzuilde samenleving reageert op het ontstaan van een geloofsgemeenschap* (Amsterdam, Het Spinhuis).

Rietveld-van Wingerden, M., Sturm, J. & Miedema; S. (2003) 'Vrijheid van onderwijs en sociale cohesie in historisch perspectief', *Pedagogiek 23* (2), 97–108.

Scheffer, P. (2000) 'Het multiculturele drama' in: *Nieuwe Rotterdamse Courant*, 29 januari.

Thurlings, J. & Van Vugt, J. (1997) 'Van schoolstrijd naar schoolstrijd? Twee eeuwen worsteling met cultureel pluralisme, 1795–1995' in C.A.M. Hermans & J.P.A. van Vugt (Eds.) *Identiteit door de tijd* (Den Haag/Nijmegen, ABKO//Katholiek Studiecentrum).

Vreeburg, B. (1993) *Identiteit & het verschil. Levensbeschouwelijke vorming en het Nederlands voortgezet onderwijs* (Amsterdam, Universiteit van Amsterdam).

Westerman, W. (2001) *Ongewenste objectiviteit. Onderwijs in Geestelijke Stromingen in historisch en vergelijkend perspectief* (Kampen, Kok).

Geir Skeie

Religion and Education in Norway

Introduction

Through most of the last 150 years the position of Christianity has been an important symbolic and ideological issue in Norwegian educational politics, while there has been less interest in the classroom practice of religious education. Some decades ago this started to change, and the last ten years have been a significant turning point. 'Christianity' is now substituted with 'religion' and when questions of religion and education are raised the focus is usually on religious plurality. Religious education research is flourishing in spite of limited funding and there is an increasing interest in classroom research as well as cooperation between teachers and researchers. Even academics from other disciplines than theology and religious studies (law, political science, sociology, pedagogy) are getting more interested in religion and education. The following will present the background of these changes as well as the most important issues one has, by which to familiarise oneself in order to understand the complexities, challenges and possibilities that is part of the relationship between religion and education in Norway.

Historical Background of Religion in Education

The recent changes in Norwegian religious education have contributed to a renewed interest in the historical background of religion in education (Hovdelien, 2003; Haakedal, 2001; Aadnanes, 2000). The first school system, established by law in 1739, was in many respects a church system. Reading was mainly taught in order to ensure knowledge about the basics of the Lutheran religion and confirmation was the final school exam. In spite of some modifications and slow development of school infrastructure in terms of school buildings, this system dominated in Norway for at least 100 years, not altered by Norway entering into union with Sweden.

In the second half of the 19th century forces of modernisation started to make their influence felt. In the beginning it was through the books used for reading exercises that the scope of learning content was widened into subject areas like nature/science, history and literature. In spite of opposition especially from the revivalist lay church movements the direction of development was clear. Influenced by general political democratisation, institutional secularisation, and the striving for national independence, school laws in 1889 introduced a school ethos much more directed towards the general education of the nation's citizens. Even if the school still was Christian in formal terms, and religious education still was seen as a part of Church education, a more democratic ethos had replaced the earlier authoritarian state-church control. The direct link between religious education and confirmation was lifted but the church had kept a right to inspect religious education, mostly performed through the local pastor. Other school subjects got a stronger position than before and teacher education was regulated by a separate law for the first time in 1890.

In 1905 Norway got its independence from Sweden after a period of political struggle and national and cultural revival. The Constitution, dating back to 1814, was seen as radical for its time, and a focus on democracy was part of the process of independence. Women got full voting rights in 1913, which was relativity early and the rapidly growing labour movement was about to become the most radical in Scandinavia. In 1918 Labour argued that religious education should be objective and part of history education; later this was modified into the traditional social-democratic position of non-confessional teaching. Even though the state-church system survived, the school was more and more seen as an institution for the general education of all citizens. The Church of Norway continued to consider religious education in primary school as part of its religious nurture, and from the 1930s there was a right of exemption for children who were not members of that church. In 1969 the Parliament explicitly stated that religious education was not to be seen as part of the religious nurture of church members and that the school subject was an educational task. The name of the subject was still "Christianity", but at this time school also started to teach about other religions and worldviews, mainly within the social sciences.

The national curriculum of 1939 represented ideas coming from the pedagogical thinking of Dewey and other reform oriented thinkers, focusing on the activity of pupils and their learning process more than the subject content. Schools maintained their Christian nature, but in religious education there was a broader Christian profile with less emphasis on the Lutheran confession. In addition it was underlined that the teacher should be aware of the fact that parents had different thoughts about the questions that were taken up in religious education. This opened religious education a little more towards a plural society. At the same time the hours allocated to religious education were reduced. The 1939 curriculum was, however, not really put into practice until 1945 because of World War two.

During 1940–45 Norway was occupied by Nazi Germany and during these years there was a united front against Nazi ideology and certain regulations from most religious leaders and teachers. The confrontations this brought with the occupation regime, contributed to a stronger sense of national community, and Christianity was vitalised as national heritage. Leaders from lay church movements, bishops and pastors as well as prominent figures within the radical Labour movement got to know each other in prison and this paved the way for a somewhat milder ideological climate after the war, even if the old controversies were still recognisable.

After the gradual change of school ethos towards education as general education for citizens of the democratic Norway, most clearly defined from 1939, the controversies over religion in education have mainly been focusing on two issues. Firstly, there have been controversies over the preamble to the school law on whether Christianity should be mentioned as part of the overall aim of education, or not. On this issue all the political parties apart from the left wing of Labour and the Socialist Left Prty have agreed to keep the formulations, but mainly as an expression of Norwegian cultural heritage. Secondly, and most often, the debate on religion and education has circled around the content and volume of religious education as a school subject. Both these issues can be seen as ways of dealing with plurality, and new research suggests that there has been two main political positions in this area the last 50 years; one arguing along communitarian lines, with an emphasis on Christianity as cultural heritage, and another using mainly liberal arguments based on human rights, with emphasis on enlightenment and tolerance (Tuastad, 2006).

The national association of secular humanists (Norwegian Humanist Association) established in the 1950s, had for a long time argued against the position of Lutheran Christianity in school, as this was displayed in the religious education subject, 'Knowledge of Christianity' ('Kristendomskunnskap'). The Norwegian Humanist Association argued that there should be a common subject for all dealing with world-views and ethics. In 1974 a syllabus for such a subject, called 'Orientation about life-stances' ('Livssynsorientering' later 'Livssynskunnskap'), was established by the Ministry of Education. It was an optional subject for those pupils who were not members of the Church of Norway and therefore could get exempted from 'Kristendomskunnskap'. The optional subject was left for the local communities to put into practice depending on a certain proportion of pupils demanding the subject, and this happened in many local schools, particularly in towns. From the mid–1970s onwards the vast majority of pupils attended 'Kristendomskunnskap', but a growing group went to 'Livssynsorientering' and quite a few had no alternative at all; either they were too few, or simply did not see 'Livssynsorientering' as an alternative for themselves.

Another change in religious education came from within, resulting from the observation that adolescents in particular lacked interest in the school subject. This coincided with a stronger interest in the individual pupil from educational theory, often based on psychological research. International impulses and a growing research in Scandinavian religious education indicated that renewal of teaching was both needed and possible by adapting teaching, as well as the teaching material, more to the situation of the young people (Asheim, 1976; Bugge & Johannessen, 1974). In Sweden there were efforts to base religious education on the questions of young people themselves, while the most visible change this brought about in Norway was the change in textbooks. They had been remarkably unchanged for 100 years, but in the early 1970s a modern type of textbook appeared, with different sorts of illustrations, questions for reflection and suggestions for activities that were designed to engage the pupils more in their learning.

Twenty years later, in the middle of the 1990s, a growing immigrant population belonging mainly to Islam, but also Hindus and Buddhists challenged the whole parallel system of 'Kristendomskunnskap' and 'Livssynskunnskap'. The religious minorities were still small, but very visible in the relatively homogenous Norwegian society, and nominally strongest in Oslo, the capital. After a process of investigation Parliament finally decided to change religious education, and from 1997 a completely new religious education subject became compulsory for all, regardless of its focus on world religions, secular worlds views, ethics and philosophy, was first called Kristendomskunnskap med religions-og livssynsorientering' (literally: Knowledge of Christianity with orientation about other religions and world views'): in 2002 it was changed to 'Kristendoms, religions- og livssynkunnskap' (literally: 'Knowledge of Christianity, religions and worldviews'). The official English name is 'Christian Knowledge and Religious and Ethical Education'. In Norwegian the abbreviation 'KRL' has been used all the time. The name clearly reflects the complexity of the political negotiations leading up to and following the 1997 decision, which was a decisive turning point.

Religious Schools

The private school sector in Norway is very small with about 2% (15 000) of all children in the 166 private primary and lower secondary schools.[1] This is less than half that of Sweden, while Denmark has by far the largest private schools system in Scandinavia with over 12% of all pupils. Within Norway, the majority of private schools are in Oslo, with a smaller proportion in other parts of the country. The sector is increasing, and has doubled since 1985. The public sector consists of 607 000 pupils in 3 246 schools.

The emphasis in Norwegian school policy has been on the public school for all, mainly represented by the Labour party, but gradually supported by other parties as well. The Christian Democrats who support religious schools have earlier allied with Conservatives who support a more liberal policy on private ownership and there have been plans for more liberal laws on this issue. At the same time there are widespread worries in Parliament that private schools may become a profitable market. There is already a tendency that some of the private schools appeal to well-off parents who think that they will get high quality schooling for their children in a private religious school, even if they have no particular interest in the school's religious ethos.

For many years Norwegian legislation only allowed public support for private schools if they were a real alternative to the public sector, in terms of parental choice. They should have a special pedagogical, philosophical or religious ethos. Today the clear majority of private schools are Christian, mostly with a conservative-evangelical profile. About 25% are Waldorf schools and around 10% are Montessori schools. The only religious schools are Christian. There was a Muslim school in Oslo 2002–2004, which was closed down mainly because of internal problems, but also the background history shows how demanding it was to get it started in the first place (Grytnes, 2004). There are plans to start Muslim schools in several places in the near future, but this will also depend on local educational authorities that have not always been sympathetic to such plans. One reason for some Muslims wanting to have private schools is worries they have about religious education in the public school being biased.

Religion in Norway – Some Sociological Remarks

In Norway 85% of the population are members of the state-church and apart from weddings (46%), a high proportion of the total population make use of the church rituals like baptism (76%), confirmation (66%), and burials (93%). This should perhaps be taken as

---

1   Statistics Norway: http://www.ssb.no/english/subjects/04/02/20/privgrs_en/ (accessed 28 August 2006). Also the GSI–05 is used, which is an official information base in Norwegian language: http://www.wis.no/gsi/ (accessed 27 November 2006).

a warning against applying a secularisation thesis too far in Norway and Scandinavia. The majority population is also less homogenous in many more ways than often presented. In Norway particularly, the tension between the centre and the periphery has a long history, and still manifests itself on many issues. This tension is often interpreted in terms of power. In addition to this there are also other differences between parts of the country that influences issues of both education and religion and that are interpreted more as horizontal differences. Both these dimensions should be reflected in a contextual approach to religion and education in Norway.

Some regions of the country are marked by considerably higher religious activity than others. These are the regions with a history of strong lay church movements related to missionary organisations or others with a focus on revival and evangelisation in Norway. Historically, the religious activity has been strongest in the prayer house, not in the church. Particularly on the south west coast the lay church movement had a cultural hegemony in many local communities. Both in these areas and in the Norwegian 'public mind' this has contributed to a picture of high religious activity as being combined with rural areas, puritan life style, conservative attitudes to dogmatic and ethic issues, concerns for poor people and the third world. Local church congregations have partly lived in some tension with lay church movements, partly in close cooperation. Changes in church working style from the 1970s have led to more activity-oriented congregational life, while some of the prayer houses and their communities have gone into decline. There is also a noticeable difference between regions in terms of lay church influence. The south and west coasts have been quite dominated by this, while eastern, middle and northern parts are less influenced. In these areas there is a 'silent' support for the local church, but often little congregational activity.

Northern Norway has a lay church revivalist movement, Laestadinaism, which is particularly strong in many areas with a Sami population (Kristiansen, 2005). The old Sami religion was oppressed and seemingly wiped out by Norwegian authorities generations ago, but still people continue to uphold some of the old practices, and today there is a revitalisation and increasing interest in old Sami religion. Laestadianism started in the 19th century and has today spread in many countries. It emphasises conservative Lutheran theology and the community of the traditional gatherings, and the life style is often very modest. All thorough the history of the movement the use of the Sami language in preaching has been a central part of many congregations.

The interpretations and explanations of religious life and religiosity in the Nordic countries are much discussed among sociologists of religion (Henriksen & Krogseth, 2001; Henriksen & Repstad, 2005; Repstad, 1996, 2000; Repstad & Henriksen, 2005). There is not space to go deeper into this here, only to mention that instead of focusing only on secularisation, other concepts arc often suggested; religious change, retraditionalisation, religion as a thin layer, individualisation, privatisation, and not least: pluralisation.

Cultural and Religious Plurality in Norway

The majority population has been the main focus in the historical and sociological perspectives above. We are now turning towards a wider plurality, starting with the immigrant population as such.[2] In 2006 there were 285,300 persons registered with an immigrant background from a non-western country, which is 6.1% of the total population. Those immigrants who had a western background counted for 2.2%. Lately, there has been an increase in immigrants of an average 0.5% per year. In 2001, the total immigrant population was 6.6% of Norway's population, of these 2.1% had a western background and 4,5% had a non-western background.

A closer look at the statistics shows that the immigrants' national background is manifold. The largest immigrant group, among those who are born in Norway, is Pakistanis who are well established since the early 1970s, but also quite a lot come from Vietnam, Turkey and Sri Lanka. Looking at those who have moved to Norway themselves, the largest groups are from Sweden, Denmark, Iraq, Somalia, Bosnia, Iran and Germany.

The immigrant population is not spread evenly all over the country. The capital, Oslo is a special case with almost 20% immigrant population from non-western countries. Also some other municipalities in the Oslo area have between 10 to 15% non-western immigrants. In this area live about ¼ of the total Norwegian population of 4.5 million. The cities following in size have significantly smaller numbers; Bergen (6%), Trondheim (5,4%), Stavanger (7,6%). If we turn to western immigrants, however, the picture is different. They are much more evenly spread, with about the same percentage all over the country, quite close to the national average of about 2%. These figures mean that a multicultural society is much more visible in the central areas of the country where political, economical and ideological power is concentrated. Having the centre-periphery tension in Norwegian society in mind, it is not surprising that many in the periphery consider the multicultural society to be an "Oslo-phenomenon". Similarly, seen from the Oslo-perspective it is easy to forget that the situation in the capital is not typical for the rest of the country.

The *religious plurality* is, like ethnic and national plurality, limited. It is also quite difficult to find reliable figures. The allocation of public support is dependent on registered members, and this varies a lot between the groups. Based on membership we find the following figures from 2004: Muslims 80,000, the Humanist Association (70,000), Pentecostals (50,000), Catholics (45,000), Free Lutheran Church (20,000), Jehovas Witnesses (15,000), Methodists and Baptists (12,000), Buddhists (10,000), Hindus (3,000) and Sikhs (3,000).[3] Several of these numbers are probably too low; Buddhists are at least 15,000 and Hindus probably around 10,000.

To put the figures into perspective: In 2006 the Church of Norway had 3,9 million members, which is 85.7% of the population and this is an increase of 0.6%, or 22,203 members over the last three years. On the one hand all religious minorities are very

---

2   For the following, Statistics Norway: http://www.ssb.no/english/subjects/02/01/10/innvbef_en/ (accessed 27 November 2006).

3   Statistics Norway: http://www.ssb.no/english/subjects/07/02/10/trosamf_en/ (accessed 27 November 2006).

small, on the other hand, a minority can become more visible in homogenous surroundings. The picture given of the geographical distribution of the immigrant population can
to some extent be found also in the case of religion. Different Christian denominations
are much more spread out in the country, partly following patterns of regional history.
The same goes for members of the Humanist Association. When it comes to non-
Christian religions, it is different.

It is difficult to get precise numbers on the municipal level, but there is a breakdown
on county level from 2004.[4] A closer look at these shows that of the almost 80,000 registered Muslims at that time 60,000 lived in Oslo and surroundings which has a total population of about one million inhabitants. The counties where the other larger cities are
placed cover a much larger area of the country and have about the same total population
as the Oslo area, but less than 10,000 Muslims altogether. Of other world religions, registered members of Buddhist communities are about 10,000 for the whole country (mainly
Thais and Vietnamese), Hindus little more than 3,000 (India and Sri Lanka), Sikhs about
3,000, Jews 1,000.

The characteristics of religious, national and ethnic multiculture in Norway can be
summed up as following:

- There has been a strong increase in immigration starting early 1970s and this is still
  continuing, but the proportion of the total population is still very small.
- The immigrant population from non-Western countries is much higher in the Oslo
  area than in the rest of the country.
- Particularly the large Muslim population is concentrated in the Oslo area; this is less
  so for the much smaller Buddhist, Hindu and Sikh communities.
- Even if the other larger cities have a noticeable multicultural population compared
  with small towns and rural areas, it is still quite small compared with Oslo.
- In the large, but more scarcely populated areas of the country there are many small
  and middle-size communities with very little visible multicultural presence. The exceptions are those municipalities with receiving centres for asylum-seekers.

Relations between Religion and State

According to the Constitution the Church of Norway is the official religion of Norway. It
has to be the religion of the king as well as the majority of the government. The government appoints bishops and senior pastors and the budget of the Church of Norway is part
of the national budget.

The state church system has been modified from within in several ways since its formal establishment after the Lutheran reformation (Oftestad, 1998). For a long time it was
part of what today would be called a totalitarian system, but in the 19th century these
regulations started to loosen up. In the 1840s it became legal for other than ordained
priests to preach publicly and also for Norwegian citizens to be members of other Christian churches than the state church. In 1851 Jews were allowed to enter the kingdom of

---

4   Statistics Norway: http://www.ssb.no/english/subjects/07/02/10/trosamf_en/ (accessed 27 No-
     vember 2006).

Norway and in the 1880s non-Christian religions were allowed to organise themselves in Norway as well as catholic orders. Regulations about civil servants having to be members of the state church were removed. After 1917 teachers could be employed in public schools without being confessing Lutherans. During the 20th century the church structures were democratised and much of the social work performed by church related organisations were either taken over by the welfare state system or entered into an intimate cooperation with the state.

Since the 1870s there have been several suggestions to abolish the state-church system, mostly motivated from factions within the Church of Norway, arguing for independence from the state. Others have argued against the system on behalf of non-Lutheran inhabitants, feeling that the Lutheran confession and the Christian religion had non-justifiable privileges, or arguing out of general democratic principles that all religions and world views should be treated equally and on principles of freedom of religion. The state-church system is presently in a process of evaluation, and it may very well be abolished after some years of debate and political processes (KKD, 2006).

In debates about religion in education it has sometimes been suggested that the position of the state church and the Lutheran religion being the, 'official religion of the state' hinders a more neutral preamble in the school law. But this is not necessarily the case. The discussion about the Constitution of the European Union and a possible reference to the Christian roots of the European civilisation seems to show that the position of Christianity in Europe is not only a legal question, but just as much ideological, and that the legal arrangements are reflections of ideological positions. An interesting feature of the ongoing Norwegian debate about the future of the state-church system is that there are influential voices arguing that the state-church should be continued in order to secure democratic structures in matters of importance for the church. They see this as a radical, not a conservative position. This is a reflection of the fact that in the Nordic countries the Lutheran churches are seen as national, popular institutions, as 'folk-churches' ('folkekirke'), because the vast majority of population are members.

According to the Constitution, all religions and world-views are allowed in Norway, and all religious communities are also equally entitled to receive state grants equivalent to the funding of the Church of Norway. Some areas where the Church of Norway still may be seen to have a privileged position are:

- The role of 'Christianity' in the preamble of school laws
- The role of Christianity and Lutheranism in the KRL-subject in primary school
- The position of the Church of Norway at 'national events'
- Church of Norway counselling pastors in Army, hospitals and prisons[5]

Major Goals of Education and their Relationship to Religion

In order to understand the Norwegian school system it is important to underline the influence that the school policy of Labour since 1945 has had, both on the population, and on other political parties (Haakedal, 2001). The social-democratic ideal has been that school

---

5   KKD, 2006, chapter 4.7.6.

should contribute to the equal distribution of welfare and social and economic opportunities for a good life. School should counteract inequalities that might separate children; like social class, geography or sex. The ideal was to have the same high quality schools all over the country, and that all children in the local area should go to the same school. In one way this has made the local school an experience in how to deal with the plurality of the neighbourhood, but it also for many years meant certain scepticism towards differentiation and competition. In the present education act (last changed in 2000) the 'object of education' states the following about religion:

> The object of primary and lower secondary education shall be, in agreement and co-operation with the home, to help to give pupils a Christian and moral upbringing, to develop their mental and physical abilities, and to give them good general knowledge so that they may become useful and independent human beings at home and in society.[6]

The formulations in the Education Act are interpreted in the school curricula, and on the general level this is particularly visible in the general core curriculum, which is unchanged since 1993. Here, it is recognised that different aims of education may seem to contradict each other, and mentions 17 'dual' aims that have these tensions. One example is the following:

> ...to provide familiarity with our Christian and humanist heritage – and knowledge of and respect for other religions and faiths...[7]

Education is challenged to

> ...'balance these dual aims. The object is an all-round development of abilities and distinctive qualities: to conduct oneself morally, to create and to act, to work with others and in harmony with nature.'[8]

The fact that the national curriculum for primary school has got completely new syllabuses in 2006, without changing anything in the core curriculum from 1993, shows that the overall aims of school are the same, and that they have strong parliamentary support. From a critical point of view it can be argued that all the traditional tensions in pedagogy, educational philosophy and educational policy are built into the core curriculum, and therefore everybody can find some of their own ideas represented. Also the Sami language and culture are mentioned as part of the common heritage, and even if the Sami population have their own curriculum the core curriculum text is the same. Based on the national cultural heritage all religions and world-views are respected:

> Education shall be based on fundamental Christian and humanistic values. It should uphold and renew our cultural heritage to provide perspective and guidance for the future.[9]

---

6   Education Act) http://www.ub.uio.no/ujur/ulovdata/lov-19980717–061-eng.pdf (accessed 27 November 2008)
7   Norwegian Board of Education, 1993, p. 39
     (General Core Curriculum, p. 39) from: http://www.utdanningsdirektoratet.no/upload/ larer-planer/generell_del/Core_Curriculum_English.pdf) (accessed 27 November 2006).
8   Norwegian Board of Education, 1993, p. 40 (General Core Curriculum, p. 4) from: http://www.utdanningsdirektoratet.no/upload/larerplaner/generell_del/Core_Curriculum_English.pdf) (accessed 24 August 2006).
9   General Core Curriculum, p. 7 from: http://www.utdanningsdirektoratet.no/upload/larerplaner/ generell_del/Core_Curriculum_English.pdf) (accessed 24 August 2006).

The role of religion in education according to the central policy documents is to work as a cultural basis or resource for values and ideals vital to education and society at large. It is not the ambition to promote Christianity as a particular religious belief, but rather to insist on the specificity of the national cultural heritage. At the same time the importance of values like equality, freedom of religion and belief, tolerance and critical thinking is underlined. But if the core curriculum is interpreted through the words of the Education Act and we include in this interpretation the fact of the state-church system, it is difficult to deny that Christianity has a particular privileged position. This is the interpretation regularly voiced by representatives of the religious minorities and the Humanist Association. This is part of the background for the present government stating in its political plan (2006–2009) that the formulations about the place of Christianity in the Education Act will be 'looked through'.

After the secularisation of education, the most visible and the most debated issue related to religion in education is religious education as such. Since the new compulsory subject (KRL) appeared in 1997 this debate has mainly focused on the curriculum and practice of this school subject. Gradually however, the focus seems to open up towards a broader perspective. This is mainly a result of the debates and curricular changes related to the right of exemption.

Some Legal Issues of Religion and Education since 1997

The debate about the right of exemption from religious education has been drawing more on legal than on educational argumentation (Enger, 1998, 2001). When the curriculum of 1997 was designed there was a strong will from educational authorities to remove the earlier right of full exemption. The official justification for this was that the new subject was neutral and impartial towards religions and world-views. Another political and pragmatic concern may have been that, with all the controversy about the curriculum, a right of full exemption could have led to massive use of this right from the minorities. If this had happened, the new subject would have been a complete failure, given that a main idea behind it was to gather all pupils in the same classroom, learning about religions and world-views, learning about each other and learning to live together.

In spite of these ambitions, or maybe because of them, there was made an investigation into the international legal obligations Norway had that could be relevant in this case, and the conclusion was that full right of exemption was advisable, but not necessary (Møse & Kirke- utdannings- og forskningsdepartementet, 1997). It was also clearly stated that the religious education practice was particularly important in a situation where full exemption was not allowed, and that it would be important to follow up on the teaching of the subject. This (legal) focus on practice together with the high level of controversy about the new curriculum in 1997 formed the background for the parliamentary decision to launch a special evaluation project looking into the school realities. Two parallel evaluations were carried through and by 2001 they had delivered their results (Hagesæther 2000, j Johannessen 2000). Both showed that local practice varied, both in interpretation of aims, teaching methods, organisation and subject content, but this was interpreted in different ways. One report saw this as a result of weaknesses in the syllabus and as schools being weak in implementation. The other report tended to put more emphasis on unresolved tensions within the religious education syllabus as well as the general core curriculum. The Ministry of Education saw the evaluation as mainly positive, but also suggested some modifications; better information about the rules of exemption, less detailed syllabus and more continuing education for teachers. As a result of this process a new syllabus was put into practice in 2002.

Parallel to this process some parents had sued the State of Norway on the issue of full exemption and this was taken to the Supreme Court, which ruled in favour of the state in 2001.[10] The right of partial exemption was therefore upheld in the 2002 syllabus. But the parents took their case to The United Nations Human Rights Committee which gave a statement in 2004, mainly saying that the Norwegian religious education without right of full exemption violated the Article 18 of the International Covenant on Civil and Political Rights.[11] According to the international conventions Norway had signed, this critique from the human rights committee overruled even Norwegian law. In 2005 several changes were made in the Education Act and other regulations and new syllabuses came into being. It was underlined that KRL is still compulsory, it is a regular school subject, and that there should be good information and dialogue between home and school. The right to exemption is not any longer related particularly to religious education, but to any teaching and the parents do not need to justify their reasons, which was the case earlier. In December 2006 the same issues are considered by The European Court of Human Rights, and the effects of this are not yet known. This recent development shows that there is a slight change in the situation of religion in education from a relatively narrow focus on the religious education subject towards a broader perspective where issues of religion are related to the school situation as such. One example is debate about assemblies in school and their religious nature. Earlier many schools have included a church service in their assemblies before Christmas or summer holidays. Even if these assemblies have never been compulsory, they are now more debated. Even if the vast majority of the local community belong to the Church of Norway, it is not necessarily felt to be right for the local school to include a special 'school-church-service' in its programme. It should be noted that these debates are closely related to the traditions and cultural composition of local communities.

Debates about Aims, Content and Teaching in Religious Education

When the new religious education subject was launched in 1997 it was after a process that started with the general core curriculum passed by Parliament in 1993 and is still the same. This core curriculum covers primary, lower and higher secondary school as well as adult education. A committee was asked to revise the entire religious education on all school levels and delivered its white paper in 1995 (KUF, 1995). To the surprise of many they suggested a common religious education subject for all children in primary and lower secondary school. Also a syllabus was suggested; with the immediate result that

---

10   http://www.humanrights.uio.no/omenheten/nytt/aktuelt/Sak.pdf (accessed 28 August 2006).
11   http://www.humanrights.uio.no/omenheten/nytt/aktuelt/lerivag.pdf (accessed 28 August 2006).

discussion focused on the syllabus, more than the issues of principle. Consultations started with the religious communities and the Humanist Association and the end result was the curriculum of 1997 including the new religious education. The non-Christian minorities' organisations opposed the curriculum mainly because they felt it was giving too much attention to Christianity and to little towards other religions ad world-views, but also because it did not allow for full exemption.

In spite of opposition the subject was established and aims and content stated in the Education Act, as the only school subject. Some of the details have been changed later, but the main content still stands. The formulations today are these:

Section 2–4. Teaching in the subject Christian Knowledge and Religious and Ethical Education.

Teaching in Christian Knowledge and Religious and Ethical Education shall

- provide a thorough knowledge of the Bible and Christianity as cultural heritage
- provide thorough knowledge of Evangelical-Lutheran understanding of Christianity and other Christian denominations,
- provide knowledge of other world religions and philosophies of life
- provide knowledge of ethical and philosophical topics,
- promote understanding and respect for Christian and humanist values and
- promote understanding, respect and the ability to carry out a dialogue between people with differing views concerning beliefs and philosophies of life.

Christian Knowledge and Religious and Ethical Education is an ordinary school subject that shall normally be attended by all pupils. Teaching in the subject shall not involve preaching.

Teachers of Christian Knowledge and Religious and Ethical Education shall present Christianity, other religions and philosophies of life on the basis of their distinctivecharacteristics. Teaching of the different topics shall be founded on the same educational principles.[12]

The emphasis on Christianity (thorough knowledge) is well in tune with the formulations of the general core curriculum about national heritage. It is quantified in the religious education syllabus by instructing the schools to allocate 55% of the teaching hours to Christianity, 25% to Judaism, Islam, Hinduism, Buddhism and other religious views, and 20% to philosophy and ethics. These instructions about the content of the subject also have some consequences for aims, and religious minorities have pointed out that the syllabus is firmly based in the majority culture and religion. A small book was made to communicate the changes (Utdanningsdirektoratet, 2005)

The aims of the subject as stated in the curriculum have both individual and social dimensions. On the individual level the focus is on knowledge about religions and world-views as an important contribution to the life-interpretation of individuals and the understanding of fellow human beings. To understand Norwegian society it is also important to know the traditions and values that have shaped this country and European culture. On the social level the aims underline that general knowledge based in religious education

---

12   The official Norwegian wording is found in Lovdtata: http://www.lovdata.no/all/nl-19980717–061.html (accessed: 27 November 2006). This english text is translated by Geir Skeie, based on the Norwegian one and aided by the official translation of an earlier version of the law.

will contribute to social cohesion, dialogue between people from different backgrounds, and a chance to learn to treat each other with respect.

These aims are also reflected in the eleven general principles of education that are applicable to all school subjects, particular no. 4:

> Stimulate the pupils in their personal development and identity, an in developing ethical, social and cultural competences and democratic citizenship.[13]

Together with the questions of subject content these aims have been the focus of debate since 1997. Disagreement does not so much concern the aims mentioned, but whether the syllabus and the practical teaching really live up to these ideals. To simplify the issues a little, we may detect two main positions among researchers. One position defends the syllabus by arguing that the majority tradition (national heritage) should be dominating of two reasons; because it represents the overwhelming majority of the population and because it is the interest of the minorities to know this tradition in order to manage successfully in a majority society (Gravem, 2004). The other position is critical towards the syllabus because it is not reflecting the multicultural and multireligious nature of today's Norwegian society. This position sees the syllabus as marked by internal tensions, combining majority domination in aims and content with declaration of multicultural ambitions (Skeie, 2003, 2006; Aadnanes & Johannessen, 2000).

The debate between interest groups and involving the general public, have also raised issues about the subject. Some, particularly from the Humanist Association, have been critical towards teaching that includes experience, involvement and emotions. In their view teaching about religions and worldviews should focus on knowledge and deliberation. To some extent religious minorities have agreed in this, being worried that their traditions will not be treated with the necessary respect. Some have argued that the faith communities should be consulted in matters of teaching materials, which was the rule earlier. In other cases, local debates have started on the basis of stories about teaching practices in a particular school that parents have reacted against.

Since 1997 many teachers have increased their competence within religious education, and basic teacher training now has a compulsory course lasting 2/3 of academic year in religion and religious education. Still many teachers find that they lack knowledge of non-Christian religions, and this may influence their teaching. Talking to teachers, the impression is that religious education still has a low priority in schools. Often those who teach it have little formal education in the subject, and it is known to be one of the last subjects to get its hours fixed when planning a new year. This means that any teacher may get to teach it.

We do not know much about pupils' views on the subject, but there are indications that it is rather well received in primary school, not so well in secondary. There may be many reasons for this, not all of them having to do with religious education in itself. Taking a pupils' perspective, however, it would not be surprising if the low priority on the part of the school has consequences. Another issue that has been little looked into in Norwegian religious education for many years is the fact that a large proportion of the children are not very interested in religion. This reflects the general population and

---

13   Utdanningsdirektoratet, 2005, p. 25, translated by Geir Skeie.

means that among children and young people it is quite rare to be an active member of a religious group, and this is most pronounced among members of the Church of Norway. The focus on living religion and on religious plurality in the last ten years of religious education has largely neglected the situation of this largest 'group' of children (Skeie, 2000).

Dialogue and Conflict

The concept of dialogue has been linked to religious education since the mid-nineties when the white paper suggesting a common religious education subject was called 'identity and dialogue' (KUF, 1995). In this document 'identity' had to do with belonging to a tradition, and dialogue had to do with communication between people from different traditions. The new religious education subject should contribute to both. All pupils should engage more with their own tradition, and all should be more acquainted with the traditions of others. Parallel to the curricular debates in school 'dialogue' has been used about contact and conversations between representatives of different religious communities in Norway as well as humanists. This type of dialogue is continuing to go on (Leirvik, 2001, 2003). In school this way of understanding the concept has been less used to capture certain ways of teaching, mostly because the idea was rejected that children could be representatives of their respective communities or religions in the classroom. Today 'dialogue' seems to be used as another word for a conversation where mutual understanding is the goal. It should also be mentioned that the concept has a long history within generic pedagogy, where it has been used to underline children's agency and of education as an ethical enterprise. This tradition has not been too much used within religious education, but still the concept has been used in a fruitful way by researchers (Leganger-Krogstad, 2003; Lied, 2004).

While dialogue has been used as a positive, value-laden concept, and with several intellectual traditions to draw upon, 'conflict' seems to have been firmly on the negative side. It may be used to signify the problematic aspects of Norwegian society, and in particular the difficulties of a plural society, and even more often about situations in other countries. Turning to religious education there has been little talk on a political level about conflicts or conflict resolution. Since the majority of political parties have supported the KRL-subject from the very beginning, possible conflicts will easily be seen as a result of bad practice, not weaknesses in curriculum. The critique of religious education from minorities is difficult to handle seen from the majority point of view, because it means that the social cohesion that the new subject should accomplish has not yet been fulfilled. It is easy then, to blame the failure either on the teachers or on those who protest, arguing that they make conflict where there should be no conflict.

There have been several signs of conflict; local protests against the KRL-subject, larger actions of protest, taking the exemption rules to court, questions in Parliament. Some of these issues have dealt with aspects of schooling other than religious education, like clothing, gender mixed physical education, or what kind of common assemblies that are acceptable. But the debate about the Muslim headscarf that swept across European countries did not become an issue in Norway. Very early in the debate the education authorities clearly stated that if certain clothing was part of someone's religious identity, it should be allowed. This position had clear connotations to the original vision of KRL to promote both identity and dialogue. If the aim of the school is to support and deepen the identity of each individual child, it seems impossible to justify a prohibition against such important identity signs.

Trends in Religious Education

In the late 1960s a scientific reflection on religious education started in Norway. At this time the ambitions of religious education was mainly to renew the perspective of the traditional teaching of Christianity in school and to meet the needs and interests of children and young people through better teaching. This perspective was informed by a theological basis, and the researchers saw renewal of school religious education and church nurture as two aspects of the same theoretical basis. Based on the Lutheran perspective of Ivar Asheim (Asheim, 1961) and much inspired by German religious education there was an important improvement in reflection on issues of education from a theological perspective in the 1960s and 1970s. The first religious education textbook for students based on this was published 1976, but teaching started long before this (Asheim, 1976)

In the 1980s an alternative perspective was offered through the work of O.G. Winsnes, who argued that the religious education of school should be based more on pedagogy than on theology (Winsnes, 1984c). His ideas were informed by his empirical research of children and adults as well as epistemological and methodological reflections (Winsnes, 1984a, 1984b, 1988). Here the German theological influence of the Asheim tradition was substituted by the sociology of religion (Thomas Luckmann), research on children's philosophy of life (Sven G. Hartman), and the theological reflections seemingly mostly inspired by Paul Tillich. At this time the religious education subject in school was still confessional in its formal structure, even if the content was mainly a general introduction to Christianity. Winsnes still argued that the role of religion in school was to help children in their reflection on life questions, more than to introduce them to a specific religion.

These two traditions in religious education theory can still be detected in Norway (Lied, 2006), but there are clear signs that the Asheim-tradition is losing importance the curriculum changes of 1997. Today most religious education research in Norway reflects the socio-cultural realities of a plural society as well as the pluralistic and multireligious perspective that is built into the school religious education subject (Lied, 2006; Skeie, 2004). The new situation has been a big challenge for teacher education, and several of the religious educators working in the teacher training colleges have taken up this challenge. Most of the research in recent years has been done by this group.

An influential trend in Norwegian pedagogical thinking has been the relationship between school and local community. The national curriculum of 1987 reflected this, and many of those working in teacher education in the 1980s were influenced by several research projects developing *contextual approaches* to teaching, with a stronghold in the northern parts of Norway (Høgmo, 1983; Høgmo & Solstad, 1977; Høgmo, Tiller, & Solstad, 1981; Solstad, 1978, 1981, 2003; Solstad & Andræ Thelin, 2006) The first text book for teacher training students reflecting the 1997 perspective was partly influenced by this northern contextual perspective (Afdal et al., 1997). It was also marked by the Winsnes tradition in Norwegian religious education, and all the authors who had worked together in the northernmost county of Finmark in the 1980s. The main new idea in the book is that the religious education theory underlying teaching has to reflect on the cultural context of children. Leganger-Korgstad's empirical research showed that this was not necessarily the case for all children (Leganger-Krogstad, 1995, 1998). According to this approach teachers should teach religious education in a way that made the children capable of reflecting on their lifeworld as they experienced it daily. Initially there was not so much focus on a multireligious perspective, but the authors have continued to work contextually with dialogue (Leganger-Krogstad, 2000, 2003), with teachers' personal approaches to religious education (Haakedal, 2004) and with tolerance (Afdal, 2006). Also Geir Skeie has been influenced by contextual perspectives in his parallel work on the philosophy and epistemology of religious education (Skeie, 1997, 1998).

The curriculum from 1997 and its successors in 2002 and 2005 have focused on issues of teaching that were partly new, and partly drawn from older traditions. The white paper leading towards the reformed curriculum was called 'Identity and Dialogue' (KUF, 1995) and since then dialogue has been an important concept in the debate on religious education in addition to the emphasis on dialogue in inter-religious relations outside of school. Particularly Leganger-Krogstad and Lied have done important work investigating children's dialogue in the religious education classroom (Leganger-Krogstad, 2003; Lied, 2004): There are also research projects, which are more critical of classroom dialogue (Gullbekk, 2000). An important discussion has been around what dialogue should mean in practical terms. Initial thoughts about children representing different religions in dialogue have been criticised and instead there has been more focus on dialogue as conversation about religions and beliefs as well as the 'inner dialogue' of learning. Also inspiration from pedagogical thinking about dialogue has played a part, underlining mainly the agency of children in teaching and learning.

Another issue in the 1997 curriculum was *story*, partly inspired by narrative Christian theology, partly by a trend of storytelling, and partly by a stronger focus on national cultural heritage with focus on folk tradition like fairytales. The idea was to make use of a narrative perspective on all religions and worldviews, and by means of this, using the same teaching approach in working with different traditions. It soon became clear that this approach was not without problems. Even if most traditions contain stories in some way or another, they do not necessarily play the same role in each tradition. Against this background Nicolaysen and Breidlid have suggested an approach to the use of stories from different traditions in religious education (Breidlid & Nicolaisen, 2000). Others have criticised this approach for being postmodern, arguing that the question of truth claims was neglected (Kvalvaag, 2002). Still, the story-telling approach has contributed a lot, and many teachers use this in their classes.

Also an aesthetical approach was launched in 1997, and the challenge was picked up by teacher educators to include more of art, music and literature in the teaching (Tobiassen, 1997a, 1997b; Winje et al., 2001). This approach has inspired many teachers to take further education, but particularly the Humanist association have been sceptical of this approach.

In 1997 *philosophy* was introduced as part of the religious education syllabus, and this theme was more or less new to the teachers. Gradually an interest has been growing in taking advantage of the international *philosophy-with-children* movement, and this approach is now gaining momentum in Norwegian schools. Teachers are being trained in this, and books based on the experiences of teachers and teacher trainers are beginning to come (Bostad & Svare, 2003; Børresen & Malmhester, 2003; Schjelderup et al., 1999). The main focus in this approach is not on the history of philosophy, but on philosophical thinking. In recent discussions it has been argued that the syllabus is more oriented towards the philosophical thoughts of Socrates, Kant, Hegel etc., than on philosophical thinking with the pupils.

A Perspective ahead

A significant aspect of the last curriculum reform implemented in 2006 has to do with changes in educational policy. The centrally governed curriculum is now much less detailed, leaving more freedom to the local level. Instead attainment targets have been introduced, focusing on learning outcomes after 4th, 7th and 10th grade. Some of them are very specific, while some are more complex and leaves much to be discussed locally. This change in policy was combined with a strong emphasis on certain skills that should be promoted through teaching in all subjects: oral presentation, reading, writing, arithmetic and using digital tools. This reform has led to a large activity in the municipalities in order to construct local versions of the curriculum.

For religion in education this swing in educational policy presents both challenges and possibilities. Religious education research must work much more intensively with the schools if religious education is to be improved, and religion taken seriously as part of a broader educational perspective.

The Norwegian project in REDCo attempts to investigate how different actors see the school religious education subject, with particular interest in its contribution to dialogue and/or conflict. References to 'dialogue' or 'conflict' are certainly found in the religious education curriculum texts, and other political documents dealing with religious education in the Norwegian context. But how should such issues be interpreted 'on the ground'? One way of dealing with this is to focus on incidents or examples, more than on the different actors' opinions. But there are also more conceptual issues buried here. How do we draw the borders between 'conflict' and 'dialogue' if these are to be understood as descriptive? Is 'conflict' negative and 'dialogue' positive, and how do we demarcate the two in practice? It is possible that the two concepts should be seen as opposites in a dialectic relationship rather than opposing categories. This could mean that some sort of conflict is a necessary basis for dialogue and that dialogue here and now may lead to conflicts later, or on another social level.

The comparative aspect of the entire REDCo project will hopefully throw light also on the different ways religious education is practised in Norway. An earlier evaluation of Norwegian religious education (KRL) showed that there were distinct differences in the way the subject is taught, although no explanation was given for this. We think it is valuable to focus on *intra-Norwegian comparison* and to link this with the overall European project. It is certainly interesting if the particular way religious education is taught locally in Norway has more effect on the conflict/dialogue dimension than national curricula and educational systems, or if the national framework is more decisive for conflict/dialogue than local teaching. In Norway it is possible that regional differences in religious history and other cultural patterns may influence the interpretation of conflicts related to religious education. In some places cultural conflicts are open and part of daily life, while in other places they are hidden and only played out in sophisticated and complex ways. It is quite likely also that immigrant minorities will accommodate to such regional differences, leading to regionalised strategies of identity management. The Norwegian contribution into the REDCo project will hopefully shed light on some of the issues addressed in this article.

References

Aadnanes, P. M. (2000) Religionsundervisningens historie i norsk allmennskole. *Prismet, 51* (2000), 204–218 & 223–229.

Aadnanes, P. M., & Johannessen, K. I. (2000) *Et Fag for enhver smak? en evaluering av KRL-faget* (Oslo, Diaforsk).

Afdal, G. (2006) *Tolerance and curriculum: conceptions of tolerance in the multicultural unitary Norwegian compulsory school* (Münster, Waxmann Verlag).

Afdal, G., Haakedal, E., & Leganger-Krogstad, H. (1997) *Tro, livstolkning og tradisjon: innføring i kontekstuell religionsdidaktikk* (Oslo, Tano Aschehoug).

Asheim, I. (1961) *Glaube und Erziehung bei Luther: ein Beitrag zur Geschichte des Verhältnisses von Theologie und Pædagogik* (Heidelberg, Quelle und Meyer).

Asheim, I. (1976) *Religionspedagogikk: en innføring* (Oslo, Universitetsforlaget).

Børresen, B., & Malmhester, B. (2003) *La barna filosofere: den filosofiske samtale i skolen* (Kristiansand, Høyskoleforlaget).

Bostad, I., & Svare, H. (2003) *Samtaler om filosofi* (Oslo, Høgskolen i Oslo).

Breidlid, H., & Nicolaisen, T. (2000) *I begynnelsen var fortellingen: fortelling i KRL* (Oslo, Universitetsforlaget).

Bugge, K. E., & Johannessen, S. (Eds.) (1974) *Religionspædagogiske brydninger* (København, Nyt Nordisk Forlag).

Enger, T. (1998) Relgious Education for all pupils – The Norwegian Way, *PANORAMA International Journal of Comparative Religious Education and Values, 10* (2), 122–134.

Enger, T. (2001) Religious Education for all Pupils stands Trial – the Norwegian Experisence after three years, *PANORAMA International Journal of Comparative Religious Education and Values, 13* (2), 77–87.

Gravem, P. (2004) *KRL – et fag for alle? KRL-faget som svar på utfordringer i en flerkulturell enhetsskole* (Vallset, Oplandske bokforlag).

Grytnes, R. (2004) Muslimsk privatskole – en trussel eller et uttrykk for multikulturalisme? *Norsk pedagogisk tidsskrift, 88* (2–3), 145–156.

Gullbekk, E. (2000) *Med identitet på timeplanen: læreres arbeid med grunnskolefaget Kristendomskunnskap med religions- og livsynsorientering* (Bergen, [E.Gullbekk]).

Hagesæther, G., Sandsmark, S., Bleka, D.-A., Norsk lærerakademi & Norges forskningsråd (2000) *Foreldres, elevers og læreres erfaringer med KRL-faget.* (Bergen, NLA-forl.).

Haakedal, E. (2001) From Lutheran Cathechism to Worlds Religions and Humanism: Dilemmas and Middle Ways through the Story of Norwegian Religious Education, *British Journal of Religious Education, 23* (2), 88–97.

Haakedal, E. (2004) *"Det er jo vanlig praksis hos de fleste her –":* religionslærerrolle, livstolkning og skolekulturell ritualisering: en religionspedagogisk studie av grunnskolelæreres handlingsrom på 1990–tallet (Oslo, Unipub).

Henriksen, J.-O., & Krogseth, O. (Eds.) (2001) *Pluralisme og identitet: kulturanalytiske perspektiver på nordiske nasjonalkirker i møte med religiøs og moralsk pluralisme* (Oslo, Gyldendal akademisk).

Henriksen, J.-O., & Repstad, P. (2005) *Tro i sør. Sosiologiske og teologiske blikk på sørlandsk religion* (Bergen, Fagbokforl).

Høgmo, A., & Solstad, K.J. (1977) *The Lofoten project: towards a relevant education.* ([Tromsø], University of Tromsø Department for Social Science).

Høgmo, A., Tiller, T. & Solstad, K. J. (1981) *Skolen og den lokale utfordring: en sluttrapport fra Lofotprosjektet* (Tromsø , Universitetet i Tromsø).

Høgmo, A. (1983) The situation in primary education in the Saami area: two cases, *Scandinavian journal of educational research 27*(1), 15-34.

Hovdelien, O. (2003) Fra kristen trosopplæring til pluralistisk religionsundervisning. Den religionspedagogiske utvikling i norsk skole, *Norsk pedagogisk tidsskrift 87*(5–6), 272–281.

Johannessen, K.I., Høgskulen i Volda, Norges forskningsråd & Diakonhjemmets høgskolesenter (2000) *Et Fag for enhver smak?: en evaluering av KRL-faget, Rapport / Diaforsk; 2000:3.* (Oslo, Diaforsk).

KKD. (2006) *Staten og Den norske kirke*: utredning fra Stat – kirke-utvalget oppnevnt ved kongelig resolusjon av 14. mars 2003: avgitt til Kultur- og kirkedepartementet 31. januar 2006 (Oslo, Departementenes servicesenter Informasjonsforvaltning).

Kristiansen, R. (2005) *Samisk religion og læstadianisme* (Bergen, Fagbokforlaget).

KUF (1995) *Identitet og dialog: kristendomskunnskap, livssynskunnskap og religionsundervisning*: utredning fra et utvalg oppnevnt av Kirke-, utdannings- og forskningsdepartementet i august 1994; avgitt 3. mai 1995 (Oslo, Statens forvaltningstjeneste Statens trykning).

Kvalvaag, R.W. (2002) Er det allmennmenneskelig å være religiøs? *Religion og livssyn: tidsskrift for Religionslærerforeningen i Norge,* (2), 48–53.

Leganger-Krogstad, H. (1995) *Læstadianske oppdragelsesidealer og skolekonflikten i Alta: foreldrenes ønsker for opplæring og oppdragelse.* ([Alta], Høgskolen i Finnmark Avdeling for barnehage- og skolefag).

Leganger-Krogstad, H. (1998) Ethnic Minority in Conflict with Norwegian Educational Ideals, *PANORAMA International Journal of Comparative Religious Education and Values,* 10(1), 131–145.

Leganger-Krogstad, H. (2000). Developing a contextual theory and practice of Religious Education. *PANORAMA International Journal of Comparative Religious Education and Values,* 12(1), 94–104.

Leganger-Krogstad, H. (2003). Dialogue among Young Citizens in a Pluralistic Religious Education Classroom, in: R. Jackson (Ed.), *International Perspectives on Citizenship, Education and Religious Diversity* (London, Routhledge/Falmer) 169–190.

Leirvik, O. (2001) *Religionsdialog på norsk* (Oslo, Pax).

Leirvik, O. (2003) Muslim-Christian dialogue – global ethics and moral disagreement: a Scandinavian perspective, in: V. Mortensen (Ed.), *Theology and the Religions: A Dialogue* (Grand Rapids, Michigan, William B. Eerdmanns) 212–217.

Lied, S. (2004) *Elever og livstolkingspluralitet i KRL-faget: mellomtrinnselever i møte med fortellinger fra ulike religioner og livssyn* (PhD avhandling) (Elverum, Høgskolen i Hedmark).

Lied, S. (2006) Norsk religionspedagogisk forskning 1985–2005, *Norsk teologisk tidsskrift, forthcoming.*

Møse, E., & Kirke- utdannings- og forskningsdepartementet (1997) *Fritak for undervisning i faget kristendomskunnskap med religions- og livssynsopplæring: forholdet til Norges folkerettslige forplik[t]elser:* utredning avgitt til Kirke- utdannings- og forskningsdepartementet 22 januar 1997 ([Oslo], Kirke- utdannings- og forskningsdepartementet).

Oftestad, B. T. (1998) *Den norske statsreligionen: fra øvrighetskirke til demokratisk statskirke* (Kristiansand, Høyskoleforl).

Repstad, P. (1996) *Religion and modernity: modes of co-existence* (Oslo, Scandinavian University Press).

Repstad, P. (2000) *Religiøst liv i det moderne Norge: et sosiologisk kart* (2nd ed.). (Kristiansand, Høyskoleforl).

Repstad, P., & Henriksen, J.-O. (2005) *Mykere kristendom? Sørlandsreligion i endring* (Bergen, Fagbokforlaget).

Schjelderup, A., Børresen, B. & Olsholt, Ø. (1999) *Filosofi i skolen* (Oslo, Tano Aschehoug).

Skeie, G. (1997). Some Aspects of RE in Scandinavia and Norway. An Outline of a Cultural Approach to RE, in: T. Andree, C. Bakker & P. Schreiner (Eds.), *Crossing Boundaries. Contributions to Interreligious and Intercultural Education* (Münster, Comenius Institut/ University of Utrecht).

Skeie, G. (1998) *En kulturbevisst religionspedagogikk* (Trondheim, Norges teknisk-natur-vitenskapelige universitet).

Skeie, G. (2000) Jeg er ingenting, gjør det noe? om identifikasjon og kommunikasjon i religions-undervisninga, in: E. Birkedal, H. Hegstad & G. Skeie. (Eds.) *Forskning og fundering: religion og religiøsitet i skole, kirke og samfunn: festskrift til Ole Gunnar Winsnes* (Trondheim, Tapir Akademisk Forlag) 99–121.

Skeie, G. (2003) Nationalism, religiosity and citizenship in Norwegian majority and minority discourses, in: R. Jackson (Ed.), *International perspectives on Citizenship, Education and Religious Diversity* (London, Routhledge/Falmer) 51–66.

Skeie, G. (2004) An Overview of Religious Education research in Norway, in: R. Larsson & C. Gustavsson (Eds.) *Towards a European Perspective on Religious Education. The RE Research Conference March 11.14, 2004, University of Lund.* Edited by O. Bexell, S. Borgehammar & S.-E. Brodd. Vol. 74, *Biblioteca Theologiae Practicae.* (Skellefteå, Artos & Norma bokförlag) 317-331.

Skeie, G. (2006) Diversity and the political function of religious education, *British Journal of Religious Education,* 28(1), 19–32.

Solstad, K. J. (1978) *Riksskole i utkantstrok* (Tromsø, Universitetsforlaget).

Solstad, K. J. (1981) Locally Relevant Curricula in Rural Norway: The Lofoten Islands Example, in: J.P. Sher (Ed.), *Rural education in urbanized nations: issues and innovations* (Boulder, Colo.: Westview Press) 301-324.

Solstad, K. J. (2003) Nordnorsk utdanningshistorie – kva kan det vere?, *Skolen : årbok for norsk utdanningshistorie* (Notodden: Stiftelsen) 5-11.

Solstad, K. J., & Andræ Thelin, A. (2006) *Skolen og distrikta: samspel eller konflikt?* (Bergen, Fagbokforl).

Tobiassen, T. (1997a) Billeddidaktikk i KRL-faget, *Prismet,* 48(5), 199–210.

Tobiassen, T. (1997b) Trenger vi en kunstkanon for KRL-faget? *Prismet,* 48(5), 211–212 og 221–225.

Tuastad, S. (2006) *Skulen og statsmaktsspørsmålet. Storingsdebattar 1945–2005 om religion i skulen og om private skular i lys av normativ teori. Avhandling for graden dr. polit.* (Bergen, Universitetet i Bergen).

Utdanningsdirektoratet (2005) *KRL-boka 2005*: kristendoms-, religions- og livssynskunnskap, læreplan for 1.–10. årstrinn, læreplanveiledning og informasjon (Oslo, Utdannings-direktoratet).

Winje, G., Tobiassen, T. & Kristiansen, R. E. (2001) *Guddommelig skjønnhet: kunst i religionene* (Oslo, Universitetsforlaget).

Winsnes, O. G. (1984a) 215 småbarnsforeldre om sitt forhold til religion og til religiøs sosialisering av barn i førskolealder: frekvensopptelling fra ReSo-prosjektets fase 1, *Rapport / Prosjektet "Religion og sosialisering"* (Trondheim: Religionsvitenskapelig institutt, Universitetet i Trondheim, Norges lærerhøgskole).

Winsnes, O. G. (1984b) Førskolelærere om sitt forhold til religion og til religiøs sosialisering av barn i førskolealder : frekvensopptelling fra ReSo-prosjektets fase 4, *Rapport / Prosjektet "Religion og sosialisering"* (Trondheim: Religionsvitenskapelig institutt, Universitetet i Trondheim, Norges lærerhøgskole).

Winsnes, O. G. (1984c) *Kristendomskunnskap – erfaring – kommunikasjon en samling artikler om religionspedagogiske emner* ([Trondheim], Tapir).

Winsnes, O. G. (1988) *E' du rel'giøs, eller – ? om konseptualisering og metodologi i empirisk religionsforskning* Dr. avh. (Trondheim, Det historisk-filosofiske fakultet Den allmenn-vitenskapelige høgskolen Universitetet i Trondheim).

Thorsten Knauth

Religious Education in Germany:
Contribution to Dialogue or Source of Conflict?

A Historical and Contextual Analysis of its Development since the 1960s

The change that religion's role in the German education system has undergone since the Second World War is well demonstrated by the development of the school subject of religious education. Up to the 1960s, religious education in public schools was taught in close cooperation with established churches. It was based on dogmatic and systematic theology and familiarized students with the Bible, the hymnbook, and central parts of church history. Its stated aim was to introduce the Gospel to the (mainly baptised) pupils as the liberating Word of God.[1] Today, nearly 50 years later, religious education has opened itself to religious and cultural plurality. It defines its purpose from its standing as a school subject, and therefore in pedagogical as well as theological terms. Every religious community which carries a share of responsibility for religious education in schools thus faces the challenge of interpreting its own religious tradition in a context of religious diversity and cultural heterogeneity. Furthermore, there is increased awareness of the fact that contextual factors such as, for example, the religious composition of the student body or the religious landscape of the region are strong contributing factors to the conceptional profile and the didactic design of religious education (Heimbrook, 2004; Günther et al., 2005). By now, there is no longer a standardized model for religious education which applies to the North and South, the East and West of Germany. Instead, considerable differences between regions have developed. Apart from such regional and political differences, however, there is consensus emerging in the discussion to treat religion as a significant dimension in the field of general education (Nipkow, 1998; Elsenbast/Pithan/Schreiner/Schweitzer, 2004). Religion becomes important for the educational process inasmuch as it is able to contribute to developing value orientation and communication within a society which is threatened by processes of societal fragmentation.

In the course of this chapter I will outline the development and change which religious education in the school context underwent over the last 40 years. This reconstruction will show that the debate on religious education within the educational system has always functioned as an indicator for societal change:

Cultural modernisation and advancing secularisation made religious education receptive to society's problems and led to an increasing emphasis on ethical issues. The abandoning of traditions and growing religious diversity caused the subject to reflect upon concepts of intercultural and interreligious learning and to rethink its established denominational approach. And at present, in the shadow of an ambivalent revival of the

---

1   Compare Bolle et al., 2002 and Jahrbuch der Religionspädagogik (1995) for an overview of the concept.

public and political discourse on religion, it appears vital to strengthen those dialogical aspects which hold the potential to facilitate living together in a multireligious society in opposition to any violent instrumentalisation.

The development of religious education towards an increasing ability of the subject to address plurality and dialogue has by no means been linear and straightforward. However, eventually conceptual solutions for religious education were implemented which were able to respond to the rising societal need for cultural and religious understanding in an appropriate and critical manner and to contribute to dialogue. This was possible because, since the mid-sixties at the latest, the subject had opened up to society and its increasingly manifold and heterogeneous contexts in its conceptual orientation. Though this opening was conceived less within the context of religious hermeneutical premises than interpreted within the analytical framework of secularisation theory, the contextual conception of the subject has not changed since then. Rather, this very contextual orientation of the subject is a significant factor ensuring the contribution of religion towards an education for plurality and dialogue (Knauth, 2005, pp. 49–60).

After a brief introduction to the overall position of the subject, I will present an outline of the state of public discourse on religious education based on statements published at two different turning points in the social history of Germany. The years 1968 and 1989 are of great importance in contemporary history. They are also crystallisation points for major conceptual shifts in religious education and typical constellations of religion in the educational system. In this article they will serve as a window through which we can observe the relevant discourses on the status of religious education and religion at school. By doing so, it will become evident that the 1970s and 1990s respectively mark the beginning of many issues still informing the current debate.

On the Legal Context of Religious Education in the Federal Republic of Germany

In order to understand the specific status of religion within the educational system of the Federal Republic of Germany, we need to recall that German democracy was built upon the ruins of the Second World War and a dictatorial and fascist system of oppression. The National Socialist genocide had brought a hitherto unprecedented dimension of inhumanity and cruelty. This, it was resolved, could never be allowed to happen again. All societal and political efforts were directed to laying the moral and ethical foundations for a peaceful and humane coexistence. After the collapse of National Socialist tyranny, religion was accorded a significant public role in liberated Germany. Christian principles were to inform childrearing, schooling and education. Many people were convinced that only an education built on religious values could counteract societal decay.[2]

At the same time it was clear that the state could never again be allowed the power to define religious and ideological questions. Liberty, as a precondition to democracy, would not be possible if the state dictated religion. Especially for the very personal ques-

---

2   You will find a richly-detailed overview of the situation of religious education in the first two years after the Second World War in Helmreich (1966).

tions of ethical development and orientation in religious and ideological matters, the state needed to be prevented from imposing its will on its citizens. It needed to be prevented from dictating doctrine and content to religions. Yet at the same time it was supposed and urged to adopt a position of openness to religion as such. In fact, its highest duty was to provide a public space for the authentic self-portrayal and self-interpretation of the Religious and thus allow the free development of individual religion and world view. As a consequence, the framers of the constitution, in an attitude of a conscious self-restriction, left it to the established churches to develop the content of religious education.

That is how they came to formulate the two articles in the German *Grundgesetz* (constitution) which define the special form and status of religious education in German schools.[3] Article 4 enshrines the basic civil right of freedom of religion. Although strictly neutral in terms of religion and world view, the state provides the public space for their expression. In Article 7, chapter 3, RE is defined as a regular school subject to be taught 'in accordance with the principles of the religious communities'. This means that the state provides the formal and financial framework for it. State organs also ensure that RE follows the fundamental educational aims established in state laws on the subject. The content of RE and the accreditation of teachers, however, is left to the religious communities. They have to formulate goals and the content according to their interpretation of their faith. Owing to the standing of religious freedom as a basic constitutional right, students have the right to opt out of RE and teachers can not be obliged to teach the subject against their will.

In the process of democratisation after World War II, religious and ideological upbringing and education were interpreted in the light of fundamental freedoms and human rights, and formulated from a fresh historical experience of institutional and state structures of oppression.

Until the 1980s, it was common to assume that the 'religious communities' addressed in the *Grundgesetz* were, for practical purposes, represented by the Roman Catholic and the Lutheran churches. However, the basic idea of providing public space in the broader context of state institutions for all groups within society to enter into dialogue on their ideology and religion was included in the constitution of the Federal Republic from the very beginning.

Thus, dialogue in the context of religious and ideological plurality is a democratic heritage of the framers of the constitution. Owing to social changes and an increasing awareness of the importance of multiculturalism, it has become increasingly clear that Article 7 of the *Grundgesetz* also had to apply to religious communities beyond the established churches. They, too, could claim the right either to have their own subject in school or to participate in framing the content and teaching of RE.[4]

---

3   Basic information on the status of RE within the educational system of Germany has already been given in: Schreiner, 2000, p. 49–54. For recent information about the situation of protestant RE see also the report of the Kultusministerkonferenz of 13.12.2002: Zur Situation des Evangelischen Religionsunterrichts in der Bundesrepublik Deutschland, www.kmk.org (accessed: 29.08.2006).

4   See the article by Jozsa in this volume for a discussion of Islamic RE in Germany.

Stations of Change: Modernising RE in the Light of the Secularisation Thesis

German society has greatly changed in its relation to religion since the end of the Second World War. Only sixty years ago Germany considered itself a Christian country. Its population was deeply committed to the two main Christian denominations. In 1950, 96,4% of the population belonged to either the Protestant or the Catholic churches.[5] Church and religious life shaped biographies and lifestyles to a much greater extent than is the case today. In the fifties, denominational milieus existed throughout the rural areas of the Republic. Even though a debate on the merits of denominational schools was beginning, the Christian foundation of German schools was beyond question. This only began to change – also through impulses from the church and theology – in the late 1950s. In 1958, the synod of the Protestant church in Berlin announced its support for an open education in a free school, and sharply renounced the church imposing its will on schools and teachers.[6]

In the 1950s, the great shift towards modernisation and individualisation, the consequences of which affect today's situation lay still in the future for German society (Kaufmann, 1989; Gabriel, 1992).[7] Four decades of division into two German states in the shadow of politically and ideologically opposed systems lay ahead. These were also the four decades in which East Germany was to become the area with the highest proportion of people without religious or denominational ties (Domsgen, 2006).[8] West German society also faced several waves of politically engineered immigration to come, which turned the Federal Republic into a multicultural society within a quarter of a century.[9] Yet German society did not then think of itself as on the way towards secularisation or any change of its attitude towards the hitherto dominant religious traditions that informed its self-image. The processes of secularisation, and of an overall cultural modernisation of society, set in in the mid-sixties, a time when – parallel to similar developments in other European countries – a politicised younger generation emerged to challenge the supremacy of society's materialistic orientation. They were motivated by an

---

5   See Statistisches Bundesamt (1966): Fachserie A/Bevölkerung und Kultur/Volks- und Berufs-
     zählung vom 6. Juni 1961, Heft 5, Bevölkerung nach der Religionszugehörigkeit, Stuttgart, p. 21.
6   Kirchenamt der EKD (Hg.): Bildung und Erziehung. Die Denkschriften der Evangelischen
     Kirche in Deutschland, Gütersloh 1987, darin: Wort der Synode der Evangelischen Kirche in
     Deutschland zur Schulfrage, p. 37.
7   In his study on questions on the sociology of Christianity K. Gabriel (1992) outlined three
     phases of transformation in Christianity in the course of modernisation: a first phase of renais-
     sance and stability of a Christianity defined by established churches (up to the mid-sixties), a
     phase of disintegration of tradition and transformation of the Christian churches (from 1968
     onwards) and a phase of religious plurality and individualisation (from the eighties onwards).
8   Müller et al., 2006, p. 26 in the book published by Domsgen refer to numbers according to
     which more than 70% of the population in Eastern Germany do not belong to any denomina-
     tion: about 25% belong to the Protestant church, 3% to Catholic church. They emphasise that
     the processes of erosion of the two main denominations still continues: After 1989, the number
     of people opting out of the churches exceeded the number of people entering a church every
     year (3,5: 1 in the Lutheran church; 22: 1 in the Catholic church).
9   According to the latest statistical data, every fifth German citizen has a migration background,
     in absolute numbers that is 15,3 million people, though according to official data, only 7,3 mil-
     lion count as 'foreigners'. cf. Statistisches Bundesamt: Mikrozensus 2005.

ethic of justice and brotherhood, applying the most radical and comprehensive standards of democracy to institutions and society (Fend, 1988). Their aim was an internationalisation of their effort and solidarity with the liberation movements in the Third World and they approached politics inspired by the spirit of grassroots movements: collective self-determination and personal autonomy. To them, politics was fundamentally connected with personal life and even the most intimate and private matters had to be accounted for in a forum of political rationalism (Ziehe, 1991). Cultural historian Hermann Glaser (1991) called this nascent modernisation a, 'tremor in the underground of society'. Last but not least, it led to extensive reforms in the educational system which aimed to dismantle social inequality through participatory educational concepts. Religious education was considerably affected by this.[10] The pupils – being trained in the religious criticism of the nineteenth century – dissociated themselves from the church and extended their criticism of social traditions to religious education. As a consequence of this critical reading of religion in its ideological functions, large numbers of them opted out of religious education.

The subject had nothing to offer to them that could address their interest in current debates about politics and ethical ideas, their passion for justice at a national and international level, or their interest in cultures and religions throughout the world. By the end of the sixties, churches, schools and universities were faced with the need to revise the previous concept of religious education. Under the impression of these societal developments, decisive change in the conception and orientation of religious education took place within only a few years' time. Religious education now oriented itself towards the newly formulated objective of autonomy and emancipation in schools. It explicitly sought to enter into dialogue with the now secular schools and society, it abandoned a purely tradition-oriented, solely biblical concept and embraced debate on the political and ethical key issues of those years. In the course of an introductory political approach towards theology,[11] religious learning was seen in connection with political education and civic commitment. Religion was to contribute to a humane culture. In order to achieve this goal, it was necessary to detach the subject from its denominational limitations and define it not as an isolated field but as contributing distinctively to wider interdisciplinary approaches and discourses. The religious pedagogue Hans Stock was the first to speak of an, 'education towards orientation, open for problems', whose basic principle is dialogue in order to develop individual subjectivity by experiencing solidarity and tolerance towards the otherness of each individual person (Stock, 1969, p. 39).

This awareness that religion in school would have to enter into dialogue with secular opinions and world views, that religious education would therefore have to prove itself in a plurality of ideologies, is also reflected in church statements on religious education from the time. In a statement in 1971 which garnered wide attention, the Protestant church interpreted its understanding of denominational religious education in a very open manner and defined its duty to seek dialogue with other religions as well as with atheist views (Kirchenamt der EKD 1987, volume 4/1). The Protestant Church of Germany thus

---

10   On the societal and cultural context of this phase of religious education compare Knauth, 2003.
11   Those approaches are linked with the names of Johann B. Metz (1968, 1997) on the Catholic part and Moltmann (1972) and D. Sölle (1971) on the Lutheran part.

signalled its commitment to the societal duty of religious education to foster freedom of religion, conscience and worship of all denominations and religions in a pedagogical manner (Goßmann 1993, p. 119).

This church statement already reflected the growing importance of religious diversity in society. At this, the policy of recruiting so-called guest workers began, which would lead to a first critical debate on how to deal with families which immigrated mainly from Southern European countries, once that it turned out they were planning to stay in the Federal Republic of Germany. The educational system was unprepared for this. The first reaction was a a so-called *Ausländerpädagogik* (pedagogy for foreigners) formulated especially for the children of guest workers which in the beginning pursued a dual objective of teaching in their native language and offering adequate support programmes – thus securing the option of returning to their home countries for the immigrant children, but also preparing them for life in the host country. In the curricula for religious education, this topic was represented in units on the problem of guest workers, but conspicuously without throwing further light on the religious dimension of this issue (Knauth, 2000). The emerging multiculturalism in the Federal Republic was addressed by religious education as a socio-ethical issue. Religion, in turn, played practically no role in the development of *Ausländerpädagogik* into intercultural education in the 1990s.[12]

Yet the shift towards a problem-oriented perspective in religious education involved a first look at other world religions.[13]

The study of the other great religions – this was the title of an important textbook of religious education in the early phase – was driven by growing interest on the part of the students as well as a widening horizon of the subject from a national context to international areas of conflict and problems: in these political and problem-oriented times, world religions were looked at in connection with the problems of the world. Thus religion, the local issue of guest workers, re-entered the scene in the field of world religions, here Third World-issues. Religions other than Christianity are – in short – transferred to distant foreign countries and perceived through the medium of religious anthropology. In contrast to missionary approaches of the past, the intention to 'neutrally' inform students about other religions represented religious hermeneutical progress. Religious diversity in the pupils' immediate environment and realm of experience is still neglected at this point. Information, not dialogue, was the core aim of these models.

This is not surprising: Religious pedagogy considered the growing secularisation to be the major challenge and reinterpreted the present religious situation against the background of the so-called secularisation thesis:

The secularisation thesis was taken up by theology and religious pedagogy mainly after the Second World War.[14] It was intended to explain the changing relation between church and society, between religion as defined by the churches and the consciousness of

---

12   For an overview on the development from an 'education for foreigners' towards intercultural learning also compare Knauth, 1996, p. 45–52.

13   On the development of didactics of world religion since the seventies see Lähnemann, 1998.

14   In 1968 Karl-Ernst Nipkow published an essay with the programmatic heading: 'Christian education on faith in secular society' which intended to redefine the subject's basic religious and pedagogical orientation in the context of far-reaching social and scientific processes of change.

modern humans. It became obvious that religion bound to institutions, general cultural patterns of religion, and personal faith biographies increasingly diverged. This was due to processes of divergence in societal development which led to the dispersal of denominational milieus and to a stronger individualization of life-patterns.[15] This development was foreseen by the clear-sighted analyses of the religious sociologist Max Weber at the beginning of the twentieth century. In his analysis of Protestantism, Max Weber wrote that the modern world had been deprived of its mystical dimension through the rational organisation of society, economy and individual ways of life. This analysis of the modernisation process from the perspective of secularisation was still regarded as plausible in the 1970s – that religions would inevitably die off and society would become secularized to the degree that religion would be reduced to an individual and subjective dimension of meaning – if that – and limited to the private sphere. Generally speaking, the process of large sections of the population leaving the churches and becoming indifferent towards religion was yet to gather pace. The writings of religious sociologist Thomas Luckmann (1967) on 'invisible religion', but also the work by Peter Berger (1967, 1979) shaping the notion of the 'heretical Imperative', strengthened the conception of individualisation and pluralisation of a now private and hidden religion.

Another consequence of the secularisation thesis was that the hidden manifestations of the religious within cultural phenomena were explicitly sought out in some schools of religious pedagogy. Thus the realm of the subject was greatly expanded.[16]

Let us briefly summarise the findings: the first wave of modernisation of the subject occurs in the mid-sixties in the context of cultural and political groundshifts in the democratic societies of Western Europe. They introduce an opening of religious education to society, a connection of religion with political and ethical education and a broadening of the subject matter of religious education in school. In those years, religion in the educational system becomes associated with dialogue and a critical analysis of a society which conceived of itself as secular. Religious diversity only rudimentarily came into focus, but in twenty years' time it would be setting the tone for the debates on religious education in school.

Between Secularisation and Religious Plurality.
The Development of the 1990s

The year 1989 stands for a fundamental change which had a great impact on religious education as well. Through the political unification of the German Democratic Republic and the old Federal Republic, the question of the legal framework and the conceptual shape of religious education arose in the newly-formed federal states. Could they, and did they want to, just copy the framework of religious education as it was generally under-

---

15   This process is also illustrated by K. Gabriel (1992) in his religious-sociological reconstruction of the changing shape of Christianity in the history of the Federal Republic.

16   This was mainly the case in conceptions of problem-oriented religious education which followed the notion of religion formulated by Paul Tillich, though detaching this understanding of religion from the theological correlation of interpretation and thus neglecting the dialectics of anthropology and theology according to Tillich in favour of a purely anthropological definition.

stood in the 'old' Laender of West Germany and transfer it to the 'new' Laender of the Eastern parts of Germany? After all, the fact that atheism had been state doctrine in the German Democratic Republic had resulted in under 30% of the people in this area being church members. The future of religious education had to be discussed against the background of this profound abandonment of tradition and the highest proportion of people without religious affiliation anywhere in Europe (Domsgen, 2006). The constitution offered the opportunity to move towards a version of religious education different from the traditional denominational one in article 141 (the so-called Bremen clause)[17], but there had only been one exception in the old Laender. A second one was instituted in the state of Brandenburg where a new statewide obligatory subject with the name of 'life plans – ethics – religious knowledge' (L-E-R) was developed which was to take the place of denominational religious education and address the religious dimension by a neutral, factual education on different religions.[18]

The other 'new' federal states of the former GDR adopted religious education in accordance with article 7.3 of the constitution and in the first years also adopted parts of extant curricula and teaching material. However, in the 'old' Laender a debate arose at the end of the 1980s whether the preconditions for a denominational religious education were still met in view of the tendencies towards secularisation in young people's religious orientation with a simultaneous religious and cultural pluralisation of society.[19]

The most recent empirical studies had shown that the long-standing trend of secularisation in society extended into the religious orientation of the youth (Baacke, 1990; Barz, 1992). These studies documented that adolescents further distanced themselves from institutional religion; at the same time as they showed a growing trend to a new form of religiosity that had become radically individualized. With these new orientations, which were referred to as patchwork-religiosity, the religious field was, so to speak, conceptualised as a marketplace with a wide variety of religious offerings ranging from new religions, post-modernism, or esotericism. This diversity of religious orientations stimulated by processes of secularisation, individualisation and modernisation constitutes one facet of religious plurality. We need to differentiate between this and the ongoing immigration,

---

17   Article 141 states that those Laender who had their own federal regulation before 1st January 1949 are not compelled to implement denominational religious education according to article seven of the basic law. On the basis of this regulation, the federal state of Bremen established a non-denominational education in biblical history. That is why article 141 is also called the Bremen Clause.

18   The broad, controversial and persistent discussion on L-E-R cannot be outlined in this article (on its background and empirical findings see, for example, Edelstein, Grözinger et.al., 2001). By now the struggle between the churches and the federal state of Brandenburg on the question whether the state is allowed to implement an obligatory subject in the domain of religion and ideology has reached a compromise proposed by the Federal Constitutional Court. This compromise has been adopted into state legislation. It allows pupils to choose for themselves whether they want to participate in L-E-R if they attend religious education.

19   The volume 'Religion – warum und wozu in der Schule?' published by J. Lott, Weinheim 1992 presents a comprehensive review of this debate; also see the volume 'Dialog zwischen den Kulturen. Erziehungshistorische und religionspädagogische Gesichtspunkte interkultureller Bildung', 1994 published by I. Lohmann and W. Weisse in consideration of significant empirical studies.

which extends the spectrum of religious and cultural plurality into the traditions of other world religions, namely Islam.[20]

The theoreticians of secularisation had obviously been proven wrong. Society had not become non-religious. On the contrary, religion still played a vital role in many varieties beyond Christianity and the established churches.[21] Secularisation theory was replaced by the paradigm of plurality.[22] By the late 1990s, a heated debate arose on whether German society was able to consider itself a multicultural society or whether it still needed to learn how to become such a society.[23] It could not be denied that by now, including two generations of working immigrants as well as refugees and asylum seekers, the cultural spectrum of society had become far broader. But it also could not be denied that this development had not only led to a harmonious coexistence of cultures and religions, but was accompanied by conflicts whose cause (among other things) lay in the refusal of the autochthonous majority actively to respect the presence of people of different cultural and religious backgrounds and to appreciate them as an enrichment.

This plurality, of course, also affected the role of religion within the educational system. It posed a new challenge to religious education, namely that of integration, conflict management and communication facing a plurality which the schools were by no means easily able to cope with. This balance between dialogue and conflict in the field of religion extending to the societal level, shapes and forms the context for the German REDCo-Project. The demand for competence in dealing with religions increased. Conventional approaches to religious education had to be revised and new ones had to be developed which would allow more room for the increased demands of coordination and communication (Nipkow, 2003). This task is mainly identified as fostering independence and dialogical competence amid the diversity of competing orientations in a plural environment. Dialogue, therefore, became a key category in a concept of religious education open to plurality (Lohmann & Weiße, 1994; EKD, 1994; Weiße, 1995; Haussmann, 1994; Knauth, 1996). However, the question of which concept and model of religious education

---

20   Newer data is assuming that 32,2% f the 82 million people in the Federal Republic are Catholic, 31,7% % Lutheran (due to the immigration from Southern and Eastern Europe, East Asia and West Africa, cultural diversity in both churches is increasing); about 1,1% belong to an Orthodox church: about 3,7% are Muslims, of which 75% are Sunni, 4,5% are Shiite, 17,8% are Alevi, and 2,2% belong to Ahmdiyya (see Renz & Leimgruber, 2004, p. 24f.) It is estimated that up to half a million people profess membership of Buddhism. About 20.000 adherents each belong to Sikhism, Hinduism and Yazidism (Beuchling, 2002, p. 65f.). Recent studies have hinted at the fact that with almost one third of the population a remarkable group in Germany appears to be people without any denominational ties (see Domsgen, 2005).

21   See also the introduction by Weisse which also mentions the 'failure' of secularisation theory and the revitalisation of religion in the last decade.

22   According to Nipkow (1998, volume 1, p. 29 ff) pluralism must first be understood as an empirical term. It means a diversity of coexisting 'worships and religions (religious pluralism) of values (value pluralism) social groups (social pluralism) and forces shaping politics (political pluralism)'. Pluralism as a normative term states that the pluralism and diversity is acknowledged and welcomed and that all groups in their unique nature are equal and free in their development.

23   On the discussion of the term multicultural society compare the article by A. Schulte (1990) who distinguishes between multicultural society as a descriptive characterization of a situation and as a prescriptive-normative objective.

was most suitable to develop this dialogue, in the face of religious diversity, was very controversially debated in the early 1990s. Initially, the discussion focussed on the limitations of the denominational approach.[24] A growing number of scholars in RE critically stated that the principle of denomination was an anachronism because it implied a duality of the religious landscape, namely the assumption that all pupils would follow their parents to become Christians of one of the established churches, which suggested a parallel Catholic and Prostestant religious education (Braunschweiger Ratschlag, in: Lott, 1992, pp. 341–355; Otto, 1992, p. 364). At this point the debate was to what extent the legal requirements for religious education also allowed for the subject to open up in a way that would do justice to the existing religious plurality of the student body. The ideas ranged from an interdenominational subject to an obligatory subject of religious studies, the construction of learning domains and models of subject-groups, to implementing an interreligious education which would be jointly informed by all religious communities. The long-standing, historical practice of religious education stood opposed to these developments as both established churches had so far claimed the right to a denominational religious education from the regulation that religious education was to be taught 'according to the principles of the religious communities'. Legal precedent confirmed that this subject was to be taught with a binding commitment to denominational positions. For the Prostestant church, denominational determination meant that all teachers had to belong to this denomination and the subject matter was to be developed along lines defined by the church, while for the Catholic school, the pupils also needed to belong to the denomination in question. Following this interpretation, an interdenominational education was impossible.

This position was reinforced by a verdict by the Federal Constitutional Court in 1974 indicating that the respective denominational content was the subject matter of religious education and this should be taught as genuine truth.[25] By these lights, religious education was given as Protestant or Catholic, with the possibility of opting out. By and by, the subject 'ethics' was established as a substitute for those pupils who opted out of religious education and over time it developed into a genuine alternative. However, the position of a rigidly determined framework for religious education has been questioned by several constitutional jurists in the course of the discussion (e.g. Pieroth, 1993). The right of the religious communities to actively co-design religious education definitely includes the possibility of changing its content beyond perceiving religious education as the teaching of existing doctrines and truths. The Constitutional Law would not be opposed to the establishment of either a bi-denominational or an ecumenical, multi-denominational religious education. The churches would only have to express this intention in a legally binding manner.

Apart from this legal debate, there was also a vehement controversy on concepts of religious education. In the early 1990s, alternative concepts of religious education were

---

24   For an overview of the state of this discussion up until the mid-nineties also compare Knauth, 1996, p. 7–52.

25   Compare BverfGe 74, 244/252 H. v. Mangoldt/F. Klein: The Basic Law of Bonn, 1957, 2, Art.7, annot. IV 3.

forwarded which still affect the discussion now. The most important models will be out-lined here, including their latest developments.

a) A Cooperative Denominational Religious Education

A first step towards religious education as the joint responsibility of all religious com-munities is the introduction of cooperative denominational religious education. This means a system where different denominational schemes of religious education cooper-ate. This can expand into an advanced version where the subjects of religious education and ethics work together. We will look at this amplified model in more detail further down. The focus is now on the more limited version in which Catholic and Protestant re-ligious education formally co-operate. Religion teachers in areas where pupils of both denominations are represented in about equal numbers and both churches are willing and able to manage RE in public schools, often favour this model. Cooperation between the churches in religious education also seems to be an appropriate solution for areas where there are few pupils or an insufficient supply of teachers of religious education, making mono-denominational religious education difficult or impossible. This is often reported to be the case in the new federal states, e.g. Saxony-Anhalt (Simon, 2002, pp. 310–325; Hanisch, 2005, pp. 185–240).

After promising approaches towards ecumenical co-operation in the early 1970s, dif-ferent interpretations of the denominational adherence to religious education prevented official cooperation until the mid-90s (though 'nonofficial' cooperation has been custom-ary in school practice at all times). The principle of denominationalism was interpreted far too differently by the Protestant and Catholic churches. While the Protestant church has, since its statement of 1974, opened its religious education for all pupils, the Catholic church has continued to maintain that non-Catholic pupils would be allowed to attend Catholic religious education only in exceptional cases. In a joint statement of the German conference of bishops and the Protestant church of Germany in 1998, however, models of co-operation that preserve the denominational nature of the religious education curricu-lum were explicitly approved of (cf. Deutsche Bischofskonferenz/Evangelische Kirche Deutschlands, 1998). A scientifically supervised pilot-study on religious education in primary school was recently conducted in Baden-Württemberg under these auspices (Schweitzer et al., 2002). The programmatic title of this project 'Strengthening Similari-ties – Taking Account of Differences' is also a sign of the two churches approaching each other in their stances on religious education. More recent statements such as the joint paper on the position of the Lutheran church in Berlin-Brandenburg and the Catho-lic archbishopric of Berlin, which recommends attendance at religious education by the respective other denomination where one's own is not offered, follow the same line (Evangelische Kirche in Berlin-Brandenburg/Erzbistum Berlin, 1998).

b) The Subject Group Model: Identity and Dialogue

The model of a cooperative denominational religious education is the expression of a specific religious-pedagogical approach to religious and cultural plurality. It wants to retain the denominational profile of religious education and thus advocates the right for denominational religious education according to Article 7.3 for the non-Christian religious communities such as Judaism and Islam. On the basis of such pluralistic offerings of religious education, the model of a subject group is to address the overlap between the content of these subjects by instituting equivalent or similar units, and even joint phases of learning, in which the different perspectives can be emphasized and reciprocally explained.[26] This organisational principle of positional differentiation and integration is underpinned by a pedagogical concept of identity and dialogue which allows the pupils to identify themselves with a certain religious or denominational tradition and – if possible – find their religious home. The second step will then be to open new perspectives by a collective encounter and dialogue and discover similarities and differences between the religious and ideological traditions by means of interdisciplinary learning. A memorandum by the Protestant church formulated this position of 'identity and dialogue' in 1994, and it has been reinforced in other papers. The model has been theologically and pedagogically elaborated in detail (Nipkow, 1998). However, there are not enough verified empirical data either to show how the model allows for the proclaimed goal of interweaving religious identity formation and interreligious dialogue in practice nor its present strengths and difficulties in view of interreligious learning.[27] Irrespective of that fact, the course along which religious education – according to the scheme set forth by the Protestant church – is to develop towards plurality, is set. In Germany, apart from the city states of Hamburg, Bremen and Berlin and the smaller federal state of Brandenburg, all Laender subscribe to this model of religious education, aiming to prepare pupils to deal with religious plurality. They intend for religious education to be based on clearly outlined religious and denominational profiles. The plurality of forms of instruction according to denominations is the precondition for a dialogue that aims to strengthen similarities and address differences.

c) 'Religious Education for All' and Dialogical Religious Pedagogy

This programmatic formula is supported by the religious pedagogues who favour a model as it is has been practised in Hamburg since the early 1990s.[28] Here, dialogue between pupils of different religious and cultural backgrounds takes place within the context of one school subject. It differs from the model of a subject group primarily in the fact that the tension between the individual and the unfamiliar, the self and the other as an alterna-

---

26　Nipkow points out that the model of a subject group has been entered into the discussion of appropriate pedagogical concepts for religious and ethical learning that takes account of for the plurality of religions and ideologies as early as the early seventies (Nipkow, in Weiße, 2002, 89–92).

27　Even the advocates of this model concede this fact, e.g. Nipkow in: Weiße, 2002.

28　Compare Doedens & Weiße, 1997 as well as Weiße & Doedens, 2002 on this programmatic concept; for further conceptual elucidation also see Weiße, 1999.

tion between positional differentiation and integration, takes place within one and the same subject rather than being organized as a dialogue across the borders of different denominationally organized forms of religious education. The potential for a dialogical exchange is a constant reality due to the heterogeneous learning groups. In this model, it is necessary to didactically organize the differentiations between religious positions and traditions within a unitary subject. As in the model of a subject group, the pupils are to be given the opportunity to familiarize themselves with the various perspectives of different religious traditions and position themselves in this spectrum – however temporarily and changeably – while maintaining critical distance. Dialogue and interreligious learning are therefore vital dimensions; as such, they are also anchored in the curricula. Religious education is referred to as 'Dialogical interreligious religious education under Protestant auspices'. This designation shows that the Lutheran church in Hamburg is responsible in legal and institutional terms and orientates the subject in 'accordance with its principles'. In order to address the interreligious dimension, the development of curricula and teaching material for religious education is supported by a panel of experts drawn from the major religious communities of Hamburg which regularly holds meetings.[29] The Jewish community, the Islamic community, the Alevi community, and important Buddhist organisations favour and support this model of religious education. For years, religious education in Hamburg has been supported by numerous empirical studies by the department of religious pedagogy at the university (Knauth et al., 1994; Weiße, 1995; Knauth, 1996; Sandt, 1996; Beuchling, 1999; Knauth et al., 2000; Jessen, 2003). Its theoretical conception, especially its pedagogical and theological concept of dialogue, has also found academic support there. Dialogical religious pedagogy takes up impulses from critical educational theory, religious-philosophical theories of dialogue by Martin Buber and Emmanuel Levinas, and ecumenical theology according to Hans Jochen Margull's approach (e.g. Knauth & Weiße, 2000) and also attempts to combine the tradition of problem-oriented religious education and ecumenical learning with the aim of interreligious learning (Weiße, 1995; Knauth, 2003). The central idea of its concept of dialogue is unconditional respect for the other in his/her current self-conception. Dialogical religious education wants to give pupils who have yet to develop a religious self-conception the freedom to explore and formulate their own questions and their own conception of existence (Knauth, 1996). Based on empirical studies, the subject also invites into its dialogue pupils who develop a self-conception of religion and world-views beyond the limits of established religious traditions (Knauth & Weiße, 1995; Sandt, 1996). More strongly than in the concept of 'identity and dialogue', this approach assumes a more open concept of identity as a quest which developed through the experience of interaction and difference. The quest for identity can well take place in the context of established denominational and religious traditions and find an anchoring point in these. Dialogical religious education offers suitable opportunities for this. However, it is also mindful not to impose an unwanted and unasked-for identity on the students. It closely assiociates itself with a radical concept of communicative freedom (Knauth, 1999, pp. 144–137). Thus, this concept of dialogical RE provides an eminently suitable foil for the principal

---

29   On the work on curricula and the perspectives of different religious communities see Doedens
      & Weiße, 1998, 23–53.

questions of the REDCo-project. 'Religious education for all' in Hamburg and its concept of dialogical religious pedagogy, was the subject of strong controversy in its first years.[30] It was obviously seen as a serious alternative to denominational religious education. Therefore, the advocates of the model of a subject group and its conception of identity and dialogue, criticized the approach taken in Hamburg as a form of, 'interreligiously oriented ethics' rather than true RE (Nipkow, 1998, p. 485) or accused it of merely advocating a neutral, secularist approach to religious studies. By now, however, we can distinguish between obvious misunderstandings and legitimate criticism:

It should be made clear that the approach taken in Hamburg did not claim to be a universal remedy for addressing religious plurality in schools, but sees itself as shaped by the particular context and conditions of the city of Hamburg, which can by no means be generalized. One of those conditions is that the Catholic church has so far largely abstained from offering its own religious education in public schools.[31]

It should also be made clear that religious education as practised in Hamburg clearly differs from a religious education aiming to neutrally teach religious studies in terms of both its theological and pedagogical conception. The approach taken in Hamburg rather operates on the assumption that wherever people communicate about their guiding orientations and commitments, faith is always involved. It does not purport to be neutral. However, it is not denominational in the sense of being committed to one denomination. It is positional, or to say it with a German neologism, 'konfessorisch',[32] because from its viewpoint it can be called Protestant and Christian in the best sense to perceive and address humanity within a variety of liberal traditions. In the light of this freedom, it also encourages pupils to develop orientations and convictions in examining these traditions, embrace them, yet also respect the convictions of others.

This criticism has also shown up the questions that religious education in Hamburg will not be able to avoid in the long run. These questions address the self-conception of the subject with regard to the demands of interreligious learning. The Hamburg way of 'religious education for all' is based on the fact that the Lutheran Church – in the protestant tradition of allowing freedom and emancipation to others – deliberately cedes part of its space to other religious communities to exercise their influence on RE in Hamburg. This has been done through the *'Gesprächskreis interreligiöser Religionsunterricht (GIR)'* (panel on interreligious RE) which includes members from very different religious backgrounds: Protestants, Muslims, Jews, Hindus, and Buddhists. This group has shaped curricula for RE in Hamburg and developed teaching material. Thus there is a basis for a joint responsibility of different religions for RE in Hamburg. Nevertheless, there is need for further development in order to guarantee that teachers of different religious backgrounds can participate in giving lessons at school. As yet, there is no teacher-

30   From the number of critical objections the articles of K. E. Nipkow (1998, 2002) and F. Schweitzer 2002 as well as R. Schieder 2003 are mentioned here.
31   This could change in the years to come. The Catholic church entered into negotiations with the Senate of Hamburg, secured the right to establish its own religious education in public schools and plans to offer it – initially only tentatively – in some schools within the state. If Catholic religious education was implemented on a large scale, a new situation would emerge.
32   The term 'konfessorisch' in its meaning illustrated above – as far as I am aware – was first introduced to the discussion on denominational religious education by D. Zilleßen (1992, p. 303).

training for Muslims, Jews and Buddhists who want to become religious education teachers like there is for Lutherans. In the framework of an interdisciplinary centre 'World Religions in Dialogue' – a first step on the way to founding an 'Academy of World Religions' – there is a strong movement towards establishing Islamic, Jewish and Buddhist theology as academic disciplines. A legal opinion concluded that the law allowed for constructions of cooperative teaching by Christian, Islamic, Jewish, or Buddhist RE teachers (see Link, 2002). It further stated that the government is even bound to open up a possibility for these groups to study their religion in an academic context. Up to now, however, the Hamburg government has not taken any decisions in this matter.

Thus we see that there is an approach for a dialogical RE in Hamburg, but it needs to be developed further. The REDCo-project might help to substantiate this further development: The analyses of interaction in the classroom are necessary in order to evaluate how young people from different religious and cultural backgrounds can best interact. However, we must also see whether the Protestant principles which underpin the opening of RE in Hamburg to other religions find corresponding ideas among members of other faith groups. We must further study how the demand to establish a religiously diversified teacher-training at Hamburg University can be addressed and find ways to allow teachers of religions other than Protestant Christians to teach RE in Hamburg.

At present, efforts are being made in Hamburg to take the necessary steps towards a genuine interreligious education, to make full use of extant interpretative tolerance, and to establish the necessary structures in the university to train teachers in Islamic, Jewish and Buddhist theology.[33] In the long run, religious education in Hamburg would then reach a crucial crossroad: In order for it to develop into an interreligious education, teachers of other religious communities would have to be granted the right to teach, not only as guests, but in full responsibility as partners in a dialogical and cooperative setup. In order to allow this, the legal status of RE would need considerable redefinition.

Summary

The 1990s were marked by controversial debates about what constituted a sustainable form of religious education. These debates arose at a time when perspectives in the field shifted towards the paradigm of plurality in theology and (religious) pedagogy and they heightened awareness of the relevance of interreligious learning and dialogical concepts of religious education. Since the early nineties, a change in didactic approaches has taken place: the world-religions approach has been replaced by a perception of religions as 'neighbour-religions' (Weisse, 1999, pp. 181ff.) in the context of a multicultural and multireligious society. Interreligious learning approaches have adopted aims of ecumenical and intercultural approaches (see also Weisse, 1995) and place greater emphasis on real-life relevance and the social and cultural environment of religion; elementary activi-

---

33   That is how – after a long phase of preparation (Neumann 2002; Knauth & Weiße, 2002) – it
     was possible to establish the interdisciplinary centre World Religions in Dialogue (ZWID) at
     the University of Hamburg in early 2006. ZWID is to be be instrumental in establishing university
     degrees which will, among other things, qualify their holders to teach of interreligious education
     (see www.zwid.uni-hamburg.de).

ties of daily life take precedence over abstract constructs of education. In many interreligious teaching materials, forms of experience-oriented and dialogical learning are given priority. After an initial phase in which conceptual positions were defined through differentiation, the debate about different models of religious education in school has resulted in an awareness of the contextual justification of each position. The religious make-up of the student body as well as legal and political contexts affect the way in which the fundamental (religious) pedagogical tensions between tradition and the world of contemporary life, identity and dialogue, the self and the other, formal religious affiliation and individual faith-biographies, can be balanced out. If nothing else, the debates of the 1990s have shown that religious education in plural societies can afford neither an exclusive denominational straitjacket nor a random inter-religious mixture. Future religious education will only be able to operate in a spirit of interreligious understanding, irrespective of whether it is separated by confessions or religions, open for other religions, or takes place in a jointly interreligious education. The dialogue of religions has been recognized as an important factor of religious education.

Perspectives: Religious Education and the Shadow of 9/11

How deeply the events of 9/11 have affected the discourse on interreligious learning is impossible to fully judge even five years after the event. Concerning the debate in Germany it has to be mentioned that dialogue between religions came under harsh attack in the immediate aftermath. Supporters of dialogical concepts were accused of allowing themselves to be instrumentalized by agendas pursuing the supremacy of a fundamentally violent interpretation of Islam. The term 'dialogue industry' was coined to discredit those voices which advocated sticking to the position, claiming that there was no alternative to dialogue, especially in a tense political environment. Leaving aside the polemics of these criticisms, they can be understood as an admonition to more fully reflect the overly harmonising tendencies and not ignore the conflicts and incompatibilities, the 'hot potatoes' of interreligious dialogue in a more realistic future approach of 'tough plurality'(cf. Nipkow, 1994, p. 204). This is one of the main motivations for the dual focus on dialogue and conflict in religion that characterizes the REDCo-project.

On the other hand we cannot ignore the fact that reference to 9/11 can serve to legitimize a retreat from the troublesome business of understanding and integration in favour of attempts to separate and socially exclude religious minorities in Germany. Any debate about Islamic religious education as a school subject – an issue that has been discussed rather heatedly in past years (cf. Bukow & Yildiz, 2003; Graf, 2004; Reichmuth et al., 2006) – has to take into account the belief that Islamic religious education can be integrated into a concept of religious education that can cope with plurality and dialogue.

Efforts to counteract these tendencies have become evident in the theological and religious-pedagogical discourse lately. While the discourse about religious fundamentalism has increasingly emphasized the ambivalences of religion after 9/11, it has also led to a greater degree of reflection on the relationship between religion and violence, or religion and power (Jahrbuch der Religionspädagogik, 2004). There has also been an increasing effort to realize the contribution of religious pedagogy to peace education (cf. Handbuch der Friedenserziehung, 2006) – a discussion which had hardly come to the attention of a wider public even of experts in religious pedagogy in the past twenty years. This is an indicator for the increasing public attention devoted to the political dimensions of religious education after the subject had spent more than two decades in 'societal oblivion' (Rickers, 1987).

There is yet another aspect to illustrate that the times when religious education offered an apparent safe haven from the discomforts and demands of hard societal realities are irretrievably gone. Strong public pressure for reforms in the educational system fuelled by the findings of international comparative studies such as TIMSS and PISA create pressure to innovate and create individual school profiles while simultaneously experiencing progressively worsening working conditions among school administrators, staff, and stakeholders. At the same time, educational requirements at the curricular level are homogenized through the implementation of so-called educational standards and key qualifications, a movement which has already reached religious pedagogy (Rothgangel & Fischer, 2004; Fischer & Elsenbast 2006). There are reasons to observe this discourse critically, insofar as it introduces a concept of productivity and efficiency into the field that is not based on any genuinely pedagogical considerations but is obviously informed by an education policy dominated by a perceived need to secure a national competitive advantage in economic terms. At this point, in my opinion, objections should be raised by a critical tradition of religious education. A societal logic which is solely dedicated to the production of useful, exploitable human resources is in irresolvable conflict with an anthropology – anchored not only in religious traditions – which is based on the dignity and value of each individual, independent of its productivity. Religious pedagogy would be well advised not to lose sight of the issues of religion and society or its anthropological questions.

Finally, it should be pointed out that a pedagogy of religion dedicated to addressing plurality (Schweitzer et al., 2002) must continue to try to understand and analyse heterogeneous religious practice both in schools and classrooms and in social contexts beyond them. Fortunately, empirical research on this point has seen a marked increase in the first years of the new century, to the point that speaking of a new, 'empirical groundshift' (Wegenast, 1968) in religious education is not unreasonable. This is true for the field of didactic research as well as for empirical studies of forms of religiosity among young people, on religiosity and religious pedagogical concepts of RE teachers, and on religious education in the new federal states of Germany. An increased awareness of the degree to which religious education is shaped by its environment is reflected in the growing efforts of an empirical research which tries to understand the overall context in which it takes place. Thus the debate about religious education has gained a new dynamic which may be useful, both for realizing conceptional innovation and pilot projects and through its connection to academic empirical research. Future conceptual debates will have to be based more strongly on scientifically verified findings on the context and conditions shaping the subject and analyses of the reality of ordinary religious education as it is offered in schools. In this context it must also be part of any analysis of religious education under conditions of plurality and heterogeneity to connect religion with the social and cultural factors determining its place in society.

Research on education under these auspices will need to focus more intensely on daily school life and the realities of religious education classrooms in order to gain insight into the factors informing the teachers' actions, the pupils' perspective, and contents and interaction on the ground. Thus the research aims of the REDCo-project meet the needs of current research on RE-pedagogy precisely. At the present time, we can only say with confidence that we still know far too little about how religious education can contribute to dialogically coping with difference.

References

Auernheimer, G. (2003) Interkulturelle Pädagogik: Eine kritische Zwischenbilanz, in: *Zeitschrift für Pädagogik und Theologie*, 2, 194–113.

Baacke, D. (1990) Die stillen Ekstasen der Jugend: Zu Wandlungen des religiösen Bezugs, in: *Jahrbuch der Religionspädagogik* [JRP] 6 (Neukirchen-Vluyn, Neukirchener Verlag) 3–25.

Barz, H. (1992a) *Religion ohne Institution? Jugend und Religion*, Bd.1 (Opladen, Leske & Budrich).

Barz, H. (1992b) *Postmoderne Religion: Die junge Generation in den Alten Bundesländern.* Jugend und Religion, Bd. 2 (Opladen, Leske & Budrich).

Barz, H. (1993) *Postsozialistische Religion: Am Beispiel der jungen Generation in den Neuen Bundesländern.* Jugend und Religion, Bd.3 (Opladen, Leske & Budrich).

Berger, P.L. (1967) *The sacred canopy* (New York, Garden City).

Berger, P.L. (1979) *The Heretical Imperative* (New York, Garden City).

Beuchling, O. (1999) Buddhistische Religiosität junger Vietnamesen in der Bundesrepublik Deutschland: Eine ethnographisch-erziehungswissenschaftliche Analyse, in: W. Weiße (Ed.) *Vom Monolog zum Dialog: Ansätze einer dialogischen Religionspädaogik* (Münster/New York/München/Berlin, Waxmann), 59–89.

Beuchling, O. (2002) Interkulturelle und interreligiöse Bildung in Deutschland, in: C. Bakker, O. Beuchling, K. Griffioen (Eds.) *Kulturelle Vielfalt und Religionsunterricht: Entwicklungen und Praxis in vier europäischen Ländern* (Münster/Hamburg/London, LitVerlag), 67–73.

Bolle, R, Knauth, Th, Weiße, W. (Eds.) (2002) *Hauptströmungen evangelischer Religionspädagogik im 20. Jahrhundert:* Ein Quellen- und Arbeitsbuch (Münster/New York/München/Berlin, Waxmann).

Braunschweiger Ratschlag vom 8.2.1991 (1992) Welchen Religionsunterricht braucht die öffentliche Schule, in: J. Lott (Ed.) *Religion – warum und wozu in der Schule?* (Weinheim), 341–355.

Bukow, W.-D., Yildiz, E. (Eds.) *Islam und Bildung* (Opladen 2003, Leske&Budrich).

Deutsche Bischofskonferenz & Evangelische Kirche Deutschlands (1998) *Zur Kooperation von Evangelischem und Katholischem Religionsunterricht* (Würzburg/Hannover).

Doedens, F., Weiße, W. (Eds.) (1997) *Religionsunterricht für alle: Hamburger Perspektiven zur Religionsdidaktik* (Münster/New York/München/Berlin, Waxmann).

Domsgen, M. (Ed.) (2005) *Konfessionslos – eine religionspädagogische Herausforderung:* Studien am Beispiel Ostdeutschlands (Leipzig, Evangelische Verlagsanstalt).

Edelstein, W., Grözinger, K., Gruehn, S. et al. (2001) *Lebensgestaltung – Ethik – Religionskunde: Zur Grundlegung eines neuen Schulfachs – Analysen und Empfehlungen* (Weinheim/Basel, Deutscher Studienverlag).

Elsenbast, V., Pithan, A., Schreiner, P., Schweitzer, F. (Eds.) (2004) *Wissen stärken – Bildung klären: 50 Jahre Comenius-Institut* (Münster/New York/München/Berlin, Waxmann).

Evangelische Kirche in Berlin-Brandenburg (Konsistorium)/Erzbischöfliches Ordinariat Berlin (Abt. Religionsunterricht) (2000) *Leben mit Sinn und Verstand: Die Schule braucht Religionsunterricht* (Berlin).

Evangelische Kirche in Berlin-Brandenburg/Erzbistum Berlin (1998) *Religionsunterricht in Berlin: Schulisches Unterrichtsfach in einer Fächergruppe* (Berlin).

Fend, H. (1988) *Sozialgeschichte des Aufwachsens: Bedingungen des Aufwachsens und Jugendgestalten im zwanzigsten Jahrhundert* (Frankfurt a.M., suhrkamp).

Fischer, D.& Elsenbast, V. (red.) (2006) *Grundlegende Kompetenzen religiöser Bildung: Zur Entwicklung des evangelischen Religionsunterrichts durch Bildungsstandards für den Abschluss der Sekundarstufe I* (Münster, Comenius-Institut).

Gabriel. K. (1992) *Christentum zwischen Tradition und Postmoderne,* Quaestiones Disputatae, Bd.141 (Freiburg: Herder).

Glaser, H. (1989) *Kulturgeschichte der Bundesrepublik Deutschland,* 3 Bde. (München/Wien).

Gottwald. E., Rickers, F. (Eds.) (2004) *Die Zukunft des Religionsunterrichts im Horizont von Globalisierung und Multikulturalität* (Nordhausen, Verlag Traugott Bautz).

Gottwaldt, E., Siedler, D.Chr. (Eds.) (2001) *'Islamische Unterweisung' in deutscher Sprache: Eine erste Zwischenbilanz des Schulversuchs in Nordrhein-Westfalen* (Neukirchen-Vluyn, Neukirchener Verlag).

Graf, P. (Ed.) *Der Islam im Westen – der Westen im Islam: Positionen zur religiös-ethischen Erziehung von Muslimen* (Göttingen, V&R unipress).

Großmann, K. (1993) Die gegenwärtige Krise des Religionsunterrichts in Westdeutschland, in: K. Großmann, A. Pithan, P. Schreiner (Eds.) Im *Blickpunkt: Religionsunterricht in der Diskussion* (Münster, Comenius Institut), 119–128.

Günther, U., Gensicke, M., Müller, C., Mitchell, G., Knauth, Th., Bolle, R. (Eds.) (2005) *Theologie – Pädagogik – Kontext: Zukunftsperspektiven der Religionspädagogik.* Wolfram Weiße zum 60. Geburtstag (Münster/New York/München/Berlin, Waxmann).

Hanisch, H. (2005) 'Sie sollten die Möglichkeit haben, sich mit dem christlichen Glauben zu beschäftigen.' Die Schule als Lernort des Glaubens im ostdeutschen Kontext, in: M. Domsgen (Ed.) *Konfessionslos – eine religionspädagogische Herausforderung: Studien am Beispiel Ostdeutschlands* (Leipzig, Evangelische Verlagsanstalt), 185–240.

Haussmann, W. (1993) *Dialog mit pädagogischen Konsequenzen: Perspektiven der Begegnung von Christentum und Islam für die schulische Arbeit: ein Vergleich der Entwicklungen in England und der Bundesrepublik Deutschland* (Hamburg, ebv-Rissen).

Haussmann, W., Biener, H., Hock, K., Mokrosch, R. (Eds.) (2006): *Handbuch Friedenserziehung: interreligiös – interkulturell – interkonfessionell,* (Gütersloh, Gütersloher Verlagshaus).

Heimbrock, G. (2004) *Religionsunterricht im Kontext Europa: Einführung in die kontextuelle Religionsdidaktik in Deutschland* (Stuttgart, Kohlhammer).

Helmreich, E. C. (1966) *Religionsunterricht in Deutschland: Von den Klosterschulen bis heute* (Hamburg/Düsseldorf).

Jahrbuch der Religionspädagogik (2003) *Die Gewalt und das Böse* (Neukirchen-Vluyn, Neukirchener Verlag).

Jahrbuch der Religionspädagogik (2005): *Lernen durch Begegnung* (Neukirchen-Vluyn, Neukirchener Verlag).

Jessen, S. (2003) *'Man redet viel über Gott und so...': Schülermitbeteiligung im Religionsunterricht der Grundschule aus allgemein- und religionsdidaktischer Sicht* (Münster/New York/München/Berlin, Waxmann).

Kaufmann, F.X. (1989) *Religion und Modernität: Sozialwissenschaftliche Perspektiven* (Tübingen: J.C.B.Mohr).

Kirchenamt der EKD (Ed.) (1987) *Bildung und Erziehung: Die Denkschriften der Evangelischen Kirche in Deutschland* (Gütersloher Verlagshaus).

Kirchenamt der EKD (Ed.) (1994) *Identität und Verständigung: Standort und Perspektiven des Religionsunterrichts in der Pluralität. Eine Denkschrift* (Gütersloher Verlagshaus).

Kirchenamt der EKD (Ed.) (1997) *Religion in der Schule: Kundgebung der Synode der EKD in Friedrichroda* (Hannover)

Kirchenamt der EKD (Ed.) (2000) *Zusammenleben mit Muslimen in Deutschland: Gestaltung der christlichen Begegnung mit Muslimen: Eine Handreichung des Rates der EKD* (Gütersloher Verlagshaus).

Kirchenamt der EKD (Ed.) (2004) *Evangelische Kirche in Deutschland. Zahlen und Fakten zum kirchlichen Leben* (Hannover).

Knauth, Th. (1996) *Religionsunterricht und Dialog: Empirische Untersuchungen, systematische Überlegungen und didaktische Perspektiven eines Religionsunterrichts im Horizont religiöser und kultureller Pluralisierung* (Münster/New York/München/Berlin, Waxmann).

Knauth, Th. (1999) Anmerkungen zum Dialogbegriff im Ansatz einer dialogischen Religionspädagogik, in: W. Weiße (Ed.) *Vom Monolog zum Dialog: Ansätze einer dialogischen Religionspädagogik* (Münster/New York/München/Berlin, Waxmann), 113–138.

Knauth, Th. (2000a) Religionsunterricht und Befreiung. Anmerkungen zum unabgegoltenen Potenzial problemorientierten Religionsunterrichts, in: W. Weiße, F. Doedens (Eds.) *Religiöses Lernen in einer pluralen Welt: Religionspädagogische Ansätze in Hamburg.* Eine Dokumentation der Novemberakademie 1999 an der Universität Hamburg (Münster/New York/München/Berlin, Waxmann), 125–140.

Knauth, Th. (2000b) Dialog von Anfang an. Die Bedeutung des Ansatzes von Helmut Peukert für eine dialogische interreligiöse Religionspädagogik, in: S. Abeldt, W. Bauer, Th. Knauth, H. Tiedemann, W. Weiße (Eds.) *'... was es bedeutet, verletzbarer Mensch zu sein': Erziehungswissenschaft im Gespräch mit Theologie, Philosophie und Gesellschaftstheorie* (Mainz, Grünewald Verlag), 321–337.

Knauth, Th. (2003) *Problemorientierter Religionsunterricht: Eine kritische Rekonstruktion* (Göttingen, Vandenhoeck&Ruprecht).

Knauth, Th (2005) Religionsunterricht und Kontextualität: Der Beitrag des problemorientierten Ansatzes, in: U. Günther u.a. (Eds.) *Theologie – Pädagogik – Kontext: Zukunftsperspektiven der Religionspädagogik.* Wolfram Weiße zum 60. Geburtstag (Münster/New York/München/Berlin, Waxmann), 49–60.

Knauth, Th, Sandt, F.-O., Weiße, W. (1994) Interkultureller Religionsunterricht in Hamburg: Erste empirische Erhebungen, in: I. Lohmann, W. Weiße (Eds.) *Dialog zwischen den Kulturen: Erziehungshistorische und religionspädagogische Gesichtspunkte interkultureller Bildung* (Münster/New York/München/Berlin, Waxmann), 217–232.

Knauth, Th., Weiße, W. (1996) Lernbereich Religion-Ethik und integrativer Religionsunterricht aus Schülersicht: Empirische Erhebungen und konzeptionelle Überlegungen, in: W.Weiße (Ed.) *Vom Monolog zum Dialog: Ansätze einer interkulturellen dialogischen Religionspädagogik* (Münster/New York/München/Berlin, Waxmann), 91–112.

Knauth, Th., Weiße, W. (2000) Konzeptioneller Rahmen für gegenwärtigen Religionsunterricht: Religionspädagogische Grundüberlegungen, in: Th. Knauth, S. Leutner-Ramme, W. Weiße *Religionsunterricht aus Schülerperspektive* (Münster/New York/München/Berlin, Waxmann), 165–202.

Knauth, Th, Weiße, W. (Eds.) (2002) *Akademie der Weltreligionen: Konzeptionelle und praktische Ansätze* (Hamburg, Schriften aus dem FB Erziehungswissenschaft der Universität HH).

Lähnemann, J. (1998) *Evangelische Religionspädagogik in interreligiöser Perspektive* (Göttingen, Vandenhoeck& Ruprecht).

Link, Ch. (2002) Rechtsgutachten über die Vereinbarkeit des Hamburger Modells eines 'Religionsunterrichts für alle in evangelischer Verantwortung' mit Artikel 7 Abs.3 GG, in: W. Weisse (Ed.) *Wahrheit und Dialog: Theologische Grundlagen und Impulse gegenwärtiger Religionspädagogik* (Münster/New York/München/Berlin, Waxmann).

Lohmann, I., Weiße, W. (1994) (Eds.) *Dialog zwischen den Kulturen: Erziehungshistorische und religionspädagogische Gesichtspunkte interkultureller Bildung* (Münster/New York/ München/Berlin, Waxmann)

Lott, J. (Ed.) (1992) *Religion – warum und wozu in der Schule?* (Weinheim, Deutscher Studienverlag).

Luckmann, Th. (1991) *Die unsichtbare Religion* [1967] (Frankfurt a.M, suhrkamp)

Metz, J.B. (1968) *Zur Theologie der Welt* (Mainz, Grünewald).

Metz, J.B. (1997) *Zum Begriff der neuen Politischen Theologie: 1967–1997* (Mainz, Grünewald).

Moltmann, J. (1972) *Der gekreuzigte Gott: Das Kreuz Christi als Grund und Kritik christlicher Theologie* (München).

Müller, O., Pickel, G., Pollack, D. (2005) Kirchlichkeit und Religiosität in Ostdeutschland: Muster, Trends, Bestimmungsgründe, in: M. Domsgen (Ed.) *Konfessionslos – eine religionspädagogische Herausforderung: Studien am Beispiel Ostdeutschlands* (Leipzig, Evangelische Verlagsanstalt), 23–64.

Neumann, U. (Ed.) (2002) *Islamische Theologie: Internationale Beiträge zur Hamburger Debatte* (Hamburg, edition Körber-Stiftung).

Nipkow, K.E. (1968) Christlicher Glaubensunterricht in der Säkularität: Die zwei didaktischen Grundtypen des evangelischen Religionsunterrichts, in: *Der evangelische Erzieher, 20,* 169–189.

Nipkow, K.E. (1994) Ziele interreligiösen Lernens als mehrdimensionales Problem, in: J.A. van der Ven, H.G. Ziebertz (Eds.) *Religiöser Pluralismus und Interreligiöses Lernen* (Kampen/Weinheim), 197–232.

Nipkow, K.E. (1998) *Bildung in einer pluralen Welt,* 2 Bde, Bd. 1: Moralpädagogik im Pluralismus(a); Bd. 2: Religionspädagogik im Pluralismus (b) (Gütersloh, Gütersloher Verlagshaus).

Nipkow, K.E. (2002a) Der Weg der Fächergruppe mit einem dialogorientierten, mehrseitig kooperierenden evangelischen Religionsunterricht, in: W. Weiße (Ed.) *Wahrheit und Dialog: Theologische Grundlagen gegenwärtiger Religionspädagogik* (Münster/New York/München/Berlin, Waxmann), 89–106.

Nipkow, K.E. (2002b) Multikulturelle und multireligiöse Erziehung in der Schule, in: *Zeitschrift für Pädagogik und Theologie* [ZPT] 2, 101–118.

Nipkow, K.E. (2003) Religiöse Bildung im Pluralismus, in: L. Krappmann, Ch.Th. Scheilke (Eds.) *Religion in der Schule – für alle?! Die plurale Gesellschaft als Herausforderung an Bildungsprozesse* (Seelze-Velber, Kallmeyersche Verlagsbuchhandlung), 53–66.

Otto, G. (1992) Allgemeiner Religionsunterricht – Religionsunterricht für alle: Sieben Thesen mit Erläuterungen, in: J. Lott (Ed.) *Religion – warum und wozu in der Schule?* (Weinheim), 359–374.

Pieroth, B. (1993) Aktuelle verfassungsrechtliche Fragen zum Religionsunterricht, in: *Der evangelische Erzieher,* 45, 2, 196–211.

Reichmuth, St., Bodenstein, M., Kiefer, M., Väth, B. (Eds.) *Staatlicher Islamunterricht in Deutschland* (Berlin, Litverlag).

Renz, A., Leimgruber, St. (2004) *Christen und Muslime: was sie verbindet – was sie unterscheidet* (München, Kösel).

Rickers, F. (1987) Religionspädagogik zwischen 1975 und 1985, zweiter Teil, in: *Theologia Practica*, 22, 63–76.

Rickers, F.(1996) Evangelische Religionspädagogik in zeitgeschichtlicher Perspektive, in: *Jahrbuch der Religionspädagogik* [JRP], 12 (Neukirchen-Vluyn, Neukirchener Verlag), 29–56.

Rothgangel, M./Fischer, D. (Eds.) (2004) *Standards für religiöse Bildung. Zur Reformdiskussion in Schule und Lehrerbildung* (Münster, Litverlag).

Sandt, F.-O. (1996) *Religiosität von Jugendlichen in der multikulturellen Gesellschaft* (Münster/New York/München/Berlin, Waxmann).

Schieder, R. (2003) Schule und Zivilreligion, in: L. Krappmann, Ch.Th. Scheilke (Eds.) *Religion in der Schule – für alle?! Die plurale Gesellschaft als Herausforderung an Bildungsprozesse* (Seelze-Velber, Kallmeyersche Verlagsbuchhandlung), 31–52.

Schreiner, P. (2000) Germany, in: P. Schreiner (Ed.) *Religious Education in Europe: A collection of basic information about RE in European countries* (Münster, Comenius Institut) 49–54.

Schulte, A. (1990) Multikulturelle Gesellschaft: Chance, Ideologie oder Bedrohung?, in: *Aus Politik und Zeitgeschichte, Beilage zur Wochenzeitung: DAS PARLAMENT*, 3–15.

Schweitzer, F., Biesinger, A., Boschki, R. u.a. (2002) *Gemeinsamkeiten stärken – Unterschieden gerecht werden: Erfahrungen und Perspektiven zum konfessionell-kooperativen Religionsunterricht* (Freiburg/Gütersloh, Herder und Gütersloher Verlagshaus).

Schweitzer. F. (2002) Konfessionell-kooperativer Religionsunterricht: Die Perspektive der Kinder, in: Weiße, W. (Ed.) *Wahrheit und Dialog: Theologische Grundlagen und Impulse gegenwärtiger Religionspädagogik* (Münster/New York/München/Berlin, Waxmann), 107–120.

Simon, W. (2002) Religionsunterricht als schulisches Unterrichtsfach in den ostdeutschen Bundesländern: Ansätze fächerverbindender Koordination und Kooperation, in: A. Battke, Th. Fitzner, R. Isak, U. Lochmann (Eds.) *Schulentwicklung – Religion – Religionsunterricht: Profil und Chance von Religion in der Schule der Zukunft* (Freiburg/Basel/Wien, Herder), 310–325.

Sölle, D. (1971) *Politische Theologie* (Stuttgart, Kreuz Verlag).

Stock, H. (1968) *Religionsunterricht in der 'Kritischen Schule'* (Gütersloher Verlag).

Wegenast, K. (1968) Die empirische Wendung in der Religionspädagogik, in: *Der evangelische Erzieher*, 20, 111–125.

Weisse, W. (1995) Interkulturelles Lernen und ökumenisches Lernen: Zur notwendigen Korrelation von zwei Ansätzen, in: K. Großmann, A.Pithan, P. Schreiner (Eds.) *Zukunftsfähiges Lernen: Herausforderungen für Ökumenisches Lernen in Schule und Unterricht* (Münster, Comenius Institut), 53–70.

Weisse, W. (1999) Ökumenische Theologie und interreligiöse Dialogerfahrungen: Anstöße für die Religionspädagogik, in: W.Weiße (Ed.) *Vom Monolog zum Dialog. Ansätze einer dialogischen Religionspädagogik* (Münster, New York, München, Berlin, Waxmann), 181–202.

Weisse, W. (Ed.) (1996) *Vom Monolog zum Dialog. Ansätze einer interkulturellen dialogischen Religionspädagogik* (Münster, New York, München, Berlin, Waxmann), zweite erw. Auflage 1999.

Weisse, W., Doedens, F. (Eds.) (2000) *Religiöses Lernen in einer pluralen Welt: Religionspädagogische Ansätze in Hamburg: Novemberakademie '99* (Münster/New York/München/Berlin, Waxmann).

Weisse, (Ed.) (2002) *Wahrheit und Dialog: Theologische Grundlagen und Impulse gegenwärtiger Religionspädagogik* (Münster/New York/München/Berlin, Waxmann).

Wermke, M. (2006) *Evangelischer Religionsunterricht in Ostdeutschland: Empirische Befunde zur Teilnahme thüringischer Schülerinnen und Schüler* (Jena, Verlag IKS Garamond).

Ziehe, Th. (1991) *Zeitvergleiche: Jugend in kulturellen Modernisierungen* (Weinheim/München, Juventa).

Zilleßen, D. (1992) Konfessioneller Religionsunterricht in multikultureller Lebenswelt?, in: J. Lott (Ed.) *Religion – warum und wozu in der Schule?* (Weinheim), 301–320.

Siebren Miedema

Contexts, Debates and Perspectives of Religion in Education in Europe

A Comparative Analysis

> La faculté d'accéder à la globalité de l'expérience humaine, inhérente à tous les individus doués de raison, implique chemin faisant la lutte contre l'analphabétisme religieux et l'étude des systèmes de croyances existants. (Régis Debray, 2002, p. 39)

In the introductory chapter of this book it was clearly stated that the aim of our REDCo-project is to analyse conceptual and practical approaches to mutual understanding in the field of religion in education. Referring to empirical research we pointed to the shown correlation between low levels of religious education and a willingness to use religion as a criterion of exclusion and confrontation. In the context of different understandings of what 'religion in education' might mean in different regions of Europe, all the members of our research group are convinced that religion in education can serve as a foundation of the peaceful co-existence of various religious or philosophical worldviews and to justify respect for the human dignity of others, regardless of their religious, philosophical and political convictions. Religious education in the form of interreligious education, as well as in the form of cultural education about religion, has been shown to be able to contribute to intercultural understanding, tolerance and harmony. However, we are also realistic and down-to-earth enough to know about the possible dangers arising from religious isolation and confrontation and from the instrumentalization of religion for political purposes.

As a research consortium we share an appreciation of religious and cultural differences as a positive factor, as well as a collective concern for the question about common values. By means of theoretical, conceptual and empirical analysis we want to lay the foundation for an adequate understanding of the contribution religion in education can make towards the current transformation processes in various European countries. Along these lines, we want to gain the necessary historical perspective and analytical clarity to address the core questions of dialogue and conflict in Europe and to find ways to stimulate a process of growing European identities. Our project represents a necessary approach to address the following core question: 'How can religions and values contribute to dialogue or tension in Europe?' In particular, we are concerned with how 'religious education', which we prefer to see in an inclusive way,[1] contributes to these processes.

Of course, religion and religiosity may also get attention in other subjects, and may also be considered at the level of school organization and governance; in other words, religion may be part of the school's identity *in toto*. 'Religious education' covers both academic teacher training as well as philosophical and practical aspects of religious and values education in schools. By using this embracing concept of religious education, we

---

1   See Jackson (Chapter 2 above) for a discussion of different uses of the term 'religious education' in Europe.

both focus on understanding religions and its role in personal development and its contribution to social responsibility and social cohesion.

In this concluding chapter I reflect on the contributions to this book, compare them and formulate a preliminary summary.

Trends and Tendencies within the European Context

In Part I, entitled 'European Horizon', our focus was on European discussions as the background against which our project is situated. Here we will highlight a few notable trends and tendencies within the European context that we have learned from the three chapters in this section.

The first chapter by Robert Jackson shows that, after a period of time in which religion was not officially dealt with in the public domain and in public education in many countries, religion has established a more prominent place in recent years, both in the public sphere and in education.[2] It is traceable both in the discussions on intercultural education and on citizenship education. This change is strengthened too by developments in the European Union. This is especially so in the way that this is emphasised in the preamble of its first constitutional treaty and in article 10 of that constitutional treaty, respectively pointing to the cultural, religious and humanist inheritance of Europe, and to the freedom of thought, religion and conscience. Also, the recent developments in the field of education in the Council of Europe are a real reinforcement of this change, both in the projects on Intercultural Education and the Challenge of Religious Diversity and Dialogue in Europe, and on Education for Democratic Citizenship. Within the format of fora and working parties on intercultural and religious education, the Council of Europe has, in recent years, brought together specialists in the field of both intercultural education and religious education who had not previously worked together. This work has strengthened the view that religion is, at the least, a cultural factor, and it has convinced intercultural educators that most religious educators in theory and practice are seeking to present religious material impartially, that is they are in favour of a non-confessional in contrast to a confessional approach to religious education in public education.

Although I agree with the view that religious education is not the same as citizenship education, there are fruitful possibilities now to link these two fields further. One option might be, as is described by the authors of the chapter on the Netherlands, to strengthen the view that every child and youngster in every school should be able to develop her or his personal religious identity or personhood. Religious edification ('Bildung') could then be interpreted as an integral part of an embracing concept of personal identity development. An embracing concept of citizenship education then implies that religious education and development is part and parcel of citizenship education and should form a structural and necessary element of all citizenship education.

This view is also combinable with – following McLaughlin's distinction – what is called a 'maximal interpretation of citizenship education' in contrast to a 'minimal inter-

---

2   See also Miedema (2006a) for the importance of religion in the public domain and the interrelationship between public, social and individual perspectives on religious education.

pretation of citizenship' in which the subject is presented in a purely knowledge-based way and with a particular civics-related content to be transmitted in a formal and didactic manner. Such a maximal conceptualization of citizenship education is characterized by an emphasis on active learning and inclusion, is interactive, values-based and process led, allowing students to develop and articulate their own opinions and to engage in debate. That view is also compatible with religious education when the aim of the subject no longer will be an education into a religion. Rather, when educating about religions, it will be conceptualised as a function of an education 'from religions', that is enabling pupils to develop their own point of view on matters of religion in the context of plurality (see Doedens & Weisse, 1997; Jackson, 1997; Wardekker & Miedema, 2001).

Following the train of thought of the philosopher and pedagogue John Dewey, it is, pedagogically speaking and from a societal perspective, desirable that children already, in the embryonic society of the school, experience or are confronted by and should become acquainted with other children's backgrounds, ideas, experiences and practices, including the religious ones. Seeing the impact of the religious domain on political, cultural and economic areas, they can also benefit from such experiences and insights when they encounter religious 'others' in society at large (see also Miedema 2006b).

In the second chapter, Jean-Paul Willaime's focus is on the relationship of religious education and schools in the European context. In his general observations he concludes that: i) a strong tie between national identity and a particular confession or an articulated view on religions, has a notable effect on religious education in schools; ii) regardless of how different a particular national constellation, in respect of state-church and school-religion, might be, all European countries have to face a set of challenges or constraints, for example secularisation, strong Islamic minorities and religious pluralization; iii) there is a European consensus on the necessity to strengthen the role of knowledge about religions in public school education.

Dealing with this last comment, there is a certain correspondence here with Jackson's above-mentioned observation with respect to the developments in the European Union and in the Council of Europe. However, Willaime is not renouncing his French background and is stressing, in line with a laical and non-confessional view on religious education, the role of knowledge about religions. So, he is taking the subject-matter of religion as the criterion from a cultural and historical point of view and argues for a socio-historical objectivity towards religion. Jackson, in contrast, is in favour of a combination of educating about and from religions. For him, the aim of religious education is both to develop knowledge and understanding of religions and to enable pupils to develop their own point of view on matters of religion. So, he is combining a constructivist view on learning and teaching with a hermeneutical and dynamic view of the relationship between the religiously learning and developing person and the relevant selection of issues of tradition(s). We notice here that the particular national, professional and personal niches of the two researchers may have their own vibrating effect on their evaluations.

Based on his analysis and the research of others, it is Willaime's contention that there is a growing tendency in Europe to integrate religious education with the overall goals in education and with the school's mission. That is an interesting statement. It is, in a certain sense, in line with the use of the concept of 'religious education' in our REDCo-project as it was outlined in the introduction of this chapter, stating that religion and religiosity may get attention in other subjects too, and also as part of the school's identity. Whether there will be still a place for a specific subject named as 'religious education' in such a development, for different pedagogical and didactical reasons, is an interesting question. This is especially so for a country like France, because there is no religious education in public sector schools at present.

As a second tendency, he points to is an increasing openness to religious and philosophical plurality in Europe. In his view, the United Kingdom currently is expressing this tendency best and this is embodied in the multi-faith religious education approach and through the internal secularization of religious education courses. It is his expectation that such an approach, due to the fact that "it is becoming ever more difficult not to approach religious faith in all its diversity in the school environment", requires a socio-historical objectivity towards religion. Such an approach is at the moment at best to be found in the laical approach in France. However, the tension between the view of Willaime and Jackson, as we outlined above, respectively in terms of 'educating about' and 'educating about' combined with 'educating from', poses at least some questions with regard to such a seemingly flexible integration of the English and Welsh system and the laical French system, as Willaime characterizes these two systems himself.

In my opinion, Willaime is fully right in expecting that the two tendencies in Europe, respectively to integrate religious education with the overall goals in education and with the school's mission and the increasing openness to religious and philosophical plurality, will lead to a third one, that is that these will also cause tensions and conflicts.

The contribution of Dan-Paul Jozsa, in the third chapter of Part I, deals with a theme of great topicality for religion and education all over Europe – that is Islam in relation to education or religious education in schools. Particularly focusing on Austria, England, France, Germany and the Netherlands, his conclusion is that, although it is possible to identify neither a general European trend nor the desire for convergence in the direction of a homogenous European model in relation to law, there is a central theme in the debate – that is the emphasis on the importance of integrating Islam into education.

It is really insightful to learn that on such important issues as Islam and education and Islamic religious education, or the positioning of Islamic religious education and other religions, it is not easy, even for a specialist in the field, to formulate a European trend or desirability. The comparison between the different countries mentioned makes it clear, in my opinion, that a careful in-depth study of and comparison between the German case (including the particularities in the different federal states [Bundesländer]) and the astonishingly progressive and articulated Austrian case, possibly can shed light on the important stance of future desirable configurations of Islam and education. It is evident that a lot work still needs to be done on these issues.

Historical Background, Institutional Frameworks and Potential in Education in Eight European Countries

In the preceding chapters of the main section of this book, the chapters constituting Part II, historical and contextual analyses of religion in education in the different countries, were presented while directing our attention to the following basic topics:

- The historical tradition and socio-political background of religion in education, including church/religion-state-relations, goals of education in state, family and church, and the geographical position.
- The present context of religion in education, including the nature and degree of multiculturalism, the impact of globalization and pedagogical trends.
- The aims and debates of religion in education, including changing aims of RE and open questions, especially referring to the legal framework, policies and pedagogies that address issues of dialogue and conflict.
- Perspectives on the potential of religion in education to make a contribution to dialogue in school and society.

Historical Tradition and Socio-Political Background of Religion in Education

Under this heading, I especially want to focus on the relationship of church and state from a historical point of view, and take France and England as two extreme positions between which I will position the other six countries participating in the REDCo-project.

The French Constitution of 1958 describes *France* as a laïque (that is secular), democratic and social Republic. The basis is the law of 1905 with a few addenda to some of the articles of that law in later years. This law ensures the freedom of conscience and the free exercise of all religions, but at the same time does not recognize or subsidize any religion. The state is neutral in religious matters and does not pay the ministers of any religion, although there is the possibility to subsidize the chaplaincy in and the free exercise of religious practice in public institutions like primary schools, hospitals, asylums and prisons. The state or lower governmental bodies, may, due to their lawful ownership, also wish to subsidize the conservation of religious buildings. Crucial for politics in France is the fact that the regulation by the state of religion is very strong in terms of reducing its social importance as an institution in the public domain. This has, more than in the other participating European countries, strengthened the privatization of religion in France. The conceptualization of laïcité has changed during the twentieth century from a militant form to a management form after the Second World War. This change is characterized as the secularization of laïcité. The former was more of a counter-system, anticlerical, with a negative form of neutrality towards religion and a controlling role with respect to religion. The latter's connotation is a more positive form of neutrality, less aggressive towards religion and offering a regulating framework in the pluralist democracy for the pluralism of both religious and non-religious worldviews, and seeking to find a place and a role in society for religious facts, including in school, with the impulse given to the study of religious facts in the students' curricula.

Compared to France, the historical and socio-political background in *England* is completely different. Since the nineteenth century there has not been a separation, but, on the contrary, a partnership between state, school and church. With regard to state funding for religious schools, support was provided for Roman Catholic and some Jewish schools, as well as for a significant number of schools of the established Church of England and a small number of other Christian schools. In 1997, state funding was extended to schools of other faiths, such as Islam and Sikhism. In relation to the majority of schools, the fully state-funded schools (designated as county schools in the 1944 Education Act, but now called community schools), syllabuses for religious education were agreed by a conference consisting of committees representing the Church of England, other (Christian) denominations, teachers and local politicians. Since the Education Reform Act of 1988, other religions represented in the locality have been included in the 'other denominations' committee. One can see how the close relationship between state, school and religious traditions has enhanced the development of multi-culturality and multi-religiosity in society.

Based on the law of 1870, religious instruction in the privileged religion of Christianity in state-funded schools could be given in the form of either Bible teaching as denominational instruction or without denominational instruction. A conscience clause gave the parents the opportunity to withdraw their children from religious instruction. In England there is the long lasting tradition that syllabuses for religious instruction, later on changed into religious education, are always drafted by participants representing different interest groups, for example teachers, denominations and religions and politicians.

In the early 19th century, as a spin-off of the French occupation, *the Netherlands* had more or less the same system as France had until 1882. The curriculum was oriented towards moral and religious education and there was no separation between religion and state. But with the constitution of 1848, the still existing, dual educational system was introduced with a distinction between religiously neutral state schools and denominational private schools. These schools, since 1917, have been equally funded by the state. From that time on, the Dutch system adopted a stance which represents, more or less, a mid point between the English and the French systems. There is at least one important difference to the English system. Until 1985, the state did not take any explicit responsibility for religion in education. With respect to the subject matter of religion in education, the full responsibility in the *civil society* was delegated to the school organisations in the social domain. State schools did not have a particular responsibility qua content, but were only obliged to accept students with all kinds of religious or worldview backgrounds. Denominational schools were free to give form and content to the religious education of their particular denomination, and the governmental principle with respect to the denominational schools was: Hands off of any religious matters!

Until the 1960s there was much similarity between the *German* and the English systems. There was an established relationship between school, church and state with respect to the whole system of religion in education. After the Second World War, religion was perceived to play an important role in rebuilding a democratic Federal Republic of Germany. Religious education was defined as a regular part of the curriculum to be taught in accordance with the principles of the established religious communities. Until the 1980s the established churches were the Roman Catholic Church and the Protestant Church, and from then on also Islamic communities became participating parties.

Due to the experiences during the National Socialist period, where the state dictated doctrine and content of religions, in post-war Germany the state was not given any power over the content of religious education. This was left to the established churches, while the state provided the public space in the schools for religious education. So, the role the state could play in England and Germany has been rather different.

Since 1492 state and church in *Spain* have formed a nearly incontestable bond, forming together an institutional linkage as well as strengthening Castilian nationality, coined as National Catholicism. The net effect was that the Catholic Church had a monopoly of power and influence in educational, cultural and ideological affairs. Even under Franco's dictatorship there was a strong alliance between the Vatican and the Spanish state. In different shapes this lasted until the end of the Franco period in 1975. Then the secularization of the Spanish state, the transition towards democracy, took place, and at the same time the religious pluralization in Spain increased with a strong presence in society of Muslim, Protestant and Jewish religious communities along side Catholic communities.

From the perspective of the state-church relationship, Spain today is developing in the direction of neither a completely laïcist nor a completely confessional state. The state is obliged to guarantee religious freedom, to consider the majority of religious beliefs in the Spanish society, and to co-operate in an active way with the existing religious communities. Also, the state is secular and neutral with regard to religion. However, the Catholic Church still holds a privileged position: it is the only religious community explicitly mentioned in the Constitution, and the state completely funds all the expenses of this church. These practices have stimulated a debate on the relationship between the state and the church in favour of a neutral and secular approach. The growing detachment of Catholics from their church, and the growing number of non-Catholic immigrants, has given an extra impetus to this debate, as well as persistent forms of historically and trans-generationally transmitted forms of stigmatisation of 'others' on the basis of different nationalities, ethnicities and religions.

It is not easy to position Spain between France and England. In my opinion, the very strong relation of church and state in Spain reminds us of the situation in France before 1882 and of England during the 19th and early 20th centuries, when, respectively, the Roman Catholic Church and the Church of England held a privileged position. Whether Spain will develop further in the direction of France or England is, at this stage, unclear.

According to the Constitution, the Church of Norway is the official religion in *Norway*, but according to that same Constitution all religions and worldviews are allowed and all religious communities receive the same state grants as are given to the Church of Norway. There are only a few more privileges for the Church of Norway. Christianity and Lutheranism are, for example, prominently mentioned in the preamble of school laws and in the statements on religious or word-view education in primary schools. From 1870 until the present day it has been suggested, for different reasons, to change this particular state-church system. At the moment the system is being evaluated again, and this might lead in due course to such changes that make this part of the Constitution and the political practices more in line with each other. In principle and in practice, the Norwegian system comes close to the English system, because it does not deal exclusively with Christianity, but with religion and religious plurality as reflected in contemporary Norwegian society.

Until the first decades of the 20th century, there was a strong relationship between the Lutheran Church and the public school with respect to religious education in *Estonia*. The Constitution of the new Republic of Estonia implied the separation of state and church and the separation of church and school. This finally led, in 1920, to the exclusion of religious education from all primary schools, and left a place for religious education on an optional and voluntary basis in secondary schools. Due to widely supported protest in society in 1923, religious education became optional for primary school students as well. Thus, primary and secondary schools were obliged to offer optional religious education lessons to students. During the Soviet occupation that started in 1940, religious education in school was banned and replaced by the teaching of an atheistic world-view. Religion was completely pushed back into the private domain, and church membership among Estonians gradually declined.

Following the Soviet period, the church became very popular, but this popularity decreased dramatically after a few years. Today Estonia is one of the most secularized countries in Europe. However, the Constitution of 1992 declares that there is freedom of religion, that there is no state church, and that the state gives space for religiosity in both the private and public domains for both religious institutions and religious communities. Co-operation between state and churches is allowed, and this also holds for the domain of religious education.

Finally, we turn to our last participating country in the REDCo-project, *Russia*.[3] Russia is the only country in our project that in the 20th century experienced thirty years of a totalitarian regime. It also experienced the longest period of peaceful co-existence between Christians and Muslims in one state, and it is the most multicultural and multi-ethnic country of all participating countries in the project. Moreover, it is just sixteen years ago that the atheist ideology was put aside. After a long period in Russian history of being a state religion, the separation between the Orthodoxy and the state began after the revolutions in 1917, and continued through the new Russian Constitution of 1993. However, after 1993, there has been a completely different societal and political setting, and this calls for a new positioning of the church in relationship with the state and civil institutions. This also affects the domain of religious education.

The Present Context of Religion in Education

I started the former paragraph with the historical background of the different conceptions of the relationship of state and church in France, and I will now first begin with a sketch of the present context of religion in education in that country, and then successively point to some notable aspects of the present context of religion in education in the other countries too.

---

3   The reader should be aware that the Russia of the Soviet Union has a different composition to that of the Russian Federation.

The above described separation of church and state in *France*, as it was fixed in the law of 1905, was preceded by the separation of school and church stated in the law on obligatory primary schooling of 1882. Schools were freed from any institutional religious tutelage by the church. Although the school's programme retained 'duties before God', the hard core of the curriculum became moral and civic instruction, instead of the former moral and religious instruction. In the first two decades of the twentieth century, and partly under the influence of a positivistic conception of science which also included the view that religion was only something of the past, there was a broad plea for moral education and for the teaching of religious history only. With the reorganization of the primary school system in 1923 the phrase 'duties before God' disappeared, and the focus of the curriculum became secular moral instruction without explicit references to religion. The complete separation of school and religion, both in its institutional forms and in general, was realized.

The return of religion to the public schools took place at the end of the 1980, and this was particularly triggered by the growing pluralism of religions in French society. Should religious matters be the responsibility of the family only or should schools also take responsibility here? So, the question of religion at school was put anew on the political agenda, now with an eye to knowledge of religious cultures as a, pedagogically speaking, necessary pre-requisite for the understanding of society's past and present. An extra impetus came shortly after 9/11 in 2002 from the report on the teaching of religious facts in laical schools written by Régis Debray for the Minister of National Education. The two socio-political conceptions of 'militant' and 'management' laïcité mentioned above, are paralleled in Debray's report on education and schooling in a laïcité of ignorance, with no concern for religion whatsoever, versus a laïcité of understanding in which the knowledge of religious facts and cultures and respect for the religious 'other' is seen as a duty. This change, according to Debray, should affect both the curricula and the programmes for teacher training (Debray, 2002).

How about the present context of religion in education in *England*? During the last three decades of the twentieth century, religions other than Christianity received a significant place in the curriculum of state funded community schools, and also provided representatives to participate in Agreed Syllabus Conferences. The Act of 1988 even strengthened the place of religion in schools. The notion 'religious instruction' was replaced by the concept of 'religious education'. In community schools, the focus in religious education moved from the study of religions, taught in a cognitive and phenomenological manner, to studies of religion that related to the experiences of the students, contributing to their personal development, while preventing indoctrinatory teaching. Religious education is related to the whole curriculum of the school and is also defined in more broad civic terms. It should promote the embracing (spiritual, moral, cultural, mental and physical) development of the students at school and of society. Crucial to these developments is the emphasis on the educational or pedagogical nature of religious education, and also attention to the major religions in local syllabuses. Both the model syllabuses of 1994 and the non statutory National Framework for Religious Education of 2004 show the Government's interest in enabling local syllabus conferences to do their job. They also might indicate a development towards a future national syllabus. With regard to the (minority) mainly state funded religious schools, the Government is keen that they should be outward looking and provide places for students from a mix of religious backgrounds. The government clearly takes an active stance towards religion in school, and is not afraid to put disputable issues on the agenda in relation to religious education in schools and faith based schooling.

In case of *the Netherlands*, a remarkable turn of the Dutch governmental policy with respect to religion in education took place in 1985. Then the government decided that a new and obligatory field should be introduced in the curriculum of every state and de-nominational primary school, called 'Religious and Ideological Movements'. Due to the growing multiculturality of the Dutch society, the government's view was that students should have some knowledge of the main beliefs systems of the world religions and of their diverse religious practices, norms and values, in order to be able to participate ade-quately as citizens in the pluralistic Dutch society. It was the government's aim that reli-gious traditions and worldviews should be presented in an objective way. So, the distinc-tion between religious education and this new field could be articulated by use of the di-chotomy between subjective and objective approaches.

Another notable intervention of the Dutch government, with respect to the relationship of state and religion in education, was that in 2003, during the debates on Islamic schools and religious lessons in Islamic schools, the Minister of Education ordered the schools' inspectorate not to evaluate the religious lessons of denominational schools structurally, but only if there were signs that children were being influenced towards attitudes of ha-tred, or in cases where there were other things going wrong with these lessons. Interest-ingly, the Minister of Education has recently also declared that she will prepare an amendment to the law to make it possible for the schools' inspectorate to evaluate also the lessons in Christian religious education, Islamic religious education and humanist world views education that are given on an optional basis *in* state schools and during school time, but which are not part of the responsibility of the state schools. So, there is the tendency now in the Netherlands for the government to take more and more responsi-bility for the adequacy of religious education in schools, without having any religious preference itself.

The present context of religion in education has been shaped in *Germany* in two waves. The first one took place via the societal developments in the mid-sixties in terms of individualization, democratization, secularization and emancipation. It opened up reli-gious education for these developments in society and resulted in a stronger linkage of religious education with political and ethical education. So, a theological perspective merged with the perspective of a secular critical theory of society with an emphasis on dialogue, solidarity and critical analysis of societal processes and practices.

The second profound change, with respect to religious education, took place after the unification of former East and West Germany in 1989. Although the new federal states of the former East Germany adopted the system for religious education operative in the fed-eral states of the former West Germany, in the 1980s some of the former West German states started to debate the prominent position of the established religious communities in relation to religion in education. They pointed to the growing religious and cultural plu-ralization of society, the secularization in society, the diminishing influence of the institutional religious communities, and the rapid growth of individualized forms of religiosity, among youngsters as well as among adolescents, as important changes in the German context. These are changes that should be expected to have an effect on the form and content of religious education in general. The federal state of Brandenburg, for example, replaced denominational religious education by 'life plans – ethics –religious knowledge' (L-E-R), a form of teaching about ethical and religious systems in the form of neutral, factual education on different religions and/or ethical systems.

The above described social-political background in *Spain*, has had and still has a tremendous impact on the school today. The school became a battlefield between political parties and religious communities, and between the state and religious communities. The debate on the present and future of religion in education is, of course, an integral part of that debate. One of the issues is the overt and only presence of Catholic religious symbols, practices and festivals in public schools. Recently, this has been criticized by non-Catholics parents and also gradually by parents who are members of other religious communities (Protestant, Jewish, Muslim). The reform of a non-Catholic religious education in the public school system is proceeding only very gradually, and non-Catholic religious education (Protestant, Islamic or Jewish religious education) is realized in public schools in Spain in only a few places. One of the great obstacles is the still ambivalent position of the state towards the Catholic Church, grounded in the constitution and linked to the still privileged position of that church in Spanish society.

The context for religious education in *Norway* nowadays is heavily influenced by the change of the national curriculum in 1997. In that year the Norwegian parliament accepted a brand new curriculum for religious education, first named (literally translated) as 'Knowledge of Christianity with orientation about other religions and word-views', and in 2002 renamed as 'Knowledge of Christianity, religions and world-views' (Kristendoms, religions- og livsynkunnskap, abbreviated as KRL). So, since the 19th century, religious education in Norway changed from being a church-bound subject leading to confirmation, to a subject that is fully dealing with the broad multi-religious character of contemporary society from both a theological and a pedagogical perspective, a subject that in principle is compulsory for all students.

As we have noted above, there has been, constitutionally, since 1990, enough space for religion and religion education in *Estonia*. However, the long lasting effects of the communist regime are still traceable, for example in the alienation of many Estonians from religious practices and religious institutions, and in the lack of knowledge about religions resulting in a form of religious illiteracy. Religion in education, and so religious educators, can profit from the theory and method of religious education already developed in the period between the First and Second Word War by Põld and Kõpp with the aims of strengthening the religious literacy of Estonian students and increasing the competence of the teachers. Fortunately, government officials, officials of religious institutions and academic scholars in the field of religious education are jointly working together now in the domain of religious education for schools. Religious education is perceived as important for identity building, moral development and for preparing students to live in a pluralistic society. However, much need to be done in terms of the construction of suitable methods, teacher training, and developing students' religious sensitivity, as well as providing enough allocated time in the curriculum for religious education.

As indicated above, since 1993 a complete different societal and political setting is at stake in *Russia*, and this also affects the domain of religious education. Although Russia has always been a multicultural and multi-religious society, before 1990 religious pluralism was not welcomed nor theologically justified by the most powerful church in Russia, the Russian Orthodox Church. The situation with respect to religious pluralism has changed since 1990. Inter-religious cooperation started in 1998, stimulated by the state and religious organizations, and has resulted in the Inter-religious Council of Russia in which representatives of Christianity, Islam, Judaism and Buddhism work together. In particular, St. Petersburg is developing into a prominent centre for inter-religious activities in the field of religious education. Important for inter-religious dialogue is the vehicle of Christian ecumenism, but this, since 1990, has met severe criticism from within the Christian churches themselves. Fortunately, this critique is diminishing currently, but still much needs to be done to pave the way for a nation-wide, increased inter-religious dialogue.

Aims of Religion in Education

After a long period of time, the beginning of the 21st century marks the return of religion to the school in *France*. Knowledge of religious facts should foster the understanding of religious cultures and practices, and also respect for the religious 'other'. In the chapter on France, three aims are mentioned: 1) an education in the symbolic language of religions; 2) a contribution to the understanding of and insight into cultural heritage; 3) a contribution to civic education. Already in 1882 civic education was prominently on the agenda in France, but then related to moral instruction and, in contrast to the time before, no longer explicitly related to religious instruction. At the beginning of the 21st century both civic education and knowledge about religious facts are together on the pedagogical agenda of schools in France. The aim is fostering understanding and respect in religious matters. In France itself, there is hardly any doubt over whether an objective religious education is possible. However, following the line of thought of Debray (see Debray, 2002), some voices can also be heard stressing the insight that, next to the knowledge of religious facts, the attitudes of believers and their piety and spirituality must be taken into account in presenting such facts. The important pedagogical question arises here as to whether this turn to religious practices, rituals and spirituality is fully compatible with the concept of teaching about religious facts as the fundamental aim of religious education in France.

In *England* there was a crucial change in respect to the aims of religion in school in terms of a replacement of religious *instruction*, with stress on the deliberate transmission of religious beliefs, by religious *education*. Here, the focus is on learning about religions and also learning from them, in the sense of relating studies of religions to the experiences of the students and to the students' own personal development with respect to values, spirituality, religion or worldview. So, instead of a teaching *into* a particular religion or a teaching *about* religions in terms of surface knowledge of religious phenomena, now the aim of religious education consists of a combination of teaching about religions (religious studies) with teaching from religions (young people's personal development). The criteria for successful religious education include both knowledge and understanding of religions and the construction by the student of her/his personal views in relation to religion, her or his actorship and authorship with respect to religious matters.

With respect to the aims of religious education, there is again some similarity between *the Netherlands* and England, especially when we focus on denominational or 'faith based' schools. In the Netherlands, following a long period when teaching into the beliefs of a particular denomination was at stake, a combination of teaching about religions with teaching from religions – with an eye on the development of the personal religious identity of the students – is now the main aim (see Miedema, 2006b). Only a minority of so-called closed denominational schools (Protestant, Roman Catholic, Evangelical, Islamic) is still aiming at teaching into a particular belief system. Since 1985 state schools focus on teaching about religions and worldviews but, interestingly enough, the consensus is growing that it is important to strengthen also in state schools the development of a personal worldview with the aim of fostering autonomy and social commitment, which can lead to the humanizing of the world and to meaning construction of the individual (see Veugelers, 2003). In *England*, we have already discussed the aims of religious education in the (majority) community schools as combining 'learning about' and 'learning from' religions. The approach to religious education in the (minority) faith based schools in England varies, partly according to denomination and partly according to the degree of theological liberalism or conservatism associated with the school. All faith based schools would aim to nurture faith among adherents to the religion of the school. However, it is policy within the Church of England to include the study of other religions as part of religious education, and many Church of England schools use the local agreed syllabus, written for community schools. Regardless of religion, theologically conservative schools tend to play down or even to avoid intercultural and multi-religious approaches and contacts. However, it is current government policy to encourage all faith based schools to be outward looking, to include studies of other religions and cultures, to build links with other communities and to accept some students from religious backgrounds other than that of the school.

At the moment the aims of religious education in *Germany* can be defined in at least three different ways. i) A separate religious community can provide the subject-matter from its own denomination; ii) it could be interdenominational or even a step further be inter-religious; in the last case religious education is jointly informed by different religious communities, and can eventually get the form of a dialogical religious pedagogy as it is for instance practised in Hamburg; or iii) it can have the form of L-E-R. The first modus has some similarities with the closed denominational model of the Netherlands. The second modus shows some similarity with the English, with the Dutch form for the main group of open denominational schools and hopefully in due course also for state schools. The third form, however, comes in my opinion closer to the French laïcal form, and this is also due to a greater influence of the federal state on the content of L-E-R.

The situation in *Spain* is very unusual. Still supported by state regulations, the Catholic Church is again and again trying to defend its presence in public schools and to continue its influence in the form of Catholic religious education there. But the Catholic church also defends the existence of fully state subsidized private Catholic schools, meant for Catholics only (by means of an exclusivist admissions strategy) and only offering Catholic religious education. The religious minority communities try to cash their legal right of designing, organising and teaching their own religious education in public schools. For some others, and among them our Spanish colleagues in the REDCo-project, the aim is the development now and in the future of dialogical forms of inter-religious education in both private and public schools. That is, in my view, an attempt to launch a strategy for religious education in the direction of, for example, the latest developments in England. However, the great constraint here is the still existing state-church relationship, not adequately adapted to the current societal circumstances.

We have seen above that, since 1997, KRL is the format for religious education in *Norway*. In the literal translation the notion 'knowledge of' as an aim is very prominent. However, the section on 'Major goals of education and their relationship to religion' in the chapter on Norway, shows that it is not just teaching about that is at stake in Norwegian KRL. Reading the text of the Education Act, with its focus on education and society at large, the aims of religious education, although not clearly stated, can be interpreted in the developmental terms of ability, attitude, identity formation and citizenship education. An issue, especially brought to the fore by non-Christian minorities, is that the new curriculum for religious education in the form of KRL still gives too much attention to Christianity and less to other religions and world-views.

In formulating the aims of religious education, *Estonia* can still use the ideas developed by Põld and Kõpp in the period between 1920-40 stating that the aim of the subject is to give first-hand knowledge about Christianity and other world religions, and to support the students' moral development. In that way religious education builds bridges between the content of religious education and the daily life world of the students. This definition could be extended with reference to more recent formulations that emphasize the relevance of religious education in developing among students the ability for dialogue and understanding between different world-views as a means to resist fundamentalism, discrimination and intolerance. Very important in the recent proposals for religious education, is the contextual approach as proposed by our REDCo colleague Pille Valk. It implies that the questions of the students themselves as well as the particular societal circumstances are fully taken into account in an adequate conceptualization of religious education. In my opinion, this approach in its final ends, is highly compatible with the English and Dutch combination of teaching about and teaching from religions because, in addition to the cognitive element, emotions, affections, and experiences are also included.

The main aim for religious education in *Russia* has not in the first place to do with the subject-matter or methodology of religious education in schools, but rather with the task of realizing the circumstances in which religion can secure a regular place in the curriculum of schools or may become part of a school's specific identity. These provisions need to be addressed first, because – as the chapter on Russia has made clear – religious classes and religious schools have not become an integral part of the school system in post-Soviet Russia. However, the possibilities for this, although supported by law, are not yet realized. This is also due to the fact that, at the moment, Russia is at the crossroads of making a decision about which direction to take: following the line of France with a strict secularism in school, or going the way Germany went, with influences of different religious communities in the school, including the influence of Orthodoxy. Until this decision is made, the place and role of religion in education will still be unclear and underdeveloped.

Potential of Religion in Education: The Way ahead

This first REDCo book has shown that in the field of religion in education a great deal is going on at the moment in the eight European countries participating in our research.

Our conclusion can be that religion in education is an important issue in all of these countries. However, the historical background, especially the particular configuration of the relationship of state and church and school and church, differs greatly, as well as the present context of religion in education in these countries. We can, nevertheless, also conclude that there is a strong convergence with respect to the aims of religion in education. With an eye on the growing religious plurality in each country, and in Europe *in toto*, teaching about religions and worldviews is seen as a necessary condition for an adequate conceptualization of religious education – a necessary condition, but in most of the participating countries, not a sufficient condition. That is why the concept of teaching and learning from religions and world views is combined with a variant of teaching and learning about religions.

In order to distinguish such teaching and learning from religions and worldviews clearly and distinctly from any, even sophisticated, form of teaching into a religion or world view, we should, from the very outset, find clear and effective pedagogies for combining knowledge and understanding of religions with opportunities for personal reflection and response that do not direct students to reach particular conclusions.

In such approaches, the relatively autonomous status of the school as a societal institution should be emphasized, implying that churches and religious organizations can be interesting and relevant partners of state and denominational schools, but that there should not be any institutional bond between churches or religious organizations and a school. The Spanish case can be illustrative here of the need of such a clear stance.

Seeing the importance of the relationship between state and church, this should, in my opinion, be combined with a political-theoretical approach in which the role, the place and the pedagogical responsibility of the state in the public, social and private domains are carefully scrutinized. The criterion for the domain of religion in education could be whether the state is fostering or hindering the realization of the aims of religious education formulated above in a particular country. An example of a fruitful state practice along this line is, for instance, the report of the commission led by Machelon in France on the relationship between the religious communities and religious organizations and the state (see Machelon, 2006). Another recent example is also an extensive report published by the Dutch Scientific Council for Government Policy (WRR) in December 2006. The advice to the government puts the issue of the place of religion in the public domain back on the agenda, in a way that is explicitly theoretically and empirically related to several developments in the Netherlands and to events taking place on a European and a global scale. The focus is especially on the role of the state in matters of religion at the beginning of the 21st century, and the conclusion is that the state, still being neutral, really has a responsibility with an eye to the place and role of religion in the public sphere (see Van de Donk et al., 2006).

In the contributions of this volume, it has been stated that there is the expectancy that the theoretical as well as empirical research that will be carried out in our REDCo-project these coming years should have a significant impact on the theoretical, practical and political debates in the participating countries. We hope to be able to define how conditions in the pedagogical field should be shaped, in order that religion in education serves as a factor for mutual understanding, respect and dialogue. We also will be considering how the issue of religious conflict can be dealt with adequately in education, whether in religious education specifically, in other related fields, or through the organisation of the school.

This book shows the differences and commonalities of religious education in different countries of Europe in recent history and at the present time. We have to be aware of them in order not to formulate unrealistic and monolithic aims for future developments in religion in education in Europe. Being aware of the different developments and contexts in European countries, we will nevertheless contribute by our research over the next three years to identifying a European outlook for religion in education in public and denominational schools. In our opinion the differences could be regarded as resources, in order to shape future European developments in ways that promote dialogue and reduce conflict.

References

Debray, R. (2002) *L'Enseignement du fait religieux dans l'école laïque* (Paris, Odile Jacob).

Doedens, F. & Weisse, W. (Eds.) (1997) *Religionsunterricht für alle. Hamburger Perspektiven zur Religionsdidaktik* (Münster/New York/München/Berlin, Waxmann).

Jackson, R. (1997) *Religious education: an interpretive approach* (London, Hodder & Stoughton).

Machelon, J.P. (Ed.) (2006) *Les relations des cultes avec les pouvoirs publics. Rapport au Ministre d'Etat, ministre de l'intérieur et de l'aménagement du territoire* (Paris, Ministre d'Etat). (Downloaded from internet on 06-12-2006 http://www.Ladocumentation francaise.fr/ rapportspublics/064000727/index.shtml)

Miedema, S. (2006a) Public, Social, and Individual Perspectives on Religious Education. Voices from the Past and the Present, *Studies in Philosophy and Education*, 25, 111-127.

Miedema, S. (2006b) Educating for Religious Citizenship. Religious Education as Identity Formation, in: M. De Souza, K. Engebretson, G. Durka, R. Jackson & A. McGrady (Eds.) *International Handbook of the Religious, Spiritual and Moral Dimensions of Education. Vol. I & II.* (Dordrecht, Springer), 965-974.

Wardekker, W.L. & Miedema, S. (2001) Identity, Cultural Change and Religious Education, *British Journal of Religious Education*, 23, 76-87.

Veugelers, W.M.M.H. (2003) *Waarden en normen in het onderwijs. Zingeving en humanisering: autonomie en sociale betrokkenheid* [Values and norms in school. Meaning construction and humanizing: autonomy and social commitment] (Utrecht, Universiteit voor Human-istiek).

Van de Donk, W.B.H.J., Jonkers, A.P., Kronjee, G.J. & Plum, R.J.J.M. (Eds.) (2006) *Geloven in het publieke domein* [Religion in the public domain] (Amsterdam, Amsterdam University Press).

List of authors

Dr. Ina ter Avest is Senior Researcher in Religious Education at the Faculty of Psychology and Education at the Vrije Universiteit Amsterdam and Research Lecturer in Denominational School Identity at CHN University at Leeuwarden, the Netherlands. E-mail: kh.ter.avest@psy.vu.nl.

Dr. Cok Bakker is Professor in Religious Education at the Faculty of Humanities (Sub-Faculty of Theology) at Utrecht University, the Netherlands.
E-mail: cbakker@theo.uu.nl.

Dr. Gerdien Bertram-Troost is post-doc Researcher at the Faculty of Psychology and Education, Vrije Universiteit Amsterdam, The Netherlands.
E-mail: gd.troost@psy.vu.nl

Dr. Vladimir Fedorov is Professor of Theology, Director of the Orthodox Research Institute of Missiology, Ecumenism and New Religious Movements and Vice-Rector of the Russian Christian Academy for Humanities (St Petersburg).
E-mail: vffedorov@gmail.com

Dr. Gunther Dietz is Professor of Social Anthropology at *Universidad de Granada*, Faculty of Education, in Granada (Spain) and Research Professor at *Universidad Veracruzana*, Institute of Educational Research, in Xalapa (Mexico).
E-mail: gdietz@ugr.es and gdietz@uv.mx

Dr. Robert Jackson, D.Litt., is Professor of Education and Director of the Warwick Religions and Education Research Unit in the Institute of Education, University of Warwick, U.K. He is Editor of the *British Journal of Religious Education*.
E-mail: r.jackson@warwick.ac.uk

Dan-Paul Jozsa is Researcher in Religious Education, Islamic Theology and Philosophy at the Münster University, Center for Religious Studies and lecturer at the Hamburg University. E-mail: paul.jozsa@googlemail.com.

Dr. Thorsten Knauth is Researcher and lecturer in Religious Education at the University of Hamburg. E-mail: knauth@erzwiss.uni-hamburg.de

Dr. Fedor Kozyrev is Assistant Professor in St. Petersburg Christian University and Director of the Religious Pedagogy Centre at the Interchurch Partnership "Apostolic City" (St Petersburg). He is head of the Religious Pedagogical Department of the Russian Christian Academy for Humanities. E-mail: fkozyrev@yahoo.co.uk

Dr. Siebren Miedema is Professor in Philosophy of Education at the Faculty of Psychology and Education, and Professor in Religious Education at the Faculty of Theology at the Vrije Universiteit Amsterdam, the Netherlands.
E-mail: s.miedema@psy.vu.nl.

Dr. Kevin O'Grady is Head of Religious Education and Citizenship at High Storrs
School, Sheffield, and Associate Fellow in the Warwick Religions and Education
Research Unit in the Institute of Education, University of Warwick, U.K.
E-mail: ogradykevin@yahoo.co.uk

Dr. Geir Skeie, Associate Professor, is teaching and researching Religious Education at
the University of Stavanger, Norway. E-mail: geir.skeie@uis.no

Dr. Pille Valk is Associate Professor of Religious Education at the Faculty of Theology
at University of Tartu, Estonia. E-mail: pille.valk@ut.ee

Dr. Wolfram Weisse is Professor of Religious Education at the University of Hamburg,
Director of the interdisciplinary centre „World Religions in Dialogue" and coordinator of REDCo. E-mail: weisse@erzwiss.uni-hamburg.de

Dr. Jean-Paul Willaime is Professor and Research Director at the Ecole Pratique des
Hautes Etudes, Department of Religious Studies, Sorbonne, Paris. He is Director of
the European Institute of Religious Studies and Director of Groupe, Sociétés, Religions, Laïcités Research Centre (Paris). E-mail: jean-paul.willaime@gsrl.cnrs.fr

Religious Diversity and Education

ed. by Cok Bakker (Utrecht), Hans-Günter Heimbrock (Frankfurt a.M.), Robert Jackson (Warwick), Geir Skeie (Stavanger), Wolfram Weisse (Hamburg)

Waxmann

In dieser empirischen Studie werden Ausschnitte von der Wirklichkeit in der niederländischen Schule beschrieben, um zu verdeutlichen, wie und unter welchen Umständen beim Unterrichten mit dem gleichen interkulturellen und interreligiösen Schulbuch die Begriffe „Religion" und „Verantwortung für religiöse Bildung" durch die Lehrkräfte normativ ausgefüllt werden.

Being tolerant is considered important by most people. Tolerance is about navigating in societies of increased differences. The larger the differences in a society, the more pressuring the issue of tolerance.

This study raises the question what tolerance means in a specific multicultural context, namely education. What does tolerance mean to teachers? And does tolerance mean the same for teachers as it is defined in national curricula and in theories of tolerance?

■ VOLUME 1

Erna Zonne

Interreligiöses und interkulturelles Lernen an Grundschulen in Rotterdam Rijnmond

Eine interdisziplinäre religionspädagogische Studie des Umgangs mit der Pluralität der Weltanschauungen

2006, 382 S., br., 29,90 €
ISBN 3-8309-1652-3

■ VOLUME 2

Geir Afdal

Tolerance and Curriculum

2006, 365 p., pb., 29,90 €
ISBN 3-8309-1704-X